Dual Justice

The Chicago Series in Law and Society

Edited by John M. Conley, Charles Epp, and Lynn Mather

ALSO IN THE SERIES:

Big Money Unleashed: The Campaign to Deregulate Election Spending
by Ann Southworth

*The Making of Lawyers' Careers: Inequality and Opportunity in
the American Legal Profession*
by Robert L. Nelson, Ronit Dinovitzer, Bryant G. Garth,
Joyce S. Sterling, David B. Wilkins, Meghan Dawe, and Ethan Michelson

The Crucible of Desegregation: The Uncertain Search for Educational Equality
by R. Shep Melnick

Cooperation without Submission: Indigenous Jurisdictions in Native Nation–US Engagements
by Justin B. Richland

BigLaw: Money and Meaning in the Modern Law Firm
by Mitt Regan and Lisa H. Rohrer

Union by Law: Filipino American Labor Activists, Rights Radicalism, and Racial Capitalism
by Michael W. McCann with George I. Lovell

Speaking for the Dying: Life-and-Death Decisions in Intensive Care
by Susan P. Shapiro

Just Words: Law, Language and Power, Third Edition
by John M. Conley, William M. O'Barr, and Robin Conley Riner

Islands of Sovereignty: Haitian Migration and the Borders of Empire
by Jeffrey S. Kahn

Building the Prison State: Race and the Politics of Mass Incarceration
by Heather Schoenfeld

Navigating Conflict: How Youth Handle Trouble in a High-Poverty School
by Calvin Morrill and Michael Musheno

The Sit-Ins: Protest and Legal Change in the Civil Rights Era
by Christopher W. Schmidt

Additional series titles follow index.

Dual Justice

America's Divergent Approaches to Street and Corporate Crime

ANTHONY GRASSO

The University of Chicago Press
Chicago and London

The University of Chicago Press, Chicago 60637
The University of Chicago Press, Ltd., London
© 2024 by The University of Chicago
All rights reserved. No part of this book may be used or reproduced in any manner whatsoever without written permission, except in the case of brief quotations in critical articles and reviews. For more information, contact the University of Chicago Press, 1427 E. 60th St., Chicago, IL 60637.
Published 2024
Printed in the United States of America

33 32 31 30 29 28 27 26 25 24   1 2 3 4 5

ISBN-13: 978-0-226-82904-3 (cloth)
ISBN-13: 978-0-226-83559-4 (paper)
ISBN-13: 978-0-226-83558-7 (e-book)
DOI: https://doi.org/10.7208/chicago/9780226835587.001.0001

Library of Congress Cataloging-in-Publication Data

Names: Grasso, Anthony, author.
Title: Dual justice : America's divergent approaches to street and corporate crime / Anthony Grasso.
Other titles: Chicago series in law and society.
Description: Chicago ; London : The University of Chicago Press, 2024. | Series: The Chicago series in law and society | Includes bibliographical references and index.
Identifiers: LCCN 2024010226 | ISBN 9780226829043 (cloth) | ISBN 9780226835594 (paperback) | ISBN 9780226835587 (ebook)
Subjects: LCSH: Criminal justice, Administration of—United States. | Equality before the law—United States. | Commercial crimes—United States. | Criminal justice, Administration of—United States—History. | Progressivism (United States politics) | Eugenics—Political aspects—United States. | United States—Politics and government.
Classification: LCC HV9950 .G74 2024 | DDC 364.973—dc23/eng/20240326
LC record available at https://lccn.loc.gov/2024010226

♾ This paper meets the requirements of ANSI/NISO Z39.48-1992 (Permanence of Paper).

Contents

Crime, Ideology, and Inequality
in American Politics

Laws are like cobwebs, which may catch small flies,
but let wasps and hornets break through.
JONATHAN SWIFT,
"A Tritical Essay upon the Faculties of the Mind" (1707)

September 26, 2016, was the first presidential debate between Hillary Clinton and Donald Trump. About a third of the way through, the candidates turned to the topic of Trump's tax returns. Clinton, noting that all presidential candidates for the past forty years had released their returns, questioned what Trump might be hiding. When she stated that the few returns Trump had chosen to release showed he paid no federal income tax, Trump interjected, "That makes me smart," dismissing the insinuation that this could constitute illegal activity by framing it in terms of business acumen and savvy.

About fifteen minutes later, the moderator, Lester Holt, shifted gears to race relations. He asked Trump, "How do you heal the divide?" Trump used the phrase *law and order* five times in his reply, forcefully promising to "bring back law and order" in crime-ridden cities.[1]

These statements highlight the hypocrisy of calling large-scale tax avoidance smart while demanding adherence to the law, but Trump's rhetoric reflected a contradiction that is deeply embedded in American politics. Through the era of mass incarceration, lawmakers have occasionally condemned corporate lawlessness in the wake of scandals like the savings and loan (S&L) crisis of the 1980s and the financial crisis of 2007–8. But the story of boom, bust, and reprimand is one we have seen before. It is a recurring historical pattern for policymakers to "discover" the problem of corporate crime during a crisis, provide a limited short-term solution, and forget about it only to "discover" it again during the next scandal.[2] Through these crises, the American state has never developed an ongoing capacity to prosecute corporate crime.

The broader development of the criminal justice system has followed a different trajectory. As the global leader in incarceration, America locks up its own citizens at a rate that dwarfs that of any other developed nation. As of 2021, the US incarceration rate stood at 639 people per 100,000, a rate that outpaces every other country in the world and registers as more than four times larger than that of any Western European nation.[3] The rise of America's "carceral state" is one of the most serious social and political problems of our time. In recent years, it has shifted from being purely an academic concern to being a political issue at all levels of government, visible in everything from the election of reformist district attorneys in major cities to the scrutiny of presidential candidates' criminal justice records. Yet, while racial minorities and the poor fill prisons and jails for property crime, drug use, and violent crime, the state routinely fails to prosecute high-ranking executives who break the law, a reality laid bare after none of the executives who facilitated the 2007–8 financial crisis faced serious repercussions. Even with the emergence of a sprawling carceral apparatus, the US government struggles to criminally punish corporate lawbreakers, often letting them walk away from crises with golden parachutes rather than criminal charges.

Therein lies the motivating question of this book: Why does the American state excessively incarcerate the poor and racial minorities for street crimes while turning a blind eye to the crimes of corporate executives?

Most scholarship treats questions about mass incarceration and the state's lenient treatment of corporate wrongdoing in isolation, but this book unearths the interconnected roots of these phenomena in over a century of ideological and institutional developments that have shaped how America conceptualizes and governs criminality. By juxtaposing historical institutional analyses of the carceral and regulatory states, it illustrates that the contrast between the mass incarceration of poor and minority Americans, on the one hand, and the state's limited capacity and unwillingness to punish executives, on the other, exemplifies something more than modern hypocrisy. While the carceral state has evolved to govern street-level criminality harshly, American law has historically defined corporate lawbreaking as a regulatory problem best managed by administrative agencies via technocratic interventions rather than punitive sanctions.

By analyzing intellectual history, policy debates, political economic change, and institutional development from 1870 to the present day, this book demonstrates how these punitive class biases in US policy emerged and took root through the development of the carceral and regulatory states. This reveals that the state's divergent treatments of street crime and corporate crime share common and self-reinforcing ideological origins. The political development of the carceral state and the political development of the regulatory state have been, not autonomous and disconnected threads, but related processes that reflect and reinforce common politically constructed understandings about what causes and constitutes crime and who counts as a criminal.

The Shared Roots of Carceral and Regulatory Development

This book traces the connected origins of carceral and regulatory development to formative moments in the Progressive era. During this period, scholars and lawmakers drew on intellectual discourses about criminality rooted in evolutionary and eugenic theories of human difference to justify harsh justice policies for the poor and regulatory controls for corporate executives who violated the law. In doing so, they packaged determinist ideas about human behavior into twin ideological frameworks that they deployed to design and defend differential responses to street and corporate crime.

This story begins in the early Progressive era, when the criminal justice system and the regulatory state began to take on their modern forms. In 1870, American penology experienced a major shift when rehabilitation became its guiding ideal. Reformatories capable of holding large numbers of offenders proliferated across the country, accompanied by practices familiar to modern observers like parole, probation, early release incentives, and discretionary sentencing practices that displaced determinate systems.[4] At the same time, the roots of the modern regulatory state emerged in the birth of national regulatory institutions. Business misconduct and market regulation were not new in the Progressive era—banking speculation had prompted economic panics before, and early nineteenth-century municipalities regulated markets locally.[5] However, the rise of the large corporation and the nationalization of the political economy altered the scope of corporate abuse as a social and political problem, prompting lawmakers to undertake a national-level regulatory response. These developments in rehabilitation-oriented criminal justice and regulatory governance were not entirely unrelated. In these seemingly distinct policy areas, political actors drew on common discourses about eugenics and human difference to construct institutional arrangements designed to punish the poor while steering the wealthy away from prison.

Understanding these developments requires understanding American eugenics. An intellectual and political movement aimed at purifying the nation's racial stock, Progressive era eugenics championed policies designed to prevent the reproduction of the "unfit" and "defective" classes—such as the poor, the working class, minorities, and criminals—through policies like compulsory sterilization, segregation, and containment. Scholars across the disciplines of sociology, anthropology, economics, law, and race science incorporated and elaborated on eugenic theories in their scholarship. Their ideas gave lawmakers simple means to identify who was "fit" or "unfit" on the basis of physical, racial, and class traits. Eugenics became intertwined with criminology through the rise of criminal anthropology in the late nineteenth century. Criminal anthropology was a school of thought founded by the Italian criminologist Cesare Lombroso, who posited that the criminal was a naturally occurring phenomenon with a biological constitution predisposed to criminality.[6] Turn-of-the-century scholars embraced Lombrosian theory and blended it with an established body of American race science and sociological scholarship attributing poverty and inequality to individuals' biological dispositions, front-loading their research with assumptions that those most likely to be criminals were the poor and racial minorities.

Progressive era scholars and policymakers packaged these ideas into a deceptively compassionate-sounding rehabilitative ideology of punishment. The rehabilitative approach reflected the precepts of Lamarckian evolutionary theory, a school of thought postulating that traits acquired during one's lifetime become heritable, meaning that if prisoners could be reformed, their criminal traits would not be passed on to their offspring. However, these scholars and policymakers also reasoned that while some lawbreakers could be rehabilitated, those who proved unreformable must be the born criminals of Lombrosian thought—"incorrigibles" so biologically inclined to crime that they could not be changed, warranting containment or eugenic treatment. As lawmakers deployed rehabilitative ideology to reform the justice system, the rehabilitative mission became a sorting project. Prison administrators and justice system officials were tasked with identifying and separating redeemable inmates from the incorrigibles requiring draconian controls. This brought new techniques, strategies, and mentalities to criminal justice that utilized racial and class traits and factors like criminal history to diagnose incorrigibility. These seeds of punitiveness were sown into rehabilitative ideology from its origins.

On the other hand, scholars articulated a mirrored logic to explain the behavior of the "robber barons" helming large corporations. Eugenic and Social Darwinist scholarship was interpreted as proving that the cutthroat businessman's combative nature was not a symptom of degenerate criminality; instead, it was seen as a manifestation of a vigorous competitive disposition, leaving him naturally well suited to market struggle. Actions that bore similarities to theft or fraud but were committed by respectable individuals in market environments were interpreted as healthy manifestations of the laws of nature. The businessman was a natural capitalist motivated by spirited self-interest, not a born criminal driven by a deviant temperament. This was the foundational rationale of a regulatory ideology suggesting that harmful actions of capitalist elites operating in markets should be managed via regulatory administration, as corporate leaders were driven by innate entrepreneurial spirits warranting encouragement and guidance rather than criminal temperaments warranting rehabilitation or punishment. Any objectionable behavior on the executive's part was deemed a consequence of the economic system's incentives and imperfections seducing his ambitious nature, giving his transgressions different substantive meanings from the crimes committed by the Lombrosian criminal. This rationalization of market conflict allowed corporate wrongdoers to evade the punitive determinist logic that bore so heavily on street criminals—they simply lacked the instincts prison was designed to eliminate through rehabilitation or containment. By defining corporate criminality as a regulatory problem, lawmakers siphoned corporate malfeasance into regulatory venues designed as alternatives to the criminal justice system for a distinct class of offenders.

By politically mobilizing these ideologies, Progressive era political actors lodged them within the foundations of American legal and political institutions. The following chapters shed light on the enduring consequences of their decisions. Since the Progressive era, rehabilitative and regulatory ideologies infused with racialized and class-skewed ideas about criminality have been adapted, repurposed, and put into action by political actors of varied political persuasions to shape the carceral and regulatory states and ensnare or exclude different populations from their grasps. Studying the origins of rehabilitative and regulatory ideologies and their political use over time illustrates how they have been deployed to delineate the parameters of carceral and regulatory institutions and define who gets punished and how.

Defining Rehabilitative and Regulatory Ideologies

In the following pages, *ideology* refers to a system of ideas providing understandings, beliefs, and vocabularies for people to make sense of their everyday reality via a coherent interpretation of the social world and its problems and prescriptions for making it better.[7] Both rehabilitative ideology and regulatory ideology outline specific understandings of human nature and the state's role in providing social control. They constitute related visions for governing the harmful behavior of different people in different ways, and political actors have activated them at various moments in time to design and shape American governing institutions. Thus, staking out how Progressives initially defined them is necessary for understanding their impact on political development.

Rehabilitative ideology is a system of ideas proposing that the penal system should transform inmates into law-abiding and productive citizens through

programs aimed at adjusting their behaviors and skill sets to reduce their likelihood of reoffending. It expresses the notion that all elements of punishment—
including sentence length, access to rehabilitative programs and behavioral
incentives, and parole and probation considerations—should be tailored to an
individual's needs and perceived potential for reform. Rehabilitative justice relies on indeterminate sentencing systems in which sentences are given as time
ranges rather than as fixed terms, permitting prison administrators to grant
individuals early release or continue their detainment depending on their rehabilitative progress. Therefore, people convicted of the same crime but diagnosed with different rehabilitative prospects warrant different sentences under
the rehabilitative approach.

Alternatively, regulatory ideology is a system of ideas dictating that the
state should rely on specialized regulatory bodies to control undesirable conduct in market spheres. It expresses the notion that such behaviors are unavoidable side effects of allowing corporate elites' innovative and competitive
qualities to thrive in the marketplace. It prescribes regulatory interventions as
the preferred remedies for controlling harmful behaviors so as not to quash
productive traits under punitive sanctions. Accordingly, laws should either
designate harmful corporate activity as noncriminal and subject only to regulatory oversight or specify that certain corporate activities are criminal but
grant regulators discretion to choose from regulatory, civil, and other measures to manage the behavior in lieu of prosecution.

While it is useful to provide these basic definitions of each ideology,
deeper analysis reveals their complexity. Importantly, neither warrants too
tight a definition beyond their essential features since the transition of both
into political practice has not been seamless. Both emanated from Progressive era politics and eugenic ideas, and both have been altered over time as
political elites have used them to market diverse policies to the public and
reshape the bounds of the prison system and the regulatory state. But scrutiny
also reveals that both ideologies rest on interconnected theoretical groundings and share a priori assumptions about human nature and criminality that
have proved tenacious.

First, both ideologies adhere to the ethic of individual responsibility and
emphasize the moral and social worth of individuals as a primary explanation
for their behavior and status, thereby legitimizing the inequalities of capitalist
society. The poor, criminal underclasses are in their position because of their
natural deficiencies. If rehabilitative interventions cannot help them overcome their marginality, the only explanation for their failures becomes their
incorrigibility, a logic that ignores how socioeconomic forces generate crime
and inequality by valorizing microinterventions aimed at improving the indi-

vidual as the solution to those ills. Meanwhile, motivated business leaders are driven by an energetic temperament, rendering their occasionally harmful actions by-products of natural forces that produce social goods. Although this book addresses the rise of the corporate form as an important development in American law, the regulatory ideological framework that emerged from eugenics emphasizes the behavior of *individual* executives. It treats corporate criminality as a misguided cousin of the entrepreneurial spirit that can be corrected via administration without suffocating enterprising characters under threat of prosecution.

Second, both ideologies have a basis in eugenics. While each was influenced by various ideas from economics, anthropology, sociology, and law, in crucial ways both rested on a common eugenic bedrock and evolved as frameworks to manage people differently depending on assumptions about their natural predispositions. As a result, they facilitated biopolitical modes of governance. Owing to the work of Michel Foucault, biopolitics is a political rationality in which state power is exerted to promote the health of the population under its jurisdiction. The biopolitical state adopts technologies of governance to classify and control the population according to social standards of health and normalcy, targeting weak or deviant members for control under the assumption that they threaten the well-being of the collective social body.[8] The biopolitical mentalities of rehabilitative and regulatory ideologies dictate that incorrigibles are naturally inferior threats requiring stern control, reformable offenders can be normalized via rehabilitation, and corporate malfeasants should be regulated to allow their desirable traits to flourish safely. While the ideologies no longer require eugenic politics to thrive, their underlying principles carry a lingering eugenic character into contemporary American law.

Third, rehabilitative and regulatory ideologies rest on racial and class assumptions. Progressive era scholars attributed myriad social and economic inequalities to eugenic variables and meshed those ideas with the "born criminal" concept, turning poverty, racial inequality, and criminal incorrigibility into products of a common set of inherent personal defects. Alternatively, White corporate elites were racialized as natural capitalists. As Foucault states, biopolitics consists of a war waged "by a race that is portrayed as the one true race, the race that holds power and is entitled to define the norm, and against those who deviate from that norm."[9] The biopolitical framework has clear value in explaining the stigmatization of incorrigibles, but it also integrates the regulatory control of corporate crime with the racial history of the carceral state. The state's inability and reluctance to prosecute corporate criminality consistently is the extreme end of a governing philosophy defining punishment in racialized terms. The poor, racialized, Lombrosian body is the core of rehabilitative ideology on one end of this axis, but on the other is the naturally strong, sanguinary body of the White corporate raider whose natural tendencies make him champion of the market jungle. The full story of race and punishment in America is not just one of punishing the racialized criminal body but one in which racialized bodies requiring punishment are distinguished from racialized bodies that do not.

Rehabilitative and regulatory ideologies subsequently advocate different solutions. Rehabilitative ideology articulates a two-pronged solution—a "benevolent prong" premised on reforming and releasing inmates who can be transformed, and a "punitive prong" promising punishment for incorrigibles. This sorting feature of rehabilitative thought spoils it at its root; rehabilitation has never embraced the possibility of redemption for all. It has always been dedicated to distinguishing a corrigible class definable only in contrast to incorrigibles requiring punishment, allowing rehabilitative ideology to operate as a punitive force behind gentle rhetoric. This book shows how numerous contemporary penal techniques and practices are legacies of rehabilitative ideology's emphasis on meting out punitive or rehabilitative remedies on the basis of assessments of defendants' reformative potential, keeping the justice system preoccupied with detecting the incorrigibles among us.

Regulatory ideology has no duality, instead adopting a singular approach. Since business actors are driven by traits that produce desirable social goods, their wrongdoing must be a result of market forces playing on vulnerabilities of character by generating temptations that lead ambitious characters astray. This framing presents corporate lawbreakers as redeemable, rational, and undeserving of full blame, warranting the use of regulation to govern misconduct interpreted as incidental effects of positive traits not requiring rehabilitation or punishment. The regulatory approach aims to keep corporate actors in line not through intensive individual-level supervision, but through regulation of the structural conditions of the marketplace to ensure that economic dynamics do not entice market participants to engage in illicit behavior.

Rehabilitative and regulatory ideologies bolster a vision of social control that punishes the poor and minorities ruthlessly for their wrongs and manages the misconduct of capitalist elites administratively, generating predictable but intractable inequalities in the process. They reflect a consensus on a constructed image about what counts as crime and who counts as a criminal, naturalizing the crime problem as a class and race problem. In other words, rehabilitative ideology has been deployed to control the poor and people of color punitively because of who they are for fear of what they *might* do, while regulatory ideology has been deployed to eschew punishment for capitalist elites because of who they are in spite of what they *actually* do.

Exposing the inequalities sustained by rehabilitative and regulatory ideologies opens up new conversations about reforming American law, and one potential interpretation of this analysis could be that the punitiveness afforded to street crime should be applied to corporate wrongdoing to align the governance of corporate misconduct with the punitive streak of American politics. But equalizing justice this way would be a shortsighted solution that is out of step with this book's central contention that the prison system must be scaled back. Instead, the comparison of rehabilitative and regulatory ideologies can be used to advance a more positively constructive resolution. Specifically, literature on the sociology of crime and critical analyses of the carceral state often insist that crime should be treated as a function of economic conditions requiring reform, not a product of individual choices deserving punishment. This book demonstrates that incorporating this notion into governing practice is not a quixotic proposition. That premise has existed within an influential ideology that has been historically present throughout the carceral state's rise—the one shaping the regulation of business. This book challenges us to think of how techniques of regulatory control can be extended to manage undesirable behavior outside corporate boardrooms without punitive sanctions. American law cannot be fully comprehended without studying how rehabilitative and regulatory ideologies have been used to establish unequal legal arrangements, but assessing their development together reminds us that the hard work of challenging the inequalities they perpetuate must rely on measured rather than rash solutions.

Approach

This book adopts historical institutionalist methodologies to trace the origins of rehabilitative and regulatory ideologies and their roles in carceral and regulatory development. It utilizes literature on ideas and institutions in American political development to examine how political actors have deployed, modified, and contested these ideologies at discrete moments to build coalitions, challenge existing structures, and pursue institutional and policy change.[10] A range of ideas has shaped American law since the colonial era, including Puritan morality, utilitarian theory, retributivist philosophies, and libertarian ideals, among many others.[11] Neglecting to examine these influential ideas in favor of focusing on rehabilitative and regulatory ideologies is not to presume that all policy developments in criminal justice and regulation are reducible to their influence. Rather, this book shows how rehabilitative and regulatory ideologies emerged and evolved as related governing mentalities that have historically served as weapons political actors have used to pursue distinctive goals at different moments.

The book begins by assessing the work of prominent Progressive era scholars of criminal anthropology, race science, prison administration, eugenics, law, and economics to excavate the interrelated origins of rehabilitative and regulatory ideologies.[12] It then traces how these ideas spread to a broader network of scholars, activists, and practitioners in law, economics, and criminal justice. Later chapters connect rehabilitative and regulatory ideologies to political development by studying how they were given meaning by political actors from the Progressive era to today. This requires qualitative analysis tracking how political actors cited and used the ideas of scholars who first articulated these ideologies and how later political actors called on and modified them to justify change and transmit them into institutional designs.

Given the book's scope and foci, it relies on diverse sources to study political development in different times and places. Ideologies travel through changing hands over time, and tracking their trajectories requires attention to the shifting arenas of conflict across the local, state, and federal policymaking venues where political actors have mobilized them. In the Progressive era, rehabilitative ideas often appeared in state board of charities (SBC) reports. State legislative records are largely unavailable from this period, but SBCs served as advisory bodies for state lawmakers regarding state social policy. Their reports outline the progression of state debates over sentencing and reformatories in which rehabilitative ideology was heavily featured. Analysis of Progressive era criminal justice also considers publications from the Eugenics Record Office (ERO), state court cases, and writings of leading penal practitioners to map the influence of rehabilitative ideology. Floor statements from the *Congressional Record*, legislative committee hearings and reports, federal court cases, and agency reports are the primary resources used to analyze how regulatory ideology manifested in Progressive era debates over the regulatory state. At the turn of the century, economic regulation became a national issue while street crime remained a state and local problem, requiring analysis of federal politics to understand the influence of regulatory ideology and state and local politics to track rehabilitative ideology.

Analysis of the twentieth and twenty-first centuries necessitates attention to different resources as institutions like SBCs and the ERO closed. Fortunately, legislative records, court cases, crime commission publications, and correctional department administrative records from mid-twentieth-century state governments are readily accessible for analyzing the path of rehabilitative ideology. The *Congressional Record* and legislative committee hearings and reports also become important resources with which to study rehabilitative ideology as crime control became a federal responsibility in the twentieth and twenty-first centuries. Federal administrative and legislative records remain the primary sources for tracing how regulatory ideology manifested throughout this period. Analysis of these resources is complemented throughout the chapters by consideration of media coverage, think tank and activist organization reports, and state and federal case law.

Given this framework, the book offers various insights into how ideas shape political development. First, it illustrates nuances in the relationship between ideas and power. Ideas do not exist separately from structures of power and are infused with effects of power only when advanced by political actors and institutions.[13] But political actors must choose from a universe of competing ideas when communicating their policy preferences and must make strategic choices by speaking within those ideational frames they believe have a feasible chance of being accepted and transmitted into favorable policy.[14] This book illustrates how ideas color the exercise of power by influencing the terms on which actors engage in political action, bringing the properties, premises, and qualities of those ideas into political conflicts that produce change.

This elucidates subtleties in how political actors exercise their power. For instance, attributing the outcomes of regulatory debates to the power of big business overlooks nuances in how firms wield their influence. Careful analysis of moments in regulatory development uncovers disagreements within and across industries that can be missed if big business is treated as a homogeneous bloc. Typically, advocates of regulatory governance have prevailed in political conflicts over firms demanding pure laissez-faire or incarceration for corrupt competitors because they did not bluntly resist change or attempt to upend all the features of the political climate that they found inconvenient, but instead maximized their leverage by couching their goals within prevailing discourses. Such scrutiny shows how even actors with enormous power direct that power in relation to their ideational context.

Second, ideas exist both in theory and in practice. While their core qualities can structure political conflicts, they are mediated by relations of power and evolve from their abstract forms when transferred into political spheres by actors who reconsider their meanings and purposes.[15] Rehabilitative and regulatory ideologies have proved malleable in the hands of lawmakers seeking varied objectives, and the chapters pay careful attention to the political context of each era to highlight the social and economic factors that conditioned how political actors deployed them. In different contexts, the ideologies were framed variously as revolutionizing forces, as moderate solutions, or in substantially modified forms. Since they have been espoused by shifting political ensembles with differing aims, their developmental pathways have not played out straightforwardly, highlighting the creative tension between abstract ideas and their political use.

Third, when ideas are entrenched within institutions, their meanings are expressed and sustained as people interact with those institutions.[16] Rehabilitative and regulatory ideologies are more than false narratives concocted by ruling classes. They consist of intellectual and political propositions that provide the public with commonsense validations of their everyday experiences as produced by institutions built on their principles. In other words, they are self-rationalizing systemic logics.[17] The development of carceral and regulatory institutions has hardened the ideological premises on which they rest because institutional practices associated with rehabilitative and regulatory ideologies continue to reflect and reinforce their underlying assumptions in the present, giving them a tenacity that keeps a eugenic stamp imprinted on the modern carceral project without the baggage of eugenic politics.

For instance, consider America's unusually heavy emphasis on criminal history in sentencing in comparison to nations abroad.[18] This practice, which generates racial and class disparities behind the seemingly neutral metric of criminal history, is traceable to the rehabilitative mission of identifying and punishing the incorrigible class and keeps the myth of incorrigibility alive. Alternatively, while no judge today justifies short sentences for corporate offenders on the basis of their racial superiority, judges often rationalize leniency by concluding that corporate offenders' clean criminal histories render them unlikely to recidivate.[19] But the administrative approach keeps corporate crime undercounted in official data sets, giving corporate recidivists misleadingly spotless criminal records.[20] Regardless of lawmakers' intentions in promoting rehabilitative and regulatory ideologies—whether because they genuinely believed in them or because they saw them as tools with which to achieve something else—their choices embedded particular understandings about criminality within institutions that now bolster those ideas. This shows how institutions can keep the ideas that undergird them alive and uncritically accepted by the public through their regular operations.

Finally, it is important to note that political development is volatile. Laws and institutions are products of conflicts in which competing ideas clash, giving them an incoherent character as contradictory ideas prevail in different moments.[21] Rehabilitative and regulatory ideologies have sometimes collided with incompatible ideas, been interpreted and mobilized in divergent ways by actors with dissimilar motives, or been deployed to unintentional effects. They have thus played dynamic rather than static roles in political development.

This clarifies how and why the ideologies have sometimes been activated to unintentional or contradictory effects. For instance, while rehabilitative ideology has often been like a Rorschach test for lawmakers in that they find in it what they want to justify sinister policies, not everyone endorsing rehabilitation has punitive ulterior motives. Chapter 7 discusses how contemporary civil rights and criminal justice reform organizations committed to shrinking prison populations by espousing ideals of human redemption have supported laws promising rehabilitative reform, although those laws have since produced punitive outcomes. Such groups are not deploying rehabilitation as a smoke screen for harsh penality of the variety this book ascribes to the rehabilitative ideal; they are contesting precisely that approach. However, this book illustrates that such well-intentioned actors do not recognize how America's carceral landscape is mired in ideological premises committed to *sorting* corrigibles and incorrigibles, not providing redemption for all. Championing human redeemability amplifies rehabilitative ideology's benevolent prong, but it also opens the door to a heavy-handed punitiveness for incorrigibles. Such actors are not duplicitous, but in an institutional terrain built on the duality of rehabilitative ideology, even their sincere appeals to rehabilitation risk exacerbating our carceral crisis.

Attending to the volatility of change also highlights moments when the ideologies conflicted with new ideas. For example, the regulatory approach to handling corporate misconduct was contested in the Progressive era. As president, Theodore Roosevelt proposed a federal corporate licensing system that constituted a different model for managing the economy and was framed as a means of attributing criminal liability to executives hiding behind the corporate form. That it never came to fruition was due to a series of political missteps on Roosevelt's part and the outcome of the 1912 presidential election. Such moments underscore how the trajectories of these ideologies have rested on contingent political occurrences and rarely played out in clearcut fashions.

Race, Class, and the Carceral State

This book intervenes in numerous debates about the development of the carceral state by offering an alternative to prevailing genealogies of mass incarceration. It most significantly departs from existing literature by examining the carceral and regulatory states as related institutions. Scholars typically divorce their analysis of the carceral state from considerations of corporate crime and regulation. This perspective fundamentally limits our understanding of mass incarceration by overlooking the fact that before contemplating whether and how to punish given behaviors, lawmakers must first decide whether behavior should be controlled via criminal sanctions or other techniques. Explaining the punitive present only by studying punitive policies adopts a restrictive analytic lens.[22] If we never look at what was excluded from, separated from, or channeled away from the carceral landscape, we will never fully appreciate how it came to be. This book distinctively studies criminal justice and regulatory administration as systems built on related ideological visions, revealing a wholly new perspective on the carceral state.

Many scholars endorse a standard story explaining the onset of mass incarceration as prompted by the collapse of postwar liberalism and penal welfarism. According to this account, mass incarceration's proximate origins lay in the repudiation of the rehabilitative ideal during the conservative backlash to the civil rights movement and the Great Society.[23] This narrative has been challenged by scholars arguing that rehabilitative logic has been harnessed to punitive ends during the era of mass incarceration, but this book unpacks a far deeper and darker history behind the rehabilitative ideal.[24] The rehabilitative approach emerged within a punitive eugenic ideology with Progressive era roots. Contrary to explanations that it promoted penal welfarism through the twentieth century, coexisted uncomfortably alongside punitive policies, or has recently been twisted to serve the carceral state, this book shows how political actors have activated rehabilitative ideology's punitive logic to construct the carceral state incrementally since the late nineteenth century.

Recent scholarship has shown that the carceral state's emergence was more than a toxic breakdown of penal welfarism. Historical accounts of law-and-order campaigns by the Left and the Right chronicle choices made across the political spectrum that laid the foundations for the carceral state well before penal welfarism's demise.[25] Sharing this orientation, this book illuminates deep bipartisan roots to the carceral state. The historical record reveals that punitive practices and assumptions have been smuggled into the criminal justice system behind rhetorical promises of rehabilitation from the late nineteenth century to the present day. Rehabilitative practices still infect the justice system with ideas of innate criminality and have long kept lawmakers of diverse partisan affiliations tied to determinist assumptions about incorrigibility.

Other accounts of mass incarceration's roots trace the poison back to the legacies of slavery, Jim Crow, and racializations of crime predating the punitive turn by centuries.[26] Identifying historical links between racism and pun-

ishment is a moral imperative given the racial profile of the prison population, and race and racism warrant thorough conceptualization as totalities of
diverse social and material forces unique to their historical context. Racial
labels manifest as "taxonom[ies] of ascriptive difference" that construct and
sort human populations into "hierarchies of capacity, civic worth, and desert
based on 'natural' or essential characteristics."[27] Historical analysis reveals that
racial categories are sites of contestation with meanings that change in relation
to shifting inequalities in power and privilege. And, as racial labels evolve,
racism—the prejudiced use of social, political, and legal instruments based
on presumed racial differences—brings racially patterned inequalities to life.[28]

This clarifies rehabilitative ideology's role in fueling the racial injustices
of mass incarceration. Intellectual endeavors ranging from Progressive era
race science through modern biocriminology share uncomfortably similar
premises about racial difference and incorrigibility. Contemporary intellectuals eschew the racial taxonomies of their forebears, enabling them to insist
that they are objective scientists, but modern biodeterminist scholarship still
treats race as an essentialist analytic category to reach racialized conclusions
about crime. Meanwhile, techniques of risk assessment and sentencing based
on criminal history inherited from the rehabilitative approach have evolved
to appear race neutral until their underlying assumptions are scrutinized,
allowing them to produce racial inequalities targeting modern-day incorrigibles through seemingly unbiased procedures.

While many have attended to the carceral state's steep racial biases, scholars often disagree over the degree to which racial and class forces are causally
determinative of the prison boom. This book adopts a class-driven perspective highlighting how racism and class control have intersected in the politicization of rehabilitative ideology. Intertwined material and racial inequalities
have marched together throughout the carceral state's development, and this
book shows how by emphasizing the far-reaching harm rehabilitative ideology has inflicted on people of color, immigrants, and those at the bottom of
the class hierarchy alike. This perspective clarifies the book's account of racial inequality by demonstrating how racial inequalities exist within webs of
economic relations, illuminating how material inequalities contribute to the
racial injustices of criminal punishment.[29]

Directing attention to the relationship between the prison system and
political economy complements critical criminological scholarship assessing
the carceral state through a structural Marxist lens. This work contends that
the state politicizes crime to legitimate capitalist social relations by framing the
poor as individually responsible for their wrongs without considering the economic conditions that cause crime. Carefully executed critical frameworks

stress how racial and class dynamics interact as the carceral state compels an increasingly Black subproletariat to transform into diligent worker-citizens or face incarceration.[30] This book connects critical criminological and historical institutionalist frames to show how ideological constructs of criminality have been used to imbue crime with racialized and class slants by politicizing poverty, racial inequality, and criminality as products of a common set of individual failings requiring stringent controls. Ideologically compromised science has historically rationalized oppression across racial and class dimensions as the label *natural criminality* and its variants—*born criminal, incorrigible*, and *habitual offender*—have been populated with various undesirable racial and class groups in different times and places.[31] This illustrates how projects of class and racial control have been fused through the politicization of rehabilitative ideology.

Importantly, there are some scholarly exceptions to the trend of studying mass incarceration separately from white-collar crime.[32] In *The Rich Get Richer and the Poor Get Prison* (2016), Jeffrey Reiman and Paul Leighton advance criminological and philosophical arguments that the justice system is designed to fail at reducing street crime, misleading the public into thinking that the poor are society's criminal threats while hiding the crimes of the wealthy.[33] In *Who Are the Criminals?* (2010), John Hagan argues that scholarly ideas of crime have historically been linked to shifts in policy and that structural criminology fostered progressive crime politics during the "age of Roosevelt" (1933–73) while "career criminal criminology" produced punitive policies for street criminals and leniency for white-collar offenders in the "age of Reagan" (1974–2008).[34] And, in *The Illusion of Free Markets* (2011), Bernard Harcourt details how libertarian ideals and free market economic theory have kept the market monitored by the gentle touch of the invisible hand while the state employs a heavy fist to enforce crime policy.[35]

This text builds on these accounts but asks different questions about the related origins, ideological character, and developmental trajectories of carceral and regulatory institutions. It takes seriously John Braithwaite's call to study business regulation in relation to punitive street crime governance, doing so on a hitherto unexplored scale utilizing historical institutionalist methods to examine political developments from the late nineteenth century to the present day.[36] Doing so unearths Progressive era ideological and political developments that have generated linked developmental patterns in American law, punishment, and regulatory governance that have been overlooked in existing scholarship. This provides novel insights into how the principles underpinning rehabilitative and regulatory ideologies have shaped the development of carceral and regulatory systems, rendering them institutional relatives and carrying a eugenic spirit into contemporary legal norms and practices.

Rethinking Corporate Crime and the Regulatory State

Fully grasping the nature of regulatory governance requires examining how corporate lawbreaking has been disconnected from punitive mentalities and subsumed under administrative controls. Corporate crime scholars have offered many explanations for the infrequency of corporate prosecutions, but they detach their analyses of corporate crime from the wider criminal justice universe. Meanwhile, political scientists examining the regulatory state's development either overlook its crime control functions or treat them as peripheral responsibilities of institutions designed for economic management with no significant connection to crime politics. These narrow perspectives produce incomplete accounts of corporate criminal punishment and regulation by studying them in isolation rather than as branches of the state's larger governing framework for controlling misconduct.[37] Comprehensively understanding them requires attention to the entire system of interconnected roots and branches that shapes the social control framework in which they exist.

In comparison to street crime, white-collar and corporate crime have garnered attention from American criminologists only relatively recently. This scholarly tradition is traceable to Edwin Sutherland's *White-Collar Crime* (1949). In this landmark text, Sutherland studied 980 legal decisions against seventy corporations and found that roughly 20 percent were handled in criminal court and that 80 percent were handled through regulatory, civil, or equity proceedings, even though most of the cases involved violations of criminal law.[38] Over time, the book has been acknowledged for revolutionizing criminology, and controlling corporate crime through regulation is now considered "the American way."[39] More current criminological scholarship emphasizes other factors to explain the infrequency of corporate prosecutions, including that judges sentence white-collar defendants leniently by virtue of their personal traits, which they believe render them unlikely to recidivate, and that prosecutors are regularly outmatched by highly paid legal teams representing corporate clients.[40] Other scholars pinpoint structural explanations, including the fact that concerns over the economic impact of prosecuting executives dissuade the state from taking legal action, that deregulation and financialization since the 1980s fostered corporate cultures that normalize lawbreaking for profit, or that executives use their clout to shape policy favorably.[41] These are valid arguments, but this book is directed toward the different aim of exploring the development of the regulatory institutions within which these patterns have emerged, unpacking the regulatory state's deeper relationship to the criminal justice system and forging a clearer understanding of its political and ideological foundations.

Political scientists depict the regulatory state as a creature of the unique dynamics of American politics and capitalism and as an alternative to public ownership of industries built to stabilize rather than restructure capitalist markets.[42] Scholars of American political development have uncovered various roots to the regulatory state, showing that at the end of the nineteenth century, reform-driven professionals, judges, corporations, and political elites with varied motives facilitated the development of a corporate capitalist economy monitored by a regulatory state.[43] This literature illustrates that the emergence of the regulatory state was an institutionally and politically mediated response to the structural dilemmas posed by industrialization and the nationalization of the political economy. But, while this scholarship reveals important realities about the regulatory state's origins, it does not explore how crime politics shaped its development. Doing so recasts the regulatory state as more than a mechanism of economic management; it is also a counterpart to the criminal justice system that operates as an alternative mode for controlling misconduct. This reinterprets debates over whether US government agencies are uniquely antagonistic or feeble in comparison to their analogues abroad, a scholarly dispute that sometimes fosters all-or-nothing statements about the regulatory state being too lax or punitive by minimizing the nuanced realities of regulation.[44] The regulatory state has both pro- and antibusiness dimensions as it was built to sustain capitalism through regulatory controls designed as relatives of crime control tools.

While powerful corporate interests have played essential roles in shaping regulatory development, this book cautions against reductionist explanations attributing regulatory policy outcomes solely to the intervention of powerful firms.[45] The political influence of business interests has historically fluctuated, often in counterintuitive ways, depending on the economy's health.[46] Coalitions of business interests have deployed regulatory ideology to pursue their goals in different political economic climates, with varying degrees of success. Further, political economic structures evolve. While economic elites have played central roles in championing regulatory ideology, the economic elites of one era are rarely the same as those of the next.[47] Over time, the leading advocates of regulatory ideology have changed to reflect relative power shifts within the political economy. Each time regulatory ideology was employed by new actors, it was modified. Additionally, presenting corporate interests as all-powerful risks treating the business community as monolithic, glossing over how firms sometimes concentrate their power and sometimes fracture into rival coalitions.[48] Asking which businesses have won over time and why highlights subtleties in how firms deploy their power.

The development of the large corporation is key to understanding how American law manages corporate malfeasance. Corporations were vital in the early republic but came into being through state charters and legislative acts defining their obligations and rights, keeping them tied to the state. As states passed general incorporation statutes in the late nineteenth century, corporations became large autonomous creations of contracting market participants bound to the interests of shareholders and corporate leadership rather than the public welfare. Then, in 1909, the Supreme Court ruled that corporate entities could be punished criminally for the actions of their agents.[49] These significant developments are considered in this book, but, given its focus on the regulatory ideology that emerged from eugenics, most attention will be directed toward evaluating how and why the state regularly fails to punish *individual* executives by virtue of who they are.

Important to note is that this book's analysis of regulatory ideology directs its focus on corporate crime rather than white-collar crime. Definitions of *white-collar crime* often encompass offenses neither isolated to economic elites nor overseen by regulators, such as forgery, identity theft, and occupational malpractice. *Corporate crime* encapsulates crimes committed either by a corporate entity or by individuals within a corporation engaging in criminal conduct through their occupation. This book's case studies largely emphasize financial wrongdoing given that regulatory ideology presumes that an individual's ability to produce wealth is a desirable trait warranting controls that are less punitive. However, chapter 6 explores how regulatory ideology's blurred distinctions between corporate criminality and entrepreneurialism have seeped into social regulations governing conduct related to nonfinancial features of the production process.

Ways Forward

The dysfunctions generated by rehabilitative and regulatory ideologies are disheartening. If all we can do is demand more rehabilitation and regulation to challenge the status quo, it signals that a certain ideological dominance has taken hold of the body politic. However, this analysis also illuminates paths toward a different future. These routes are briefly reviewed here and discussed in greater detail in chapter 8.

First, subjecting corporate offenders to the instincts powering mass incarceration is an unwise remedy that would counterproductively grow the carceral state. Juxtaposing regulatory and carceral development is intended to highlight the inequalities produced by these institutions, not spark categorical anger at regulatory governance. It is important to critique these inequalities without overlooking how effective regulation can ameliorate economic conditions that cause crime without punitive sanctions. Rather than dismissing regulatory ideology as a hypocritical sham, a more productive critique is that only a select few benefit from its application.

This perspective facilitates a different prescriptive move than embracing a vindictive egalitarianism exposing corporate offenders to the punitive impulses afforded to everyone else. Idealized aspects of the regulatory approach—like imposing noncriminal sanctions as initial responses to wrongdoing and correcting economic forces that generate misconduct—offer a constructive blueprint for resolving maladies in criminal justice. American carceral and regulatory institutions perpetuate enormous inequalities that are worthy of criticism, but the path to equality should "level up" by expanding dignified treatment to everyone rather than "level down" by affording the most degrading penalties to all.[50] The proactive and risk-preventative character of regulatory governance has the potential to reform criminogenic conditions in poor communities through economic management rather than punitive controls. The logic that crime is a consequence of economic circumstance undergirds the regulatory approach, and critics of mass incarceration would be wise to expand its reach.

This is not a far-fetched idea. State-level developments legalizing and regulating marijuana already partially reflect this notion, but there are bigger possibilities. Many hardships faced by the poor can be attributed to unregulated dimensions of modern capitalism, and research reveals that generous social welfare is linked to reduced crime rates by remedying structural economic inequalities that cause crime.[51] In communities with surplus populations trapped in poverty and exploitation, guaranteeing a livable wage or access to public goods like affordable housing can be conceived of as regulatory forms of economic management that proactively offset the conditions of poverty that cause undesirable conduct. Federal jobs programs have similar potential given the relationship between unemployment and crime.[52] New Deal era programs employing millions in federally regulated public works projects have been credited as crime preventative by providing jobs to otherwise unemployed individuals susceptible to criminogenic economic pressures during the Great Depression.[53]

Second, critiquing rehabilitation is not a call to make prisons less humane. It can be jarring to hear that rehabilitation should be renounced as a guiding objective of the prison system owing to its promise to punish incorrigibles harshly, but this does not mean that the interventions that we call *rehabili-*

tative should be eliminated from prisons. Rather, they should be framed as means of recognizing the human rights and dignity of those behind bars, not as means of fixing deviant people. Chapter 8 explains how presenting measures like in-prison educational and vocational programs in this way would detach them from assumptions about innate incorrigibility, de-emphasize the importance of recidivism as a metric for evaluating their efficacy, and create space to reimagine parole and probation.

Third, this book contends that governing corporate misconduct requires a combination of regulatory and prosecutorial controls. Research on deterring corporate wrongdoing shows that "a mix of agency interventions" tailored to the frequency and severity of infractions maximizes deterrent effects.[54] This aligns with the "responsive regulation" model advocated by Braithwaite and Ayres, which posits that regulators should utilize a hierarchical "sanctions pyramid" beginning with mild administrative interventions to manage minor and first-time infractions before escalating to punitive tools for serious wrongdoing. They theorize that milder regulations serve as deterrents only if prosecution is perceived as a credible threat.[55] Deterrence research supports this view by indicating that combining administrative interventions with consistent punishment in serious cases, not excessively severe or overly frequent use of punishment, best deters corporate misconduct.[56]

The book endorses the responsive regulation framework to emphasize the complementary roles of prosecution and regulation. The absence of prosecutions after the financial crisis has raised serious concerns about the erosion of the rule of law in America's boardrooms. The state risks undercutting public faith in the legal system if it fails to secure meaningful accountability from corporate lawbreakers. But prosecution alone cannot manage intricate economic systems without robust regulatory controls, a reality illustrated by the S&L crisis discussed in chapter 6. Prosecution and regulation are integrated components of one system, not mutually exclusive strategies, and both are necessary for managing corporate activity in a complex economy.

Notably, deterrence research belies the idea that regulation is merely a convenient answer to the structural predicament lawmakers face when industry leaders commit crimes. This mentality suggests that holding executives criminally accountable risks harming the economy more than benefiting it and that regulation gives the state an expedient way to do *something* about corporate malfeasance without hurting itself by prosecuting vital economic resources. But this assumes that leaving corporate misconduct unpunished serves the institutional interest of avoiding economic harm when scholarship indicates the exact opposite: markets are less stable and healthy if prosecution of wrongdoing is not seen as a credible threat.[57] Put simply, consistently prosecuting corporate malfeasance *helps* the economy. Reasoning that corporate misconduct should go unpunished so as not to inflict economic harm, despite evidence to the contrary, only underscores the dominant hold that regulatory ideology exercises over our political imagination.

Fourth, the strategies detailed above are worthwhile but insufficient solutions on their own because rehabilitative and regulatory ideologies sustain deeper pathologies in the political economy. Fully undoing their legacies requires shifting focus toward transforming the broken economic system that they prop up.

Rehabilitative ideology assumes that vulnerable populations can lift themselves out of marginality through individual empowerment, leaving intact the unequal economic structures of modern capitalism. It rests on the misguided assumption that all causes of crime exist at the individual level and can be corrected through individual-level solutions. This logic disregards the enormous obstacles rehabilitated individuals face when released to disadvantaged communities with limited opportunities for success. What follows is a self-fulfilling punitive politics. Any findings that in-prison rehabilitative programs do not correlate with long-term behavioral change become justification to lock up incorrigibles and throw away the key. But truly empowering individuals requires macroeconomic reforms giving returning offenders real chances for success following their time behind bars. Instead of trying to fix people, we should fix the chronic structures of marginality that drive crime where people live. In this light, the regulatory philosophy provides a valuable schematic for thinking about how a politics focused on economic management as crime preventative can give people genuine chances to succeed.

Meanwhile, even a thoughtful mix of regulation and prosecution cannot contain the corporations that now exert vast power over all dimensions of society. Regulation and prosecution are crucial governing instruments in a complex economy, but they can do only so much to improve American life if they stabilize an inequitable and dysfunctional economy. Solutions like breaking up big banks, federal chartering systems, and nationalization strategies can make the economy more manageable and functional. Recognizing the limitations of prosecution and regulation in controlling the contemporary economy opens the door to these more radical ideas.

Book Structure

This book explores how political actors have used rehabilitative and regulatory ideologies to build institutions that channel lower-class offenders toward the prison and corporate lawbreakers away from it. It does so by examining three intertwined historical narratives—the development of rehabilitative and regulatory ideologies, the development of the carceral state, and the development of the regulatory state.

Chapter 2 excavates the intellectual origins of rehabilitative and regulatory ideologies in eugenic currents in Progressive era social, legal, and economic theory. Chapter 3 then traces the significance of rehabilitative ideology to Progressive era politics. It examines Zebulon Brockway, the "father of the rehabilitative ideal," who pioneered the rehabilitative paradigm at New York's Elmira Reformatory. Analysis of the reformatory movement illustrates how state legislators across the country replicated Brockway's model. It then examines the racial and class biases of rehabilitative ideology through its impact on vagrancy laws, which were reformed in thirty-two states to enhance punishments for vagrants who exhibited class and racial traits associated with born criminality. The chapter ends by studying links between rehabilitation and the eugenics movement.

Through examinations of the 1887 Interstate Commerce Act (ICA) and the 1914 Federal Trade Commission Act (FTCA), chapter 4 traces how regulatory ideology shaped Progressive era politics. In the 1880s, railroad officials regularly testified before Congress about the ICA, which initially included strict criminal prohibitions on railroad industry activities. They insisted that executives were more respectable than common criminals since they were driven by a competitive ethic, not a criminal disposition, and advocated for the Interstate Commerce Commission to monitor markets through administrative tools instead. Debates over the FTCA were similar, but the players involved reflected a power shift within the political economy as the financial industry took center stage. In both instances, a case was made for including statutory criminal sanctions on common market tactics, but industry elites and their political allies advocated within regulatory ideological terms to monitor market crimes through administrative governance.

Chapter 5 illustrates how rehabilitative ideology fueled punitive outcomes through the mid-twentieth century and the subsequent rise of the carceral state. It explores the proliferation of state-level habitual offender laws from the 1920s through 1970s, with case studies of New York and California illustrating how these laws were rationalized as components of rehabilitative politics. This discussion is followed by an analysis of the federal sentencing guidelines of the 1980s, which did not completely reject the rehabilitative ideal but subtly repurposed its most punitive elements.

Chapter 6 examines three pivotal moments in the twentieth century when corporate crime provoked public outcry and regulatory ideology conditioned the path of political change. It first analyzes Congress's investigation into the

1929 economic crash, which uncovered substantial evidence of wrongdoing on Wall Street. But Congress and the Justice Department relied on modified interpretations of regulatory ideology to elevate regulation over prosecution in the Securities Exchange Act of 1934. The chapter also explores the consumers' movement of the 1970s, when demands for criminal law enforcement clashed with existing institutional arrangements governed by regulatory principles. Finally, it studies the S&L crisis, noting that the over one thousand federal prosecutions it prompted illustrates that the state can punish corporate crime under certain conditions. But this prosecutorial enthusiasm should not overshadow that deregulation permitted the industry's problems to grow and overwhelm federal prosecutors with an unmanageable caseload once the industry collapsed. This underscores the need to understand regulation and prosecution as complementary components of a unified system.

Chapter 7 examines how rehabilitative and regulatory ideologies persist in new forms today. It traces how conservative think tanks and knowledge-producing institutions are modifying rehabilitative and regulatory ideologies to pursue neoliberal agendas of cost-efficient governance while biological analyses of crime are resurfacing, even though they are not necessary for justifying the neoliberal rebranding of rehabilitation and regulation. Next, the chapter studies the First Step Act of 2018. The law's laudable changes are compromised by its reliance on a racially and class-biased risk-assessment tool couched in a commitment to rehabilitation. The chapter then studies post-2000 trends in regulation, particularly emphasizing the Dodd-Frank Wall Street Reform and Consumer Protection Act of 2010.

The concluding chapter details how the harmful legacies of rehabilitative and regulatory ideologies can be excised from American politics through institutional reforms. It also discusses how both ideologies sustain deep economic inequalities and argues that we must abandon the idea that we should control people to fight crime and instead rectify the economic structures that produce crime in the first place.

Evaluating the developmental threads of the carceral and regulatory states illustrates how they have evolved to work together in defining what it means to be a criminal in America. Their related ideological roots must be laid bare and fully understood if they are to be transformed.

Ideological Formation: Constructing Rehabilitative and Regulatory Ideologies

The tramp and the millionaire have always existed. . . . [P]ut them down side by side naked and helpless on a desert island; and in one year the one will be what he was at first, namely, a pauper, while the other will have become a capitalist.
"Tramps and Millionaires," *New York Daily Tribune*, July 26, 1887

The late nineteenth century and the early twentieth were times of upheaval in American life. Violent class conflict, Jim Crow segregation, industrialization, the rise of the large corporation, and the emergence of the administrative state were just a few of the major changes that unfolded over only a few decades. The following three chapters direct attention to the politics of crime and social control in this tumultuous context. This chapter illustrates how currents in political and social theory about criminality, government power, and human difference became intertwined during this time in ways that have had lasting consequences for American political development.

The chapter explores the origins of the Progressive era ideologies of rehabilitation and regulation. The rise of each was driven by varied political, social, and economic forces, but their geneses also had common ideational groundings in eugenic and Social Darwinist thought about what constituted crime, drove criminal behavior, and warranted punishment. They reinforced shared notions about who did and did not count as criminal, which had manifold consequences for economic elites, the urban poor, immigrants, and freed slaves.

The intellectual history assessed here shows how thinkers in eugenics, sociology, anthropology, economics, race science, and legal realism built common eugenic assumptions about crime and human behavior into the foundations of both rehabilitative and regulatory ideologies. Later chapters illustrate how political actors mobilized these ideologies in diverse ways in policy debates, establishing distinctive developmental pathways for rehabilitation and regulation that have since unfolded in relation to evolving contingencies of power, politics, and institutional conditions. But this chapter specifically examines the theoretical construction of the ideologies, illustrating how their core premises rested on shared elements of liberal, eugenic, and Darwinist thought. Criminality and the competitive ethic were both deemed individual attributes that conditioned how one experienced life in liberal democratic society, both traits were explained as heritable in eugenic terms, and the criminal underclass and the capitalist class were both racialized as products of nature. The ideologies thus prescribed policy solutions that sustained the racial and economic status quo.

This historical perspective highlights how dynamics of race and class overlapped in these governing ideologies and how they shaped the foundations of the carceral and regulatory states. The ideologies have been mobilized and adjusted over time by various political coalitions to shape structural features of criminal justice and regulatory institutions, but this chapter shines a light on their core qualities, properties, and premises that have conditioned American political development. Understanding their shared ideological roots enables us to see how punishment and regulation are related visions of social control meant to govern dangerous behavior and why the regulatory state and criminal justice system must be understood as institutional relatives.

The construction of rehabilitative and regulatory ideologies cannot be divorced from the social, political, and economic currents of the late nineteenth and the early twentieth centuries, and the chapter begins by detailing how and why biodeterminist and Darwinist theories became popular at the turn of the century. It then explores the origins of the born criminal idea before analyzing how the era's political and social theorists embedded the idea into rehabilitative ideology. The final sections discuss how intellectuals used the same determinist understandings of human behavior to depict the cutthroat businessman as an inversion of the born criminal—a virtuous man whose actions were the result of a naturally competitive disposition rather than a criminal one.

Natural Selection in American Political Thought

The political terrain of the late nineteenth and the early twentieth centuries provided a favorable environment for a political consensus to emerge embracing biodeterminism, natural selection, and Darwinism. But the era was characterized by intense political conflict as industrialization and urbanization rapidly unfolded and capital-labor conflict became commonplace. These battles engaged some of the era's most powerful coalitions—Populists challenging the inequalities of industrialization and conservative economic elites prioritizing free markets. Driven by agrarian discontent and labor unrest, the

Populists articulated a class politics promoting regulation, antimonopolism, and redistribution, pitting rural farming communities and organized labor against capital.[1] They made inroads in terms of checking corporate power, but their fiery rhetoric also hardened conservative commitments to markets, and powerful business coalitions were often able to limit the impact of the fragmented working class.[2] Further, given the emergence of unprecedently large corporations with immense power and influence, those business forces were difficult to challenge in political spheres. Alfred Chandler's theory that large enterprises emerged organically at this time to coordinate the nationalized market has been refined by political scientists showcasing how the choices of judges, administrators, and political elites—notably, Republicans linked to financial and manufacturing interests—facilitated the growth of a minimally regulated national market dominated by large corporations.[3] But, while populism and conservatism were in conflict, they also shared affinities in how they conceptualized human behavior and difference.

In the closing decades of the nineteenth century, the tenets of Darwinism proliferated across the academy, offering convenient rationalizations of systems of racial and economic inequality. Scholars of race science—the pseudoscientific discipline arguing that there existed natural racial hierarchies among humans—interpreted Darwin's evolutionary theory as validation of the premise that natural competition among humans could promote racial improvement. Tying Darwinism to the imperatives of scientific racism made it orthodoxy among scholars of anthropology, phrenology, and the various disciplines race scientists used to study human life.

Darwinism's appeal was not limited to intellectuals. As Rogers Smith has written, "Across the spectrum . . . from laissez-faire enthusiasts and white supremacists through Socialists and black separatists, leading writers accepted evolution in ways that permanently altered how they understood even the features of American life they endorsed." Embraced by proponents of diverse political persuasions, evolutionary theory simultaneously fueled radical demands for social equality and the racist, nativist, and classist sentiments that sustained systems of inequality.[4]

Richard Hofstadter famously argued in 1955 that the Populists embraced nativist and racist ideas legitimated by scientific racism.[5] His thesis has since been critiqued for conceptualizing the Populist movement overbroadly, misrepresenting the Populists' radical politics as uneducated opposition to progress, and exaggerating their racist tendencies. As Thomas Frank has explained, the Populists often fought for immigrant votes and were not so much opposed to economic progress as hostile to how the robber barons directed it.[6] Still, like almost all the era's coalitions, the Populist movement was infused

with principles of Darwinism and race science that validated essentialist narratives of group difference. Darwinism was not a Populist consensus, but a
national consensus.[7]

Social Darwinism especially served diverse political purposes. Attributed
to English scholar Herbert Spencer, the theory applied the principle of natural selection to social and economic contexts. Social Darwinism has historically been used to validate state racism, imperialism, and various oppressive
political projects.[8] In the late nineteenth century, it became a variant of political economy that naturalized economic inequality as conservatives found a
scientific ally in Spencer and his rationalization of laissez-faire.[9] While the
era's populism portended the emergence of a redistributive and bureaucratic
state, the upper classes clung to free market ideologies by legitimating them
through theories valorizing the competitive ideal.[10] For Spencer, applying
evolutionary theory to economics necessitated the endorsement of minimally
monitored markets characterized by unrestrained competition and opposition to assistance for poor populations that had proved themselves unfit.[11]

The economist William Graham Sumner was the most prominent voice
connecting Social Darwinism to economics. Interpreting natural selection as
an unsentimental science, he critiqued social policy and defended free markets by claiming that society "does not need any care or supervision" to lead
to the emergence of a "natural social order." He wrote, "Let us translate [my
theory] into blunt English, and it will read, Mind your own business."[12] Markets unfettered by state intervention would naturally sort people into classes
as pecuniary success was the result of thrift and poverty the result of natural
defect. Sumner's application of Social Darwinism to capitalism thus entailed
embracing unbridled individualist economics as natural law in the economic
jungle, thereby promoting racial improvement.[13] Captains of industry followed suit by using Social Darwinism to justify assumptions about their inherent superiority, criticize welfare as aiding the defective, counter critiques
of corporate power, and vindicate the inequalities of capitalism by legitimating the economic status quo behind the language of science.[14]

Populists and economic conservatives were just two coalitions that drew
on Darwinism, but they were fundamental forces that structured the era's
debates over economic and social policy around these ideas. Their impact
was not fleeting. Influenced by the political and economic debates of the
late nineteenth century, the Progressive movement inherited an ideological
legacy emphasizing Darwinism that contributed to the development of rehabilitative and regulatory ideologies of governance. The bounds of the Progressive era are debatable, often being treated as roughly spanning the 1890s
to 1920s, but fully understanding the movement requires eschewing blunt

periodization and acknowledging that the movement's seeds were sown well before 1890.[15]

Progressivism has had multiple meanings throughout American history, and during the Progressive era the word had broad application. In 1912, the three major presidential candidates, all from different parties, identified as Progressives. *Progressivism* generally referred to a collection of ideas about the role the state should play in solving problems associated with industrialization, urbanization, and corruption. Progressives critiqued the influence of parties and bossism while advocating for a state administered by professionals, advised by knowledge-based communities, and anchored in science. They believed that experts and professionals would run the state more efficiently than officials handpicked by party leaders would.[16] But, like proponents of laissez-faire and Populists, Progressives also drew from a historically specific set of scientific discourses including evolutionary theory, natural selection, Social Darwinism, race science, and eugenics.[17]

It should be noted that eugenics and race science, both influential in the Progressive era, were distinct but interdependent projects. While race science was a centuries-old intellectual discipline dedicated to hierarchizing racial categories, the eugenics movement emerged out of Francis Galton's nineteenth-century research and aimed to improve the human race through selective breeding. The movement was a substantial political force in the United States. In the early twentieth century over thirty states established eugenics programs compelling the sterilization of unfit populations. Eugenics and race science shared assumptions about racial difference but had distinct political goals. In the late nineteenth century, race science rationalized a "survival-of-the-fittest" approach to economic and social policy, delegitimizing the state as a corrective force and painting it as a disruption to natural competitive processes. Eugenicists alternatively called for a vast expansion of state power, believing it was the state's duty to identify and sort out the unfit to promote racial progress. Pure natural selection was thereby replaced with a project of state-administered selection enforced by experts distinguishing the fit from the unfit. This enabled Progressives to defend oppressive legal regimes including Jim Crow, immigration quotas, compulsory sterilizations, and repressive policies for the poor, women, and unfit in the name of racial improvement. Progressives consequently defended uplift for some and repression for others by relying on discourses lending scientific credence to hierarchies of race, class, and gender.[18]

As Daniel Rodgers has written, Progressives embraced the "rhetoric of the moral whole."[19] This was apparent in their inclination to describe American society anthropomorphically as a living organism.[20] Protecting the social organism required exclusionary politics; undesirables were diseases threat-ening collective national health.[21] As a biopolitical governing mindset, this meant that protecting the social body was best achieved by preemptively removing the unfit before reproduction, prompting eugenicists to rely on taxonomic hierarchies of naturally occurring human types to guide decision-making about compulsory sterilization, antimiscegenation, and segregation. Prioritizing collective well-being over the individual thus rationalized the imposition of extensive state controls over individuals as means of pursuing collective health objectives.[22]

Progressives' emphasis on science was not purely academic. Progressive intellectuals also believed that it was their duty to be public figures, prompt-ing them to intervene in public policy debates, hold government positions, and take leadership posts in prominent academic associations. Believing that experts should identify the public good and instruct the public through ser-vice, they ensured that eugenics traveled from intellectual to policy circles.[23]

Progressive scholar-reformers also brought their ideas to debates over economics and regulation. The field of economics grew in prominence in the early twentieth century as the American Economic Association (AEA), founded in 1885, evolved into a powerful political outfit. Richard Ely, a pro-fessor of political economy at the University of Wisconsin, became the AEA president in 1900, and the AEA has been under the control of academics ever since.[24] Ely called economists a "natural aristocracy," claiming that they were incorruptible because their authority was derived from science and they were committed to disinterested truth seeking, which Ely said differentiated economists from capitalists or politicians and made them essential to policy debates.[25]

Progressive economists thought that they could promote market effi-ciency through state regulation. This was not as sharp a break from classical economics as it appears; they criticized Gilded Age capitalism by contend-ing that the acolytes of Sumner and Spencer mistook the robber barons for the fittest market players when in reality some were unscrupulous players whose behavior distorted the market's natural selection forces.[26] Progressives believed that regulatory oversight could ensure that market competition was fairly conducted. Much as they believed that eugenics would improve the effi-ciency of natural selection without displacing it, they believed that regulation would improve the efficiency of markets without displacing competition. Ex-perts, they reasoned, would direct market participants' competitive instincts in healthy directions. In this way, eugenics and regulation were both pro-grams designed to enforce and enhance, not replace, the dynamics of natural selection in their respective spheres.

Within eugenic discourse, Progressives articulated a naturalized understanding of capitalism. Economic inequality was explained as a result of healthy competitive dynamics, rendering voracious competition a social good that enabled elites to rise to the top of the social ladder. It was only because Progressives acknowledged that a small handful of industrial titans attained their status through illicit means that they deemed pure laissez-faire unsound. Consequently, their faith in the state's "visible hand" to correct for market failures included weeding out the dishonest from the honest market players, a task best conducted by administrative experts isolated from electoral pressures.[27] But one of the many motivating purposes driving the adoption of national market regulations was that they protected industries from unethical players who lowered competitive standards by compelling otherwise ethical market participants to engage in illicit practices to survive, without dampening the competitive dynamics of the marketplace. Regulators were empowered to rectify the harm done by unethical competitors and channel the impulses of market actors in constructive directions without chilling their capitalist instincts. Progressives thus sought a careful balance when designing regulatory institutions, empowering them to intervene when market participants stepped out of line but in ways that did not leave industry actors fearful to engage in risk-taking.

Rehabilitative and regulatory ideologies were not the only ideological frameworks that developed within this ideational milieu. Various discourses about race, immigration, and sex were imbued with similar principles.[28] But understanding the inequalities of American crime policy requires comprehending how these discourses shaped the development of rehabilitative and regulatory ideologies and sowed individualistic, determinist, and racially and class-biased premises in their foundations.

Cesare Lombroso and the Reorientation of Penology

Nineteenth-century theories about criminality rooted in biodeterminism challenged established ideologies that had previously defined American criminal justice. Particularly, Cesare Beccaria's *On Crimes and Punishments* (1764), which depicted crime as a function of free will that could be deterred through clearly defined terms of punishment, had been a significant influence in America. This utilitarian philosophy was adopted by most states from the Founding through the nineteenth century via determinate sentencing systems. Determinate sentences were designed to deter would-be criminals by signaling that criminal acts would be met with swift and certain punishments of fixed lengths.[29]

The fundamental assumption undergirding utilitarian deterrence theory—that each offender was a rational actor responsive to incentives and capable of making the calculations required for law to have deterrent force—was upended by determinist scholarship theorizing that criminality was a natural trait. This was driven by the rise of Cesare Lombroso's school of criminal anthropology. An Italian criminologist, Lombroso argued in *Criminal Man* (1876) that biological defects rendered some people atavistic evolutionary throwbacks unable to control their violent, selfish, and amoral dispositions, earning them the classification *born criminal*.[30] Such individuals were criminal by nature rather than by choice and could not be deterred. Criminal anthropology quickly eclipsed deterrence theory in influence as Lombrosian theory became popular in America in the late nineteenth century.

Lombroso's theory was individualistic and determinist. In *Criminal Man*, he conducted phrenological and anatomical analyses of convicted criminals in Italy, concluding that various physiological stigmata like skull thickness and protruding ears were indicative of a primitive biological inheritance that left individuals predisposed to deviance. He claimed that 40 percent of offenders were born criminals. The final edition of *Criminal Man* concluded that "born criminals must be interned in special institutions for the incorrigible."[31] His future work extended the label *born criminal* widely. In an 1891 study of Italian revolutionaries, he concluded that 34 percent of anarchists had born criminal stigmata and theorized that the same dispositional instinct drove political radicals and criminals.[32] He also identified Black men as innately criminal, writing in 1897, "[T]he great obstacle to the negro's progress [in America] is the fact that there remain latent within him the primitive instincts of the savage." He attributed high homicide rates in America to Black criminality and atavism.[33]

Aside from reframing crime as a function of biology, Lombroso's work sparked the onset of criminological positivism. Positivist criminology asserts that through the scientific analysis of crime, the various causes of criminal behavior can be identified and understood. Whereas utilitarianism focuses on punishing actions with clear and fixed deterrent sanctions, the positivist perspective emphasizes tailoring punishments to the particular drivers of someone's criminality. In short, it targets the *criminal* more than the *crime*. By the end of the nineteenth century, state-level Beccarian determinate sentencing systems began giving way to indeterminate models in which punishment could be adjusted for each individual.

By aiming to punish the criminal rather than the crime, Lombrosian theory articulated a constructed image of the likely criminal type. Having the traits of this criminal type became a more important metric for determining whether people deserved punishment than their behavior. Lombroso suggested that punishment should be meted out most harshly against born criminals and emphasized property and violent crime in his analysis, allowing what we would now call *white-collar crime* to evade his logic. By emphasizing specific types of crimes, Lombrosian theory rested on class-skewed a priori assumptions about what counted as crime and who was likely to commit it. While it is unsurprising that Lombroso's conception of crime was colored by such premises, it is important to recognize them in order to understand how those who built on his ideas inherited comparable assumptions.

Lombroso's research has long been discredited as empirically unsound, but when it was published his work resonated with American scholars who similarly suggested that criminals were biologically defective. In his 1877 *The Jukes*, Richard Dugdale traced the ancestry of the "Jukes," a New York "hill family," and concluded that they were biologically predisposed to crime. Though often read as purely biodeterminist, the book noted that environments can "produce bad habits which may become hereditary." This reveals Dugdale's commitments to Lamarckian theory, which allowed him to acknowledge the variety of factors that caused crime while insisting that criminality was hereditary. He concluded that reform was possible for some but that "perpetual imprisonment" was necessary for "habitual criminals" for whom "we cannot accomplish individual cure." Permanent incarceration, Dugdale believed, would "organize [the] extinction of their race" by socially separating habitual criminals from the population.[34]

American criminal anthropologists were intellectual descendants of Lombroso and Dugdale, adopting determinist frameworks viewing criminals as pathologically distinct from ordinary individuals. But they situated these ideas within an endorsement of prison programming designed to rehabilitate curable offenders and incarcerate the incurable.

The Origins of Rehabilitative Ideology
and the Naturalization of Criminality

In 1870, the American Congress of Corrections held its first-ever annual meeting in Cincinnati. Attended by penal scholars and practitioners, the congress presented its "Declaration of Principles" establishing the rehabilitative ideal as the guiding principle of American prisons.[35] The declaration directed prison administrators to implement indeterminate sentencing, moral training, and educational programs behind bars.[36] It sharply diverged from Beccarian principles. In *On Crimes and Punishments*, Beccaria wrote, "punishments are to be estimated, not by the sensibility of the criminal, but by the injury done to society."[37] The second of the Congress's thirty-seven principles took the exact opposite view: "[T]reatment is to be directed to the criminal rather than the crime."[38]

One of the principal organizers who helped write the declaration was Zebulon Brockway. Brockway went on to receive national praise for his implementation of these techniques at New York's Elmira Reformatory during his tenure as the institution's warden from 1876 to 1900, earning him the nickname "father of the rehabilitative ideal." Nearly all the reformatories that opened across the nation in subsequent decades emulated Brockway's model.[39] Scholarship often asserts that from Brockway's time at Elmira through 1970, rehabilitation was the dominant philosophy of punishment in America. While rehabilitation waxed and waned in popularity, took root in certain regions more than others, and existed alongside the diverse penological ideas that characterized American criminal justice during this time, it remained a significant influence on penal practice through these years.[40] But a complete picture of rehabilitative ideology is more complicated than is often believed.

Several features of rehabilitative ideology's structure were essential to shaping Progressive era criminal justice. Rehabilitative ideology had a Lamarckian influence conceptualizing criminality as an acquired trait for some people that could be reformed away before the individual in question reproduced. But related to this was the Lombrosian assumption that there existed immutable biological roots of criminality for others—the born criminals who were so prone to crime that they were rendered irredeemable incorrigibles. These premises rested on a series of racial and class assumptions about who required social control. Just as biodeterminist theories legitimated socioeconomic and racial inequality, they had similar consequences in criminology. Because the rehabilitative perspective encouraged lawmakers to punish the criminal rather than the crime, traits associated with born criminality such as being poor, unemployed, or of a certain race became signs of an incorrigible criminal disposition. Meanwhile, wealthy White businessmen acting in market contexts did not have these qualities. These premises rendered rehabilitative and regulatory ideologies counterparts for governing undesirable behavior along a racially and class-skewed axis.

Rehabilitative ideology embodied two ideological prongs relying on coercive state interventions to control individual-level defects—one premised on reforming and releasing inmates and the other on incapacitating and punishing incorrigibles. This duality forms the core of rehabilitative thought. The prescriptive practices attached to rehabilitative ideology—the indeterminate sentence, parole, probation, and the like—are tools designed to sort the corrigible from the incorrigible populations and determine who deserves access to rehabilitative ideology's benevolent prong and who requires the punitive prong. Both are integral components of the rehabilitative model; the rehabilitative ideal is fundamentally committed to offering hope for a reformable population whose mutability is defined only in contrast to the presumed incorrigibility of others. In other words, neither prong of rehabilitative ideology can operate without the other. While it is reasonable to wonder whether incorrigibility was fundamental to rehabilitative thought or an idea tacked onto it later, analysis of intellectual history shows that the idea of incorrigibility is foundational to rehabilitative ideology and cannot be separated from it. Rehabilitative ideology and its core policy innovations are defined by this sorting-focused duality, which is why even the most well-intentioned efforts to reclaim the rehabilitative ideal today are doomed to fail in an institutional context built on these double-edged premises.

Lamarckian and Lombrosian theory imbued rehabilitative ideology with a durable set of assumptions that have had enduring consequences for American crime policy. First, the ideology rests on individualizing assumptions that rehabilitative microinterventions can empower people with enhanced knowledge and skills to change their ways, ignoring how socioeconomic marginality creates knowledge and skill deficits before people get to prison. This allows lawmakers to explain recidivism as a consequence of personal failings rather than of the structural economic conditions of high-crime communities. Second, rehabilitative ideology's determinist premises that certain wrongdoers are driven by naturally criminal temperaments has ensured that rehabilitative logic always retained its punitive duality even in the absence of eugenic politics. Policymakers throughout the twentieth century and into the twenty-first have recurrently whipped up anxieties about incorrigibles or habitual criminals as distinctive criminal types requiring punishment alongside promises to extend reformative opportunities to the deserving. Third, the ideology's linking of incorrigibility and racial and class traits persists today in seemingly benign practices that are legacies of the rehabilitative approach and promote its two-pronged sorting logic of redeeming the redeemable and punishing the incorrigible. This renders rehabilitative discourse an inadequate tool for challenging the logics sustaining the carceral state.

Brockway is a good starting point for understanding rehabilitative ideology's emergence. Elmira's day-to-day operations under his watch did little to justify the nickname "father of the rehabilitative ideal." Despite his reformative posturing, Elmira's staff psychologically and physically abused inmates while "reforming" them into working-class citizens.[41] His embrace of both rehabilitation and harsh justice can be understood only by examining his conception of criminality. Like Dugdale, Brockway endorsed Lamarckian theories conceptualizing degeneracy as an acquired trait that could become a hereditary cause of crime.[42] He suggested that a "lack of proper education and other unfavourable circumstances" could create biologically transmittable defects in one's moral and mental faculties. But he qualified this by claiming that environmental factors contributed to crime only by altering biology and that merely 4 percent of criminals sprang from "healthy stock."[43] His embrace of Lombrosian theory also colored his rehabilitative project. He stated that inherently criminal types could be identified by physiological traits.[44] He said that such "defective fellow beings" were driven by "undeveloped, incongruous, or unbalanced condition[s] of their higher mental faculties" that left their "animal instincts" unchecked, rendering them incurable and warranting their extended or permanent containment.[45] He claimed that eliminating criminal traits through a combination of rehabilitation and containment would produce "a perfect race."[46]

Given the Lombrosian and Lamarckian currents in his thinking, Brockway coupled his defense of rehabilitation with a promise of indefinite containment for born criminals. His implementation of indeterminate sentencing, the cornerstone of his rehabilitative model, is revealing of this double-edged logic. In an address before the National Prison Congress in 1898, Brockway defended the indeterminate sentence as a repressive and curative instrument. He explained that indeterminate sentences should offer opportunities for inmates to reform but only while being used indefinitely to contain incorrigibles so naturally deviant they were immune to reformative interventions.[47] In his memoir, his discussion of the Elmira inmate Macauley—a man committed first for burglary, then twice for parole violations—illustrates his thinking. Brockway suggested that Macauley typified the class of "incorrigible criminals" and that "such offenders, could they be committed under the absolute indeterminate sentence plan, would be continuously held under enough of custodial restraint to protect the public."[48]

Brockway's ideological duality conditioned the work of intellectuals drawn to rehabilitation and Lombrosian theory. In *Creating Born Criminals* (1997), Nicole Hahn Rafter identifies several influential Progressive era scholars who built on Lombrosian theory—including Arthur MacDonald, Henry Boies, Charles Henderson, August Drahms, William McKim, G. Frank Lydston, and Philip Parsons.[49] Close analysis reveals that they also built on Brockway's rehabilitative philosophy. Consistent with Progressive era trends combining expertise with politics, these men frequently held posts with institutional authority. For instance, Arthur MacDonald held a federal appointment with the US Bureau of Education, and Henry Boies served on the Pennsylvania Board of Charities, which oversaw state social policy and advised the state legislature, for sixteen years.[50] Charles Henderson, one of the nation's most respected sociologists, served as president of the National Conference of Charities, American commissioner to the International Prison Commission, and president of the International Prison Congress. While this chapter focuses on processes of ideological construction within their intellectual work, it is important to emphasize that these men broadcasted their ideas from positions of institutional power, advantaging them over those advocating alternative perspectives and keeping scholars of color and female academics at the margins of debate.

Arthur MacDonald's 1893 *Criminology*, one of the earliest American texts in criminology, is a prime example of the influence of Lombroso and Brockway on American scholarship. The book's introduction was written by Lombroso, to whom MacDonald dedicated the book. Lombroso wrote that it was impossible to "deny the organicity of crime, its anatomical nature and degenerative source." In the book, MacDonald insisted on the construction of special institutions for incorrigibles just as Lombroso did.[51] That same year, in *Prisoners and Paupers*, Henry Boies asserted that "a large proportion" of prison inmates "were born to be criminals."[52] Also in 1893, Henderson and Boies both argued that criminals should not reproduce until they are rehabilitated so that their children would not inherit criminal tendencies.[53] This joint endorsement of Lamarckian and Lombrosian theories within the context of pursuing rehabilitation reflects the influence of Brockway on their thinking.

Scholars' support for the rehabilitative model was clear in their criticisms of determinate systems for offering inadequate behavioral modification incentives.[54] Alternatively, the indeterminate sentence was consistently praised for providing reformative opportunities and motivation to demonstrate good behavior while serving as a long-term containment tool.[55] For example, MacDonald stated, "The indeterminate sentence is the best method of affording the prisoner an opportunity to reform, without exposing society to unnecessary dangers," because it permitted long-term detainment for incorrigibles.[56] In 1900, August Drahms claimed that the permanent containment of incorrigibles was a more important purpose of indeterminate sentencing than rehabilitation, and in 1893 Boies wrote that three criminal convictions, regardless of the severity of the underlying offenses, warranted life incarceration.[57] In 1901, Boies wrote that "the reformatory . . . will operate as an institution for sorting and separating corrigible and incorrigible subdivisions." He further claimed, "[T]hose who can be cured will be cured before liberation. The chronic incorrigibles will be found to consist of two classes: the incurably vicious, the physical, mental, and moral imbeciles; and those whose organization is so defective as to be incapable of restoration. . . . [T]hey should be confined under entirely different conditions."[58] Boies's language revealed that, at its core, the rehabilitative project was designed as a sorting program to distinguish the corrigible from the incorrigible, not a benevolent endeavor founded on a universal faith in human redemption.

McKim, Lydston, Parsons, and Drahms transported Lombrosian ideologies into the twentieth century.[59] In 1900, McKim expressed some skepticism of Lombroso but endorsed the consensus that "the tendency to crime is essentially inborn."[60] In 1906, Lydston suggested that "undue importance" was assigned to Lombrosian theory but included a chapter in his book phrenologically analyzing criminal crania. He insisted that Lombrosian physiological stigmata were indicative of "mental and moral defects" associated with criminal behavior.[61] These scholars situated themselves in slight contrast to Lombroso, but they differed from him only trivially, leaving intact the causal arrow from biology to crime. They still paired biodeterminism with rehabilitation, supported the indeterminate sentence as reformative and punitive, and proposed eugenic solutions for born criminals, including indefinite containment, sterilization, and extermination.[62] Their work maintained the marriage of an ostensibly progressive rehabilitative discourse to punitive policy.

The scientific racism in this literature is apparent. Khalil Gibran Muhammad has illustrated how racialized crime policy in the North and the South during the Progressive era was shaped by ideologies about innate Black criminality, most famously through Frederick Hoffman's fusion of White-supremacist discourse and Lombrosian theory in service of the argument that Blacks had "a decided tendency towards crime."[63] Unsurprisingly, such ideas about race, crime, and biology were manifested in rehabilitative scholarship. For instance, in a chapter titled "The Negro Element of Increase" in *Prisoners and Paupers*, Boies made a distinctively Lamarckian argument insisting that inbreeding and "generations of slavery" have "obliterate[d] all consciousness of *meum* and *tuum*" in Blacks. Boies's rationale was that, because they had lived as slaves, over time Black men and women lost their biological ability to distinguish private property, which developed into a hereditary criminal trait.[64] Similarly, Henderson explained the degree of crime among Blacks as a function of "racial inheritance, physical and mental inferiority, barbarian and slave ancestry culture."[65]

Subtler than the race claims were the links between economic class and crime in the works of rehabilitative theorists. Brockway directly linked the disposition of poor populations to criminal behavior. He claimed that "habitual improvidence, with its attending poverty," was a primary cause of crime.[66] Linking poverty and crime to a shared biological constitution implied that being poor was an indicator of criminal propensities. Lydston claimed to have uncovered shared defects in the crania of tramps (unemployed men wandering between cities) and born criminals.[67] Poverty and criminality both were rationalized as functions of a singular biological predisposition indicative of limited reformative potential.

Prisoners and Paupers powerfully highlights the class character of the rehabilitative ideational framework. In it, Boies proposed that there were two classes of paupers: those with physical or mental impairments and the "incorrigibly idle, dissolute, and criminal," including "beggars, vagrants, and tramps." He insisted that these populations must be "transformed into honest self-supporters" or incarcerated "for life" if they proved unreformable.[68] This provides stark insight into the rehabilitative ideal's class ideology—successful rehabilitation required transforming into a self-supporting worker, and failure to do so was evidence of incorrigibility.

Identifying patterns of natural criminality across class also complemented popular currents in Social Darwinism. In his depiction of social and economic hardship as incidental to natural selection, Sumner provided a cosmic rationale for inequalities common among the criminal classes. He criticized leniency toward crime, arguing that it is a "false doctrine" that "criminals have some sort of a right against or claim on society."[69] Linking class and crime, he argued that if the state were to disperse the "poverty-stricken, vicious, and criminal inhabitants" from urban slums, they would enter a society where they would either be "crushed by the competition of life" or incarcerated.[70]

American scholars connected class, race, and crime via biology as far back as Dugdale, but such ideas resurfaced in rehabilitative scholarship, which incorporated them into policies like the indeterminate sentence. The translation of these ideas into concrete institutional reforms laid the groundwork for key elements of the modern justice system, but it is unappreciated how this institutional system was built on eugenic notions of criminal behavior. Through eugenic discourses, behavioral patterns and traits common among the poor, minorities, immigrants, workers, and other undesirable populations were pathologized as signs of an incurable criminal disposition. Determinist ideas and ascriptive ideologies of class and race were not appended onto the rehabilitative ideal following its design—they were basic ingredients of its structure.

Eugenics, Economists, and Rehabilitation

Determinist framings of criminality in the rehabilitative ideal provided fertile ground for various ascriptive ideologies to flourish and justify punishment for a broad range of groups deemed incorrigible. But while rehabilitative ideology could not have thrived in the United States without the dominance of race science and natural selection, it received its biggest political boost from the eugenics movement, particularly from the sociologists, hereditarians, and economists espousing eugenic ideas in their work.

It is worth recognizing that eugenics encountered intellectual challenges. Research on culture disputed eugenic explanations of difference, depicting behavioral variations across race and class as outcomes of social forces understandable only via reference to histories of group marginalization. But cultural schools failed as counterdiscourses in the face of eugenics' unshakable appeal. Khalil Gibran Muhammad explains why in *The Condemnation of Blackness* (2010), highlighting W. E. B. Du Bois's *The Philadelphia Negro* (1899) and Franz Boas's *The Mind of Primitive Man* (1911) to make his case. A foundational text of cultural anthropology, Boas's book argued that perceptions of racial inferiority and differences in crime rates were outcomes of social neglect that conditioned the development of distinctive racial cultures.[71] But Muhammad argues that Boas "erased the color line and replaced it with a culture line" by linking crime to Black culture, fostering a discursive shift to cultural essentialism that retained assumptions of racial determinism.[72] Du Bois's *The Philadelphia Negro*, a study of race in Philadelphia, had similar faults. The book powerfully reformulated the concept of race, though at the time scholars dismissed Du Bois's most insightful claims.[73] Nonetheless, Du Bois still treated Black crime as a distinct social problem and even entertained determinist notions. Four years later in *The Souls of Black Folk*, Du Bois wrote, "[S]ome [Blacks] were fitted to know and some to dig."[74] Through these examples and others, Muhammad illustrates why cultural theory failed to discredit eugenics.[75]

A more popular school of thought that emerged in the late nineteenth century was hereditarian theory. Tied to the eugenics movement, hereditarian theory was often presented as a challenge to Lombrosian scholarship. The alleged difference of the hereditarian perspective was that the atavistic features of Lombrosian theory were hypothesized not as directly indicative of criminality, but as signs of low intelligence or moral defects that *correlated* with criminality. This was a distinction of trivial import as hereditarians still maintained that criminality was congenital and identifiable via the traits cataloged by Lombroso. The more important difference was that hereditarian theory implied the necessity of a large state role in selecting out the unfit before they reproduced, providing intellectual grounding for the eugenics movement.

Stephen Jay Gould's *The Mismeasure of Man* (1981) tracks the development of hereditarian scholarship and the eugenics movement. Hereditarian research had its origins in the work of the French psychologist Alfred Binet, who developed mental tests to quantify intelligence. Binet was an "antihereditarian" in that he measured mental capacity not to uncover inherent developmental ceilings, but to identify individuals' educational needs.[76] But American scholars quickly perverted his work to serve the imperatives of eugenics, interpreting his tests as proof that people had natural limits. H. H. Goddard and Lewis Terman linked this to criminality in their research on feeble-mindedness. At the time, *feeble-mindedness* was a clinical term encompassing degrees of social, mental, and cognitive deficiency and a range of psychological disorders. Concepts like feeble-minded and mental defective emerged in these intellectual traditions independently from debates about crime, but this scholarship routinely blurred the lines between intelligence, mental illness, and criminality by treating the feeble-minded, the insane, mental defectives, and epileptics as interchangeable criminal types.

For instance, in *The Kallikak Family* (1912), Goddard asserted that "Lombroso's famous criminal types . . . may have been types of feeble-mindedness on which criminality was grafted."[77] He said that "[t]he so-called criminal type is merely a type of feeble-mindedness," estimating that 25–50 percent of people in prisons were mental defectives "incapable of managing their affairs with ordinary prudence."[78] Lewis Terman built on Goddard's ideas in *The Measurement of Intelligence* (1916), identifying intelligence as the most relevant heritable trait explaining crime. Like Goddard, he saw himself as modifying Lombroso, stating that "[t]he physical abnormalities which have been found so common among prisoners are not the stigma of criminality, but the physical accompaniments of feeble-mindedness."[79]

The assertions of Goddard and Terman that Lombrosian stigmata were indicative not of a criminal biology, but rather of defective intelligence correlated with criminality, simply added a step to Lombroso's causal claims. It is unsurprising that they endorsed the same harsh policies as Lombroso, Brockway, and their adherents, including permanent custody for incorrigible lawbreakers.[80] Scholars endorsing rehabilitation had also long supported eugenic solutions for incorrigibles, including sterilization and extermination.[81] These ideas were quickly picked up by eugenicists who saw affinities between rehabilitative ideology and their goals. Active players in the movement funded research projects exploring these ideas and solidifying the union between eugenics, hereditarian theory, and rehabilitative ideology.

Consider the Eugenics Record Office (ERO). Established in 1910, the ERO proclaimed itself the national center for the study of human heredity. Founded by Charles Davenport, it served as an organizational center for the eugenics movement by producing and funding research while conducting lobbying and advocacy campaigns. It claimed that the most defective 10 percent of the human population, including the feeble-minded, the poor, and criminals, among others, should be targeted for compulsory sterilization. Insisting that the "fact of incorrigibility" mandated the sterilization of criminals, Davenport argued that the ERO should target a range of criminals from vagrants to felons for long sentences with sterilization being a condition of release.[82]

The ERO's research activities exemplify how the eugenics movement imported Lombrosian and Lamarckian theories about criminal incorrigibility into hereditarian scholarship. For instance, studying "degenerate families" in the tradition of Dugdale remained popular among eugenicists. In 1912, Arthur Estabrook and Charles Davenport copublished *The Nam Family* through the ERO, studying crime and degeneracy in a mixed-race German–Native American family.[83] Four years later, Estabrook published a follow-up study of Dugdale's *The Jukes* under the ERO's auspices. Titled *The Jukes in 1915*, the book connected Dugdale's work to the theories of Terman and Goddard in a reexamination of the Juke family. Estabrook cautiously distanced himself from Lombroso but noted that there is a "close correlation between feeble-mindedness and crime." He concluded that "the eradication of crime in defective stocks depends upon the elimination of mental deficiency" and made a notable shift by defending sterilization as a form of rehabilitation, arguing that it would "interfere with the real liberty of the individual less than custodial care."[84] Goddard similarly studied degenerate families, explaining in *The Kallikak Family* that "Lombroso's famous criminal types" were just "types of feeble-mindedness."[85]

In *The Passing of the Great Race* (1916), arguably the most authoritative American text on eugenics, Madison Grant made comparable claims. He wrote that sterilization "will in self-defense put a stop to the supply of feebleminded and criminal children of weaklings," describing it as "a practical, merciful, and inevitable solution" that "can be applied to an ever-widening circle of social discards, beginning always with the criminal, the diseased and the insane."[86] Similarly, Davenport linked crime, feeble-mindedness, poverty, and heredity, bemoaning that "criminality is ascribed to poverty, to bad example, to bad or inadequate education, despite the fact of incorrigibility," while insisting that eugenicists provided "a more fundamental explanation for these non-social traits" than did scholars of culture or sociology.[87] He believed that eugenicists should be public intellectuals to ensure that the "public spirit is aroused" and "crystallized in appropriate legislation." He defended sterilization, claiming that "incurable and dangerous criminals . . . may under appropriate restrictions be prevented from procreation—either by segregation during the reproductive period or even by sterilization."[88] These ideas also had influential supporters outside the academy. Theodore Roosevelt famously endorsed eugenics on multiple occasions, even bluntly writing in a public letter in 1914 that "criminals should be sterilized."[89]

The hereditarian theories undergirding the eugenics movement naturally complemented the findings of scientific racism. The term *race* had multiple meanings at the time, with Progressive era race scientists using it to refer to the human race, national races, or phenotypic racial categories in different contexts, but the eugenics movement focused on preserving the White American race by keeping non-Anglo-Saxon elements separated from native White racial stock. Rather than assessing racial differences between Blacks and Whites, early eugenicists often focused on European immigrant populations that threatened Anglo-Saxon purity and connected those deemed non-White to criminality.[90] As a result, southern states relied on different measures than did northern ones in the eugenics movement's early stages—like antimiscegenation laws and racially motivated vigilante violence—to protect the White racial stock until eugenic studies of Black inferiority facilitated compulsory sterilizations in the early years of the twentieth century.[91]

The links between race science and eugenics are predictable, but less appreciated is how eugenics and rehabilitative ideology became popular among economists. Thomas Leonard has shown how Progressive era economists like Richard Ely, John Commons, and Edward Ross favored facially progressive reforms that subtly promoted social exclusion by uplifting the worthy and excluding inferiors.[92] These scholars adopted the Progressive rationale that criminals were pathologies afflicting the social body and that, since criminality was a tendency common among the poor, criminals were also economic burdens and impediments to society's productive capacities.

For instance, in *An Introduction to Political Economy*, Richard T. Ely said that "the dependent and criminal classes . . . impair the productive power of the community."[93] Elsewhere, he wrote that there were three divisions of unemployable citizens, "the defective, delinquent, and dependent," before arguing that these classes were "incurable" and "should not be allowed to propagate their kind."[94] The economist Frank Taussig similarly argued that there existed two classes of unemployables—the aged and disabled, on the one hand, and, on the other, the "feebleminded," consisting of "irretrievable criminals and tramps" who were "tainted with hereditary disease" and should be "prevented from propagating their kind."[95]

Edward Ross regularly made connections between criminality and economic health. He argued that the criminal law should not punish a crime in proportion "to the measure of harm" it incurred, a practice common in "rude communities" that oversympathized with victims. Alternatively, he said that "offences should be repressed *according to the badness of character they imply.*"[96] His emphasis on tailoring punishment to character rather than actions reflected the transition from utilitarianism to rehabilitative ideology. In an 1896 article, he wrote that society should focus on the "moulding of the individual's feelings and desires to suit the needs of the group." He claimed that "insuring greater harmony of social life by segregation of the insubordinate and elimination of the criminal, aims . . . at progress."[97] In *Social Control* (1901), he framed his conclusion explicitly within rehabilitative ideology: "[A]s to the mass of small-witted, weak-willed, impulse-ridden human 'screenings' that collect in prisons, our care should be to reform the reformable and to hold fast the incurable the rest of their days."[98]

Scholars like Ross argued that eugenics improved the process of natural selection.[99] Ross supported "the sterilization of all congenital criminals as the only means of thinning out the bad breeds."[100] In 1914, he defended Wisconsin's sterilization law by connecting it to crime prevention, stating that "[s]terilization is not nearly so terrible as hanging a man, and the chances of sterilizing the fit are not nearly so great, as are the chances of hanging the innocent."[101] John Commons wrote that "[w]e cannot placidly rely on any abstraction of natural selection to wipe out crime."[102] Ely also pointed to "the superiority of man's selection to nature's selection."[103] Through this logic, economists justified state sterilization of populations viewed as economic burdens, including criminals.

As the social sciences evolved in the twentieth century, a diverse group of scholar-reformers elaborated rehabilitative ideology through eugenic work in criminology, race science, and economics. And, as academic disciplines professionalized at universities like Columbia and Wisconsin, social scientists evolved into drivers of reform. But their work legitimated the nativist, racist, classist, and other ascriptive impulses embedded in rehabilitative ideology through a veneer of scientific objectivity.

The Origins of Regulatory Ideology and the Naturalization of Market Competition

While determinist constructs of behavior predominated in the era's crime scholarship, combining eugenics and Social Darwinism with individualist economics also appealed to leaders of nineteenth-century corporations and their allies who sought scientific validation of the inequalities of capitalism and the natural superiority of economic elites. It was in this context that regulatory ideology took shape. By presenting the harmful actions of economic power holders as natural functions of healthy capitalist self-interest rather than deviant dispositions, regulatory ideology depicted such behavior as less criminal than street criminality. Because desirable competitive instincts were at the root of this behavior, gentler interventions were proposed to control market forces that tempted the entrepreneurial spirit toward wrongdoing without instilling anxiety in markets through threats of prosecution. Importantly, the scholars who advocated for a eugenics-infused rehabilitative program were the same ones depicting corporate lawbreakers as requiring lighter regulatory controls, showing how rehabilitative and regulatory ideologies were infused with eugenic and Darwinist assumptions by the same sets of thinkers.

When it came to naturalizing the rigors of free markets and their resultant inequalities, Sumner led the charge. He claimed, "[M]illionaires are a product of natural selection. . . . They may fairly be regarded as the naturally selected agents of society for certain work." He wrote that while the "intensest competition" may produce inequality, "the bargain is a good one for society" because it ensures that "all those who are competent for a [given] function will be employed in it."[104] Scholars across disciplines similarly fused commitments to liberal economics, Social Darwinism, and determinist understandings of behavior in ways that legitimized the arguably immoral actions of corporate leaders as natural and healthy manifestations of their competitive vigor.

Inheriting the class-skewed foci of Lombroso and Brockway, it is surprising that discussions of economic crime appeared in criminological scholarship at all. But commitments to liberal economics were apparent in this research as scholars who endorsed rehabilitation and Lombrosian theory simultaneously rationalized market crimes as products of the distinctively spirited rather than criminal dispositions of successful capitalists operating in market contexts. For instance, Charles Henderson claimed that ruthless competition among industry leaders was normal and beneficial. In an 1896 issue of the *American Journal of Sociology*, he wrote, "It would be strange . . . if the 'captain of industry' did not sometimes manifest a militant spirit, for he has risen from the ranks largely because he was a better fighter than most of us." He reasoned that "[c]ompetitive commercial life is not a flowery bed of ease, but a battle field where the 'struggle for existence' is defining the industrially 'fittest to survive.'" He went on to write that market competition requires a "peculiar type of manhood, characterized by vitality, energy, concentration, skill . . . great foresight . . . [and] integrity." He finished by drawing a sharp line between business leaders and criminals, concluding that "the sense of fairness and justice is strong in business men."[105]

G. Frank Lydston's *The Diseases of Society* (1904), which included phrenological comparisons of criminals and the poor, also differentiated the behaviors of economic elites from crime. In the book, Lydston distinguished corporate rapacity from crime by emphasizing the character of business leaders. He defended businessmen accused of wrongdoing by noting that "none of them had a previous criminal record" and that they "were respected citizens," reflecting the rehabilitative practice of using past behavior to measure individual worth and estimate criminal inclinations. Lydston claimed that businessmen swayed toward crime were driven by a "great inherent capacity for good, and the force of character that makes men great." He argued that if a businessman committed a crime, he was led to it by instincts of ambition not found in ordinary criminals. He wrote, "Whether ambition results in great crimes or in good deeds, the individual will be found to be of a forceful character. The petty thief is not impelled by it." Given that the capitalist lacked the typical criminal instincts, "[c]ertain influences may divert the force of a strong character in the direction of criminality."[106] This was a crucial component of the regulatory ideological framework; when corporate criminality occurred, it was a function of structural economic forces seducing ambitious characters toward crime.

This position severed corporate criminals from rehabilitative ideology by suggesting that exogenous forces typically drove their illicit behavior and that the inherent traits fueling their misconduct were desirable. It implied that businessmen needed neither rehabilitative nor punitive interventions and shaped the policy prescriptions of regulatory ideology—because businessmen were inherently good people, their behavior could be guided through regulatory rules. By challenging attacks on the robber barons and defending their allegedly criminal behavior as healthy, crime scholars excused the misconduct of economic elites as by-products of market conditions and, if anything, rendered them sympathetic figures.

These ideas found relevance among defenders of free market economics. For instance, during a banquet honoring Herbert Spencer's visit to New York in 1892, the Richmond and Allegheny Railroad executive Eugene Leland said that businessmen "give nominal adherence" to laws governing markets because such policies are typically "wholly inconsistent" with the realities of market operations. He claimed that "the fundamental laws upon which the doctrine of evolution rests" always bore more on the choices of business leaders than man-made law.[107]

The scientific validation of laissez-faire resonated with the common sense of superiority shared by industry giants like John Rockefeller in oil and Andrew Carnegie in steel. A good case in point is a famous speech Rockefeller delivered in which he declared that "[t]he growth of a large business is merely a survival of the fittest." Employing Darwinist metaphors, he stated, "The

American Beauty rose can be produced . . . only by sacrificing the early buds which grow up around it. This is not an evil tendency in business. It is merely the working out of a law of nature and a law of God."[108] In 1889, Andrew Carnegie penned a defense of laissez-faire in the *North American Review* rooted in the logic of Sumner and Spencer. He dismissed critics of the free market's inequalities, stating that "[i]t is a waste of time to criticise the inevitable." He claimed that laissez-faire was not just economically sound but necessary to promote racial progress. Carnegie wrote, "[Laissez-faire economics] is here; we cannot evade it; no substitutes for it have been found; and while the law may sometimes be hard for the individual, it is best for the race, because it insures the survival of the fittest human in every department." He thus insisted that "[w]e accept and welcome, therefore, as conditions to which we must accommodate ourselves, great inequality of environment, the concentration of business, industrial and commercial, in the hands of a few, and the law of competition between these, as being not only beneficial, *but essential for the future progress of the race.*" He went on to say that "not evil, but good, has come to the race from the accumulation of wealth by those who have the ability and energy that produce it."[109] Carnegie's claims were rooted not only in market logics, but also in scientific racism. This naturalization of the capitalist class made for a sharp distinction from the idea of the born criminal, but both ideas were rooted in common trends in social theory that proffered racialized and class-skewed ideas about whose behavior counted as criminal, whose did not, and how each should be managed.

During these years, the cornerstones of the regulatory state were built, indicating that the scientific naturalization of free markets did not dissuade policymakers from intervening as the laissez-faire economy evolved into a corporate capitalist one. Debates over creating regulatory agencies were shaped by leading industrial interests, including railroads and the financial and banking sectors. But, as support for unadulterated laissez-faire became politically untenable, corporate leaders viewed regulation as preferable to criminalization and politicized ideas about the naturally competitive businessman to ensure that regulatory bodies had carefully limited prosecutorial powers, thus designing regulatory institutions to make free markets operate better without restructuring markets or inhibiting competition through excessive prosecution. The Progressive era's leading economists were crucial in advancing this logic.

Progressive economists questioned the efficacy of market selection processes, concluding that some champions of market competition were unethical players who damaged economic health. As AEA President Richard Ely wrote in *An Introduction to Political Economy*, "Competition, if unregulated, tends to force the level of economic life down to the moral standard of the worst men who can sustain themselves in the business community."[110] Edward Ross made similar claims, linking wealth accumulation to his concerns about racial progress. In 1903, he wrote, "The struggle for wealth does not bring to the top the intellectual aristocracy. . . . The plutocracy of to-day is far, very far . . . from favoring the multiplication of the best."[111] Out of this logic came the acknowledgment that concepts of fitness in Social Darwinist thought were contingent constructs. Economic luminaries like Lester Frank Ward, Henry Carter Adams, and John Bates Clark challenged Spencer and Sumner by revealing natural selection in economic contexts to be environmentally conditioned.[112] Like Darwinist apologists for laissez-faire, Progressives argued that those who succeeded in business were naturally distinct human types, but, unlike laissez-faire adherents, they claimed that some market victors could be unprincipled. The most successful capitalists were often products of skill and intelligence, but others were occasionally products of dubious ethics.

The Progressive regulatory project thus became impelled by the impulse to protect law-abiding businessmen. Most economists believed that most players in the marketplace were good people and proposed a regulatory approach to protect ethical actors from their competitors who, fueled by a combination of their ambitious natures and market incentives, veered into crime and lowered the ethical bar of competition. Regulation would improve the moral quality of economic competition without deterring morally sound businessmen from risk-taking. Absent regulation, as Ely said, economic life would be brought down "to the moral standard of the worst men who can sustain themselves in the business community." He claimed that such men "have not been able to endure" the temptations of material power.[113] John Commons made similar claims, writing that, without regulation, all employers are "forced down to the level of the most grasping."[114]

The economic realities of the growing nationalized market raised genuine complications for lawmakers as they grappled with the challenges of monitoring industry wrongdoing and holding respectable executives accountable for their behavior without deterring risk-taking. Richard Ely offered an answer. He stated that, in its ideal form, "regulation, well enforced, would simply confirm the efforts of the most intelligent and most just employers" in the market.[115] He described how, in a regulatory model, "what is required with respect to them [businesses] is that sort of regulation which, without destroying competition, will raise its ethical level," and how "[r]egulated competition within its own proper sphere is one of the conditions of social progress."[116] The goal was to raise the "ethical level" of industry, not to identify and punish the most severe wrongdoers. This required gentler interventions, not crimi-nalization, to reward ethical actors and encourage unethical ones to be more honest and productive.

This logic elucidated several features of regulatory ideology. First, regula-tory ideology assumed that economic actors who resorted to illicit practices were not naturally deviant but that their competitive ethic had become com-promised by market temptations or the need to compete with unscrupulous rivals. The "ethical level" of competition was, thus, remediable. Mirroring the shift in punishment toward tailoring sanctions so that they were based on judgments of individuals and their personal traits, regulatory ideology ex-cused the actions of corporate wrongdoers by virtue of their personal traits. Second, since economic elites were driven by competitive rather than crimi-nal natures, their most harmful behaviors could be discouraged by prevent-ing market conditions from deteriorating into unscrupulous competition via regulations and gentle course corrections.

One of the clearest explications of regulatory ideology came from the ju-rist Louis Brandeis. Before serving on the Supreme Court, Brandeis worked in Woodrow Wilson's White House and was a key player in structuring the Federal Trade Commission (FTC), as discussed in chapter 4. As Gerald Berk has written, he endorsed a model of regulated competition in which federal economic regulation was designed to enhance the quality of market com-petition.[117] But his philosophy rested on crucial assumptions—namely, that corporate lawbreakers were not as blameworthy as common criminals and that they could be guided via regulation. His philosophy offered a coherent distillation of the regulatory ideological vision that focused on regulating competition to improve it without resorting to punishment.

In 1913, Brandeis laid out his thinking clearly. In a piece for the *American Legal News*, he wrote that the "regulation of competition" was "essential to the preservation of competition and to its best development." He considered his approach "distinctly a constructive policy" rather than a punitive one.[118] When he testified before Congress on the FTC bill, he linked this proposal to his belief that corporate leaders who broke the law were rational, good people whose behavior could be righted without punishment. He stated that business leaders engaging in questionable activities "could by exercising their powers in the right direction aid the community mightily" but "are led by a bad system to do the things that are harmful to the community." By blaming market forces rather than the individual, Brandeis concluded that business offenses are "not like those cases where the offense involves a moral taint in the individual." This led him to state, "Our aim should not be to instill fear, but to so develop the commercial conditions that crime becomes unnatural."

Consequently, he favored regulation of market illegalities with minimal use of prosecution.[119] Brandeis's statements offer the clearest example of regulatory ideology being mobilized to enhance market dynamics via management of structural economic conditions.

Brandeis's statements also show how Progressives concerned with promoting market ethics via regulation still accepted ideas about the natural and essentially good character of lawbreaking capitalists. The impetus to protect law-abiding capitalists from lawbreaking ones was not akin to the eugenic-rehabilitative sorting rationale treating the good as reformable and the bad as incorrigible. Even the worst corporate offender was assumed to be morally rescuable and responsive to reasonable incentives and rules. As Brandeis expressed, corporate offenders' actions were attributable to economic conditions, not a "moral taint." Similar to what Lydston had written years earlier, Brandeis felt that their criminality was explainable as a consequence of structural forces guiding strong characters in criminal directions. In this logic, business elites should not be punished not only because good people who resorted to crime to compete with unethical rivals did not deserve harsh justice, but also because the bad competitors were driven toward crime by economic conditions and a desire to succeed rather than immutable faults. In other words, bad businessmen were not innately bad but were simply led astray by the interaction of their strong personalities with market forces.

Regulatory ideology thus had distinctive policy implications. First, it was directed toward saving markets rather than restructuring them. The central aim of regulation was not to protect the public from market predations, but to protect businessmen from succumbing to market pressures and to save capitalism from itself without dampening competition. Second, regulatory agencies typically retain power to refer cases for criminal prosecution. But regulatory statutes often include criminal referrals as discretionary options for regulators to deploy in lieu of pursuing administrative, civil, or equity sanctions for the same behaviors. This range of options should not be mistaken as analogous to alternatives to incarceration sometimes made available for certain street offenses, like fines or probation, which still carry the stigma of criminality through conviction. Granting regulators discretion to determine when to punish specified behaviors through criminal, civil, equity, or administrative tools means that actions defined as criminal in statutory text may not be treated as such. And it is often the case that criminal referrals target not the actual undesirable behavior but a corporate actor's disregard of a regulator's administrative order, meaning that prosecutions often punish noncompliance with an agency directive rather than the actual underlying behavior targeted in the first place. This means that corporate offenders can repeatedly break the law without ever being labeled as criminals if regulators consistently resort to noncriminal sanctions in exercising their discretion. These procedures became the primary policy approaches justified by regulatory ideology.

Importantly, regulatory modes of governance were more than a product of eugenic ideologies of criminality. Progressive era lawmakers were faced with what many likely felt was one of the most significant political problems of their time—finding a way to hold business leaders accountable without undermining the value they saw in industrialism, the corporate form, and a nationalized economy. The compromises and choices they made when designing the regulatory state were driven by a range of institutional, political, and economic considerations. In this light, regulatory ideology was a tool that helped corporate interests and their allies champion their desired policies in a common language with broad appeal, but that does not mean that regulatory ideology should be dismissed as a rhetorical front. With national lawmakers pressured to act, corporate powerhouses and their political friends had to speak within discourses that had appeal and made sense to those outside their own coalition. Aware of growing populist critiques of corporate power, politically effective business coalitions dulled the force of anticorporate politics by deploying and shaping regulatory ideological ideas to advocate for acceptable policy outcomes rather than by pushing a purist commitment to laissez-faire ideals unlikely to garner broad support. This is not to suggest that corporate actors do not have outsized political power—they certainly do—but to emphasize that, at any given historical moment, they operate within the same political universe as everyone else and remain bound by the constellation of ideas prevailing in that particular place and time. The strategic choice to mobilize regulatory ideology served the goals of powerful interests, but the ideology colored political development as its premises and assumptions shaped debate and became lodged within the foundation of the regulatory state.

While there are many reasons that corporate offenders evade punishment, the focus of this book is on the development of ideologies that have led us to build institutions locking up the poor and minorities for street crimes while channeling corporate offenders away from the prison on the basis of determinations of who is bad and who is good that are dependent on individuals' racial and class traits. In this light, it must be stated that the ascendance of regulatory ideology was not inevitable. There were real ideological alternatives offering greater justification for punishing wealthy lawbreakers, including some from Cesare Beccaria's work that was so influential in early America. In a chapter in *On Crimes and Punishments* titled "On the Punishment of Nobles," Beccaria insisted on punishing wealthy elites equally with the rest of society. He not only wrote that "the injury done to society" by a criminal act should be the determinant of a sentence; he also stated that "injury is augmented by the high rank of the offender," suggesting that wealthy and powerful wrongdoers deserve sterner punishment than most because their actions inflicted greater damage.[120] While Beccaria was an advocate of economic regulation, his criminological work shows that he also saw value in instituting meaningful criminal sanctions for corporate wrongdoing to deter crime and preserve the rule of law.[121] His utilitarian vision, which strongly emphasized the importance of clarity and consistency in punishing crimes to secure deterrent effects, differed sharply from a regulatory regime in which regulators exercised broad discretion to manage criminalized activities through a range of alternative mechanisms.

One Progressive era economist also proposed an alternative. In 1907, Edward Ross made a case for punishing the corporate wrongdoer.[122] He upbraided Americans for holding permissive attitudes toward what he called the "quasi-criminal" or the "criminaloid." Criminaloids included "prosperous evil-doers that bask undisturbed in popular favor [and] have been careful to shun—or seem to shun—the familiar types of wickedness." They "are not culpable in the eyes of the public and their own eyes" and are "fortified by [their] connections with 'legitimate business'" so that "their spiritual attitude is not that of the criminal." Nonetheless, Ross noted that the criminaloid was not driven by a criminal nature:

> The director who speculates in the securities of his corporation, the banker who lends his depositors' money to himself under divers [sic] corporate aliases, the railroad official who grants a secret rebate for his private graft, the builder who hires walking delegates to harass his rivals . . . these reveal in their faces nothing of wolf or vulture. Nature has not foredoomed them to evil. . . . They are not degenerates tormented by monstrous cravings. They want nothing more than we all want—money, power, consideration—in a word, success; but they are in a hurry, and they are not particular as to the means.

He attributed economic elites' misconduct to the allure of wealth and power, enticements he suggested everyone can understand, not inherent criminal tendencies. That even Ross expressed these ideas showcases the breadth of the consensus that corporate lawbreakers were relatable figures naturally distinct from pathologically deviant criminals. However, he reached a different conclusion than did his contemporaries. He stated that the "criminaloid," being of sound mind and constitution, is "society's most dangerous foe" as "he sports the livery of virtue and operates on a Titanic scale."[123] Because such lawbreakers were rational, Ross's contemporaries believed that they would be responsive to lesser sanctions, but Ross believed that these traits made the corporate criminal uniquely blameworthy since his crimes were acts of choice.

Ross was a lonely voice in his day, and academic analysis of what modern observers would consider white-collar crime would not resurface until Edwin Sutherland took up the cause in the 1940s. But Ross was influential, even receiving letters from President Theodore Roosevelt and Supreme Court justice Oliver Wendell Holmes Jr. praising his scholarship.[124] Given Ross's unique position at the time as a eugenicist willing to condemn corporate lawbreakers, Roosevelt's admiration of him makes sense in light of the president's support for eugenics and his support for reforms making it easier to hold executives criminally accountable, as discussed in chapter 4.

The ideologies of rehabilitation and regulation perpetuate pernicious inequalities, and a system built on their principles deserves critical consideration. But it bears repeating that the inequalities are the problem, not the mentality of regulatory administration on its own. Dismantling regulatory systems in favor of punitive strategies would not only undo valuable regulatory systems that should exist as complements—though not as wholesale replacements—to criminal controls; it would also neglect to draw lessons from institutions built on the very logic most critics of the carceral state wish to apply to all forms of crime. The regulatory strategy—especially as articulated by those like Brandeis aiming to ameliorate the economic conditions that encourage wrongdoing without punishing the individual wrongdoer—offers promise as an alternative to the punitive strategies used to manage street crime. The following chapters detail how regulatory and rehabilitative ideologies have legitimated offensive inequalities, but anger at those inequalities should not cloud our vision from seeing the regulatory approach's potential as a strategy for governing all forms of crime via economic management rather than harsh justice.

Regulatory ideology was built on the logic that administrative interventions could correct economic conditions and solve the problems of market crime without disrupting market dynamics via the heavy hand of punishment. Its focus on fixing economic conditions without constraining industrialists' capitalist natures stood in sharp contrast to rehabilitative ideology's emphasis on fixing or punishing street criminals' deviant natures. When regulatory ideology became entrenched in the state's regulatory architecture, it brought these contradictions into the fabric of institutions as the regulatory state became a relative of the criminal justice system.

Punishment and Ideology

Both rehabilitative and regulatory ideologies were consistent with traditions of liberal individualism by isolating the individual as the target for social control, and racially and class-biased currents in Darwinism and eugenics undergirded both frameworks. But these shared assumptions pushed in divergent directions; the naturally avaricious disposition of the capitalist class needed to be cultivated and directed appropriately, while the naturally criminal disposition of the marginalized classes needed to be eliminated through rehabilitation and harsh justice.

Through rehabilitative and regulatory ideologies, a subjective judgment of the individual became a lens for interpreting an individual's actions. The robber barons were deemed good people by virtue of their status regardless of what they did, while the poor were deemed likely criminals by virtue of their status regardless of what they did. By dressing up the era's commonsense class and race assumptions in scientific language, rehabilitative and regulatory ideologies internalized, reproduced, and validated capitalist class relations and racial hierarchies.

As Progressive scholars waded into public and political debates over social and regulatory policy, they brought these ideological frameworks with them, transforming them from ivory tower constructs into political realities. A range of political actors found value in rehabilitative and regulatory ideologies, including lawmakers, penologists, eugenicists, and advocates of corporate capitalism. The next two chapters show how these ideologies were politically mobilized in Progressive era politics. The meanings and purposes associated with the ideologies evolved over time as political actors altered their character in pursuit of particular policy goals, but putting them into practice transmitted fundamental attributes of their ideological structure into the political sphere, conditioning the direction of policy change and institutional development.

Entrenching Rehabilitation:
Pathology and Punishment in the Progressive Era

> The vagrant, the man without a permanent abode or visible means of support, is nec-
> essarily a dangerous element, whether or not, or even before, he blossoms out into a
> professional criminal.
> "Crime and Vagrancy," *New York Times*, May 2, 1907

In 1911, Cesare Lombroso's daughter Gina published a book summarizing her
father's research. Although it was often confused for her father's original work,
only the book's introduction was written by Cesare. In it, he bemoaned the
cool reception his work received "from all quarters of Europe." However, he
recognized that his ideas were implemented almost perfectly in one country:
"One nation, however—America—gave a warm and sympathetic reception
to the ideas of the Modern School which they speedily put into practice, with
the brilliant results shown by the Reformatory at Elmira."[1] At Zebulon Brockway's Elmira, the birthplace of the rehabilitative ideal, Lombroso proudly saw
his theory influencing penal practice.

Accounts of mass incarceration often suggest that the repudiation of penal rehabilitation in the 1970s ignited the rise of the carceral state.[2] A growing
literature is revealing a more complicated story, highlighting the historically
fluctuating influence of the rehabilitative ideal and its regionally diverse impacts.[3] But Lombroso's praise for Elmira underscores how the rehabilitative
ideal was never a foil for punitive ideologies.

This chapter traces how Progressive era policymakers used rehabilitative
ideology to shape development across three domains. First, it examines the
origins of the rehabilitative ideal, specifically how Zebulon Brockway used
rehabilitative ideology to establish a new paradigm of punishment that sup-
planted and subsumed older approaches while also instituting new practices
and techniques. Known for his pioneering use of the indeterminate sentence
as the warden of New York's Elmira Reformatory from 1876 to 1900, Brockway employed the indeterminate model to serve two purposes—to rehabilitate curable inmates and to incarcerate born criminals for as long as possible. The chapter details the influence of this model on the Progressive era's

reformatory movement, tracing how Brockway's ideas were adopted by states that built reformatories. Second, the chapter examines how rehabilitative ideology fueled a spate of reforms to state-level vagrancy laws. Forty-six states reformed their vagrancy laws in punitive directions, with most billing their revamped laws as "antitramp acts" designed to lock up incorrigible vagrants for extended periods because vagrancy was deemed an indicator of inherent criminality. The eugenic racial and class biases undergirding the rehabilitative perspective helped construct punitive vagrancy laws designed to control poor White and immigrant populations, recently freed slaves, and organized labor in different contexts. The mobilization of rehabilitative ideology in the service of vagrancy law reform was often a move to control labor populations on behalf of capitalist interests, but the politics sustaining this wave also tied the determinist premises of rehabilitation to racial control goals. These racial and class dynamics were mutually reinforcing and illuminate the complexity and versatility of the rehabilitative ideational framework when it was transferred into political practice. The chapter concludes by outlining the links between rehabilitative ideology and the eugenics movement as constructs of incorrigibility helped justify sterilization as a punishment for crime in twenty-eight states. The eugenic underpinnings of rehabilitation legitimized conceptions of criminality, inequality, and group difference that validated widely held, commonsense cultural presumptions about race and class in Progressive era America.

The Proliferation of the Rehabilitative Model

Ideas of rehabilitation and born criminality intuitively seem incompatible, but they were inseparable to turn-of-the-century penologists. Rehabilitative ideology did not accommodate Lombrosian theory; it hinged on it. The spread of the rehabilitative ideal in the late nineteenth century and the early twentieth entrenched determinist conceptions of criminality in state penal systems. Where the indeterminate sentence took root, it was geared as much toward containment as toward rehabilitation. The idea of incorrigible criminality had massive political value to lawmakers capitalizing on law-and-order impulses. Politicians would likely have articulated similar ideas in the absence of the rehabilitative ideal, but rehabilitative ideology offered something unique by enabling politicians to reap benefits on polar ends of the spectrum of crime politics by selling themselves as tough on crime while maintaining an air of benevolence by speaking within a rehabilitative discourse. This empowered lawmakers to cultivate public images as both criminal justice hardliners and compassionate forward thinkers by rationalizing state control over

incorrigible racial and class populations alongside promises to extend rehabilitative opportunities behind bars. It thus offered a compelling framework
within which lawmakers could justify discarding Beccarian theory's postu-
lation that all offenders were equally deterrable, along with its generalized
assumptions of human rationality, while reorienting penal systems toward
individualizing sentences based on assessments of defendants' characters and
dispositions according to the pathologizing premises of Lombrosian theory.

The rehabilitative ideal also diverged from the management styles of the
famous "separate" and "silent" prison systems. In Pennsylvania, Philadelphia's
Eastern State Penitentiary long practiced a separate system of strict solitary
confinement, embracing Quaker ideals in the hope that isolating inmates
would promote contemplation, moral reflection, and divine redemption. In
New York, Auburn Prison's silent system kept inmates in solitary confinement
in the evening and forced them to perform group work in silence during the
day. But the ideas that religious salvation or hard labor could set someone on
the right path were subsumed into the broader rehabilitative enterprise of
reformatories like Elmira as potential avenues for reform rather than the sole
solution.[4] Instead of religious authorities helping inmates undergo penance
or officers compelling work, rehabilitative institutions were run by professional state bureaucrats equipped with ostensibly scientific knowledge of the
criminal. They relied on education, vocational training, physical recreation,
behavioral incentives, and therapeutic treatments to transform inmates while
also offering them work opportunities and religious outlets, arming prison
administrators with an array of tools to deploy in their attempts to reform
offenders diagnosed with diverse and unique needs.

The reformatory movement as described by Alexander Pisciotta (1994)
spanned the forty years following Elmira's opening from 1876 to 1916. During this time, seventeen states and Washington, DC, opened reformatories
emulating Brockway's model to varying degrees (fig. 1). It is unsurprising
that the model developed most thoroughly in the Northeast and the Midwest. Western states lacked the resources and institutional capacity to operate
robust penal systems, while vigilante lynch mob justice was common as an
alternative to formal institutions for Blacks accused of crime in the South.
The distinctive emphasis on extralegal racial control in the southern states
inhibited them from developing a reformatory movement to the extent that
northern states did.[5]

Pisciotta and Nicole Hahn Rafter have demonstrated how the ideas of
criminal anthropology influenced the development of state reformatories.[6]
Building on this work, this chapter illustrates how states followed New York's
lead by coupling indeterminate sentencing with their reformatory systems

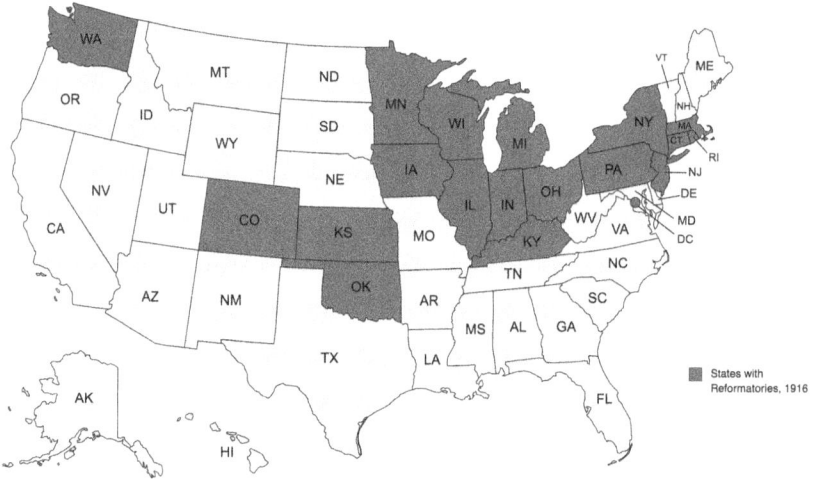

FIGURE 1 States with penal reformatories, 1916. (Data from Pisciotta, *Benevolent Repression*, 81–126. Map created with mapchart.net.)

to pursue the joint goals of rehabilitation and punishment. State legislative records from these years are largely unavailable or nonexistent, making it difficult to track legislative debates over indeterminate sentencing statutes, but documents from state boards of charities (SBCs) are available. SBCs were state institutions that oversaw welfare and social policy and served state legislatures in advisory capacities, writing annual reports analyzing policies and proposals. Analysis of SBC reports reveals that rehabilitative ideology was a fundamental driver of the shift toward indeterminate sentencing. This section relies on SBC documents from five states in the Northeast and the Midwest where the ideal took hold—Illinois, Indiana, Ohio, Pennsylvania, and New York—to analyze the spread of the indeterminate sentence.

New York led this movement. In 1901, Brockway's methods were highlighted in the *Washington Post*. The article noted that while Brockway endorsed rehabilitation, his philosophy insisted that "evildoers do not respond to any general influence of the good." The rehabilitative model left it to prison authorities—"who have better chances for studying the criminal"—to determine an individual's sentence. Under this approach, "future criminals will find themselves under such restraint that they will cease to do wrong," while, for those who can be reformed, the "chief concern" will be "to redeem the prisoner and teach him to be self-supporting."[7]

Ohio became one of the first states to follow New York's lead and pass an indeterminate sentencing law in 1885. The law granted judges the discretion to sentence third-time felons to life imprisonment and was later amended to include three-time petty thieves who "failed to reform" and needed to be "permanently secluded" as eligible for life sentences. Increasing sentences for repeat offenders was a common development during the reformatory movement as tailoring punishment to individuals required an evaluation of their reformative capacity and a criminal record was strong evidence of incorrigibility. The Ohio board's 1891 report specifically cited Brockway's advice on how to structure an indeterminate system, and in 1892 the SBC praised the state for operating on "substantially the same plan as that of New York" by sorting inmates into divisions of incorrigibility.[8] In 1899, the board commended Pennsylvania, Illinois, Michigan, Minnesota, Kansas, and Indiana for making early release through the indeterminate sentence available to only "a limited class of prisoners."[9]

Indiana's SBC advocated for an indeterminate sentencing law for years prior to its passage in 1897.[10] The board insisted that indeterminacy protected society through "the detention of the incorrigible and the release of the reformed criminal."[11] Citing Elmira as proof, it claimed that indeterminate sentencing has "proven [to be] the most successful" means of "reforming the corrigible criminals and permanently containing the incorrigible."[12] Illinois's SBC similarly cited Elmira as evidence that indeterminate sentencing provided "a safeguard and security to the public" by permitting prisons to hold "the most dangerous criminals" for extended periods.[13] Three years later, the board stated that such "born criminals" necessitated "incarceration for life" under such a system.[14] In 1891, Illinois enacted an indeterminate sentencing law that the SBC later claimed embodied "the nobler purpose . . . to reclaim as well as punish."[15] The board cited Arthur MacDonald and Charles Henderson in discussing prison reform and the need for a national laboratory to study the criminal class.[16] The Pennsylvania board on which Henry Boies served defended indeterminate sentencing, which the state implemented in 1889, by praising how it permitted "indefinite" terms for incorrigibles and increased the average length of confinement in the state.[17] New York's SBC supported Brockway's model, even after it conducted an investigation into allegations of abuse at Elmira in 1894 that exonerated Brockway and the staff, praising his indeterminate model for enabling the state to identify "those who are fitted for release, [and] those who by defect of character or constitution may need longer or even permanent detention."[18] In 1905, it approvingly informed the legislature that "in every state where the indeterminate sentence has been given trial, the average term of imprisonment has increased."[19]

The Illinois board was careful to note that while a "theoretically correct" indeterminate sentencing scheme would confine incorrigibles for life, in "popular usage" such a system assigns only a long "maximum limit" on detainment.[20]

The indeterminate sentence was not implemented to this theoretical extreme until 1907, when New York passed a habitual offender law detaining fourth-time offenders for life. For years preceding the law's passage, the SBC advocated for it by drawing on rehabilitative ideology. The 1905 report concluded that the law was necessary because "incorrigible offenders should be permanently segregated by the state" and that consequently the indeterminate sentence "should be relieved of its maximum limit."[21]

The indeterminate sentence is often thought of as a gentle alternative to determinacy, but from its inception it embodied dual commitments to reform and containment, with this flexibility permitting movement in punitive or reformative directions on the basis of evaluations of an individual's reformative capacity. This has had deeper consequences than just driving the reformatory movement. Criminal history persists as a powerful consideration in American sentencing because it is a legacy of the rehabilitative ideal and acts as a proxy for incorrigibility, carrying the eugenic assumptions undergirding rehabilitative thinking into modern practice. While the rehabilitative ideal has oscillated in appeal and influence, its underlying assumption that sentencing should be tailored to the individual on the basis of considerations that we take for granted—such as criminal history—is a feature of rehabilitative ideology that has become entrenched in the justice system's operations.

Vagrancy and Incorrigibility

When combined with commonly held prejudices and social assumptions, rehabilitative ideology served to reconstruct criminal law into a class and racial control tool. This is clear in the reformation of vagrancy laws. America inherited vagrancy laws from England, but unlike English statutes, American vagrancy laws became potent mechanisms of crime control.[22] Before the mid-nineteenth century this was not the case as vagrancy laws were generally used to manage the flow of migratory labor. When discovered by police, jobless transients were often not punished but instead housed overnight in station houses.[23] Urban police departments, which had not yet evolved into professionalized crime control forces, were sometimes tasked with such social welfare functions.[24] But industrialization and urbanization in the late nineteenth century sparked heightened anxieties over the impoverished and working classes in the Northeast and industrial Midwest, while in the South lawmakers sought mechanisms for controlling Black populations following emancipation. These anxieties fomented a toxic political reaction in which the determinist ideas of rehabilitative ideology were directed toward remaking vagrancy laws into punitive instruments.

As inequality intensified in the late nineteenth century, the idea of natural criminality helped restructure public policy to control the "dangerous classes." This group included undesirables like the urban poor, the working class, immigrants, and Blacks. The overhaul of vagrancy laws was tied to these varied political imperatives as lawmakers sought to justify punitive control over poverty in some times and places and over Blacks, immigrants, and organized labor in others. Blending vagrancy laws with rehabilitative ideology thus solved multiple political problems. Infusing revamped vagrancy laws with the idea of incorrigibility advanced certain class interests by legitimating the aggressive management of surplus labor while also achieving racial control in regions where lawmakers sought methods for controlling recently freed slaves or arriving immigrants. Rehabilitative ideology's determinist biases established a foundation from which these different species of punitive control could grow.

After the Panic of 1873 made urban poverty a visible social problem, it ignited larger political debates about poverty that drove vagrancy laws in punitive directions.[25] The panic generated anxieties over a "tramp army," an imaginary revolutionary force consisting of homeless men threatening the nation's social stability. In combating this "tramp crisis," the idea of incorrigibility became a tool to stigmatize the poor as criminal threats.[26] The application of the label *incorrigible* to the unemployed and impoverished classes can thus be understood as a mechanism for managing surplus labor and as a response to public concerns prompted by urbanization and the economic stresses of the changing political economy. But the retooling of vagrancy laws was in part a consequence of the politicization of a popular law-and-order campaign through which lawmakers could demonize vulnerable poor populations and punish them to allay public fears. And while varying terms for the poor emerged in Progressive era discourse—such as *hoboes* (who wandered between cities seeking transient work), *tramps* (who traveled between cities to avoid work), *vagrants* (the chronically unemployed who survived by begging), and *paupers* (who were simply poor)—the poor were typically treated in political discourse as one mass of deviants, and these terms were often used interchangeably.[27]

Vagrancy law reform was linked to assumptions about poverty and criminality embedded in rehabilitative ideology. Dugdale, Brockway, and their protégés sowed these seeds. In 1877, Dugdale argued that the Jukes' criminality could be attributed to the same traits that contributed to their pauperism.[28] In 1898, Brockway advanced the Lamarckian argument that "the deprivation and dissipations of the improvident class" produced degeneracies that were "transmitted to generation after generation." He concluded that, if provided with money, poor inmates would "squander [it] before exerting themselves for a living" because "habitual improvidence, with its attending poverty, must constitute one of the chief causes of the condition of mind we are considering."[29]

Brockway and Dugdale were not alone in making these connections, as chapter 2 explained. Again, Henry Boies categorized paupers into two natural classes, one consisting of the physically and mentally impaired and the other populated by the "incorrigibly idle, dissolute, and criminal," including "beggars, vagrants, and tramps." The existence of this latter class could be attributed to poor heredity, and Boies advocated for its members' permanent incarceration if they could not be rehabilitated as productive members of society.[30] As discussed earlier, G. Frank Lydston argued there were common physiological patterns in the skulls of tramps and criminals.[31] Philip Parsons called tramps "a distinct social peril" and "iniquitous menace[s] to life and property," while Charles Henderson described them as "corrupting and diseased" individuals posing "grave evils" to society.[32]

In 1877, the Annual Conference of State Charities focused its deliberations on tramps. With attendees from several SBCs, the meeting brought the social sciences to bear on the problem.[33] Members were convinced by Dugdale's presentation of his *Jukes* research and focused on the tramp's defective biology, not the conditions that caused poverty.[34] Perhaps no one was more responsible for linking poverty, crime, and biology than Francis Wayland III, the dean of the Yale Law School. Arguably the most nationally respected expert on poverty, Wayland argued that 94–99 percent of tramps were natural criminals and described the tramp to conference attendees as "a lazy, shiftless, sauntering or swaggering, ill-conditioned, irreclaimable, incorrigible, cowardly, utterly depraved savage." He warned that the tramp "seems to have wholly lost all the better instincts and attributes of manhood" and "will outrage an unprotected female, or rob a defenceless child, or burn an isolated barn, or girdle fruit trees, or wreck a railway train, or set fire to a railway bridge, or murder a cripple, or pilfer an umbrella, with equal indifference, if reasonably sure of equal impunity." He concluded, "Having no moral sense, he [the tramp] knows no gradations in crime." Wayland repeatedly drew on rhetoric that lent scientific credence to social apprehensions that tramping was a precursor to serious crimes like rape and murder.[35]

The *Journal of the American Institute of Criminal Law and Criminology* regularly published scholarship linking poverty and crime. In a study of New York's municipal lodging houses published in the journal's September 1914 issue, Robert Gault argued that "[a] large proportion of vagrants" were "pathologic" and that 12 percent "showed definite evidences of defective mentality."[36] In the November 1914 issue, John Lisle wrote that the tramp class "must be destroyed" because "[tramps'] delinquency is not due to their failure to bear their share of the social burden . . . , but in their dangerous characters."[37] These ideas justified proposed bills to create a laboratory in the Justice Department to study criminals and paupers.[38]

Economists validated popular notions about class and criminality in their research on labor. Richard Ely wrote in 1891 that there are two classes of paupers, one that is willing to work but has not yet learned any usable skills and another that is "practically impossible" to reform and "belongs to the criminal class."[39] In *Principles of Economics* (1911), Frank Taussig tied "criminals and tramps" together as feeble-minded populations that are "unemployable."[40] President William McKinley's Industrial Commission directly applied these ideas to its analysis of prison labor, identifying Elmira as a useful paradigm. Through the "reclaiming of the younger lawbreakers, who could not be properly classified as . . . incorrigible criminals," the commission endorsed putting reformable inmates to work. It suggested that reformatories follow Elmira by grading convicts into tiers of reformability, with "the incorrigible" being "kept in confinement" and "at such labor as practicable."[41] It supported the indeterminate sentence, stating that if people "are becoming habitual criminals, they can be sent [to reformatories] for a longer time, even to the extent of a life sentence," a practice that should "be applied to all delinquents, including the pauper."[42] The commission's detailed listing of state-level convict labor laws highlighted the common practice of putting the poor to work behind bars under the assumption that they required compulsion to work.[43]

This research legitimated public assumptions linking poverty and criminality that appeared in journalistic outlets. The term *tramp* first appeared in an American newspaper in 1875 when the *New York Times* described tramps as willing to "do anything mean or disagreeable to maintain themselves in a condition of idleness."[44] In 1877, the *Chicago Daily Tribune* cited New York's enhanced vagrancy law as a laudable reform meant to "check the extent of pauperism, thereby of course checking the extent of crime." The article described vagrancy as a "growing evil" that could "result in a frightful increase of crime."[45] Later that year, a *Tribune* article made the case for "putting a little strychnine or arsenic in the meat and other supplies furnished to tramps" to send "a warning to other tramps to keep out of the neighborhood."[46] In 1894, the *North American Review* included an article claiming that "[t]he relation of the vagrant to the criminal class . . . is of the closest character; it is hard to say where the one begins and the other ends" and that tramps deserved to be "severely punished, and by force exterminated."[47]

Hostility to the poor remained tangible through the Progressive era even as popular culture transformed conceptions of poverty in the early twentieth

century—vaudeville comedy began depicting tramps as fools that made audi-
ences laugh rather than recoil. But even this did not erase the links between
poverty and criminality; romanticizing poverty relied on exploiting assumptions about the criminality of the poor. For instance, Charlie Chaplin's famous
Little Tramp character was an amusing trickster, but the films in which he was
featured regularly revolved around the character being a thief and a con artist.[48] This nostalgic imaging easily coexisted with ideologies justifying harsh
antitramp policies. The *Los Angeles Times* acknowledged this in 1901, claiming that "[t]he hobo of the comic page is an amiable soul, with a tomato can,"
but that "the hobo of real life . . . is thoroughly vicious, degraded and dangerous," before warning that "[a]n epidemic of crime invariably follows the
coming of the tramps." The *Times* attributed California's recent crime wave
to an influx of tramps and praised Pennsylvania's antitramp law as a model
solution.[49] In 1907, the *New York Times* stated that the vagrant "is necessarily
a dangerous element, whether or not, or rather even before, he blossoms out
into a professional criminal."[50]

Individuals with real institutional power outside the academy applied
ideas about criminal incorrigibility to their assessments of tramps. Particularly remarkable is a statement from James Forbes, the director of the National Association for the Prevention of Vagrancy. Quoted in the *Washington
Post* in 1911, Forbes suggested that his association had limited ability to affect
change, asserting that "[i]t is practically impossible to reform a tramp."[51]

Demands for antitramp legislation were wrapped into arguments about
indeterminate sentencing. The motivating rationale was that laws punishing
the poor should similarly extend their potential maximums to contain incorrigibles for longer. For instance, in 1892, the Ohio SBC suggested that recidivist misdemeanants were members "of the incorrigible class" and should
receive "indefinite sentences" under the indeterminate model.[52] Indiana's
board made comparable recommendations in 1891.[53] In 1896, Pennsylvania's
SBC suggested that "better results would come from longer periods of detention" for paupers and serious criminals alike.[54] At the 1892 National Prison
Congress, Francis Wayland defended "perpetual imprisonment" for "habitual
criminals, paupers, and drunkards," echoing his earlier advocacy of punitive
vagrancy laws on the grounds that "tramping, such as we have seen it, if not a
crime at first, soon becomes one."[55]

This conflation between tramps and criminals resulted in a wave of reforms
to vagrancy statutes. Under vagrancy laws, lacking visible means of support
constituted a criminal offense, but the content of those laws changed radically
in the late nineteenth century. During that time, forty-six states revamped their
vagrancy laws, with many being rebilled as antitramp acts.[56] Designed to pun-

ish tramping for fear that tramps inevitably produced crime waves, antitramp acts constituted restructured vagrancy laws reliant on punitive sanctions.

Reformed vagrancy laws varied. As of 1916, thirty-seven states' vagrancy laws authorized incarceration in penal institutions as a punishment. While some states treated incarceration as a first option, some fined tramps before incarcerating them (although fines often led to incarceration when they went unpaid), and others mandated labor.[57] The laws articulated expansive definitions of vagrancy, extending beyond disorderly conduct to wandering without work. Some laws also converted certain misdemeanors into felonies if committed by tramps.[58] By the 1890s, many observers went so far as to advocate for a national antitramp act.[59]

Statutes varied in severity:[60]

- Two (Indiana and Texas) imposed only a fine.
- Two (Tennessee and Virginia) had no authorized maximum sentences.
- Eleven (Arkansas, Delaware, Kentucky, Mississippi, Missouri, Nebraska, North Carolina, North Dakota, Oklahoma, South Carolina, and South Dakota) imposed maximum sentences of under three months.
- Nine (Arizona, Colorado, Idaho, Minnesota, Montana, Nevada, New Mexico, Utah, and Wyoming) imposed maximum sentences of three months.
- Eleven (California, Florida, Georgia, Illinois, Iowa, Louisiana, Maine, New Jersey, Oregon, Pennsylvania, and Washington) imposed maximum sentences of between six and ten months.
- Four (Alabama, Connecticut, Kansas, and Maryland) imposed maximum sentences of one year.
- Five (Massachusetts, Michigan, New Hampshire, New York, and Wisconsin) imposed maximum sentences of two years.
- Two (Ohio and Rhode Island) imposed maximum sentences of three years.[61]

By 1916, twenty states had authorized a maximum sentence of between three and ten months for tramping, while eleven had authorized maximums of anywhere from one to three years.[62] And states got creative; New Hampshire and Pennsylvania paid the public for information on the whereabouts of tramps, while Connecticut and Nevada gave police and prosecutors monetary incentives for catching them.[63]

The reconstruction of vagrancy laws entailed changes in urban policing. The growth of urban police departments far outpaced the growth of city populations from 1882 to 1909, and victimless disorder offenses topped their lists for arrests.[64] Increased crime rates at the turn of the century were not simple results of urbanization but a reflection of changes in criminal law.[65]

An 1897 survey of antitramp acts found that sentences were most severe in the Northeast industrial core states.[66] This makes sense since tramps were often understood to be White urban industrial workers. But given the nativist overtones in Progressive era discourse, it was also presumed that tramps consisted of indolent immigrants intermixing with the White populations in industrial states. The natural criminality of immigrants was also verified in rehabilitative scholarship. Brockway claimed that immigrants affected "the volume of crime in our own country" while bringing "dangerous tendencies" into the American gene pool.[67] McKinley's Industrial Commission made specific claims about immigration's impact on labor markets, writing that Italians, Hebrews, and Irish were prone to pauperism and criminality.[68] In his testimony before the Industrial Commission, the economist John Commons insisted that "foreigners and children of foreigners are the worst element which we have in this country" and should be put to work in prison.[69]

Scholars of immigration made similar connections, condemning immigrants as the "dangerous classes" and "barbarians."[70] Arguing that the races were not "equally endowed," Daniel G. Brinton told the American Association for the Advancement of Science in 1895 that "the black, the brown, and red races" each had a "peculiar mental temperament which [had] become hereditary" and rendered them "recreant to the codes of civilization, and therefore technically criminal."[71] So not only was exclusive immigration policy necessary to control immigrants, but so too was enhanced crime control. After the lynching of eleven Italian men in New Orleans in 1891, the largest mass lynching in American history, Representative Henry Cabot Lodge (R-MA) stated that the tragedy's underlying cause was "the utter failure of any laws or regulations which we now have to exclude members of the criminal classes."[72] Theodore Roosevelt, serving on the US Civil Service Commission at the time, famously referred to the lynching as "a rather good thing."[73]

In northeastern states with high immigrant populations, antitramp acts were linked to these attitudes. But vagrancy laws served different purposes elsewhere. Many southern states authorized fines as punishment for vagrancy in lieu of incarceration, creating an appearance of leniency.[74] In reality, this is because southern vagrancy laws were uniquely designed to stock the convict-lease system. They were integral to the Black Codes and helped control recently freed slave populations while providing southern economic elites a soft landing as they transitioned out of a slave-based economy.

The convict-lease system served the twin goals of racial control and supplying cheap labor to southern industries. Crimes such as "mischief," "insulting gestures," and "pig laws" (punishing theft of farm animals) provided law enforcement with vague tools empowering them to lock up young Black men en masse. When unemployed young Black men could not pay fines for vagrancy violations, their labor would be sold to private bidders. The convict-lease system lasted until 1928, when Alabama became the last state to abolish it.[75] It was simultaneously an economic project and a racial control project legitimized in part by biodeterminist assumptions about Black criminality.

Muhammad's *The Condemnation of Blackness* sheds light on how pseudo-scientific analysis of Black criminality shaped such practices in the Progressive era, once again emphasizing Frederick Hoffman's synthesis of Lombrosian theory and race science to explain census data showing disproportionately high rates of Black crime in the United States.[76] These links between race, crime, and biology also appeared in the works of rehabilitative scholars like Henry Boies and Charles Henderson who made Lamarckian arguments suggesting that under slavery Blacks developed criminal habits that became hereditary traits.[77] This conclusion was shared by scholars of race, who identified it as a unique challenge for southern penologists. In 1891, Dr. P. D. Sims informed the National Prison Association, "We have difficulties at the south which you at the north have not. . . . We have a large alien population, an inferior race. . . . The Negro's moral sense is lower than that of the white man." He rationalized the peculiarities of southern criminal justice by insisting that southern penologists "do not yet know" how to reform Black crime. Sims's colleague, Dr. Albert Henley, seconded his concerns, explaining to attendees that "[i]t is almost impossible to reach the Negro by means applied to the white convicts."[78]

This explains both the peculiarities of southern vagrancy laws and the absence of reformatory institutions in southern states. Taxpayers in the South were resistant to spending money to house offenders in reformatories since it was believed that the southern criminal population was disproportionately incorrigible because it consisted mostly of Black offenders who could not contribute to society unless compelled. In *"Worse than Slavery,"* David Oshinsky discusses one Mississippi state legislator who hoped to save juveniles from the convict-lease system by building a juvenile reformatory. But there was decisive pushback in the statehouse, and his proposals were rejected by colleagues insisting that "it was no use trying to reform a negro."[79]

Vagrancy laws helped southern Democrats by appeasing White resistance to funding reformatories. Instead, they put the region's largely incorrigible criminal population to work by force while serving racial and economic functions by creating a controllable racialized labor pool for industry. While racial and economic dimensions undergirded the system, rehabilitative ideology justified populating it with young Black men for whom nothing but compulsion would encourage productivity. As the convict labor camp captain J. C. Powell wrote in his defense of convict leasing, "We have little material for skilled labor among the criminals of the South. The bulk of our convicts are negroes who could not by any possibility learn a trade, and how to employ them at anything save the simplest manual toil is a problem not yet solved."[80]

Convict leasing was present in the United States before the rise of the rehabilitative ideal, and along with comparable forms of racial control it would have been adopted in the postbellum South even without rehabilitative ideology, given that such policies could have readily been supported through other strands of thought in American politics. However, while convict leasing was distinct from the reformatory systems of the North, it is important to recognize that southern lawmakers explained the practice as consistent with the same systemic logics that defined the rehabilitative approach, often speaking of the innate inferiority and incorrigibility of the population subjected to the leasing system. The difference was not that southerners wholly rejected the logic underlying rehabilitative thought; rather, they understood their overwhelmingly Black prisoner population to be overwhelmingly incorrigible. By concentrating vagrancy law enforcement on Blacks, the police were already performing the rehabilitative sorting process before inmates arrived at the prison. It subsequently made sense to construct a fully dedicated system of exploitation rather than one committed to sorting when the sorting was done by law enforcement given that Blackness was understood as an easily identifiable marker of incorrigibility. The professionally staffed, expert-run reformatories of the North were consequently unnecessary in the South. Convict leasing would have inevitably been a popular practice in the late nineteenth-century South, but the fact that lawmakers presented it as consistent with core logics of the rehabilitative ideal is a testament to the political versatility of the rehabilitative ideological framework.

It was not only in the racial climate of the postbellum South that questions of race, labor, and criminality overlapped in vagrancy law reforms. As labor-capital conflicts intensified at the century's end, labor organizations were often conflated with constructs of natural criminality. Particularly, immigrants and tramps were presumed to be the drivers of labor agitation. While this narrative was widely accepted, whether such an alliance existed is questionable. Immigrants undercut the wage labor market to the dismay of some labor organizations, and the culture of tramping was steeped in notions of Anglo-Saxon masculinity and often excluded Blacks and immigrants. Some labor groups—notably the Industrial Workers of the World—attempted to connect workers and the unemployed poor, but others supported antitramp acts to differentiate the deserving and the undeserving unemployed as governments blamed labor unrest on tramps.[81] However, these nuanced realities did little to counteract popular assumptions lumping these groups together.[82]

Spurious connections between labor and natural criminality appear in the intellectual foundations of rehabilitative ideology. Brockway noted that "the labor question . . . bears directly upon crime" since his research indicated that 82 percent of prisoners were laborers.[83] In 1893, Henry Boies linked labor unrest in American cities to urbanites' habit of welcoming "criminals, anarchists, and ferocious beasts of prey."[84] G. Frank Lydston deployed particularly unusual language in *The Diseases of Society* to imply a relation between atavism and political radicalism. In distinguishing "the social instinct of the lower animals" from that of humans—who, despite being driven by "selfish and sordid ambition," he emphasized were more capable of complex reasoning and moral judgment—he noted that paleontological analyses of mammoth and mastodon fossils indicate that they huddled together for protection, suggesting that "among the lower animals true communism of interests is found."[85] While Lydston may have used *communism* simply to signify an instinctual regard for the collective, the phrase unmistakably bore sociopolitical significance and imbued his argument with implications connecting primitive animal instincts to dangerous radical ideologies.

When the United States experienced a nationwide strike in 1877, the propertied elements panicked, fearing that a criminal army of tramps was threatening the nation's social and political structure by orchestrating labor agitation. The strike began with railroad workers in West Virginia in July, but thousands of workers across the nation promptly joined the cause. Federal troops were sent to seven states and state militias into more. By August, over one hundred were dead and thousands injured.[86] That tramps were absent from the strike did not prevent them from being politicized as its villains.[87] Francis Wayland insisted that the whole series of events was caused by a "standing army of professional tramps" who were "at war with society."[88] Newspapers described tramps as the proletariat's "lowest layer," claiming that they would "gladly participate in any mob action" while wearing "badges of red."[89] Other observers—including Allan Pinkerton, who founded the Pinkerton Detective Agency, which became crucial in businesses' efforts to privatize labor control—argued that labor unrest and crime was due to Communists and "professional tramps" who do "the chief criminal work of this age."[90] Many workers involved in the strike were arrested on vagrancy charges.[91]

Linking labor unrest to populations associated with innate criminality opened the door to revisions in criminal law after the strike. Many states expanded their criminal conspiracy laws, empowering courts to inhibit labor coordination if it was shown that a strike could damage a business's "probable expectancies." This allowed would-be strikers to be arrested and summarily tried for contempt before organizing. Many state militias were expanded with subsidies from businesses, and corporations also hired private police to fight labor, leading to abuses of workers' rights.[92] Private organizations like the American Protective League were paid by firms to infiltrate labor organizations with the endorsement of the Department of Justice, demonstrating how intertwined the interests of business, the police, and the state became in controlling labor through criminal law.[93] Meanwhile, Populists like William Jennings Bryan inadvertently helped legitimize the expansion of state policing institutions by objecting to the privatization of police in favor of public policing.[94]

The 1894 Pullman strike was a particularly crucial moment in criminalizing labor. Owing to wage cuts, three thousand employees in the Pullman Car Company went on strike in June 1894. The American Railway Union (ARU), led by Eugene Debs, carried out sympathy strikes in twenty-seven states and territories. After the activist Jacob Coxey led a march of ten thousand men on Washington the year before to demand unemployment relief—the march ended with thousands of vagrancy arrests of participants in "Coxey's Army"— public anxieties were piqued at the manifestation of a "tramp army" making radical demands, and public support swung in favor of the railroads.[95] With the support of Attorney General Richard Olney, the railroads' General Managers Association secured injunctions hampering the strike. In total, 190 strikers were indicted and 515 arrested, many on vagrancy charges, and the Supreme Court held up Debs's six-month sentence and the three-month sentence given to his associates for violating the injunctions.[96]

The state not only used vagrancy statutes and other legal tools to criminalize the Pullman strike while ignoring the violence carried out by corporations against workers; the railroads' victory also put to bed larger debates about the economic order. The ARU was decimated after the loss, prompting organizations like the American Federation of Labor (AFL) to swing to the right to avoid the same fate. The struggles faced by the labor movement led organizations like the AFL to abandon political commitments that could have formed the basis for a working-class movement in favor of a narrow dedication to business unionism.[97] The criminalization of labor dissent stunted the development of the labor movement, motivating organizations like the AFL to pursue change within the economic system without challenging it.[98]

Perhaps one of the clearest instances of labor being linked to notions of innate criminality came years later during the nation's first "Red Scare" in 1919 when Attorney General A. Mitchell Palmer instituted a series of raids against organizations deemed radical that resulted in thousands of arrests.

Palmer drew on language from anthropological assessments of criminality to defend his actions, suggesting that, "from their lopsided faces, sloping brows, and misshapen features," anarchists and strikers arrested "may be recognized [as] the unmistakable criminal type."[99] Such durable links between organized labor and ideas of innate criminality gave the state the validation not only to punish labor, but also to defuse proworker politics. Conflating labor unrest with populations deemed criminal types—notably tramps and immigrants—legitimized the convergence of interests between the state and industry to repress labor dissent.

Ideological assumptions about innate criminality infected capital-labor conflicts in ways that not only expanded the criminal law's reach but also helped settle broader economic debates on conservative terms. The delegitimization of organized labor as an innately criminal enterprise quieted the strongest opponents of corporate power and undermined the best means workers had for challenging the inequalities of the political economy. When determinist constructs of criminal incorrigibility were politically weaponized against organized labor, vagrancy laws became cudgels the state could use against the working class to secure the outcomes desired by economic elites. In this context, the ideas of rehabilitative ideology were instruments deployed by the state to advance the underlying interests of the capitalist class against a growing labor movement. Through this process, the determinist principles of rehabilitative ideology were brought to bear on a range of economic and racial tensions that colored turn-of-the-century political life.

Reformed vagrancy laws took varied shapes and forms. In each case, rehabilitative ideology was deployed to different effects by furthering some mixture of economic and class control goals, racial control objectives, and political efforts to alleviate popular anxieties about the nation's changing economic and racial makeup through an emphasis on law and order. The story of vagrancy law reform and its connections to rehabilitative ideology illustrates the way ideology can be adjusted and put to varying purposes when it is transmitted from theoretical space into political practice.

Eugenics and Rehabilitative Ideology

The eugenics movement was a substantial booster of the rehabilitative ideal. As eugenicists gained stature in the early twentieth century, Elmira combined its rehabilitative model with a eugenics program and became a national leader in promoting eugenic policy within the context of its rehabilitative model.

The connections between the reformatory movement and eugenics opened prison doors to the influence of medical and psychological professionals.

These experts claimed that they had the requisite epistemological authority to judge the criminality of inmates and sort them into corrigible and incorrigible tiers scientifically. This further departed from the deterrence model, silent system, and separate system by introducing medical expertise into penal practice, lending a veneer of scientific objectivity to the sorting procedures at the heart of the rehabilitative mission. Chapters 5 and 7 explain how the scientized sorting of inmates is a legacy of the rehabilitative program that persists in present-day risk assessments classifying inmates into categories of reformability on the basis of dubious empirics and flawed assumptions that lawmakers and criminal justice administrators continue to insist are scientifically valid. This ever-present concern with infusing the sorting process with scientific credibility has roots in the entrance of eugenic professionals into the penal system during the reformatory movement.

Elmira led the way in enacting a eugenic-rehabilitative program. In 1910, the facility's medical staff declared 38 percent of Elmira's population mentally defective owing to either congenital or acquired defects indicative of incorrigibility. In 1917, Dr. Frank Christian became the institution's warden after serving for years as its lead physician. Putting an MD at the helm signaled the institution's increasing medicalization of crime, and under Christian's leadership the eugenic orientation of Elmira became more pronounced. By 1919, Elmira predicted a positive reformative prognosis for only 4 percent of offenders, and the medical staff explicitly advocated that the remainder be put in penal colonies or sterilized.[100] In 1920, the percentage of inmates declared subnormal, abnormal, or defective was nearly double that reported in 1910. Christian relied on instruments like the Binet intelligence test to determine that the majority of Elmira's inmates were mentally inferior, a fact that he attributed to "the effects of a damaged heredity." He internalized Lombrosian ideas, noting that the criminal "is frequently afflicted with physical deformities" that render him visibly recognizable. He praised sterilization as an instrument for handling incorrigibles, writing that it often "produce[s] excellent results." He also maintained Elmira's commitment to long-term containment by claiming that recidivists required "permanent custodial care," writing in 1921 that over 25 percent of Elmira's inmates were so defective that they required such treatment. He embraced the duality of rehabilitative logic, writing in a report to the state that "[i]t will be admitted . . . that in reformatory treatment the general character and particularly the mental characteristics of the subject are a matter of prime importance and, presumptively, the lower or more abnormal the mentality the longer it will be before his release will not be incompatible with the welfare of society, and *possibly that time may never come*."[101]

Outside Elmira, a variety of intellectuals, professionals, and reformers advocated for criminal sterilization. As discussed in chapter 2, some of the earliest endorsements of criminal sterilization came from rehabilitative theorists, and medical professionals cited their ideas about incorrigibility to defend the practice as the eugenics movement took off. In 1899, Doctor A. J. Oschner defended sterilization in the *Journal of the American Medical Association* by noting that Lombroso proved that "there are certain inherited anatomic defects which characterize . . . born criminals," who commit most crime.[102] The next year, George Makuen, the president of the American Academy of Medicine, endorsed compulsory sterilization, citing Brockway to contend that penal practice should be about caring for criminals while preventing their propagation. Makuen also referenced Boies's *Prisoners and Paupers* in claiming that "[p]auperism, criminality, [and] insanity" are "all one interdependent family" and should be grounds for sterilization. He also criticized William McKim, another disciple of Brockway, for claiming that "a gentle and painless death" should be given to incorrigibles. But he conceded that McKim's proposal revealed the "drift of thought with reference to these matters" in criminological circles and used McKim as a foil to depict sterilization as humane.[103] In the next year's *Academy Bulletin*, S. D. Risley similarly drew on McKim to depict sterilization laws as a kind alternative to extermination.[104]

Important players in the eugenics movement drew links between rehabilitation and sterilization. For instance, in 1904, Dr. Martin Barr, superintendent at the Pennsylvania Training School for Feeble-Minded Children at Elwyn, presented sterilization as a curative tool.[105] In 1908, the American Prison Association (APA) established its Physicians Association, and at the 1908 APA meeting Dr. Charles Carrington stated that he "unreservedly" supported sterilization for "habitual" and "incorrigible" offenders.[106] At the next year's meeting, several members, including APA President Charles Henderson, discussed sterilization as a means of controlling the "incorrigible criminal" identifiable by "physical irregularities."[107]

As early as 1893, inmates of US reformatories were being sterilized off the books. The physician Harry Sharp extralegally performed at least 176 vasectomies in Indiana reformatories between 1893, when Sharp earned his medical degree, and 1907, when the state finally legalized the practice in response to lobbying from Sharp and others.[108] A prominent advocate of compulsory sterilization, Sharp wrote in 1909 that "[i]n treating upon this subject [of criminal sterilization] there must ever be borne in mind the distinct understanding that degeneracy is a defect, and that a defect differs from a disease in that it can not be cured." Targeting "confirmed inebriates, prostitutes, tramps, and criminals, as well as habitual paupers," Sharp argued that the vasectomy was

the most humane means of preventing defectives from breeding. He qualified
that "this operation shall not be performed except in cases that have been
pronounced unimprovable," suggesting that traditional reformative interventions should be applied first.[109] But he noted that the "decidedly defective individual is very easily recognized" and argued that this "mental abnormality
is usually accompanied with prominent physical defects, described by Lombroso" and others.[110]

In the early twentieth century, eugenicist scholars were essential in passing state sterilization laws. Sharp played an important role in Indiana, Barr
in Pennsylvania, and Edward Ross in Wisconsin.[111] In doing so, they drew on
ideas undergirding rehabilitative ideology, and prominent eugenicists paid
attention. Invoking the notion of incorrigibility, Charles Davenport, the ERO
founder, defended sterilization as the only way to stop incorrigibles from reproducing.[112] Similarly, David Starr Jordan of the American Breeder's Association argued that the criminal "can perhaps be healed" but that, if he was incurable, "he can be kept in confinement; and to physicians, and to them alone,
the community must look for help in these matters."[113] This highlights how
eugenicists of varying stripes endorsed the logic of rehabilitation and sought
to medicalize the crime problem, but to different ends. Sharp and Davenport
viewed sterilization as a punitive solution, while others like Barr viewed it
as a rehabilitative procedure. Barr wrote, "Let asexualization be once legalized, not as a penalty for crime, but a remedial measure preventing crime and
tending to future comfort and happiness of the defective; let the practice once
become common for young children immediately upon being adjudged defective by competent authority properly appointed, and the public mind will
accept it as an effective means of race preservation."[114] Eugenicists thus drew
on rehabilitative ideology to rationalize sterilization as punitive or curative
depending on their personal views. In his typology of criminal sterilization
laws, Harry Laughlin, the ERO superintendent, noted this pattern by explaining that some laws were "therapeutic" in design (like that in California, which
called the procedure "beneficial and conducive" to the inmate) while others
were punitive (like that in Washington, which called it an "addition to such
other punishment or confinement").[115]

Laughlin's work highlighted the relationship between Lombrosian theory,
rehabilitative ideology, and eugenics. His work frequently referenced rehabilitative penologists. His treatise *Eugenical Sterilization in the United States*
(1922) pulled multipage quotes from Boies's *Prisoners and Paupers* (1893), including statements arguing that imprisonment without sterilization permitted the reproduction of "those who would perish" otherwise and that, consequently, "in no sense could the deprivation of [sexual] organs inflict injury

or damage to criminal[s]." Laughlin did this while providing a close analysis of litigation in Washington State in which the state effectively invoked Boies's work to successfully defend the state sterilization statute from legal challenge. He cited a litany of academic publications to conclude that "asexualization can only be justified in the case of born criminals."[116]

Laughlin defended the indeterminate sentence as it was envisioned by Brockway but cautioned that "[r]eformation of the individual is humane . . . but absolutely undesirable and poor sociological economy if at the expense of the rights of organized society." He thus highlighted the problem of incorrigibility as the central puzzle of rehabilitative ideology. The introduction to his book addressed this problem. Written by his friend Chief Justice Harry Olson of the Chicago Municipal Court, it stated that "the segregation of incorrigible defectives . . . as a measure of crime prevention is urgently needed." But Olson also noted that in many states "experiments have been made with sterilization" and argued that "[t]he two theories of segregation and sterilization are not antagonistic, but both may be invoked."[117]

Olson's career as a jurist shows that support for eugenics was not limited to medical professionals. In "The Two Percent Solution," Michael Willrich has demonstrated that the convergence of eugenics discourse and urban court operations in the early twentieth century facilitated the emergence of "eugenics jurisprudence," defined as "the aggressive mobilization of law and legal institutions in pursuit of eugenic goals."[118] Willrich outlines the history of Olson's Chicago Municipal Court as the prime example of eugenics jurisprudence. Olson believed that courts should use psychological testing to identify mental defectives requiring long-term confinement.[119] In 1914, the Chicago Municipal Court opened its Psychopathic Laboratory to identify genetically predisposed criminals, and tens of thousands of defendants were tested there during Olson's tenure as chief justice, which lasted until 1930. The lab assisted judges in sentencing, directed clinical research on crime, and served as a model for similar labs in other cities. Olson argued that crime control was "the first step in the eugenics programme."[120]

Olson was not alone in bringing eugenic ideas into the legal profession. Progressive era legal realists venerated the social sciences, including eugenics. Scholars of legal realism like Roscoe Pound publicly supported Olson's practices, while legal realists on the bench wove eugenic thinking into judicial philosophy.[121] Jonathan Simon has argued that Benjamin Cardozo was a particularly prominent example of this trend. Cardozo's criminal law jurisprudence, especially when he served on the New York Court of Appeals prior to his Supreme Court appointment, was instilled with a eugenic spirit that was present throughout his work.[122] In *The Growth of the Law*, Cardozo compared the judicial process to the "wise science of eugenics."[123] In his 1929 article "What Medicine Can Do for Law," he proclaimed that "the teaching of bio-chemists and behaviorists, psychiatrists and penologists, will transform our whole system of crime." He wrote that casual offenders may be rescuable but that scientific study has revealed that there exist "defective and recidivist" individuals for whom "redemption is hopeless." Making this distinction, he said, required making an "adjustment between the penal and the remedial elements in our scheme of criminology," linking eugenic assumptions to the duality of rehabilitation.[124]

The popularity of eugenics within the legal profession had significant consequences as compulsory sterilization raised constitutional questions. Sterilization policy was spreading across the states, and sixteen authorized the practice by 1922. But state laws varied substantially in design—Governor Woodrow Wilson said New Jersey's law would be directed against "the hope-less defective and criminal classes," California and Oregon passed laws in 1909 and 1917 (respectively) authorizing sterilization for third-time felons, four states vaguely targeted "habitual offenders" without offering coherent definitions of the term, and other states targeted feeble-minded populations for sterilization but not criminals.[125] The practice's popularity and variability generated legal challenges, which ended with the Supreme Court upholding the practice as constitutional in the 1927 decision *Buck v. Bell*. Although the defendant, Carrie Buck, was forcibly sterilized for feeble-mindedness, not criminality, Justice Oliver Wendell Holmes explicitly discussed criminality in the decision's most famous passage. He wrote, "It is better for all the world, if instead of waiting to execute degenerate offspring for crime, or to let them starve for their imbecility, society can prevent those who are manifestly unfit from continuing their kind. The principle that sustains compulsory vaccina-tion is broad enough to cover cutting the Fallopian tubes. Three generations of imbeciles are enough."[126] One of the most celebrated figures in US legal his-tory, and an enormously influential legal realist, Holmes had an established record of endorsing eugenics and determinist ideas of incorrigibility.[127] In his well-known speech "The Path of the Law," given thirty years prior to *Buck*, he stated that "[i]f the typical criminal is a degenerate, bound to swindle or to murder by as deep seated an organic necessity as that which makes the rattlesnake bite, . . . he cannot be improved."[128]

Holmes's decision reflected not only his personal faith in eugenics, but also broader eugenic sympathies on the Court. His majority opinion in *Buck* was signed by eight of his nine colleagues, including Justice Louis Brandeis. Even Brandeis, the Court's public interest champion, had ties to eugenics in his legal career prior to *Buck*. As a lawyer, he wrote a brief in the 1908 case *Muller v. Oregon* citing eugenic research asserting that women were biologically inferior to men in order to advocate for state regulation of women's employment. Thomas Leonard notes that while Brandeis may have just been trying to secure state protections for female workers by any means necessary, it was a dangerous move prompting the Supreme Court to cite his logic.[129] That Brandeis signed *Buck* without qualification further indicates that he accepted eugenics or, at the very least, that he had no qualms about giving it the Court's stamp of approval. *Buck* was emblematic of eugenics' broad appeal. With only one dissenting justice, who did not author an opinion explaining his reasoning, the majority spanned from the progressive Brandeis to the conservative chief justice, William Howard Taft. The decision rejuvenated the eugenics movement as a new wave of state sterilization laws raised the number of states with eugenics programs to twenty-eight by 1931, while the national rate of sterilizations soared to nearly two thousand annually after the decision.[130]

There is reason to believe that sterilizations happened more often in mental facilities than in prisons, especially since some states passed sterilization laws targeting the mentally impaired but not criminals.[131] But, as Rafter has shown, early twentieth-century eugenics research blurred the lines between low intelligence, mental illness, and criminality. Further, courts with psychopathic laboratories like Chicago's routinely sent criminal defendants to institutes for the feeble-minded. This suggests that the occupants of mental institutions where sterilizations were most common may have included many "criminal types," demonstrating how constructs of criminality overlapped with diagnoses of mental illness. While not all were convicted criminals, at least seventy thousand people were subjected to compulsory sterilization between 1900 and 1970, a number that likely understates reality since so many sterilizations went undocumented.[132]

Eugenics faded in influence over the course of the twentieth century, unlike the rehabilitative ideal, but scholars often underestimate the durability that it had. The links between crime and biology were maintained by *Buck v. Bell* and the spread of state and national crime commissions through the 1920s. Outgrowths of progressivism's reliance on scientific expertise, crime commissions were tasked with employing experts to study the crime problem.[133] Commissions had real political authority, discussing numerous reform proposals and reviewing popular theories of criminal behavior. From 1919 through 1931, at least thirty-five crime commissions were created at the state or the federal level to examine such questions.[134]

Three of the best-known commission reports were the Cleveland Crime Survey (1922), the Missouri Crime Survey (1926), and the Illinois Crime Survey (1929).[135] The reports routinely validated the ideas of eugenics and incorrigibility. The sole examination of the causes of crime in the Cleveland survey came in the section "Medical Science and Criminal Justice," which directed attention toward how health workers could detect criminality.[136] The Missouri commission also had only one chapter on the causes of crime, "Mental Disorder, Crime, and the Law," which explored "feeble-minded persons," "psychopathic personalities," and mental disorder.[137] The Illinois commission's only analysis of crime's causes was the chapter "The Defective or Deranged Delinquent," examining the "psychopathic conditions" of criminals and the psychiatric assistance provided to the Cook County courts by the Psychopathic Laboratory. The commission endorsed the "School of Modern Penology" and its logic that "uncontrollable hereditary impulses . . . [make] the commission of crime almost inevitable." The report expressed strong approval of the indeterminate sentence for increasing the average term of incarceration for inmates.[138] Similarly, the Missouri Crime Survey linked its support for indeterminate sentencing to concerns about incorrigibility, writing that repeat offenders should be "subjected to wholly indeterminate incarceration."[139]

The fact that commissions commonly endorsed eugenics highlights the tenacity of biodeterminist explanations of criminality among scientific experts in the 1920s and 1930s. Nonetheless, the eugenics movement lost steam following World War II as the scope of the Nazi regime's eugenicide became clear, prompting a shift in public opinion that left American eugenicists hard-pressed to secure research funding or find legal and political power holders receptive to their ideas. Calls for eugenic crime policies consequently quieted.[140] Notably, in the 1942 case *Skinner v. Oklahoma*, the Supreme Court struck down a state law authorizing the sterilization of habitual criminals on Fourteenth Amendment grounds. The *Skinner* ruling did not have a massive impact on the eugenics movement—the Court neglected to overturn or limit *Buck* by narrowly striking down the statute for failing to differentiate crimes of "moral turpitude" from other offenses, and overall sterilization rates actually increased following *Skinner* and persisted until the 1960s—but it signaled a developing coolness toward eugenics.[141]

Still, the movement's policy implications exhibited surprising staying power. Eugenics was quietly reframed in the postwar American South, where criminality became less of a concern as eugenics targeted Black women for sterilization without their knowledge, often on the basis of welfare and birth control considerations.[142] The last state-sanctioned compulsory sterilization in the United States was ordered in 1981.[143] And, while they are not technically compulsory, at least nine states today have programs permitting chemical or surgical castration for sex offenders, although the policies are more coercive in practice than is suggested.[144]

This history sheds light on the punitive character and eugenic underpinnings of the rehabilitative ideological framework and the damage it has done when embraced by coalitions with repressive aims. Although eugenics fell from grace in the wake of World War II, the rehabilitative program inscribed eugenic logics into the architecture of American criminal justice. A preoccupation with identifying the naturally incorrigible still colors American sentencing via risk assessments, sentencing guidelines, and criminal history considerations. Modern observers often uncritically take these practices for granted as sensible, but, as chapters 5 and 7 will argue, they are legacies of the rehabilitative paradigm's sorting mentality and frame the eugenic racial and class assumptions of rehabilitative ideology as seemingly objective calculations and commonsense conclusions about criminality.

The Reality of Rehabilitation

From its inception, the rehabilitative ideal embodied premises that laid the seeds for punitive politics. Various political actors deployed rehabilitative ideology to validate a multitude of severe penal and social control measures, including the indeterminate sentence, vagrancy law reform, and eugenic penal policies. This enabled them to stigmatize the urban poor, workers, immigrants, Blacks, and any other groups considered undesirable by branding them as incorrigible. Naturalized conceptions of criminality were not just ideological constructs but ideas that did political work legitimating the racial and class dimensions of American capitalism through scientific language.

Although rehabilitation would become unmoored from its biodeterminist foundation over the course of the twentieth century, the individualistic, determinist, and racially and class-biased logics inherent to the rehabilitative framework became durable features of American criminal justice. The notion that crime is caused by individual traits and defects best addressed through individual interventions, whether reformative or punitive, has conditioned how scholars and policymakers conceptualize criminality and directed their focus toward punishing the criminal rather than the crime in ways that have hardened racial and class distinctions. Rehabilitative ideology has long validated antipoor, anti-Black, anti-immigrant, and antiworker attitudes. Scholarship often studies the punishment of these groups separately, but rehabilitative ideology casts a wide net justifying punishment of them all.

Through debates over indeterminate sentencing, vagrancy, and eugenics, the ideas of Lombroso and Brockway served multiple political agendas and became entrenched in the criminal justice system. Even as ideas of criminal biology became discarded over time, rehabilitative ideology established legacies that continue to shape American crime politics, especially via the assumption that criminality is the result of individual defects requiring individualized solutions.

Entrenching Regulation:
Crime, Politics, and the Origins of the Regulatory State

You don't suppose you can run a railroad in accordance with the statutes, do you?
COMMODORE CORNELIUS VANDERBILT

Commodore Cornelius Vanderbilt was one of the richest men in nineteenth-century America. Having made his fortune as a railroad and shipping magnate, he has earned a contested place in American history. One historian recently wrote that "[w]hile Vanderbilt could be a rascal, combative and cunning, he was much more a builder than a wrecker," and claimed that "he possessed other admirable traits, including being honorable, shrewd, and hard-working."[1] Others are less kind. In a 1940 speech introducing his concept of white-collar crime, Edwin Sutherland cited Vanderbilt's remark that serves as the epigraph to this chapter to underscore his point that criminologists overlooked the crimes of the country's elites. As he explained, scholars missed their offenses because white-collar crime was hidden underneath layers of rules, regulations, and discretionary choices by bureaucratic agents not to prosecute the nation's wealthiest lawbreakers.[2]

Political scientists have rigorously analyzed the development of US regulatory politics but have overlooked how crime concerns factored into debates over the origins of the regulatory state. Through analyses of the 1887 Interstate Commerce Act (ICA) and the 1914 Federal Trade Commission Act (FTCA), this chapter traces how regulatory ideology shaped the development of regulatory institutions. As debates unfolded over the ICA, railroad industry leaders testified before Congress arguing against including strict criminal provisions in the bill, maintaining that executives were more respectable than common criminals and would be more responsive to the lighter hand of the Interstate Commerce Commission (ICC). Debates over the FTC followed a similar trajectory as the financial industry advocated for an independent commission in lieu of criminal controls. In both cases, serious arguments for criminalizing market practices were countered by defenses of regulatory governance, but the competing coalitions changed. Populists, a coalition of moderate Democrats and Republicans, and free market conservatives drove the ICA debates, while the FTCA debates were driven by disagreements between self-identified Populists and Progressives on both sides of the aisle. Each debate saw representatives from affected industries and their political allies fight to create regulatory bodies in lieu of direct criminal controls.

The comparison of the two debates sheds light on the contingent impacts regulatory ideology had on institutional change. During the ICA debates, regulatory ideology was in an embryonic state, but its Darwinist premises were useful for lawmakers seeking to devise a governing approach that administered competitive dynamics rather than punish wrongdoing. By the FTCA debates, regulatory ideology had become a fixture of intellectual thought in sociology, law, and economics and was established as an approach to governance given its influence on the ICA. In these debates, Louis Brandeis outlined a thorough crystallization of regulatory ideology as a governing strategy for correcting the economic conditions that drive good people to do bad things via administrative rather than punitive controls.

The politicization of regulatory ideology in these debates does not completely explain the passage of the ICA or the FTCA. Regulatory ideology was mobilized by political actors seeking specific goals, and it interacted with the range of political and economic motives driving their actions. Contests over regulatory institution building had enormous stakes hinging on fundamental structural transformations in the country's economic system as lawmakers sought solutions for managing an integrated national political economy. But, when interested parties mobilized regulatory ideology to navigate questions of punishment during these debates, it did more than serve as window dressing for other issues. It brought the ideology's properties and assumptions to bear on defining the terms of these contests, conditioning the institutions that came out of them.

By employing regulatory ideology, industry leaders and their allies recast discussions about the value or harm of certain market activities into judgments of human nature. This hinged questions about criminal punishment less on whether legislators thought executives did bad things and more on whether they judged them as bad people—that is, whether they fit common constructs of the criminal type. This encouraged the dilution of the laws' toughest features by making the debates referenda on the character of executives rather than evaluations of their behavior. This helped ensure that corporate wrongdoers evaded the determinist logic defining other forms of criminality by chalking up their crimes to the problems inherent in a national market, not the problems inherent in the people running industry. Demands to punish executives were thus absorbed into discretionary commission work on the grounds that prosecution would disturb the natural benefits secured by letting innovative business leaders compete in the marketplace.

While the regulatory state was the product of myriad factors, that it was defined from its origins as an analogue to the justice system is an important feature of its development. The decision to regulate or punish is a choice, and the application of regulatory ideology was a political choice to regulate rather than punish lawbreakers at the top of the economic hierarchy. Regulatory governance is a branch of social control, and in conjunction with the prison system it legitimated an institutional project of class sorting. Penal control was appropriate for lower-class citizens displaying traits associated with incorrigible criminality, while regulatory oversight was appropriate for economic elites driven by healthy instincts interacting with the structural vices of the marketplace. No corporate offender was incorrigible; even the worst were assumed to be responsive to reason and worth sorting away from the prison before having punitive sanctions leveled against them. The corporate lawbreaker was a natural capitalist and thus a fundamentally reasonable person regardless of what he did, while rehabilitative ideology presumed the poor and people of color to be criminals on the basis of their racial and class traits alone. Cornelius Vanderbilt could price gouge farming towns into ruin and have it explained as the result of a good man's cunning, but the tramps in those soon-to-be ghost towns would be sent to jail because their economic station indicated a natural criminality.

The chapter begins by examining the ways in which regulatory ideology was put into practice by politicians navigating Progressive era politics, detailing how it interacted with the motives driving political actors during the national economy's transformation. It then reviews the historical context of the ICA's passage before exploring how railroads and their legislative allies framed the ICA debate within the terms of regulatory ideology. It then segues into an overview of Progressive era antitrust politics, followed by an analysis of how regulatory ideology featured in debates over the creation of the FTC. There were notable differences in the designs, purposes, and powers of the FTC and the ICC, but in both cases regulatory ideology was a powerful persuasive device for corporate coalitions seeking to favorably shape regulatory bodies by positing that corporate competitors should not be punished for merely acting in accord with the laws of nature in the marketplace.

Regulation, Economic Change, and Progressive Era Politics

When lawmakers transmitted regulatory ideology into policymaking space, its ideational elements were mediated by existing institutions, economic considerations, and contingencies of power and politics. Its character evolved as political actors put it to use, as it was a malleable instrument that enabled industrial coalitions to advance their interests. But when politicians deployed the ideology, it interacted with distinctive aspects of US politics, conditioned how powerful interests defined their goals, organized the terms of these critical debates, and ensured that regulatory governance emerged as an institutional analogue to punitive punishment.

This ideational account complements existing research detailing the institutional and structural reasons for the regulatory state's emergence. Numerous scholars have shown that the construction of the regulatory state was a response to a serious political economic predicament.[3] As the national economy grew, lawmakers confronted a new market system in which the leaders of large corporations engaged in undesirable behavior. However, these actions were committed, not by easily demonized classes on the street, but by those who led the nation's engines of economic growth. It is hardly surprising that elected leaders valued the nation's business class differently than they did street criminals, as many saw large corporations as vital to national well-being and were reluctant to interfere with their operations. These structural conditions were key in driving the adoption of regulation, but the Darwinist premises of regulatory ideology remain overlooked features of the politics that conditioned the regulatory state's early design.

Importantly, while the vexing questions raised by a changing structure of political economy were not unique to the United States—industrialization and large corporations were global developments at the end of the nineteenth century—the American regulatory response was unique. Idiosyncrasies of American politics help explain this phenomenon. During this period, nations including Belgium, Prussia, France, Austria, Italy, the United Kingdom, and Canada had different responses to managing industrialization, often implementing centralized bureaucratic control over industrial policy or nationalizing key industries.[4] By contrast, Congress passed the ICA and the FTCA, which sought to sustain capitalism through administrative bodies with narrowly defined powers. Regulatory ideology excused the most harmful behaviors of corporate actors as natural manifestations of market dynamics that should not prompt the state to overreact, sidelining demands for punishment along with more ambitious proposals to restructure the political economy through strategies like nationalization. Additionally, bureaucratic development in Europe was tinged with skepticism that political bureaucracies could threaten popular sovereignty by elevating technical efficiency over democratic control of policy. This view was dismissed by American lawmakers, who believed that a nationalized bureaucracy of expert regulators would improve competition through apolitical administration while conveniently shielding elected leaders from having to make the unpopular decisions necessary to maintain the corporate capitalist economy.[5] Federalism adds yet another explanatory layer to the unique trajectory of US regulatory development. In the nineteenth century, regulatory experimentation in states like Texas and Illinois offered federal lawmakers examples of how to pursue regulatory governance once powerful corporate actors began engaging in anticompetitive conduct across state lines and made federal intervention necessary.[6] These peculiarities of American politics illuminate important structural factors undergirding the regulatory state's emergence that interacted with the political application of regulatory ideology's central features. As William Novak has written, Americans "envisioned the state not as an economic policeman or even as a countervailing force to private economic power, but as a full, interactive partner in a legal-economic vision of modern state capitalism."[7]

The mobilization of regulatory ideology was an impactful choice for industries with wealth and privilege. That businesses endorsing regulatory ideology were more successful in securing their desired outcomes than were firms advocating alternative routes to managing markets was due partially to their superior political organizing and partially to their presentation of their goals within a politically appealing and understandable discourse. In an era of hostility to business, resisting any form of state intervention and oversight of the economy was unsustainable, but invoking regulatory ideology shifted debates about corporate lawbreaking onto terms that were advantageous to businesses and agreeable to lawmakers. It permitted legislators to include prosecution as an option for wrongdoing, addressing demands to check business, while appeasing corporate constituents through the inclusion of regulatory alternatives to punishment. It thus provided industrial interests and their political allies a compelling common language with which they could all operate, publicly defend their actions, and secure agreeable policy.

Like rehabilitative ideology, regulatory ideology fueled a politics colored by a liberal individualism in which state sanctions were tailored to individuals rather than their actions. It may seem counterintuitive to claim that businessmen of the era endorsed individualist perspectives since they also frequently espoused the rhetoric of the "corporate person" in debates about economic policy and law, centralizing the corporation as the focus of state oversight rather than its leadership. Deploying language making the corporate entity the target of legal supervision crucially shaped debates about liability and social responsibility in the corporate sphere.[8] But these languages are not mutually exclusive; economic actors switched between language of the *corporate person* and the *natural capitalist* in different contexts when it suited them. In some contexts they countered proposals to criminalize executives' misbehavior with corporatist language, but in other contexts they relied on the individualistic ideas that emerged out of Darwinism and eugenics to convey a favorable racialization of the businessman as a healthy entrepreneur. That industries and their political allies embraced these ideas does not mean that they rejected ideas of the corporate person. Rather, it indicates that politically effective business interests did not attempt to bulldoze their desires through lawmaking institutions using a one-size-fits-all strategy. Instead, they strategically adjusted how they communicated their political preferences by deploying different ideational framings to maximize their odds of success in various settings.

Of course, people of high status were not rendered entirely immune from prosecution and remained subject to traditional criminal laws for violence, property crime, and the like. Regulatory ideology was deployed specifically to justify corporate rapacity in economic spheres. When it came to transactions in the market, the businessman was understood to be acting on his capitalist disposition. Judgments of his character thus became a lens through which his actions were evaluated—even if something like rate-setting abuse resembled theft, it was not criminal by virtue of his traits, which were desirable qualities for someone acting in accordance with market forces. Industry leaders found a winning strategy in using regulatory ideology's emphasis on evolutionary themes and human nature to turn debates about their actions into debates about their natures, distinguishing themselves from common understandings of criminality warranting punishment.

When put into practice, regulatory ideology embedded certain normative meanings about corporate misconduct into institutions. That the regulatory state empowered regulators to use administrative tools to control behavior defined as criminal communicated an understanding of corporate lawbreaking as undeserving of the same punitive response as street-level crime. This throws into relief how regulation relates to the arc of American penal politics. A consequence of imbuing the ICA and the FTCA with regulatory ideological principles was to institutionally express the notion that the economically motivated businessman was a mirrored inversion of the born criminal; a productive and virtuous person whose harmful behavior could be explained only through reference to market conditions interacting with his competitive instincts. Regulatory ideology provided a favorable racialization of the executive that dismissed criticism of his allegedly criminal conduct because his natural disposition made him a champion of the market jungle, not a deviant.

Carefully conceptualizing the role of regulatory ideology in this history clarifies how it helped legitimate vast inequalities via the presumption that corporate elites were a superior kind of person, a disturbing premise warranting its analysis as a feature of the racial story of American justice. There is good reason to indict a system that unforgivingly punishes poor and minority offenders deemed incorrigible for their missteps while giving wealthy offenders light administrative reprimands. But the inequality is the outrage, not regulatory governance itself. Regulation provides a valuable complement to prosecutorial controls by using proactive governing strategies to keep economic conditions safe while working collaboratively with industries to prevent undesirable behavior. It is reasonable to critique how regulatory ideology has legitimated tremendous inequalities—and how it has been exploited to render corporate prosecution an almost nonexistent threat—but the resulting frustration should be channeled toward thinking of ways to balance prosecution and regulation in markets judiciously while extending the regulatory mentality to all forms of crime. Criminal behavior at the lower end of the class hierarchy should also be empathetically understood as driven by the interaction between human nature and imperfect economic structures best governed via economic management techniques rather than punitive controls.

The choice to establish national commissions to regulate business conduct was a complex one. But by mobilizing regulatory ideology in pursuit of a certain economic vision, industrial interests and lawmakers ensured that a politics in which criminality was conceptualized in individualistic and determinist terms intersected with pressing demands for market control at a formative moment in national economic development. This imbued regulatory ideology with a unique utility for politicians looking to satiate politically unavoidable demands to check corporate power without alienating key industries. The presentation of corporate leaders as vigorous entrepreneurs rather than parasitic criminal types emerged as a powerful weapon with which to justify governing corporate misbehavior with an administrative hand. Regulatory ideology did not single-handedly dictate the outcomes in the ICA and FTCA debates, but its activation in political discourse structured the developmental path of the regulatory state in significant ways.

The Politics of Interstate Commerce

To understand the history of the ICA, it is appropriate to begin with John Reagan. A Democrat from Texas, Reagan was first elected to the House in 1857, resigned during the Civil War, and was reelected ten years later. Like

many Democrats, his election was fueled by agrarian discontent with railroads charging exorbitant and variable shipping rates. States like Texas initially passed state Granger laws to regulate rates and solve such problems.
This was consistent with the politics of the time—through the nineteenth century, states and localities maintained a regulated society through market
controls. Early corporate entities were also organized through state charters,
which allowed governments to bind them to state-dictated aims. But the
emergence of large autonomous corporations through general incorporation
statutes in the late nineteenth century created space between the corporation
and public interest. The growing autonomy of corporate actors and their increasing involvement in interstate commercial activity compelled the federal
government to take regulatory action.[9]

It was in 1877 that Reagan became the first lawmaker to propose national
regulations as a solution to the railroads' abuses.[10] Until the ICA's passage in
1887, Reagan insisted on punishing abusive rate setting. His proposal directly
criminalized every complaint that his populist base lodged against railroads,
including charging more for short than long hauls, pooling arrangements in
which railroads split competitive business, and rebating through which railroads secured business from big shippers by offering them discounts offset
by imposing higher costs on low-volume shippers.[11] Reagan's concerns were
widely shared; legislators of all regions and partisan orientations agreed that
something was needed to check the power of railroads.[12] But his proposed
solution was unique. Whether corporate wrongdoing was best understood
as criminal remained a contested question undergirding the ICA's circuitous
path to passage in part because Reagan set these terms at the outset. While his
1877 proposal initially earned support from Democrats in the populist South
and West, it was promptly killed in the Republican Senate.[13]

A window of opportunity opened for the ICA in 1885. Three political camps
emerged out of the 1884 elections that shaped debates over the ICA's criminal provisions—populist-leaning legislators hostile to corporations (mostly
agrarian-state Democrats), a tenuous alliance of moderate Democrats and
mugwumps (Republicans who backed the Democrat Grover Cleveland in the
presidential election of 1884), and the disproportionately Republican allies of
industrial interests mostly from the North and Midwest. While more populist-
oriented Democrats favored Reagan's ideas, Republicans in the Senate and a
coalition of moderate Democrats and mugwump Republicans in the House
supported creating a commission to regulate the railroads, which was proposed
as an alternative to Reagan's more punitive approach.[14]

After Reagan's bill passed the House in 1885, the Senate took it into serious consideration, signaling a new receptiveness to regulation in the chamber. But with Republicans in control the Senate moved in a different direction. Senator Shelby Cullom (R-IL) headed a Senate subcommittee to explore ways to reconstruct the bill so that it could "not possibly harm the railroads or other business interests of the nation."[15] Cullom's proposal accommodated populist demands by defining violations of the law as misdemeanors but added a commission to adjudicate disputes and provide relief through equity and civil proceedings.[16]

By 1886, a federal interstate commerce bill was all but certain, putting pressure on the House and Senate to compromise. In October of that year, the Supreme Court ruled in *Wabash, St. Louis & Pacific Railway v. Illinois* that states could not pass regulations affecting interstate commerce, effectively overturning *Munn v. Illinois* (1877) and invalidating state Granger laws, thus placing responsibility for interstate commerce regulation squarely with Congress.[17] Consequently, a conference committee ironed out the differences between the Cullom and the Reagan bills.[18] The final law signed in 1887 specified that a railroad's officers, agents, and directors could be criminally punished with a fine of up to $5,000, satisfying Populists, while creating the ICC as added by the Cullom Committee. The law defined specific actions like rebating as criminal but granted the ICC discretion over when to use criminal, administrative, civil, or equity remedies in response.[19]

There were real benefits to empowering the commission with such discretion. Equity powers enabled the ICC to prevent harmful actions proactively via interventions like injunctions, and civil suits made it possible to seek monetary damages, techniques that are well suited to managing the abuses of powerful corporate actors. These tools offered valuable ways to check market dynamics and manage harmful economic behavior before resorting to prosecution. But while regulatory ideology offers real benefits to managing a complex economy and has the potential to recast the American approach to governing street crime, its narrow application to corporate illegality promoted stark inequalities next to a criminal justice system that severely punished the poor and people of color out of an assumption that their racial and class traits were indicative of criminality. It permitted state actors to obscure the frequency and severity of corporate crime by using noncriminal sanctions to respond to market-based crimes while offenses as minor as tramping could land someone a multiyear sentence or time in the convict-lease system. This is why rehabilitative and regulatory ideologies must be studied together. As they were applied, they jointly expressed the message that corporate lawbreakers and their offenses were substantively different from common criminals and their offenses and that each deserved distinct treatment.

COMPETING VIEWS IN THE INTERSTATE
COMMERCE ACT DEBATES

Legislators had many goals in the ICA debates, including maintaining market health, imposing rate controls on railroads, and facilitating the growth of a nationalized political economy. Although whether the robber barons should be criminally punished was not the central consideration of legislators, analysis of the ICA's history reveals that it was an important one. But while regulatory ideology came to bear heavily on the ICA's design, it was not the only proposed model for balancing criminalization and regulation. Legislators and relevant parties advocated a wide spectrum of positions during the ICA debates, proposing diverse frameworks for conceptualizing and controlling corporate misconduct.

First, Reagan's approach was explicitly retributive, reflecting a retaliatory logic presenting rate-setting abuse as a moral wrong requiring punishment. A second frame endorsed by legislators emphasized deterrence. Some lawmakers believed that deterrence would be best achieved through criminal penalties, reflecting Beccarian theory, while others relied on regulatory ideology to claim that regulation was enough to deter reasonable executives. It is worth reviewing the retributive and Beccarian perspectives to contextualize this debate before exploring the arguments for regulatory ideology.

Reagan's retributive logic appealed to agrarians (mostly Democrats but also some Republicans) from the South, West, and the Plains states.[20] Because Reagan was the first to propose national regulation, his perspective became the starting point of debate and reflected populist critiques of the robber barons.[21] He remained an ardent advocate of this approach, depicting rate abuses as serious moral wrongs. In 1882, he wrote in a committee report that his bill "does not provide for punishment for anything except for manifest wrongs, which injure citizens and the public." He explained that "[i]t is framed on a theory which respects [the public's] intelligence and sense of moral right."[22] Many shared Reagan's mentality. In an analysis of roll-call votes on the ICA, Scott James has shown that agrarian Democrats consistently opposed the commission until 1887, when Democratic leaders engineered the party's capitulation to the commission bill.[23] The legislative record indicates that the resistance reflected Reagan's concerns. For instance, Senator James Beck (D-KY) was one of many who cited James Hudson's critical tract *The Railways and the Republic* (1887) on the floor of Congress to endorse Reagan's proposal. Noting the double standard of US crime policy, Beck argued that if "Western bandits" amassed the wealth large companies did through comparable means, they would be punished.[24] Some Republicans from populist regions also

bought Reagan's logic, with representatives like John Anderson (R-KS) eras-
ing the moral distinction between robbery and financial crime. Speaking on
the House floor about the price-gouging pools of the railroad magnates Jay
Gould and Cornelius Vanderbilt, who he said were widely "said to be very respectable men," Anderson maintained, "[M]orally I can see no difference between that action and absolute, naked, bald-headed robbery."[25] Partisanship
was thus not wholly determinative of one's position on Reagan's proposal,
although Democrats were more likely to share his populist roots and embrace his logic. But, despite its appeal to populations abused by the railroads,
moderate Democrats and Republicans viewed Reagan's punitive model as an
unreasonable impediment on market competition.

Other legislators spoke in utilitarian terms to emphasize that the ICA
should deter abuse rather than satiate retributive instincts. But lawmakers
disagreed over how to achieve deterrence. Legislators with populist sympathies believed that a commission would lack deterrent value. Senator Charles
Van Wyck (R-NE) lamented that the ICC's only power was to "write essays."[26]
Representative Poindexter Dunn (D-AR) insisted that the commission enabled railroads' abuses to "go unprevented and unrestrained" without robust
criminal sanctions, while Andrew Caldwell (D-TN) decided to vote for the
commission bill but expressed concern that the ICC would be a "Trojan horse
and a deception" that would close the courts to aggrieved parties.[27] William
McAdoo (D-NJ), a corporate lawyer who identified as a Populist, considered
the commission "impotent" and "a harmless safety-valve for popular and individual discontent."[28] Even some Democrats detached from populism like
Charles O'Ferrall (D-VA) agreed that penal provisions would "go much further in securing adherence to the law" than civil or equity remedies.[29] These
legislators primarily wanted the ICC to deter abuse through a balance of regulation and punishment, but this coalition expressed genuine concerns that
the commission lacked the power to punish violations of the law consistently
enough to provide deterrence.

However, deterrence frameworks cut in different ways depending on one's
perspective, as those advancing regulatory ideology to the end of narrowly
minimizing prosecutorial oversight of industry claimed that executives could
be deterred by a commission without criminal sanction. For instance, after
Reagan proposed his bill again in 1882, Chauncey Depew (who served as general counsel for Vanderbilt's railroads before becoming vice president and
later president of Vanderbilt's New York Central and Hudson River Railroad)
claimed before the House Committee on Commerce that "the open sun-
light" afforded by a commission would deter crime better than punishment, a
point echoed by the former US attorney general and chair of the Pennsylvania

Civil Service Reform Commission Wayne MacVeagh.[30] Corporate allies in Congress picked up these talking points. When the bill was debated in 1884, Representative William Rice (R-MA) stated that the ICC afforded the "sunshine of publicity" and would be "more potent to reform than fines or imprisonments."[31] Representative John Stewart (R-VT) said that a commission promoted "righteous dealing" before resorting to the "hasty action" of prosecution because regulation would give the "opportunity for retraction or correction of ascertained error" before involving the courts.[32] This logic rested heavily on the principle that railroad leaders were driven by desirable industrious instincts and would be responsive to reason.

Notably, a full-throated rhetorical equation of corporate rapacity with criminality came from the Populist Party five years after the ICA's passage. In its Omaha Platform of 1892, the party stated, "Wealth belongs to him who creates it, and every dollar taken from industry without an equivalent is robbery."[33] This language is political rhetoric lacking in legal specificity, but it signaled the party's willingness to equate corporate greed with criminality. However, the Omaha Platform also sheds light on broader dynamics shaping the ICA deliberations, including the limits to Reagan's politics and the perspectives that were excluded from debate.

Specifically, Reagan's bill would likely have crippled the formation of a national rail network. It complemented broader political aims to develop a diversified, regionally based political economy instead of a national one, but it is debatable that it would have done so effectively. It was a blunt instrument reflecting Reagan's reactionary impulse to appease populist antagonisms by criminalizing everything that angered his constituents; it was not built on a particularly nuanced understanding of the nation's changing economic structures.[34] From this perspective, the move to subsume prosecutorial action under a commission's operations was not in and of itself unwise in comparison to Reagan's approach. The problem remained that, ultimately, the embrace of regulatory ideology in this context produced sharp inequalities next to the changes unfolding in criminal justice for street-level offenders. Nonetheless, Reagan's criminalization bill constituted an alternative of questionable practicality and workability.

Further, a deeper read of the Omaha Platform throws into relief how framing this debate as one between regulation and criminalization had constricting effects. Despite its rhetorical flourishes drawing parallels between corporate greed and criminality, the otherwise sophisticated tract in socioeconomic and political analysis did not include a rigorous discussion of criminalizing corporate misconduct, even though most populist lawmakers aligned with Reagan's bill. This is because the Populists did not truly support any form of federal oversight of private railways, whether through regulatory or criminal schemes. Rather, the Omaha Platform demanded outright nationalization of the railroads and the conversion of managers into civil servants. But during the ICA debates, legislators never addressed nationalization with the seriousness they granted to Reagan's punitive proposal and the commission model, which were the positions bounding debate. Consequently, those with populist sympathies typically backed Reagan's relatively unrefined proposal, even though many likely preferred a nationalization strategy based on a more comprehensive understanding of political economics that was excluded from discussion.

There were multiple ideological frames that could have structured the ICA deliberations. But with nationalization off the table and deterrence arguments largely co-opted by an interpretation of regulatory ideology that sidelined criminal controls, the debate unfolded on a continuum bounded by regulatory ideological principles weaponized to minimize prosecution on one end and the blunt retributive populism of Reagan on the other.

ENTRENCHING REGULATORY IDEOLOGY IN THE INTERSTATE COMMERCE ACT

As regulatory ideology seeped into debate, it was predominantly pushed by probusiness Republicans allied with industry in northern and midwestern states, with mugwumps and moderate Democrats providing additional support. Corporate wrongdoers evaded the Lombrosian constructs that defined other forms of criminality for several reasons, and legislators may have sympathized with executives with whom they possibly identified. But evaluating regulatory politics as a relative of crime politics highlights that many executives and industrial allies used regulatory ideology to redirect the terms of the debate established by Reagan emphasizing the immorality of the robber barons' actions toward judgments of whether executives had fundamentally criminal characters. Not everybody accepted this interpretive frame, and it is impossible to know with certainty if individual legislators voted for the commission bill because of pressure from party leadership, personal interests, or genuine conversion to their opponents' arguments. Support for regulatory ideology could have been a post hoc rationalization of a politically calculated vote for some legislators and an expression of a genuine belief for others, but it is worth acknowledging that even some legislators with populist roots endorsed favorable constructs of corporate leaders as distinct from the traditional criminal type. This indicates that regulatory ideological frames were useful not only for legislators representing industry, but also for any legislators rationalizing their vote for the commission, rendering regulatory ideology an important feature of debate that had significant political value for the final bill's supporters.

Consider Chauncey Depew's congressional testimony. He, like many of the railroads' agents, routinely synthesized classical economics and evolutionary rhetoric, insisting that railroad men lacked the pathologies necessitating punishment. He informed the House Commerce Committee in 1882 that executives "have outlived the penitentiary for mistakes."[35] Years later, he told the committee that the bill targeted not the "convicted thief," but "as fair, as honorable, as reputable a class of our fellow-men . . . as any other."[36] Depew was not the only one to make this distinction. John C. Brown, Tennessee's former governor and the future president of the Texas and Pacific Railroad, informed the same committee that railroad managers "are just as honest as lawyers, doctors, legislators, and . . . any other class of people."[37] Albert Fink, a nationally respected railway engineering expert often brought before Congress, stated that "the evils encountered in the management of this great property in this country are not the result of any wickedness on the part of the American railroad managers."[38] By pointing to their moral senses, Depew, Brown, and Fink depicted executives as similar to well-adjusted social actors, thus not requiring punitive interventions.

Republicans representing industry from the Northeast and the Midwest made similar claims that executives should not be treated criminally by virtue of their character. Representative Roswell Horr (R-MI) panned Reagan's bill for "tak[ing] men who stand well among their neighbors, who are honored and respected by those who know them best, who are well spoken of by the entire community in which they live," and equating them with " 'cut-throats,' or . . . 'naked, bald-headed robbers.' "[39] Representative Byron Cutcheon (R-MI) similarly criticized the notion of punishing "upright and enterprising men" who have "never been accused in [their] community of being dishonorable."[40] William Rice (R-MA) alleged that "[t]he managers of these roads are no longer robber barons, but practical and able business men."[41] These legislators protested lumping executives together with criminals when their clean behavioral histories, upright characters, and normal dispositions indicated that they deserved different treatment.

Lawmakers opposed to Reagan's criminalization model praised the commission as a suitable alternative for men without criminal traits. Representative Ralph Plumb (R-IL) stated that the commission was a "practical measure" to alleviate the threat of prosecution for men who are "fair-minded and just" with "as much probity as any other class."[42] Even Albert Hopkins (R-IL), an advocate of criminal provisions throughout the debate, came to support the commission. He defended his shift by claiming "[t]hat the officers and managers of some of the great railroads of the country are just and honorable men can not be denied, and that they manage the affairs of their roads in a spirit of fairness to the public must . . . be admitted."[43]

While Democrats from populist strongholds often defended Reagan's model, their embrace of his proposal was not universal, even among those with antibusiness records. Of course, being an agrarian Democrat did not automatically require support for Reagan's approach—some likely did not join Reagan's coalition out of a distaste for his ideas, party pressure, or personal interests. But regardless of their motivations, agrarian Democrats who favored the commission articulated similar sympathetic arguments about corporate criminality. Senator John Morgan (D-AL) is a good case in point. Days before the law's passage, Morgan declared that the criminal provisions served only to "make a moral point on" an executive, "damage his reputation," and "hurt his feelings."[44] Morgan had long exhibited agrarian sympathies counterbalancing the probusiness politics of Alabama's other senator, James Pugh, but he still supported the commission and critiqued the law's criminal provisions as irrationally retributive. Similarly, Senator Edward Walthall (D-MS) opposed punishing executives, stating, "I have no word of denunciation for the railroad managers of the country as a class." He argued that railroad leaders "are just like other men."[45] Walthall was staunchly committed to states' rights except for his support for federal economic oversight, a contradictory set of views he inherited from his mentor, the popular Mississippi senator L. Q. C. Lamar. The records of Morgan and Walthall indicate alignment with the agrarian wing of the Democratic Party.[46] That they expressed these ideas despite their political track records indicates that favorable interpretive constructs of corporate criminality had substantial political, persuasive, and instrumental value even to populist lawmakers.

By arguing that criminal natures were not the cause of rate exploitation, this interpretive frame led to the conclusion that executives' arguably criminal actions must be driven by exogenous market forces interacting with competitive instincts. This reframing served multiple purposes. First, because these behaviors were depicted as by-products of forces that produced social goods, actions that may have been labeled *criminal* in other contexts took on favorable meanings. Second, even among legislators conceding that rate manipulation was morally wrong, this logic fueled anxiety that criminalization would disrupt the healthy Darwinian laws of markets by discouraging businessmen from unleashing their competitive potential.

Legislative hearings from 1882 to 1887 were replete with this reasoning. Former attorney general MacVeagh argued in 1882 that although rebates and other price discriminations may hurt shippers, they were industry norms that should not be disrupted. He argued that "no man believes that it is a crime or a wrong" for railroads to do these things and that punishment should be reserved for "manifold forms of *crime*, in the ordinary acceptation of that term."[47] In 1882, Albert Fink made similar claims. He argued that the bill targeted activities that were "inherent in the system of railroad transportation itself," not "the result of any greater wickedness" among executives.[48] Fink elaborated this argument before the House Commerce Committee in 1884, declaring that it was "a great injustice to hold the railroad companies responsible for those evils of the transportation business which are the result of the system adopted by the people in creating these railroads."[49] Testimony before Cullom's Senate committee in 1885 was no different. John Kernan, the chair of the New York Railroad Commission, argued that penal sanctions were inappropriate when it came to regulating railroads' activities "because they relate to and are a part of and share in the vicissitudes and disturbances of business." George Richardson, the president of the Northern Pacific Railroad, justified his disdain for the bill's criminal sanctions by suggesting that they disrupted the natural laws of competition in markets. He stated, "Sometimes the nature of trade is such that a man feels excused for being dishonest. It would be very difficult to enforce the [criminal] law."[50]

Comparable claims were advanced by legislators. Representative William Phelps (R-NJ) claimed that Reagan's bill foolishly attempted to "interfere with [the] general laws" of the economy, suggesting that markets were governed by natural dynamics that the state should not disrupt.[51] Without defending what the railroads did, he opposed intervention by implying that regulation would distort market operations. Senator Orville Platt (R-OH) made an emphatic defense of railroad leadership using this logic immediately preceding the law's passage. A Republican leader in the Senate, Platt opposed the inclusion of criminal provisions even as additions to commission oversight. He stated that punishment should be reserved for actions that were "inherently wrong" and "not a necessary result of the system."[52] For Platt, the actions that many of his colleagues considered criminal were unavoidable parts of the marketplace that should be permitted in order to promote economic health.

Statements from Republican leaders confirm that they largely aligned with business interests, but many moderate or probusiness Democrats expressed comparable notions. Representative Edward Seymour (D-CT) argued that "experience shows that there must sometimes from the necessity of the case be rebates and drawbacks." Channeling Sumner and Spencer, he claimed that criminalizing behaviors natural to markets constituted "an attempt to make that a criminal offense which in the very nature of things ought not to be so made."[53]

Alabama's business-aligned senator, James Pugh (D-AL), considered penal pro-visions "impracticable" because they were designed "without any regard to dif-ferences or changes in the conditions, relations, or surrounding of the twelve hundred railroads running all over thirty-eight States."[54] Representative Gilbert Woodward (D-WI) similarly argued that the behaviors targeted by the ICA were just "error[s] of judgment" that "should not be treated as a crime."[55]

Even Representative Martin Clardy (D-MO) agreed with this sentiment. Hailing from Missouri and representing a populist base, Clardy was the sec-ond longest tenured member of the House Commerce Committee in the 1880s after Reagan. But in 1885 Speaker John Carlisle minimized Clardy's role on the committee by appointing the more controllable second-term repre-sentative Charles Crisp (D-GA) to the second seat instead, believing that Crisp would accommodate mugwumps, favor a commission, and minimize the agrarian discontent he anticipated from Clardy.[56] Despite leadership's as-sumptions, Clardy criticized Reagan's assessment "as to the justness" and "eq-uity of the principle" in his proposal, insisting that the bill wrongly punished executives for errors of business judgment.[57] His statements provide an ex-ample of fractures among populist-sympathetic Democrats on the question of criminalization versus regulation, whereas a bipartisan coalition of Repub-licans, moderate Democrats, and mugwumps remained more consistently on board with the commission bill.

Anxieties that punishing executives risked impairing economic function-ality were, to a degree, a primitive variant of "too big to jail" politics as large corporations became commonplace. "Too big to jail" is not the same as "too big to fail"—corporate institutions can be preserved even when individual executives are imprisoned—but the corporate coalition of the era stoked fears that jailing executives would imminently lead to business failures and economic ruin. In this way, the rise of the large corporation discouraged the punishment of individuals in positions of leadership. In fact, railroad manag-ers pushed for the creation of corporate criminal liability rules that punished corporate entities for the actions of agents and officers, believing that it would insulate them from sanction.[58] After the Supreme Court's articulation of cor-porate criminal liability doctrine in 1909, corporate officers quickly devised ways to avoid entity liability, and the state has since struggled to use that doc-trine effectively and consistently.[59] But regulatory ideology was also deployed by lawmakers and corporate interests in these legislative contexts to resist punishing individual executives out of fear that it would topple the mighty corporations they ran.

This point was made repeatedly before the House Commerce Commit-tee. In 1882, E. P. Alexander, an executive of multiple southeastern railways, criticized Reagan's bill for treating railroad leaders as "robbers . . . of the most villainous kind" because it neglected to weigh the "compensating advantages" of their actions.[60] Weeks later George Blanchard, the director of the New York and Erie Railway, stated before the committee that "[railroad directors] are not robbers or malefactors" and that punishing them would interfere with the "great public trusts and benefits" they provide.[61] Later during those hearings, Albert Fink suggested that the "evils of the transportation business have been magnified . . . by interested classes" who have represented those evils "as a great mountain, and its benefit as mole-hills." He said that an accurate picture would depict the benefits as "a great mountain chain" while the evils would be a molehill.[62] Legislators of varying partisan allegiances accepted this logic. As early as 1884, James Pugh defended Fink's concerns in the Senate, claiming that the Reagan bill would "impede the whole transportation of business of this country."[63] Representative Jonathan Rowell (R-IL) qualified his support of the bill by criticizing the penal provisions and asserting that "[t]here is another class of men who see only a set of robbers in transportation companies" and that those who seek to punish them forget "that a bankrupt railroad company is like any other kind of bankruptcy, a bad thing for the community."[64]

In the days before the final vote, Senator Joseph Brown (D-GA) made an argument that few advanced during these debates. He blamed most serious corporate wrongdoing on a minority of market participants. But while he did not give an unequivocal defense of railroads, he expressed that there "is no reason why Congress should seriously cripple all the great railroad interests of this country" owing to the actions of "a few bad men."[65] Consequently, he endorsed a commission through reasoning that was inconsistent with what most of his colleagues presented. He argued that the wrongdoing of a few actors did not warrant overzealous prosecutorial interventions that could seriously damage the economy by discouraging risk-taking and vigorous competition among honest market players. While conceding that significant wrongdoing occurred in the industry, he nonetheless concluded that a commission was still preferable to a law based on strict criminal sanctions. This illustrates how bringing the collateral economic consequences of prosecution to center stage persuaded some on-the-fence legislators to endorse the commission bill.

With corporate executives politically defined as natural competitors rather than natural criminals, regulation became less about protecting the public from corporate wrongdoing. Rather, regulation was framed as an alternative to empowering an uninformed public to indulge its rash populist impulses through prosecutions against corporate officers. This was a spurious argument—Populists and Grangers championing populist causes long demonstrated a capacity for knowledgeable social, economic, and political inquiry—

but it resonated with widespread fear of the "uninformed" masses.[66] In this light, railroad executives were not potential criminals, but potential victims of a vindictive public that did not understand the nuances of business. For instance, representing several midwestern railways, Darwin Hughes told the House Commerce Committee in 1882 that penal provisions would create "a hungry and mercenary swarm of informers and spies."[67] Albert Fink similarly argued that executives would "be treated as criminals" owing to the allegations of people "entirely ignorant of the facts and the principles" of business. He warned that this would "ruin the railroad companies" and that "the railroads have been wronged, not the people," because the public has condemned them as criminals out of "misapprehension and ignorance."[68] John C. Brown stated that the punitive elements of the bill were "calculated to make railways and their officers and agents the prey of a horde of harpies."[69] Two years later, he repeated that penal provisions would "crowd the dockets with blackmailing informations" because they offer "a premium for men to become spies."[70] Lawmakers thus dismissed demands for punishment by minimizing the early Populist and labor movements as irrational. Representative Roswell Horr (R-MI) suggested that the bill's supporters have "mistaken . . . local clamor for genuine public sentiment."[71] Edward Seymour (D-CT) feared that, without a commission, the bill "tempted a new swarm of spies and informers" and cautioned that "to make him [the businessman] a criminal is extravagant."[72] Senator John Morgan (D-AL) worried that the criminal sanctions exposed corporations "to a set of men who have no other interest in the world in the matter than to levy blackmail and to profit."[73]

A coalition of probusiness Republicans and moderate Democrats successfully promoted regulation in the ICA not only as economic policy, but also as an alternative to criminalization. By speaking to prevailing ideological currents, railroads and their legislative allies shaped institutional structures to reinforce the idea that lawbreaking economic elites were different from the criminals targeted by the justice system. Depicting executives as foils to standard constructs of criminality rationalized regulation as a mode of management for people who did not need or deserve punishment.

The creation of the ICC cannot wholly be explained by the appeal of regulatory ideology, but questions about criminality undeniably shaped the debate. Whether lawmakers supported, opposed, or were indifferent to railroad executives, they had to grapple with questions about whether their behavior should be treated as criminal. The law's final design—making criminal sanction a possibility but only as an option among interventions the ICC could deploy that did not impose the label of criminality—was largely justified by the favorable construct of corporate criminality attached to regulatory ideology that prevailed over populist depictions of the robber baron. It treated the corporate executive as distinct from the common criminal, and in giving the ICC the discretion to respond to criminal acts through noncriminal means, it imbued those acts with noncriminal meanings. This prompted Representative Thomas Wood (D-IN) to say that it was a "farce" to "declare certain acts and practices of railroad companies wrong and a crime and then leave it out to a commission to investigate."[74]

The final bill enjoyed broad support, passing 219–41 in the House and 41–15 in the Senate.[75] There remained some opposition to it from rank-and-file agrarian Democrats in both chambers, but most yielded to the commission bill owing to the political maneuvering of party leadership.[76] The ICC was the product of a totality of political considerations and economic circumstances, but debates about corporate criminality and the mobilization of proregulation industrial interests were essential in shaping the law. Legislators may have been citing regulatory ideology as a rationalization for other choices rooted in political, economic, or material interests or emphasizing it out of a sincere belief in its value, but regardless, they produced an institutional regime that was rooted in the ideology's premises.

It matters that the early foundation of the regulatory state was in part built on this ideology because it expresses and validates the racial and class inequalities that define American penality. Regulatory bodies are complex institutions that do valuable work through nonpunitive forms of social control, and critics of the prison system would be well-advised to keep this in mind. But in conjunction with concomitant changes to the criminal justice system, which internalized inverted and insidious assumptions about people with different racial and class traits, the choices undergirding its origins turned the regulatory state into a part of the state's social control architecture and not just a technical market management mechanism. The application of regulatory ideology in this context reflected and reinforced a disturbingly racist and class-skewed approach to governing socially undesirable behavior that validated the idea that people with certain qualities deserved different and less punitive treatment than those with others. The problem with regulatory ideology is not its reliance on nonpunitive sanctions to manage behavior, but how it shaped the regulatory state to operate alongside the criminal justice system in ways that perpetuate an unequal two-tiered approach to governing misconduct.

The Politics of Antitrust and Competition in the Progressive Era

In subsequent years, antitrust law became a significant part of American corporate law as the trust-busting age took shape. But in the Progressive era there was no clear consensus on how to manage trusts as Progressives, Populists, and conservatives endorsed variants of antimonopolism, industry nationalization, or regulation of big businesses.[77] Through this context, regulatory ideology persisted as a presence in institution-building politics. In creating the FTC to regulate restraints of trade, prevailing lawmaking coalitions continued to distinguish businessmen from common criminals and built institutions that avoided punishing executives for pushing their competitive impulses to the point of producing anticompetitive concentration.

The FTC's design was closely tied to other policy developments, including the passage of the Clayton Antitrust Act (CAA) of 1914, which was proposed as a supplement to the Sherman Antitrust Act (SAA) of 1890. The CAA statutorily specified anticompetitive practices and sanctioned them through criminal punishments, but a diluting of the Clayton bill paved the way for a trade commission built around the ideals of regulatory ideology to emerge as a complement to the law. However, this outcome was not inevitable, and the CAA was not the only development that set the stage for the FTC's creation. Antitrust politics were convoluted and contested during this era, and the FTC's construction hinged on an array of legal, economic, and political circumstances that established the conditions for its emergence.

ANTITRUST POLITICS AND THE CONTEXT FOR THE FEDERAL TRADE COMMISSION ACT

The enactment of the FTCA was preceded by a lengthy series of political developments and debates concerning antitrust policy. Its passage was guided and influenced by these developments, which included the adoption of the SAA, early twentieth-century evolutions in trust-busting politics, President Roosevelt's failure to secure federal licensing reform, the outcome of the 1912 presidential election, the design of the CAA, and the economic context surrounding the FTCA's ultimate passage.

Most historical accounts of white-collar crime begin with the SAA and claim that it marked the state's first attempt to monitor corporate crime by outlawing restraints of trade and empowering the Justice Department to prosecute violations.[78] But the Sherman law reflected the legacy of the ICA by defining violations of antitrust law as crimes that could be punished through myriad interventions like civil or equity proceedings. In the Senate, George Vest (D-MO) protested that this sent the message to executives that "you are a lot of criminals, thieves, and robbers, but if you will give us a thousand dollars we will let you go on robbing."[79] However, many have suggested that the SAA was never designed to rein in trusts; rather, it was meant to provide

Republicans with political cover to pass other unpopular economic policies. This allowed concentration to carry on uninhibited even before the Supreme Court constrained the federal government's power to enforce the SAA against manufacturing and intrastate commercial activity in *U.S. v. E.C. Knight Co.* (1895).[80]

What is often described as the "trust-busting" era took off during President Theodore Roosevelt's administration, but the nuances of the president's antitrust stance are often overlooked. Roosevelt did not shy away from confronting trusts and condemning the "predatory capitalist," but he also believed that industrial combination was efficient and natural. He actually critiqued the SAA for posing "a constant threat against decent business men."[81] He found the SAA unwieldy and sought other mechanisms for controlling the corporate capitalist economy. Reflecting the assumption that executives were basically decent people, his preferred mode for handling trusts was to broker informal agreements with businesses personally through the Bureau of Corporations (BOC), through which he hoped to reform wayward corporate leaders via moral suasion rather than law enforcement.[82] Established in 1903, the BOC was designed to monitor and report on major industries and monopolistic practices, and the president could release any information it gathered to publicize restraints of trade and corporate wrongdoing.[83] However, the bureau usually muddled criminal cases since its private agreements with businesses granted them immunity from prosecution.[84] Some high-profile trust prosecutions bolstered Roosevelt's trustbuster image, but his administration usually aimed to correct businessmen morally through informal negotiation.[85]

This is not to suggest that Roosevelt did not seek significant state control over the economy. One of his boldest political efforts was his failed attempt to secure a federal corporate licensing scheme, a story detailed by Martin Sklar. It begins with the Industrial Commission—created under President McKinley in 1898—which in 1902 recommended a federal licensing system requiring corporations conducting interstate commerce exceeding $10 million annually to obtain a federal license. A state bureau would collect and publicize annual reports from licensed corporations detailing their assets, liabilities, profits, and losses, withdraw or reject licenses if corporations violated federal law, and facilitate prosecutions of lawbreakers.[86]

The BOC, a product of the commission's work, had no licensing power, but it developed proposals for federal licensing in the hope that it would expose the crimes of miscreant individuals hiding behind the corporate form. In its 1906 annual report, it wrote that licensing would "restore individual responsibility and prevent the corporation from being the hiding place of the irresponsible, dishonest, or corrupt manager." A licensing system opening firms' books to state inspection would reveal the workings of "the individuals who control" them so that "personal responsibility" for a corporation's actions "can be instantly fixt upon them."[87] It was widely understood that corporate agents routinely violated the law; the BOC's 1908 report conceded that "industrial concentration is already largely accomplished, in spite of general statutory prohibition." Roosevelt informed Congress that judicial interpretation of antitrust law produced a situation in which "the business of the country cannot be conducted without breaking [the law]." These constituted stark admissions that corporations were restructuring American capitalism in open defiance of law. Roosevelt and the BOC believed that licensing would promote individual criminal accountability, restore the rule of law in a changing market, and repair public faith in the corporate form.[88]

Federal incorporation, registration, and licensing of corporations were constitutionally fraught issues at the time, but there was meaningful potential for reform. Despite entailing a vast expansion of state power over industry, federal licensing enjoyed support from significant portions of the business community. Many businesses felt that licensing could cleanse markets of corruption and provide certainty and clarity for honest market participants, underscoring the real divisions of opinion across industry actors over how to manage the corporate economy.[89] But a series of strategic missteps by Roosevelt doomed the effort. Most importantly, the president insisted on a licensing bill that relied on executive branch administration of the system with almost no room for judicial review. When an antitrust reform bill was drafted in 1908, he intervened and demanded revisions to include his preferred licensing scheme.[90]

The licensing proposal focused less on enforcing competitive dynamics than on centralizing state control over the economy by transforming corporations into entities tightly controlled by government mandates. This broke sharply from the regulatory approach by conceiving large corporations as something akin to public utilities whose activities should be made to align with the public interest via far more intensive state supervision. But despite business support for federal licensing, the bill as written experienced a quick death in Congress. It encountered considerable hostility owing not to general resistance to granting the federal government extensive licensing powers, but to a revolt against the bill's concentration of executive power. Even firms and committed Roosevelt supporters who favored a strong licensing program ultimately declined to support it, unnerved and alienated by its vast expansion of executive branch authority. What was poised to be a close game became a blowout as overwhelming opposition mobilized against the proposal.[91]

The moment was ripe for a licensing law that broke from the doctrines of regulatory ideology and enjoyed support from business. Had Roosevelt not been intransigent in his commitment to brokering his ideal bill without concessions, he may not have squandered the opportunity. That the ideals of regulatory ideology came to influence Progressive era antitrust policy was dependent on this failure, which dampened reform impulses that could have constructed a different kind of state authority over the economy and strengthened the state's power to prosecute individual corporate malfeasants.

Roosevelt's successor, William Howard Taft, was less focused on devising administrative schemes for controlling the economy. Taft preferred to rely on Justice Department authority to enforce the SAA in the hope of producing a common law of antitrust precedents to govern corporate behavior. Taft filed eighty-nine antitrust suits in four years, more than doubling Roosevelt's seven-year total. Several of these prosecutions produced major precedents, like *Standard Oil of New Jersey v. U.S.* (1908), which declared the controversial "rule of reason" authorizing judges to deem combinations illegal only if their effect was to restrain trade unreasonably.[92] Taft still condemned overly zealous antitrust crusades as an unfair "impeachment of the motives of men of the highest character," but his preferred strategy was a purely reactive law enforcement approach, as opposed to Roosevelt's preference of concentrating control over economic affairs in the executive branch.[93] Taft's course on antitrust was one of the many things that prompted Roosevelt to run as a third-party candidate in the 1912 presidential election.

The 1912 presidential election was one of the most important in US history.[94] Arguably, no other election prioritized antitrust policy as much as the 1912 presidential race. It is worth noting that the three main candidates— Roosevelt, Taft, and Woodrow Wilson—all identified as Progressives and adopted different combinations of Progressive principles. This reflected disagreements among self-identified Progressives over how to handle regulatory and antitrust policy, throwing wrinkles into the partisan landscape rendering party identification not fully reliable as a predictor of party members' positions on these issues. The political and partisan divisions that characterized the CAA and FTCA congressional debates were consequently far messier than were those that characterized the ICA debates.

There were four primary views expressed on antitrust policy in the election. The Republican Taft favored law enforcement through the SAA to prosecute and break up trusts on a case-by-case basis and build a common law of antitrust precedents. Roosevelt's "New Nationalism" platform, promoted through his Progressive Party, asserted that trusts were inevitable and efficient. The former president favored permitting large corporations to monopolize industries and then regulating them through the BOC, advocating for a revival of his licensing proposal. Some condemned him as Wall Street's ideal candidate for creating state-supported monopolies, but others derided him as a harbinger of socialism owing to his ideas' statist overtones. Eugene Debs, running as a Socialist, scoffed at the latter notion. Given that Debs was a victim of the SAA's disproportionate use against labor, he had little faith that antitrust law could be used fairly. He presented a third idea: abandoning antitrust policy and nationalizing trusts to bring them under direct public control. The Democrat Woodrow Wilson was situated between the regulatory nationalism espoused by Roosevelt and the common law approach preferred by Taft and called his stance *regulating competition*, a term shaped by the guidance of his adviser Louis Brandeis. Whereas Roosevelt wanted to regulate monopolies after their formation, Wilson wanted to regulate competition to prevent monopolies from forming at all. His synthesis of the Taft and the Roosevelt approaches led him to favor the creation of a regulatory commission to police markets (although his precise views on the commission's strength and structure would not crystallize until later in his first term) while permitting ongoing judicial review of antitrust cases.[95]

Wilson's victory ratified his procompetition administrative logic as the hegemonic scheme for regulating American corporate capitalism over the alternatives championed by his opponents, but the establishment of a commission and its particular form was uncertain in the wake of his election. Wilson had been ambivalent toward antitrust and economic regulation prior to his pursuit of the Democratic nomination, so his early views were shaped by the 1912 Democratic Party platform. But there was vast disagreement within the party over how strong a trade commission should be. Most agrarian Democrats who detested big business opposed a strong commission, fearing that it would be vulnerable to industry capture. They preferred to break up monopolies and prevent consolidation through statutory prohibitions on anticompetitive practices enforceable via criminal penalties. The CAA was intended to serve this purpose, but agrarian Democrats later begrudgingly lent support to the trade commission's creation after the CAA's criminal provisions were severely weakened. Other moderate Democrats supported corporate consolidation when they felt that it served the public interest but sought to supplement the SAA with a powerful expert bureaucracy capable of investigating concentration, enforcing the SAA, and stopping business practices that unfairly restricted competition.[96] Meanwhile, conservative Republican allies of capital sought to preserve large enterprises and coalesced in opposition to a strong commission, favoring a weak one that required businesses to submit only basic information about their operations.

When Democrats secured unified control of Congress and the presidency in 1912, agrarian Democrats seemed poised to push for their designs eschewing a strong commission in favor of statutory prohibitions. But these disagreements generated unwieldy legislative debates. Unlike the situation in the 1880s, when the Senate was a bastion of conservativism and business influence, this Democratic-controlled Senate had significant divisions. Given the overrepresentation of rural states in it, the chamber had a sizable agrarian contingent advocating for a coercive approach. But other senators representing more diverse statewide populations had to balance the conflicting views of industries and farmers through a middle position. Alternatively, the House experienced polarizing debates between representatives from industrial districts favoring a weak and advisory FTC, those from farming districts favoring the punitive approach, and those in the middle seeking a strong commission alternative. This created deep gulfs among lawmakers over how much power to grant the FTC even though Democrats retained unified control of the federal government. With the House and the Senate plagued by internal factions on the question and a president whose position on the FTC was unclear, the future of a trade commission was uncertain.[97]

By 1914, Wilson moved to a middle-ground position endorsing a regulatory commission to solve the trust problem. Part of his move was driven by economic and international events, especially the onset of World War I. Upheaval in world financial markets and shipping lines after international declarations of war raised the stakes in debates over the CAA and the FTCA. In conjunction with a domestic business depression, lawmakers were faced with circumstances that left them unwilling to experiment in financial markets at a precarious economic moment. Unsure that the nation could withstand an assault on corporate concentration with a world war unfolding, the prospects for a CAA imposing strong criminal sanctions were severely diminished, leaving Wilson open to alternatives for the trade commission's design. Internal advisers like Brandeis moved him toward a position favoring a moderately strong commission with minimal options for prosecuting wrongdoing, and congressional Democrats settled for a diluted CAA coupled with a more powerful FTC. When Wilson moved to the middle, agrarian Democrats articulating a punitive antitrust stance were unable to secure the support necessary to achieve their goals, paving the way for party moderates to deploy regulatory ideology as the structuring framework for debate.[98]

The FTC's mandate was a vague reflection of these conflicting intentions and political and economic circumstances. The FTCA enjoyed nearly unanimous support when it passed both chambers of Congress in part because of its unobjectionable nature—it offended few because it did little.[99] Roosevelt's failure to secure a licensing scheme, Wilson's 1912 election, internal party divisions over antitrust policy, economic depression, and a world war generated an uncertain state of affairs from which an FTC built on the familiar principles of regulatory ideology emerged.

REGULATORY IDEOLOGY AND THE FEDERAL
TRADE COMMISSION

The FTCA created an expert-staffed commission to monitor industry, constrained that commission's power, and permitted agency enforcement of antitrust law primarily through an administrative approach. This outcome was a compromise between those Democrats who wanted a moderately powerful commission to help enforce the SAA and those who sought legislation prohibiting specific restraint of trade practices in the CAA.[100] Once the CAA was stripped of its criminal penalties and the FTC was granted broad administrative discretion in enforcement of both statutes, these laws solidified the hegemony of regulatory ideology in antitrust law. But this was not a replica of the ICA debate. Early twentieth-century Progressives were far more skeptical of markets than were the coalitions driving the ICA debates, and they feared that unrestrained competition allowed the most unscrupulous to excel. Progressives framed their deployment of regulatory ideology as more consistent with intensive state intervention than lawmakers did in the ICA debates, in a manner similar to the way in which they reframed rehabilitative ideology from being consonant with natural selection to a tool justifying state-administered eugenic selection. As a result, regulatory ideology retained value in this new environment for Progressive lawmakers.

The FTC had a rough precursor in the advisory BOC, but a need for stronger oversight became apparent in the 1910s as public anxieties over the growth of a "money trust" spread.[101] As the financial sector became increasingly powerful, fears that a group of Wall Street financiers controlled a sprawling web of corporations amplified public concern about trusts. The money trust became the target of a high-profile 1912–13 congressional inquiry chaired by Representative Arsene Pujo (D-LA), with Samuel Untermyer serving as the committee's legal counsel. Known as the Pujo Committee, the inquiry found that the money trust not only was real but controlled over $22 billion across the mining, manufacturing, transportation, telecommunications, and financial sectors. Headed by the Morgan empire, the trust held 341 directorships spanning 112 corporations.

The Pujo hearings were replete with articulations of regulatory ideology. Those called to testify often relied on a familiar fusion of liberal economics with Spencerian and Sumnerian language to defend the money trust's behavior as healthy and natural. Consider the former New York Stock Exchange (NYSE) president Frank Sturgis. When asked by the committee about whether he approved of the money trust's aggressive manipulations of stock prices, Sturgis defended its actions, claiming that "you are asking me a moral question, and I am answering you a stock-exchange question," which he said "are very different things." When pressed on whether such behavior hurt smaller investors to the money trust's advantage, he stated, "It might. Self-preservation is the first law of nature. . . . I do not consider it wrong." Sturgis defended the money trust's actions as natural and unassailable, suggesting that the committee naively misunderstood organic market dynamics.[102] His comments prompted newspapers to run headlines the following morning claiming that "manipulation is well approved" and considered "regular and legitimate" on the NYSE.[103]

Sturgis was not alone in distinguishing questions of business sense from ones of morality on the grounds that lawmakers mistook natural market competition for immorality. The New York State Chamber of Commerce cautioned the committee against criminalizing actions like restraint of trade that were consistent with natural economic forces, arguing that doing so would actually *violate* economic law because it would "shackle the genius of this country" while being "inconsistent with moral law" for punishing actions that were not inherently wrong.[104] William Sherer, the manager of the New York Clearing House Association, informed the committee that "the average business man . . . is a person of some moral status" who is "going to do right anyway" and did not need the threat of prosecution to keep him in line.[105]

When the Pujo Committee published its final report, many lawmakers—especially populist Democrats—condemned the money trust as morally and criminally wrong. Representative Edwin Webb (D-NC) said that the trust's actions should be forbidden "in conscience."[106] Similarly, Senator James Hamilton Lewis (D-IL) argued that anything contrary to good public policy should "be treated as also a violation of public morals."[107] But in response, some of their colleagues drew on familiar ideas distinguishing businessmen as noncriminal. Representative Joseph Moore (R-PA) and Senator William Stone (D-MO) argued that the committee's suggestions would punish "the industrious and progressive business man" who "has lived an upright, moral, and manly life, building up a character that should stand in his support when accused."[108] This served as a preview of what would come during debates over the FTCA.

The Pujo Committee's recommendations led to the Clayton Act, which was supposed to aid enforcement of the SAA by specifying and prohibiting particular practices deemed harmful to the market's competitive health, such as

price discrimination, multiple or interlocking directorates, and anticompetitive acquisitions and mergers. This constituted a clear response to the Supreme
Court's ruling in the *Standard Oil* case in that it attempted to limit the judiciary's ability to distinguish reasonable and unreasonable restraints of trade.
The bill in its early form specified that directors or agents found guilty of any
violation would be punished with a $5,000 fine and up to a year of impris-
onment while also authorizing courts to provide injunctive relief on behalf of
those suffering potential losses.[109] It was thus a punitive means of controlling
anticompetitive practices standing in contrast to varying proposals for a new
regulatory authority, an ideal for agrarian Democrats. But the CAA's passage
was a rocky process driven by factions of Progressives, farmers, and labor interests. Advocates of regulatory bureaucracy in the House successfully struck
the criminal penalties, creating space for the middle-ground compromise position of handing off broadened enforcement authority to a moderately powerful
FTC. Legislators seeking a stronger commission were comfortable gutting the
CAA's enforcement provisions because they saw the FTCA as a replacement,
while those dismayed to see the CAA weakened reasoned that any new regulatory body might as well be meaningful.[110] And while Wall Street may have been
disheartened to see public apprehensions over the money trust manifested in
new market controls, the Pujo Committee failed to agree on how to define unlawful restraints of trade and suggested that the CAA should be supplemented
with a commission to identify industry-specific restraint of trade practices.[111]
This opened the door for entrenching regulatory ideology in a commission
that would coexist alongside the Department of Justice's antitrust mandate.[112]
The FTC was a response to the money trust controversy, but it was also a creature of these political contingencies.

President Wilson seized on the middle-ground solution of a moderately
powerful regulatory bureaucracy. Perhaps more than anyone else, Louis
Brandeis drove this choice. Gerald Berk has detailed how when he was an
adviser to Wilson, Brandeis articulated an economic philosophy of "regulated competition" that shaped the FTC. But at the heart of his model was an
understanding of corporate criminality that valorized regulatory guidance as
the key to promoting competition in lieu of punitively sanctioning market
participants.

Brandeis was well-known for his antimonopolist bona fides, and he was
publicly critical of trusts for focusing on consolidation over product quality
and innovation.[113] But he also wrote that the "regulation of competition" was
"essential to the preservation of competition and to its best development."
Therefore, his opposition to monopoly power manifested in a philosophy
seeking to encourage the right kind of competition through regulation.[114]

Brandeis believed that market competition could promote innovation and efficiency in some contexts but abuse and mismanagement in others. He offered a nuanced argument that state regulatory bodies should proactively manage the competitive process to guide it toward ideal outcomes by discouraging concentration, extinguishing unfair trade practices early, and working with the targets of state oversight to keep markets healthy. Consistent with the ideology of regulation articulated by Progressive era economists, his theory of regulated competition was not a way to punish wrongdoing or protect the public. Rather, it was a way of saving capitalism from itself by establishing healthy, safe, and efficient market conditions.[115]

Consequently, Brandeis's philosophy was not just rooted in economic theory. His faith in a proactive and collaborative commission rested on a series of assumptions about what caused undesirable restraints of trade that engaged with questions about human nature. Rather than condemning corporate greed as the cause of wrongdoing, Brandeis condemned the industrial system, which he believed could be corrected to avert the need to prosecute lawbreakers. His testimony before the US House Commerce Committee in early 1914 made these aspects of his philosophy clear. At this point, Congress was deadlocked over how strong to make the FTC and what to do in the CAA, but Brandeis offered language that helped resolve the debate.[116] Brandeis told the committee that "industrial crime is not a cause, it is an effect; the effect of a bad system." He reasoned, "if we adopt a good system, we are very apt not to have much of industrial criminality." He suggested that the FTC should "prevent breaches of the law and not punish breaches of the law" by "preventing the conditions which lead to the criminal tendency."[117] His interpretation of "the *criminal tendency*" is particularly telling. He attributed the executive's criminal tendency not to human nature, but to manageable industrial conditions. This is a critical point that not only distinguished corporate wrongdoing from common criminality, but also implied that market conditions rather than market participants should be the primary object of regulators.

By locating the cause of monopolistic practices in the commercial environment rather than the individual, Brandeis dismissed the notion that the commission should be punitive. He stated that the economy could be reformed so that wrongdoing becomes "unnatural" because business leaders "who could be exercising their powers in the right direction . . . are led by a bad system to do things that are harmful to the community." Advocating within the regulatory ideological framework, he stated that such men do not deserve prison because their offenses are "not like those cases where the offense involves a moral taint in the individual." He explained that "[o]ur aim [in designing the commission] should not be to instill fear, but to so develop the commercial conditions that crime becomes unnatural."[118] It is important to note that Brandeis was more willing to consider corporate rapacity wrong than were laissez-faire ideologues of the late nineteenth century, but he explicitly rejected the idea that corporate wrongs were functions of malicious dispositions and instead expressed faith that correcting market conditions would prevent the problematic behavior.

Brandeis's comments reflected a deeper concern shared by economists like Richard Ely and John Commons that an overly punitive commission would discourage innovation and risk-taking among law-abiding actors owing to the problematic habits of a few competitors. It was thus crucial that the commission be empowered to work with industry to promote efficiency and innovation *before* resorting to enforcement actions. Brandeis's assertion that restraint of trade lacked "moral taint in the individual" explicitly discouraged punishment as a solution and reflected the premises shared by Progressive economists that businessmen were generally good people dissuadable through mild administration.[119]

This is not to say that Brandeis's testimony ended the political fight as legislators also cited Roosevelt's success negotiating with trusts informally and expressed their own doubts about the Justice Department's enforcement capacity as important considerations in the FTC's design.[120] But Brandeis's testimony was vital to shaping legislative discourse around the FTC by directing lawmakers to think about regulation as a way to control competition without punishment. In subsequent hearings, lawmakers and industrial representatives argued within Brandeis's framework as agents of various oil, gas, and steel companies pleaded with legislators to create a nonpunitive commission.[121] For instance, the Columbus Steel Castings Company told the Senate Interstate Commerce Committee that criminal provisions would punish "people who had done things which were not considered to be immoral in themselves." They claimed that "it is always dangerous to attempt too closely to define acts which, while in the absence of statutory laws are neither immoral in their nature nor savor of criminality."[122]

Brandeis's framing proved an effective strategy for legislators. In the House, Representative Dick Morgan (R-OK) defended Brandeis's proposal by stating, "[O]ur criminal laws only prohibit things which are immoral; but when we come to prohibit things which are involved in business transactions, . . . we are entering not only upon a difficult but a dangerous field, dangerous to business, and very difficult to carry out without doing more injury than good."[123] Senator Albert Cummins (R-IA) of the Chamber's Interstate Commerce Committee was more explicit in his endorsement of the Brandeisian model. He expressed "a confident belief that the business men of this country

are honest, faithful men" who generally "intend to obey the law." He argued
on behalf of creating a commission to which men who "have a real desire to
uphold the law" can turn for guidance "before they are branded as criminals." He stated, "I am unwilling that the failure to obey these regulations . . .
shall make the men who conduct our business affairs criminals, without consciousness of moral turpitude or moral dereliction."[124] Tennessee Democrat
John Shields of the Senate Commerce Committee expressed similar thinking,
asking his colleagues who wanted the commission to be more coercive: "Have
our business men a lower standing than criminals at the bar of justice?"[125]

The Senate passed the FTCA in September 1914 by a 43–5 vote, it sailed
through the House on a voice vote, and the commission was launched the
next spring.[126] As stated in the 1914 statutory text, the FTC was designed to
prevent "persons, partnerships, or corporations, except banks, and common
carriers . . . from using unfair methods of competition in commerce."[127] It
was given two institutional warrants—to work with businesses to identify
industry-specific restraint of trade practices and to curb those practices
through administrative supervision, education, and information provision.
It was thought that this would preclude corporate concentration and prevent
markets from becoming criminogenic, limiting the necessity of prosecution.
The commission was to rely on the CAA and its own discretion to target
specific restraint of trade practices warranting scrutiny. While the CAA detailed some prohibited practices, the FTCA incorporated broad language empowering the commission to initiate proceedings when it believed doing so
"would be to the interest of the public," thus granting the commission wide
administrative authority to determine what constituted the national interest
or unfair competition.[128]

One of the FTC's most significant tools was the cease-and-desist order
(CDO). A CDO is a written notice from an agency directing a subject to
discontinue certain conduct and placing it under enhanced administrative
scrutiny. The FTC was statutorily empowered to issue such orders whenever
it uncovered a firm engaging in an unfair competitive practice, and it could
seek judicial enforcement of its orders. But as originally written, CDOs authorized under the FTCA and the CAA carried no immediate consequences
if violated. Rather, they were enforced through what was sometimes colloqui-
ally referred to as the "three bites at the apple" procedure. First, in order to
issue a CDO, the FTC needed to show proof of a statutory violation under
the FTCA or the CAA. The FTC could subsequently secure a judicial enforcement order for the CDO if it proved to a circuit court that the CDO
was violated—a second infraction. Then, sanctions via criminal contempt
charges could be obtained via proof of a violation of the court's enforcement

order—a third infraction. This offered wide latitude by giving offenders three opportunities to disregard legal orders before facing consequences. Narrowly written CDOs were particularly difficult; if respondents engaged in violations not included in an initial order, the FTC had to modify that order or issue a new one.[129]

Senator Francis Newlands (D-NV), the chair of the chamber's Interstate Commerce Committee, offered some insight into Congress's attitude on CDOs:

> Now, I will state that throughout this bill, so far as I am individually concerned, I have not been disposed to suggest extreme penalties. I thought it only fair that . . . to be tested through this tribunal the parties brought before it, at all events in the earlier stages, should have the opportunity without facing the penitentiary to assert their rights . . . and that the penalty should be imposed only in case of disobedience to the order of the courts. Of course we could have put a provision in the bill that after an order was made by the commission every day's failure to comply with it would involve a fine of a thousand dollars a day or a hundred dollars a day or whatever else we might make it, or perhaps imprisonment.[130]

Newlands's statement offers a window into Congress's intention of authorizing CDOs to provide additional due process protections to anyone targeted by the commission and give them multiple opportunities to right their behavior before facing penalties. There have been changes to how the FTC issues and executes CDOs—which will be discussed in chapter 6—but in this original form, an order led to criminal charges only after three violations. Those charges came in response only to disobeying a federal court order compelling obedience with a CDO after two infractions—a punishment far removed from the initial violation. The CDO was thus weak and cumbersome in its early structure. As Thomas Kauper writes about this process, "[T]he entry of a cease and desist order . . . meant little, in and of itself, to firms bent upon violation."[131]

Debates over the FTCA differed in important ways from debates over the ICA, but in both cases hinging the debate on character judgments of business leaders fostered favorable interpretations of their actions. If businessmen were good people, restraint of trade took on a substantive meaning distinct from traditional definitions of criminality. Accepting Brandeis's arguments, Congress designed the FTC as a corrective instrument to improve competition. The House Interstate Commerce Committee concluded that the FTC would produce "an elevated business standard" and "better business stability."[132] The Senate Committee on Interstate Commerce concluded that the FTC would "promote fair competition" but only because it was designed to be "persuasive and corrective rather than punitive."[133] Brandeis admitted that some trade practices were wrong and harmful, but his philosophy was that those actions were functions of market circumstances rather than a criminal human nature, meaning that we should avoid treating them punitively. His intervention in the FTCA debates shows how regulatory ideology's core tenets could be adapted in changing political contexts by coalitions demanding different degrees of regulation as he articulated an approach that appeased the warring factions of his day.

Brandeis's presentation of the regulatory model again highlights the perils and promise of regulatory ideology. Brandeis put powerful words to the reasonable notion that crime should be treated as a function of economic forces, and it is worth exploring how he successfully brought this logic to bear on the criminal justice system's institutional cousin. But his conceptualization of lawbreaking corporate leaders as well-intentioned victims of market imperfections sharply contrasted with eugenic understandings of street criminals—understandings he later validated as a Supreme Court justice when he voted to uphold compulsory sterilization policies—helping legitimate immense inequalities in law. But the notion that crime should be controlled by reforming the economic conditions that generate lawbreaking should not be rejected because of its unequal historical application. Rather, it must be expanded to create a more just legal system for all.

The Reality of Regulation

The development of the regulatory state has not been smooth; rather, it has been a story of fits and starts. These bursts of change are characterized not simply by more or less regulation, but by qualitative changes in the purposes of regulation and how administrative bodies are designed, rendering each moment of institution building different from the previous ones.[134] However, we should not miss the forest for the trees. Regulatory development has been driven by many punctuated changes, but the long arc shows some consistencies. One of those consistencies is the persistent belief that regulation should, to some extent, be an alternative to prosecution for people who do not deserve it. Regulatory ideological frameworks have appealed to diverse political actors who have mobilized and adjusted them depending on their shifting goals and political contexts, shedding new light on how and why the American state developed an anemic institutional capacity to prosecute corporate crime. The stories of the ICC and the FTC illustrate the power and appeal of regulatory ideology in different political and economic environments.

Of course, regulatory agencies change over time. The ICA was amended soon after its initial passage, and presidential appointments and unfavorable Supreme Court decisions delivered setbacks to the FTC in the 1920s.[135] But their ideological bases reveal something fundamental about the nature of regulatory institution building. By laying at the foundation of regulatory institutions, regulatory ideology works with the rehabilitative ideology woven into criminal justice institutions to reinforce a shared set of ideas about who does and who does not legitimately count as criminal.

Again, corporate actors can avoid prosecution by hiring strong legal defense teams, capturing agencies, initiating capital strikes, or buying friends in legislative arenas, but the story presented in this chapter unpacks more subtle dynamics that shape business-government relations. Businesses pursue their goals strategically and select communicative frames to convey their preferences in ways that resonate with policymakers and the public. While the creation of the ICC marked the origins of national market regulation in the United States, it was also a victory for the railroads, which deployed prevailing discourses about crime, economics, and Social Darwinism to design a new regulatory institution to their liking. Decades later, when the financial sector faced criticism during the Pujo hearings, Progressive lawmakers were receptive to regulatory ideology when it was packaged into a new expert-staffed commission tasked with enhancing the quality of competition. This illustrates how prevailing ideas and ideologies can provide powerful political actors with appealing languages and understandings they can use to express their political goals and navigate evolving political divisions among lawmakers.

Regulatory bodies like the ICC and the FTC are designed to monitor undesirable and unlawful behavior, and research on the political development of the regulatory state often ignores this. Understanding the development of regulatory governance as related to the development of the justice system illuminates how both serve to express and fortify a politically constructed understanding of criminality.

The Persistence of Rehabilitation: Criminality, Incorrigibility, and Twentieth-Century Politics

Where an incorrigible recidivist felon like Andrade shuns rehabilitation, rejects the lessons of previous punishment, and fails to be deterred, the safety and comfort of society
demands incapacitation.

Brief on the Merits of Amicus Curiae,
California District Attorneys Association, *Lockyer v. Andrade* (2002)

In November 1995, thirty-seven-year-old Leandro Andrade was caught shoplifting videotapes from a K-Mart in Ontario, California. Two weeks later,
he stole more from another store in the nearby town of Montclair. He was
arrested and charged, and with a record littered with convictions for theft,
burglary, and drug possession, he was sentenced to two consecutive twenty-
five-year prison terms. The merciless penalty was a result of California's 1994
three-strikes law, which mandated that judges issue a term of twenty-five years
to life for individuals convicted of a third felony if their two prior convictions
were designated as violent or serious under state law. Before the Supreme
Court upheld Andrade's sentence in the 2003 decision *Lockyer v. Andrade*, the
California District Attorneys Association (CDAA) submitted an amicus brief
defending Andrade's sentence as appropriate for, as the CDAA described him,
an "incorrigible recidivist" who "shuns rehabilitation," as noted in this chapter's epigraph.[1]

Not every inmate's story is like Andrade's, but his experience is not unusual in the era of mass incarceration. Many scholars suggest that severe
mandatory sentencing practices like this have been key contributors to the
carceral state's escalation by rejecting the rehabilitative ideal in favor of brute
one-size-fits-all justice.[2] But the reality is that Andrade's sentence would have
likely enjoyed support from the rehabilitative ideal's founders. Consider what
Henry Boies wrote in *Prisoners and Paupers*: "When upon a third conviction
the judicial authorities determine the prisoner to belong to the criminal class,
the law should imperatively require the sentence to be the penitentiary for
life, whatever the crime committed."[3] This 1893 statement could just as easily
have come from the CDAA's brief in Andrade's case. The determinate sentencing practices of today are often framed as rejecting rehabilitation, and the

law-and-order movement driving mass incarceration has undeniably articulated a new brand of crime politics, but it would be hasty to write off these developments as complete and unqualified rejections of rehabilitative thinking.

Scrutinizing the evolution of US sentencing through the twentieth century
reveals that rehabilitative ideology remained a consistent influence on political
development. This chapter advances two fundamental critiques of the narrative
that rehabilitative ideology dominated American crime politics from the 1890s
until its discrediting in the 1970s. First, during its dominance at midcentury, the
rehabilitative ideal did not promote benevolent policy. Rehabilitative ideology
was linked to punitive reforms such as habitual offender laws in over forty states
that looked nearly indistinguishable from modern three-strikes laws. Rehabilitation's individualizing frame neutralized the potential for social democratic
political currents and social-structural shifts in criminological theory to promote progressive crime politics during this period. Second, while penal conservatives reframed popular understandings of criminality during the punitive
turn, it is incorrect to claim their politics wholly rejected rehabilitative theory.
Law-and-order hard-liners often drew on reasoning found only in rehabilitative ideology to justify harsh justice policies. This is particularly clear in the
promulgation of the 1987 federal sentencing guidelines. While the guidelines
are often treated as a historical pivot marking the death knell for rehabilitation,
key features of them were built on facets of rehabilitative thought.

This history illustrates the flexibility and tenacity of the rehabilitative ideal.
Rehabilitation became unmoored from its eugenic roots but persisted in evolving forms. The ideal's determinist premises were kept alive through ideas of
inherent incorrigibility that lawmakers mobilized in new ways to shape central
components of the modern carceral regime. These ideas eschewed a biological
character but left a eugenic mark on American criminal justice. Factors that
seem more neutral than eugenic variables—most notably criminal history—
have become racially and class-skewed stand-ins for incorrigibility. This appears less clinical than earlier instantiations of rehabilitative ideology, but statutes and guidelines schemes designed to ratchet up prison terms for those with
lengthier records achieve the same basic goal of sorting people into categories
of reformability and incorrigibility for differential punishment.

As mass incarceration took shape during the course of the twentieth century, the politics of crime was convulsive and multifaceted. The expansive and
disparate features of the carceral state cannot be explained by one common
denominator, and various developments that laid its foundations were tied to
ideas and political motives other than rehabilitative politics. Early twentieth-
century prohibitionists carved out a new role for the federal government
in crime control while establishing a model for the modern war on drugs

through campaigns steeped in religious moralizing.[4] The racialized crime politics following the civil rights movement cannot be understood without considering the era's political realignments, regionally patterned racial attitudes, and changes in race relations that prompted policy entrepreneurs to link race and crime in new ways.[5] And certain developments in sentencing—such as the constitutional approval of mandatory life-without-parole sentences for particular nonviolent offenses—eschewed rehabilitative notions about sorting and sentencing individualization.[6] These examples clarify that the carceral landscape is a product of a vast and conflicting array of ideas. The history detailed in this chapter does not propose that rehabilitative ideology was the *only* factor driving mass incarceration, that mass incarceration would not have emerged in some form absent rehabilitative ideas, or that rehabilitative ideology has prevailed every time it was deployed. Rather, it argues that during the course of the twentieth century, political entrepreneurs regularly and effectively mobilized rehabilitative ideology as one ideational tool of many to justify carceral expansion. America's carceral regime is not wholly a product of rehabilitative politics, but its character cannot be fully recognized without unpacking the role rehabilitative ideology played in its design. Key punitive developments shaping the carceral state were presented not as exceptions to or rejections of rehabilitative penology, but as consistent with it. This should be not discounted as a novelty, but instead considered as an alarming fact for reformers advocating for the revival of rehabilitation.

The chapter begins by outlining academic perspectives on early to mid-twentieth-century crime politics and the rehabilitative ideal's dominance. It then explores the tenacity and adaptations of rehabilitative practices in the twentieth century and argues that the individualizing frame of rehabilitation muted emergent structural currents in criminology and New Deal era politics that could have promoted a progressive understanding of criminality. Next, it analyzes the spread of habitual offender laws across the states through the 1940s—specifically through case studies of New York and California—to demonstrate how these three-strikes precursors were often grounded in rehabilitative theory. The punitive turn of the late twentieth century is then examined with an eye toward understanding how, despite articulating a facial rejection of rehabilitation, penal conservatives drew on ideas from rehabilitative ideology in their politics to design the federal sentencing guidelines.

An Overview of Rehabilitation in the Twentieth Century

The rehabilitative ideal's rise and fall unfolded from the 1920s through the 1970s. As the ideal spread across the states during these years, criminal justice became a national issue. Prohibition set the stage for the federal government to assert a new degree of authority over crime and the policing of public morals, yielding an enhanced federal law enforcement apparatus and a legacy of expanded police powers.[7] When the National Crime Commission of 1929 (known as the Wickersham Commission after its chair, George Wickersham) was appointed by President Herbert Hoover to study the crime problem, it questioned the value of Prohibition but still defended an enhanced federal role in crime control. Subsequently, national lawmakers began discussing crime as a problem requiring federal intervention.[8] After the commission put the crime problem in the national spotlight, Franklin Roosevelt and his attorney general, Homer Cummings, secured several crime control packages in the 1930s, vastly expanding the federal criminal justice system.[9]

In many ways, the Roosevelt administration's policy programs provided opportunities to institutionalize a new model of American life rooted in the social democratic pursuit of an egalitarian society. Under Roosevelt's leadership, the austere individualism of traditional liberalism gave way to a more socialized understanding of liberalism in which the individual was to be liberated through the protection of social necessities and economic security. Perspectives holding that Roosevelt's election constituted a durable regime change suggest that this governing mentality had powerful structuring effects on politics from roughly the 1930s through the 1970s.[10] This is the logic implicitly accepted by scholars who endorse the rehabilitative narrative; rehabilitative penology was popularized during an era characterized by progressive policy shifts, helping to moderate penal policy.[11]

While the New Deal's social democratic commitments shaped political change in many ways, numerous scholars argue that the regime's egalitarian rhetoric did not translate into compassionate policy for all, often disadvantaging marginalized populations, including immigrants, African Americans, and women.[12] Criminal justice was no exception. The New Deal approach to crime had an unapologetically punitive undercurrent clear in the tough-on-crime philosophy fueling the Roosevelt administration's policies criminalizing kidnapping, sex crimes, organized crime, and juvenile delinquency.[13] Even the Truman administration's criminal justice reform efforts, which were intended to ameliorate racial inequality, relied on procedural reforms that bolstered the tenacity of the nation's punitive justice system.[14] Despite the meaningful social and economic achievements of the era, New Deal politics remained less progressive on criminal justice.

This history complicates claims advanced by advocates of the rehabilitative narrative who suggest that New Deal progressivism included a compassionate approach to punishment. Scholars endorsing this logic typically link midcentury crime policy to shifts in criminological thinking, reasoning that these ideational developments fueled temperate crime politics. For instance, John Hagan's analysis of crime politics during the New Deal era (which he defines as the period 1933–73) concludes that innovations in criminology locating the causes of crime in social structures and economic relations softened the state's approach to punishment. Hagan illustrates how scholars like Clifford Shaw, Henry McKay, Robert Merton, and Edwin Sutherland redirected attention to the role that material conditions played in generating crime.[15] Central to this ideological milieu was a resurgent interest in rehabilitation, and David Garland has written that core features of the rehabilitative program like sentencing individualization were part of a "broad professional consensus about the basic framework within which crime control should operate" through this period. This is to suggest not that there was no contestation over crime policy during these years, but rather that such contestation often occurred within a prevailing rehabilitative framework. Garland writes that the rehabilitative ideal served as "the hegemonic, organizing principle, the intellectual framework and value system that bound together the whole [penal] structure" from "the 1890s to the 1970s."[16]

Hagan and Garland correctly identify meaningful trends in criminological thinking and rightly consider rehabilitative ideology a primary organizational principle of the prison through the period. But rehabilitative ideology often contributed to cruel rather than compassionate penal policy during these years while muting the potentially progressive impact of social-structural criminology. The individualized and determinist premises embedded in rehabilitative ideology—that rehabilitation is an individual process, failure to reform is indicative of natural incorrigibility, and the racially and economically marginalized are the likely incorrigibles—neutralized the effects of the era's social democratic politics and the structural revolution in criminology on crime policy. In the process, it kept lawmakers and criminologists focused on the atomized and pathologically flawed individual as the root explanation of criminal behavior.

The Evolution of Indeterminate Sentencing and Risk Assessments

As the linchpin of the rehabilitative ideal, indeterminate sentencing spread with the popularization of rehabilitation and was adopted in all fifty states and the federal system by 1970.[17] Designed to give judges and administrators discretion to tailor prison terms to individuals' reformative potential, it brought its duality into the twentieth century. Associated with these changes was the emergence of actuarial assessments of defendants' risk of criminality, tools that foreshadowed modern risk assessments, which further cemented rehabilitative ideology's racial and class assumptions in the punishment process.

It is useful to begin this analysis with the 1949 Supreme Court case *Williams v. New York*, which upheld the constitutionality of indeterminate sentencing and exhibited rehabilitative ideology's enduring duality. In the case, a New York judge imposed the death sentence on a defendant on the basis of information not presented to a jury, which had recommended life imprisonment. The Supreme Court upheld the sentence by grounding its analysis of indeterminate sentencing in rehabilitative logic. In the opinion, Justice Hugo Black wrote that "[r]eformation and rehabilitation of offenders have become important goals of jurisprudence." Discussing rehabilitation might seem outlandish in a capital case, but Black explained that an assumption of the rehabilitative approach was that "punishment should fit the offender and not merely the crime." For Black, rehabilitation was not synonymous with compassion; it was about individualizing punishment to the person, punitively or mercifully. He concluded that sentencing judges should be virtually unlimited in what they can consider when tailoring sentences to a defendant. Information never presented during trial, including details about a defendant's life or conduct unrelated to the conviction at hand, was deemed relevant in customizing a sentence to a defendant's rehabilitative potential. Black concluded by stating that "[t]oday's philosophy of individualizing sentences makes sharp distinctions between first and repeat offenders."[18]

While the Supreme Court explicitly noted the duality of rehabilitation in *Williams*, one might hope that because the period from the 1930s through the 1970s witnessed the emergence of criminological theories explaining crime as a function of social and economic relations, rehabilitative instruments would incorporate the consideration of material and social inequalities as mitigating factors.[19] But rehabilitative ideology's emphasis on tailoring punishment to an individual's traits and personal deficiencies had the opposite effect, leading judges to interpret social and economic inequalities as evidence of individual defects and a criminal disposition. Deeper analysis of Black's ruling in *Williams* provides insight. Black emphasized that a system operating on the principle that "punishment should fit the offender and not merely the crime" must give judges access to "the fullest information possible concerning the defendant's life and characteristics," considerations that he deemed "highly relevant—if not essential—to [a judge's] selection of an appropriate sentence."[20] He wrote that judges should rely on presentence reports (PSRs) written by probation officers when sentencing defendants. Probation in America dated to the 1840s, but it became prominent with the rise of the rehabilitative ideal.

In the twentieth century, most states with indeterminate sentencing statutes passed accompanying probation laws, and Congress passed the Federal Probation Act in 1925.[21] Probation officers became involved in preparing PSRs for sentencing judges that included sentencing recommendations and broadranging background information on offenders for sentencing judges to consider when assessing their risk of future criminality. Black cited a publication from the Administrative Office of the US Courts that summarized the purpose of the PSR: "[The PSR's] primary object is to focus light on the character and personality of the defendant, to offer insight into his personality needs, to discover those factors underlying the specific offense and his conduct in general, and to aid the court in deciding whether probation or some other form of treatment is for the best interests of both the offender and society." The report, the authors said, would assist in "rehabilitative efforts" and help reformatories "in their institutional classification and treatment programs."[22] The publication opened by stating that the PSR was designed to uncover information about the "character" of the defendant and "his personality needs." The PSR assessed evidence of an individual's criminality and reformative potential across thirteen dimensions: "(1) Offense; (2) Prior Record; (3) Family History; (4) Home and Neighborhood; (5) Education; (6) Religion; (7) Interests and Activities; (8) Health; (9) Employment; (10) Resources; (11) Summary; (12) Plan; and (13) Agencies Interested." These factors were examined with an eye toward "an interpretation of the defendant's problems and needs" and an "evaluation of [the] defendant's personality."[23]

The attention paid to an individual's criminal record and behavioral history was crucial. The authors clarified that a record of prior convictions was an important sentencing consideration and that "a long succession of misdemeanors, even though the final disposition was 'discharged,' tells a lot about the defendant." This focus on the individual's background was a legacy of the rehabilitative model. Past convictions, personal traits, and even discharged conduct were considered evidence of individuals' natural disposition and indicators of their reformative potential that should shape their sentence in the case at hand.[24]

It is worth noting that in the PSR, employment, education, neighborhood conditions, and other social factors were listed as considerations, indicating that material conditions were recognized as explanations for an individual's deviant behavior. However, economic circumstances were treated not as mitigating factors, but as signs of personal defects requiring individualized punitive sanctions. For instance, questions in the PSR about educational background were related not to the quality or availability of schooling, but rather to the "defendant's own reaction to school," "likes and dislikes," and personal

"history of truancy." The section on employment considered not regional labor market conditions, but rather the "kind of work" for which the defendant
is "best adapted," the "occupational skills" the defendant possesses, and "the
employer's evaluation of the defendant's personality, capabilities, punctual-
ity, [and] reliability." The section on employment stated that if defendants
were unemployable, the "nature of [the] handicap" rendering them unable to
secure work should be discussed in the section on health.[25] Later versions of
the report made similar recommendations, aiming to "present the respective
problems and needs of the individual offender in a meaningful way," including his or her "needs, capacities, and problems."[26]

What is notable about the PSR is how factors emphasizing economic structures were incorporated into rehabilitative frameworks as individual problems requiring individualized solutions. In the realm of punishment, social-
structural ills that increased one's risk of criminality—including poverty or
unemployment—were viewed as manifestations of individual failings requiring microinterventions rather than as products of structural inequalities requiring macro–political economic reforms. The dominance of rehabilitative
ideology was key to this development as the rehabilitative ideal limited the
potential for a progressive crime politics by reinterpreting the era's structural
and economic explanations of criminality through an individualistic risk-
predictive lens. This excised social democratic instincts from the logics that
could have shaped crime and penal policy. When social-structural explanations of criminality were channeled through rehabilitative frameworks, they
were reinterpreted to rationalize individualized sanctions by locating the
causes of crime and inequality in the person rather than in the material conditions of the political economy.

The federal PSR represented broader trends in the legal system toward
systematically assessing defendants' criminal risk on the basis of subjective
analysis of their personal traits. More methodical actuarial approaches to penal decisions explicitly rooted in social science were taking hold at the state
and local levels, serving as precursors for contemporary risk assessments in
sentencing and punishment. But while modern risk-assessment metrics are
critiqued for legitimating racial and class biases through ostensibly neutral
mechanisms, their historical antecedents explicitly considered racial traits in
evaluating an offender's risk of criminality.[27]

Bernard Harcourt has shown not only that actuarial prediction in criminal justice has had a lengthy and fraught history predating the rise of modern risk assessments, but also that racial considerations have always been
embedded in risk assessments. The nation's first supposedly scientific tool
for making parole decisions—created by the sociologist Ernest Burgess in the

1920s—relied on twenty-one factors to predict individuals' success when on parole and their risk of recidivism. When Sheldon and Eleanor Glueck published their landmark *Five Hundred Criminal Careers* in 1930, they offered a prediction tool that relied on only seven factors. Both models explicitly considered an offender's race and parents' nationality. Illinois and California were among the states that designed risk-assessment tools based on this work, and both deemed being Black predictive of future violation and being White predictive of success. California's tool made sentencing and release recommendations by assessing only prior commitments, offense type, number of escapes, and race, and it remained in operation into the 1970s.[28] The rise of actuarial risk assessments in sentencing and release decisions, which complemented the era's attempts to proceduralize criminal justice in the name of progressive reform, ultimately reinforced the system's racial biases.[29] Burgess and the Gluecks and the jurisdictions that enacted their ideas thought they were relying on cutting-edge science to turn penal determinations into objective calculations, but their work was infused with prejudiced assumptions about incorrigibility. Attempts to predict criminal risk scientifically—and doing so with racial bias—have had a long history linked to rehabilitative thinking about incorrigibility.

This history sheds light on why the progressive currents driving other aspects of New Deal politics did not translate into benevolent crime policy. Punitive politics remained consonant with state commitments to rehabilitation during the era of the rehabilitative ideal's dominance, a fact that was especially clear in the spread of habitual offender laws.

Habitual Offender Laws

Habitual offender laws, popular among the states from the 1920s through the 1940s, were designed to target recidivists with long prison terms. Rehabilitation, indeterminate sentencing, and habitual offender laws were seen, not as contradictory policies, but as complementary components of rehabilitative systems distinguishing curable from incurable inmates. While habitual offender laws seem fundamentally contrary to rehabilitative values, close analysis shows how they were often understood as the hard end of the rehabilitative program.

New York ignited the spread of habitual offender laws with the passage of the Baumes Laws in 1926. Sponsored by New York state senator Caleb Baumes, these reforms reduced behavioral early release incentives for inmates, increased sentences for recidivists, and instituted life sentences for fourth felony convictions. Rebecca McLennan presents the Baumes Laws as a deviation from New York's larger emphasis on managerial penology, a philosophy of prison administration focused on managing rather than reforming inmates.[30] This is true; the ideology underpinning the laws ran contrary to the managerial currents also shaping New York penal policy, contributing to an incoherent vision of justice in the state. Baumes defended the laws bearing his name by stating that their purpose was providing "protection to the public" against "incurable" offenders, not prison management.[31] In 1927, the New York State Crime Commission reiterated Baumes's arguments, claiming that the laws' purpose was to contain offenders who "cannot be changed by reform." The commission's report noted that the laws implemented ideas rehabilitative criminologists long articulated, particularly that "punishments should be made to suit the criminal, not the crime."[32]

The commission stated that "there is nothing new about this statute" because it simply replicated New York's 1907 habitual offender law, which had gone unenforced owing to poor recordkeeping and failures in communication between prosecutors, the police, and the courts.[33] The history behind the 1907 law highlights deeper links to rehabilitative ideology. For years preceding its passage in 1907, New York's state board of charities (SBC) advocated for it through rehabilitative theory. The 1905 SBC report cited Brockway's use of indeterminate sentences at Elmira to release reformed offenders and provide "permanent detention" to "those who by defect of character or constitution" required containment. It concluded that a habitual offender law was necessary because "incorrigible offenders should be permanently segregated by the state" and that the indeterminate sentence "should be relieved of its maximum limit."[34] The 1907 SBC report supported the new law, citing scholars like Dugdale and Lombroso as proving that habitual criminals are a "distinct class" requiring long-term and potentially permanent restraint. It praised the implementation of a "genuinely indeterminate sentence" for incorrigibles.[35] This 1907 statute, which the Baumes Laws copied, was understood as a logical extension of indeterminate sentencing.

The laws' connections to rehabilitative ideology were made clear in the first prosecution under them. After holding up a store, a twenty-one-year-old man was sentenced to life under the statutes in August 1926. At his sentencing, the judge cited his failure to reform during his prior stays at Elmira: "Hanson, you have four other complaints against you in addition to the one older offense. You had punishment when you were sent to Elmira Reformatory. It did you no good. You are no good to yourself or society. I sentence you to life imprisonment and direct that you be kept there for the natural extent of your life."[36] In design and implementation, the Baumes Laws were tied to rehabilitative aims. Speaking before the New York State Bankers'

Association, Baumes stated that the laws were "not retributive nor vindictive" and explained that "[t]hese laws may provide the last and only chance for the redemption of hardened criminals, because if these men go to prison for life they must go to church."[37] Baumes's religious spin on rehabilitation demonstrates the malleability of the ideology as he framed his policies as a component of the rehabilitative model paving a path to divine redemption. But underlaying his statement was an unshakable assumption of incorrigibility—he said that his laws "may" offer individuals a last chance at redemption, acknowledging that not all will succeed.

The New York Court of Appeals upheld the Baumes Laws in 1927. It noted that rehabilitation was an important goal and that early release incentives often promoted "the rescue and reformation of the individual," with the qualification that "the laws enacted for the reformation of the criminal should be administered with caution and circumspection." To ensure that punishment is dispensed when necessary, a habitual offender law was a necessity. The court stated that in determining a sentence, the defendant's past convictions and behavior "have much to do with the way he should be treated," whether that entails rehabilitation or a life sentence.[38]

Three years later, the Supreme Court of New York further showed how integral the laws were to rehabilitative pursuits. In *People v. Spellman* (1930), a judge sentenced a defendant convicted of several concurrent felonies to a life sentence under the Baumes Laws. The individual had only two priors, but the sentencing judge determined that the concurrent offenses triggered both the third and the fourth convictions, thus warranting a life sentence. But the New York Supreme Court reversed, saying that the Baumes Laws "humanely and justly required a mandatory life sentence only after three or more fully completed, legal, prior judgments of conviction, *separated sufficiently to offer opportunity for the felon to reform*."[39] In other words, the defendant would have to serve his sentence for these offenses and be convicted on a fourth occasion after his release—squandering his third rehabilitative opportunity—to trigger the Baumes Laws' most severe solution. The laws were, thus, interpreted as giving the state a mechanism for distinguishing those still deserving rehabilitative opportunities from those who no longer did.

On several occasions through the twentieth century, the Supreme Court of New York recognized that the Baumes Laws were grounded on rehabilitative theory. It noted that the "theory of . . . the so-called Baumes Laws . . . is that they [repeat offenders] have not reformed since their first offense but have persisted in breaking the law."[40] As a primitive form of three-strikes sentencing, the Baumes Laws treated individuals' third failure to rehabilitate, not their third offense, as the third strike. This is a nuanced but important distinction underscoring how the habitual offender law was rationalized as a necessary counterbalance to the indeterminate sentence within the rehabilitative scheme.

Race and class considerations were crucial to the trajectory of the Baumes Laws, but their roles in this history were intricate. The laws were written largely to target gangsters during Prohibition, but in effect they disproportionately ensnared destitute low-level White offenders, prompting some backlash. There were high-profile instances of jury nullification in Baumes Laws cases, and some criminal justice officials expressed distaste for them. Fears that the laws would significantly harm a generation of young White men prompted then governor Franklin Roosevelt to reform them by replacing the mandatory life sentence for fourth-time offenders with a fifteen-year minimum while reinstituting some early release incentives. These racialized concerns over the laws' target population tempered their most punitive elements.[41] However, even after the reforms, punishments were still unduly harsh. A fifteen-year minimum was hardly generous for laws with a clear record of targeting poor offenders with records of petty crimes. The reforms did not erase the laws' brutal class effects; they merely shaved down their fangs without removing them, leaving intact their potential to deliver a painful class bite. The laws' underlying logic that repeat offending and poverty were evidence of incorrigibility persisted in drastic sentencing enhancements for individuals with records full of past convictions for even minor offenses. But these minimal reforms were too little, too late anyway as the Baumes Laws became a model for other states.

One of those states was California. While New York was *a* leader, California was arguably *the* leader of penal reform in the mid-twentieth century and was "ground zero" for the era's rehabilitative movement.[42] California's Youth Authority (YA) and Adult Authority (AA) put the Golden State at the forefront of prison reform in the 1940s. Established by the Prison Reorganization Act of 1944, the YA and the AA were to be exemplars of progressive corrections. They were tasked with classifying adult and juvenile offenders on the basis of their criminal tendencies and matching them to a correctional institution suited to their needs. Both functioned like parole boards, determining the length of an inmate's stay under the indeterminate sentence. The AA recognized the 1944 Reorganization Act as laying the foundation of the state's correctional treatment program dedicated to the "rehabilitative treatment of men and women committed to the prisons of California."[43] However, after the authorities' creation, California saw its prison population rise from 5,700 in 1944 to 19,202 in 1958.[44] Scrutiny of the state's habitual offender law and its implementation by the YA and the AA offers insight into how California's

attempts to individualize treatment brought more sophistication in predict-
ing risk, promoting a focus on reducing recidivism by preemptively identifying incorrigibles.

These dynamics appeared in the 1944 California Department of Corrections (CDOC) "Progress Report." The report described the AA as embodying
"a new approach to the problems of reformation and rehabilitation." It laid
out four guiding principles for the AA. The first two were the "preparation of
the offender for his return to society" and the identification of "the underlying causes of criminality in each case" to provide individualized treatment.
The second two highlighted the harsh duality of rehabilitation: the identification of inmates who "can reasonably be expected to go forth and become
useful, law-abiding citizens" and the identification of "those prisoners who,
because of mental abnormalities or deeply rooted criminal behavior patterns,
would constitute a menace to society" and "should be held as long as is possible under their commitments."[45]

The AA and the YA helped design California's base expectancy tables,
the risk-prediction instrument intended to categorize inmates on the basis
of a multifactor scale quantifying criminal risk.[46] The tables were intended
to guide sentencing, release, and the sorting of inmates to institutions.[47] The
model explicitly included only four factors—prior commitments, escapes, offense type, and race—but left room for administrators to consider other factors like misbehavior at school or psychological evaluations.[48]

The AA acknowledged that it had "positive instructions" to manage rehabilitative programs and a "negative purpose" to incarcerate incorrigibles. A
1951 AA report stated:

> [C]lassification is the study of the individual prisoner for the purposes of un-
> derstanding his needs and of providing an administrative procedure for car-
> rying out a program for his rehabilitation. . . . [T]he program of the prison
> is aimed, therefore, toward the understanding of the individual in order to
> insure his best possible training and treatment in the institution and to facili-
> tate his adjustment later in society. The negative purpose of classification is,
> however, not to be overlooked. Those exceptional inmates whose criminality
> seems relatively incurable in terms of present-day knowledge, are assigned by
> classification procedures to humane, but also secure, custodial care.

The report also stated that the AA's tasks should be administered with "a view
to [the inmate's] reformation and to the protection of society" and that "classification is regarded as the foundation in the California prison system." It
tasked the director of corrections with collecting data on inmates in order to
systematically engage in the "scientific study of each prisoner, his career and

life history, the cause of his criminal acts and recommendations for his care, training, and employment with a view to his reformation and to the protection of society."[49]

Two years after the creation of the AA, its chair worked with the state's director of corrections to conduct studies of habitual criminals at several state institutions. The studies were "of great value to members of the legislature in considering the passage of an improved Habitual Criminal Law."[50] Passed in 1946, the habitual offender statute gave judges the ability to give a life sentence to third-time felons. It included exceptions permitting habitual offenders to be considered for parole under specific circumstances, but it remained an early version of a three-strikes law tied to the logic of rehabilitative ideology.

California courts upheld the state's habitual offender law on grounds comparable to those used by New York courts. In *People v. Richardson* (1946), the California Court of Appeals dismissed arguments that being punished more severely for previous behavior constituted a violation of double jeopardy because habitual criminality was "a status," not an offense. This status aggravated the sentence because the defendant "comes within the classification of those who probably may never be reformed."[51] California courts repeatedly ruled against claims that habitual offender laws violated double jeopardy because the laws created a status specifically for those "who have proved immune to lesser punishment."[52] Courts in Washington, Minnesota, Nebraska, and New Jersey rejected double jeopardy challenges to their habitual offender laws on similar grounds.[53]

In 1967, the California Court of Appeals rendered a ruling that was almost a replica of *People v. Spellman*, in which a defendant was sentenced to life after committing three offenses simultaneously. The court ruled that for the habitual offender law to apply, a defendant's convictions must be separated to provide "two chances of rehabilitation." It stated that the purpose of "any" habitual offender law "is not obscure." Such a law serves two purposes: "(1) to act as a deterrent to repeated criminal acts while affording the criminal two . . . opportunities to rehabilitation, and (2) to protect society against the incorrigible recidivist." Concurrent crimes did not constitute proof of *habitual criminality* because that label applied only to those who have experienced "separate terms . . . for separate offenses separately sentenced" that "have been followed by separate chances at rehabilitation." The court concluded that "the third time around defendant, to adopt the vernacular, 'has had it.'"[54]

As in New York, racial considerations influenced the law's evolution in California, but racial dynamics pushed officials in different directions. From the 1940s through the 1960s, California prison administrators fought to limit the power of treatment staff by pushing electric shock, hydrotherapy, and other forms of harsh justice as "treatment." This abuse intensified the already-aggravated racial tensions between the mostly White prison staff and the largely Black and Latino prison population. Minority inmate coalitions subsequently organized to demand improved treatment and a host of other rights, prompting inmate strikes at multiple institutions and exacerbating existing antagonisms. But the self-advocacy of Black and Latino inmates boomeranged to the state's advantage—their actions validated the popular racist assumptions of risk that got the inmates institutionalized in the first place. Correctional administrators won the public relations contest by insisting that a law-and-order approach was necessary to control the recalcitrant prisoners.[55] This illustrates how racial and class factors undergirding separate states' rehabilitative models manifested in different ways, leading to divergent outcomes.

New York and California were not the only states that saw value in Caleb Baumes's ideas. Over the two decades following the passage of the Baumes Laws, forty-two states and Washington, DC, passed legislation based on them.[56] Five states attempted to pass versions of the Baumes Laws only one year after New York.[57] In 1927, the county prosecutor in Minneapolis said that the state's proposed version of the Baumes Laws "gives prosecuting attorneys the power to deal severely with the man who will not reform."[58] Thirty-two states authorized life sentences in varying circumstances—including for a fourth, third, or, in the case of Arizona, a second felony—with different degrees of judicial discretion. Figure 2 outlines these variations.

Academic analysis from the time suggests that these laws were broadly understood as consistent with the rehabilitative mission. For example, George Brown wrote in 1945 that habitual offender laws were "regarded as a reformatory measure." He described them as the logical end of the indeterminate sentence, claiming that "the indeterminate sentence affords the best opportunity" for the treatment of "recidivists who are reformable" but that "those lacking reformable characteristics . . . would be restrained for life" via the habitual offender law. He explained that this understanding of habitual criminality was "no doubt" traceable to "the work of Lombroso."[59]

The analysis in this chapter scrutinizes only New York and California, and it remains uncertain whether other states adopted habitual offender laws on the basis of rehabilitative logic or alternative reasons. Brown's work suggests a connection, but it would be overreaching to suggest that every state integrated its habitual offender law with a rehabilitative correctional system as states likely had varied understandings of their laws' purposes. But, as two of the era's national leaders in criminal justice reform, New York and California illustrate what is possible when the punitive prong of the rehabilitative ideal is

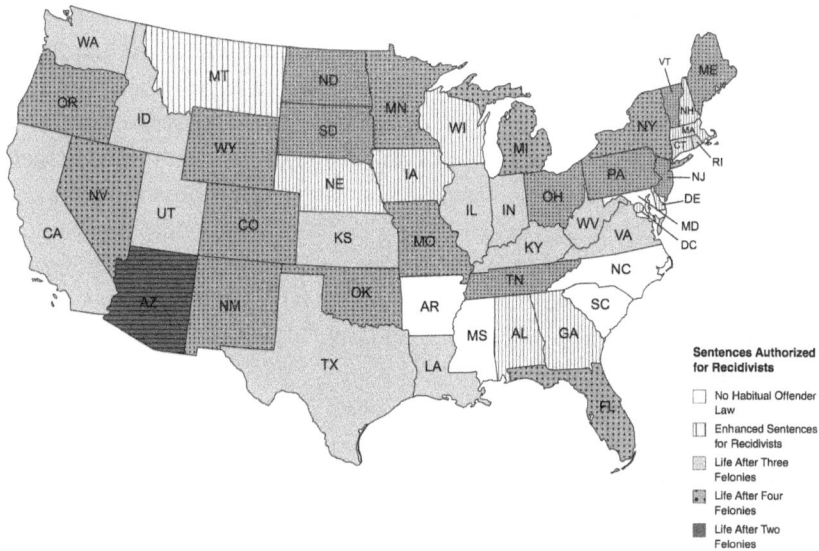

FIGURE 2 Map of habitual offender laws authorizing life terms, 1947. (Map created with mapchart.net.)

taken to its extreme. In these states, habitual offender laws were understood, not just as consistent with rehabilitative ideology, but as its logical end.

Figure 2 indicates that southeastern states were less likely to adopt stringent habitual offender laws than were their northern counterparts, but this should not be interpreted as a sign that southern justice was particularly kind. Previous chapters have explained that rehabilitative ideas took hold differently in the South, where disproportionately Black criminal populations were controlled through convict leasing, segregation, and extralegal mechanisms distinct from those of northern reformatories but still understood as consistent with components of rehabilitative philosophy. Southern lawmakers may have viewed habitual offender laws as unnecessary as southern Blacks accused of crimes were still often subjected to vigilante White-supremacist violence rather than being brought to court and rarely were treated fairly when they did get trials.[60] Southern states also led the charge in death sentencing during this era, which disproportionately affected Black defendants.[61] And, in the postwar South, eugenics reemerged as a means of racial control—especially against Black women—even as its popularity diminished elsewhere.[62] This suggests that political and racial conditions unique to the South explain why social control instincts connected to rehabilitation did not produce the same changes seen elsewhere. But today, southern states have some of the most punitive three-strikes laws in the nation, which look just like midcentury habitual offender laws. As was the case with indeterminate sentencing, antitramp laws, and eugenics, habitual offender sentencing was delayed in reaching the South. This is evidence of a common historical trend in which southern states are slower to embrace punitive innovations linked to rehabilitative ideology. Instead, they have tended to remain committed to older forms of racial control on the grounds that such techniques are appropriate for managing their overwhelmingly incorrigible criminal population until those practices become politically indefensible, prompting them to adopt punitive programs dressed in rehabilitative language that were already popularized elsewhere.

This history lays bare how core assumptions of Lombrosian theory remained embedded in rehabilitative philosophy. Habitual offender laws did not produce mass incarceration at midcentury, given the limits on prison capacity and the high cost of institutionalizing that many people, but their popularity illustrates that a politics for mass incarceration rooted in rehabilitative ideology existed long before mass incarceration emerged. The midcentury resurgence of rehabilitation revitalized its core individualistic and determinist principles, with state lawmakers articulating these ideas to justify the harsh policies accompanying rehabilitative programs. But once critical empirical evaluation was reapplied to the rehabilitative model in the 1970s, the punitive facets of rehabilitative ideology were amplified to a new degree by the tough-on-crime movement.

The Punitive Turn and the Federal Sentencing Guidelines

When the influence of the rehabilitative ideal reached its zenith in the early 1970s, indeterminate sentencing was the rule in every state and at the federal level. But in contrast to earlier scholarship identifying the 1970s as a moment when the rehabilitative ideal was abandoned in favor of punitive politics, more recent scholarship illustrates how rehabilitative logic has been interpreted as consistent with various punitive policies and practices in the modern era.[63] This section shows how seeds for the punitive turn were sown in rehabilitative ideology, which was discreetly repurposed rather than rejected in the immediate lead-up to mass incarceration.

The rehabilitative ideal long defined itself as an evidence-based project offering ostensibly scientific means for separating corrigibles and incorrigibles in order to maximize recidivism reduction. As the CDOC wrote in 1948, "The objective of our correctional system is to return to society a better product than was received. All of the study, education, treatment, and training that a man receives in an institution will be lost and the time and effort expended wasted if the paroling process is not an effective one."[64] By adopting the language of scientific efficacy and objectivity, the rehabilitative ideal disguises how distinguishing corrigibility from incorrigibility always requires subjective value judgments. And by adopting recidivism reduction as a key measure of effectiveness, the rehabilitative project sets itself up for failure since criminality is not merely an individual pathology (as the rehabilitative framework assumes), but a product of a totality of circumstances. When rehabilitation was empirically assessed by social science in the 1970s and deemed ineffective, the tough-on-crime movement capitalized on the ideal's punitive elements.

During the years of the Great Society and the civil rights movement, liberals reinvigorated talk of rehabilitation. In a 1967 report, President Johnson's Crime Commission endorsed funding for in-prison rehabilitative interventions like education and parole while stressing the continued importance of classifying offenders by needs and corrigibility in order to individualize treatment.[65] The National Council on Crime and Delinquency's "Model Sentencing Act," published five years later, articulated a similar logic, stating that "persons convicted of crime shall be dealt with in accordance with their potential for rehabilitation, considering their individual characteristics, circumstances, and needs," while emphasizing that "dangerous offenders shall be identified, segregated, and correctively treated in custody for as long terms as needed."[66]

This revitalization of rehabilitation paved the way for the famous critique of the rehabilitative ideal advanced by Robert Martinson, a professor at the City College of New York. Martinson's 1974 article "What Works?" detailed what he deemed inadequacies in the rehabilitative approach. He opened by noting the centrality of rehabilitation to American penal practice, stating that "American prisons, perhaps more than those of any other country, have stood or fallen in public esteem according to their ability to fulfill their promise of rehabilitation." But his analysis of multiple institutions employing diverse rehabilitative strategies uncovered little evidence of recidivism reduction, leading him to conclude that there existed "very little reason to hope that we have in fact found a sure way of reducing recidivism through rehabilitation."[67]

Martinson's work was widely criticized, and he retracted many of his claims within a few years.[68] But the damage was done. His conclusion was dubbed the "nothing works" doctrine and was embraced by penal conservatives energized by empirical grounding to discredit rehabilitative interventions.[69] The conventional story concludes that this embrace of "nothing works" led to the abandonment of the ideal. It is true that a new coalition of conservative intellectuals and tough-on-crime lawmakers weaponized Martinson's work to reframe popular understandings of criminality to justify the punitive turn. But their politics—and many punitive post-1970 reforms—drew on logic directly traceable to rehabilitative ideology.

Martinson's study prompted a barrage of conservative intellectual reassessments of rehabilitation. Two years after "What Works?," the report *Doing Justice* was published by the Committee for the Study of Incarceration with funding from the Field and the New World Foundations. The authors wrote, "To our surprise, we found ourselves returning to the ideas of such Enlightenment thinkers as Kant and Beccaria—ideas that antedated notions of rehabilitation that emerged in the nineteenth century."[70] The committee's director, Andrew Von Hirsch, became a leading scholar of just deserts, a philosophy of punishment rooted in Kantian retributivism that interpreted punishment as a form of moral condemnation commensurate to the immorality of the offense. Beccaria, the committee's other source of inspiration, famously theorized that in order to achieve deterrence, punishment should be swift, certain, and proportionate to the crime. These ideas differed from rehabilitation by directing sentences to be tailored to the offense, reorienting attention back onto the crime rather than the criminal.

One of the most significant players in the Right's intellectual crusade was James Q. Wilson, who advocated for a new brand of crime politics by blending classical deterrence theory with notions of the naturally incorrigible criminal. His book *Thinking about Crime* (1975) clearly outlined the punitive discursive shift sought by the Right.[71] In the book, Wilson insisted that "[w]icked people exist" and that "[n]othing avails them except to set them apart from innocent people."[72] The second edition of *Thinking about Crime* incorporated a chapter discussing studies validating the "nothing works" doctrine and claiming that indeterminate sentencing rested on "heroic assumptions" about reformability.[73] Decades later, as debate over the infamous 1994 federal crime bill was wrapping up, Wilson continued to sound the alarm with searing rhetoric painting young offenders as atavistic degenerates through language recalling the Lombrosian incorrigible. He wrote that innocent people walked the streets terrified of being shot "by youngsters who afterward show us the blank, unremorseful faces of seemingly feral, presocial beings."[74] His language previewed the oncoming moral panic over juvenile "superpredators" that would grip the nation in the 1990s and facilitated severe juvenile justice policies out of fears that a generation of morally bankrupt young men would wreak havoc on the nation by doing, as John DiIulio wrote, "what comes 'naturally': murder, rape, rob, assault, burglarize, deal deadly drugs, and get high."[75] Wilson thus endorsed determinate sentences limiting judicial discretion and early release opportunities as the answer to the crime problem.

This gave the conservative law-and-order movement intellectual ammunition to link liberal welfarist and civil rights commitments as misguided attempts at social benevolence that increased crime. The Right's outward rejection of rehabilitation had evident racial and class dimensions. The GOP sought to connect the civil rights movement to urban crime in order to stoke racial anxieties among southern Democrats displeased with the party's support for civil rights.[76] Meanwhile, Republicans attacked the War on Poverty for failing to produce an immediate reduction in crime via welfare, allowing the GOP to contend that crime was a personal choice among poor populations who proved unworthy of state generosity in the wake of these allegedly failed attempts at liberal egalitarianism.[77] It was in this context that the work of Martinson, Von Hirsch, and Wilson found a receptive audience hostile to liberal social programs and happy to write off the crime problems of inner cities as manifestations of Black and poor urbanites' personal faults.[78]

The story of Martinson and the rehabilitative ideal's fall from grace is well-trodden history for most scholars of American criminal justice, but an unappreciated aspect of this saga is that Martinson was anything but a law-and-order zealot. He was a left-leaning academic and civil rights activist who spent time incarcerated for protesting segregation.[79] His 1974 article was never intended as a harsh justice screed. Instead, he hoped that his research would help shut prisons down, not turn them into human warehouses. By showing that prison rehabilitation was ineffective, he meant to argue that attempts to reform prisons and make them humane rehabilitative institutions were futile, concluding that prisons "cannot be reformed and must be gradually torn down."[80] But despite his intentions, his radical recommendation to shutter prisons never took hold in the public zeitgeist. Once his work entered the political arena, his ideas ricocheted in unanticipated directions and were harnessed by a movement with an entirely different understanding of his work's implications. His research unintentionally legitimated the aims of a conservative law-and-order coalition bent on pushing the message that it was not prisons that were unsalvageable, as Martinson had claimed, but people.

Martinson's story reminds us that the rehabilitative ideal's influence on American political development has been anything but clean. It has always been deployed in contested environments populated by actors with competing political motives. This underscores the challenges that well-intentioned reformist actors face when navigating the politics of rehabilitation. Martinson's conclusion that prisons should be shuttered because they could not rehabilitate offenders was doomed to backfire as a critique of institutional arrangements built on the rehabilitative ideal's dual premises. Martinson misunderstood that the American correctional system's commitment to the rehabilitative ideal never embodied a promise of redemption for all; it was always a commitment to sorting the corrigible from the incorrigible. In this context, no one read Martinson's work as evidence that prisons should be dismantled.

Instead, it was interpreted as proof that conservatives were right in claiming that the prison population had been badly misjudged. A far greater proportion of inmates was incorrigible than anyone had ever imagined.

As the conservative shift gained traction in the mid-1970s, leftist intellectuals and politicians joined the cause. Citing mounting social science research, liberal scholars and practitioners like Marvin Frankel and Charles Silberman became critical of rehabilitation. Senator Edward Kennedy (D-MA) famously criticized indeterminate sentencing on the grounds that it produced inconsistent and arbitrary outcomes, notably across racial dimensions. His rejection of rehabilitation was less rooted in punitiveness, but his impulse was to move in the same direction as conservatives by condemning indeterminate rehabilitative models. This broad alliance rendered rhetorical opposition to rehabilitation the only viable political position by the late 1970s. This established the context in which the federal sentencing guidelines—largely Kennedy's brainchild—became law, a fact that many scholars interpret as a final blow to the rehabilitative ideal.

The popularization of mandatory sentencing schemes like the federal guidelines followed the discrediting of indeterminacy. The Sentencing Reform Act (SRA) of 1984 created the US Sentencing Commission (USSC), which was tasked with promulgating sentencing guidelines for federal judges. The eventual guidelines were, as Michael Tonry noted, "oriented more toward toughness than toward fairness" given how dramatically they increased sentences.[81] But the legislative development of the federal guidelines was a messy affair, not a beeline toward punitiveness or uncontested application of rehabilitative ideology's harsh qualities. Naomi Murakawa has shown that over the bill's life Kennedy made concessions that jettisoned notable anticarceral features in his original proposal. His early bill retained parole and good time credits, included alternatives to incarceration for certain offenders, and directed the USSC to produce guidelines that did not exceed prison capacity. But as the country moved to the right, Kennedy compromised by abandoning his support for parole, good time credits, and alternatives to incarceration while the USSC was authorized to recommend expanding prison capacity rather than being bound by it.[82] This route to the final guidelines was a circuitous one, but within this thicket, lawmakers effectively mobilized the punitive prong of the rehabilitative ideal to justify specific policy choices. While the guidelines were a product of diverse forces, it is worth exploring how principles of the rehabilitative ideal were adapted and deployed to shape them.

Notably, guidelines are diverse. Numerous states have guidelines, and not all followed the same path as the federal system. Some states use guidelines that have functioned without promoting an escalation of prison capacity comparable to what has unfolded at the federal level, while others adopted systems similar to the federal guidelines and witnessed spikes in their prison populations.[83] But while state guidelines are built on varied ideas, it is important to realize that lawmakers and political interests advocating for the punitive federal guidelines effectively deployed precepts of rehabilitative ideology to sell their preferred policies and incorporate them into the system. The rejection of the indeterminate sentence represented a denunciation of the core policy of rehabilitation, and it would be reasonable to expect that the guidelines would be built on theories of punishment that, if not Kantian or Beccarian, at least eschewed rehabilitation. But ideological innovations of rehabilitative ideology—notably, the predictive containment of incorrigibles based on reformative potential—remained central to the SRA and the federal guidelines as criminal history became a surrogate for incorrigibility. This embrace of the rehabilitative ideal's punitive logic was hidden underneath rhetoric damning its redemptive features.

A good case in point is in the testimony of Stephen Trott, the assistant attorney general, to the House Judiciary Committee about the 1984 law. Trott provided testimony riddled with contradictory assertions rejecting the rehabilitative ideal in the abstract while simultaneously endorsing certain aspects of it. He told lawmakers that "it has been generally concluded that there exists no satisfactory means of inducing rehabilitation," directly citing Martinson and Von Hirsch to make his case. But he abruptly changed course later by couching a defense of a punitive position within the rhetoric of rehabilitation. Specifically, he attacked proposed provisions that would forgive defendants for not admitting prior convictions under court order. He explained that forgiving defendants for lying or omitting such information was inconsistent with "the interests of encouraging rehabilitation of offenders" and risked "the potential for causing public harm," thus warranting sentencing enhancements under these circumstances.[84] Therefore, for Trott, rehabilitative considerations were irrelevant unless they justified a more punitive outcome.

Benjamin Baer, the chair of the US Parole Commission, similarly harbored support for rehabilitative ideology that could be missed given his rhetorical denunciation of the ideal. Baer emphasized that decades of empirical research "generally fail[ed] to demonstrate that institutional rehabilitative programs are effective." He went on to claim that issuing sentences with uncertain release dates inflicts harmful "psychological stress" on inmates and is therefore "morally unjustifiable." These problems "render[ed] the argument for an increase in determinacy compelling." But he then suggested that under determinate models "participation in prison rehabilitative programs may show more positive effects since such participation will be voluntary, not merely to impress the parole board."[85] People would have the chance to rehabilitate themselves in Baer's preferred system but with reduced incentives for early release, which he believed rendered inmates' rehabilitative efforts superficial attempts to please prison administrators. Baer explicitly defended harsh determinate sentencing, a direct reversal of rehabilitative penology's core approach to punishment, but as a way to *improve* rehabilitative outcomes rather than abandon them.

Congress also heard from the Pennsylvania Guidelines Commission when contemplating the design of the federal guidelines. In a summary of Pennsylvania's system, state officials explained their rationale for including a defendant's criminal history score to determine a sentencing range, a design choice that was incorporated into the federal guidelines. The summary clarified that a criminal history axis was included so that "the recidivist [would] be given priority in being allocated prison space, even if this means that a first time felon remains in the community, because recidivism is the best predictor of future criminality."[86] This indicates that concerns over rehabilitative potential were not discarded by lawmakers in the 1980s.

It is undeniable that the indeterminate sentence—the rehabilitative ideal's flagship policy innovation—was deemed a failed project. The consequence was a reining in of the justice system's flexibility to adapt sentencing on the basis of corrigibility determinations. But to suggest that this constituted a wholesale rejection of the rehabilitative ideal oversimplifies the complexities of sentencing, the nuances of rehabilitative ideology, and how deeply rooted the ideal's assumptions were in the American legal system by the 1980s. Concerns about future criminality, potential for reform, and criminal history remained central to the lawmakers crafting the guidelines in the 1980s. But in the era's political climate, it was assumed that a heightened proportion of inmates was incorrigible. To borrow Wilson's language, too many people were simply "wicked," thus legitimating enhanced punitiveness and shifting sentencing practices.

As the law neared passage, lawmakers endorsed rehabilitative ideology behind seeming denunciations. In a 1983 report about the SRA, the Senate Judiciary Committee wrote that "imprisonment is not an appropriate means of promoting correction and rehabilitation."[87] The House Judiciary Committee similarly specified that "[t]he bill prohibits the use of rehabilitation as a rationale for imprisonment."[88] However, neither report wholly rejected rehabilitation, noting that circumstances existed under which rehabilitative goals were appropriate sentencing considerations. The Senate Committee clarified that "the Committee does not suggest that efforts to rehabilitate prisoners should be abandoned" and acknowledged that although "arguments were

advanced that rehabilitation should be eliminated completely as a purpose
of sentencing" during hearings, "[t]he Committee has rejected this view." The
report stated that the law required judges to consider "the four purposes of
sentencing," which included "to provide rehabilitation," while the House Judiciary Committee report similarly stated that rehabilitation was "a permissible
reason for imposing a sentence."[89] Both committees recognized the value of
rehabilitative goals in sentencing but believed that rehabilitative aims were
ill served through incarceration and should instead be served in other ways,
often alternative sanctions that were available only under narrowly limited
circumstances. This logic relied on distinguishing the reformable offenders
granted noncarceral sentences from the incorrigibles for whom incarceration
was appropriate. Therefore, when the act charged the USSC with the duty
of writing the guidelines, Congress left it room to incorporate rehabilitative
considerations.

When the Supreme Court upheld the constitutionality of the SRA in
Mistretta v. U.S. (1989), it interpreted the legislative history as a rebuke of
the rehabilitative ideal, concluding that all evidence suggested that "the efforts of the criminal justice system to achieve rehabilitation of offenders had
failed." Given the "shameful" disparities and inconsistencies of indeterminate
sentencing, the Court explained that Congress replaced it with guidelines
designed to "establish a range of determinate sentences for categories of offenses and defendants according to various specified factors."[90] It is some-
what strange that the Court claimed that the guidelines constituted a categorical rejection of rehabilitation given what the USSC said in the manual it
published to accompany the guidelines. The first page of the 1987 guidelines
manual explicitly stated four purposes of punishment: "deterring crime, incapacitating the offender, providing just punishment, and rehabilitating the
offender." These purposes, including rehabilitation, were repeated throughout the manual. Confinement in halfway houses, substance abuse centers,
mental health institutions, and similar facilities as conditions of probation or
supervised release were narrowly authorized as sentencing options serving
rehabilitative goals.[91]

Published in 1987, the guidelines constructed a matrix that primarily
considered two factors—offense seriousness and an offender's criminal history—in specifying a tightly confined range in which federal judges could
sentence offenders. Predictive incapacitation, the logical reciprocal of rehabilitation, influenced the guidelines regime through this heavy emphasis on
criminal history. The USSC explicitly linked predictive incapacitation to rehabilitative ideology, criminal history, and risk prediction. Defending criminal history as an indicator of risk that warranted a lengthened sentence, the

USSC claimed that "[t]o protect the public . . . the likelihood of recidivism and future criminal behavior must be considered" because "[r]epeated criminal behavior is an indicator of a limited likelihood of successful rehabilitation."[92] This reflected the conclusions of the House Judiciary Committee, which called criminal history "one of the most reliable predictors of further criminal conduct."[93] A criminal history score was predicated not only on the number and type of past convictions, but also on "diversionary dispositions" defendants had received in state courts. Through diversionary dispositions, states authorized judges to grant noncarceral punishments for rehabilitative purposes without a formal conviction.[94] By incorporating diversionary dispositions into the criminal history score, the USSC ensured that "defendants who receive the benefit of a rehabilitative sentence and continue to commit crimes [would] not be treated with further leniency."[95] Further, the guidelines' controversial relevant conduct provision permitted judges to consider uncharged, dismissed, or acquitted conduct when determining a defendant's criminal risk, reformative potential, and sentence. In 1997, the Supreme Court upheld the relevant conduct provision by citing *Williams v. New York* (1949), which upheld indeterminate sentencing on rehabilitative grounds.[96] All this undercuts claims that the guidelines reflected an unconditional dismissal of rehabilitative thought.

At some points, the USSC suggested that considering criminal history was consonant with just deserts and utilitarian goals in addition to rehabilitative ones, but this rests on dubious reasoning.[97] Scholars of just-deserts retributivism identify a difficulty in considering criminal history within a penological frame asserting that individuals morally deserve punishments directly commensurate to the immorality and severity of their particular crimes. Incorporating considerations of past behavior into sentencing undermines efforts to customize punishment to the moral severity of each specific offense.[98] The utilitarian Wilson suggested that enhanced punishments for recidivism were unlikely to work given that recidivists are not deterrable, but he also said that "[i]t is possible that severity is the enemy of certainty and speed," citing Beccaria's axiom that excessive severity could distort the deterrent effects of punishment by twisting the incentive structure for would-be lawbreakers.[99] Increasing sentences on the basis of past behavior is difficult to square with retributivist and deterrence theories, but it was designed as an essential corollary to rehabilitation by penologists who used recidivism to identify incorrigibles.

The federal guidelines illustrate how an overwhelming emphasis on criminal history carries eugenic fictions of inherent criminality into US criminal justice. The shift from indeterminate to determinate schemes was significant, but there was continuity between the systems. Constraints on judicial discretion and early release opportunities along with the use of criminal history to in-crease sentences to an extreme degree reflected anxieties that judges routinely underestimated incorrigibility. This was a crucial achievement of the puni-tive coalition—not dismissing rehabilitation, but reframing assumptions cen-tral to rehabilitative ideology to stoke fears that the criminal population was widely incorrigible. This led criminal history to be endorsed by lawmakers on the Left and the Right as an ostensibly race- and class-neutral measure of cor-rigibility. While this approach is not the same as the pseudoscientific medi-cal techniques of the Elmira wardens or the unapologetically racist actuarial assessments of Burgess and the Gluecks, it achieves the same outcome—it organizes people into categories of risk, reformability, and incorrigibility for differential treatment. This produces profoundly dissimilar punishments for similar crimes if the people who commit them are deemed unequal in their potential for reform based on their criminal record.

Given that criminal history is skewed across racial and class dimensions owing to regional variations in law enforcement practices, it is unsurprising that the guidelines have had well-documented and painful impacts for Black, Latino, and poor populations.[100] It bears repeating that the reframing of re-habilitation took place in the context of the broader conservative Southern Strategy capitalizing on southern White backlash to the Great Society and the civil rights movement. The GOP's assertion that a massive share of the popu-lation was incorrigible was part of this scheme, and in the public's mind the image of the repeat career criminal targeted by the guidelines was conflated with the image of a poor minority urbanite.[101] Heightened concerns about incorrigibility were not unusual; throughout US history, the curative and re-pressive facets of the rehabilitative ideal have swung back and forth in sync with punitive impulses and changing perceptions of incorrigibility.[102] But in the 1980s the force of that swing was harnessed by political entrepreneurs appealing to popular racial and classist anxieties following liberal policy vic-tories in the 1960s and 1970s, helping fuel the mass incarceration of the poor and people of color.

While lawmakers might say that they did not see the law's harmful racial and class impacts coming, they were warned. During hearings on the bill, Shanara Gilbert, a director for the National Conference of Black Lawyers, argued that "[r]ehabilitation has not failed" but that "[a] political decision was made that it was no longer fashionable to discuss rehabilitation as a goal." She asked lawmakers "whether reliance upon imprisonment as a solution to criminality is acceptable in a democratic society, particularly where impris-onment results primarily in the imprisonment of non-whites and the poor, with no rational relationship to the incidence of crime."[103] In discussing the risk factors considered in calculating sentences, Professor M. Kay Harris presciently warned legislators that many factors viewed as neutral and legitimate "may result in differential impact on certain groups," especially criminal record, which is characterized by "pronounced racial differences."[104] As Bernard Harcourt has written, modern risk-assessment practices are almost entirely dependent on criminal history, rendering risk "a proxy for race."[105]

Rehabilitation-oriented indeterminate sentencing was discredited by a suite of political and intellectual strategies in the late twentieth century. The case for determinacy suggested that harsh fixed sentences were the appropriate remedy for criminality, but it also capitalized on rehabilitative assumptions regarding offender incorrigibility. The hard shift toward unforgiving rigidity exemplified not a rejection of rehabilitation, but a growing anxiety that the prison system needed to handle its predominantly incorrigible population appropriately. The apparent rejection of rehabilitation was rooted in tough-on-crime policymakers exploiting foundational ideas from rehabilitative ideology to justify their politics.

Rehabilitation in the Twentieth Century

From the 1920s through the 1970s, American penology continued its push to perfect the science of sentencing, but the spread of rehabilitation brought with it an emphasis on both punitive and therapeutic sanctions during the era of the rehabilitative ideal's dominance. The individualizing frame of rehabilitation was the lens through which new ideas about criminality were channeled, ensuring that emerging social-structural theories of crime and New Deal collectivist politics failed to dislodge the justice system's emphasis on the atomized individual. Rehabilitative frameworks treated material inequalities as individual deficiencies linked to criminality that required narrow individualized solutions, quashing the potential to frame political economic reform as a solution to criminality. Meanwhile, rehabilitative rhetoric justified the harsh punishment of repeat offenders as criminal history morphed into a blunt measure of incorrigibility. The law-and-order policymakers fueling the punitive turn of the late twentieth century used the punitive prong of rehabilitative ideology to argue that America long underestimated the incorrigibility of its prison population, thus requiring a new approach to sentencing. Their express disapproval of the rehabilitative ideal masked a politics amplifying the ideal's most punitive elements to rationalize sweeping reforms.

Attempts to revive rehabilitative logic are misguided because it was never fully abandoned. Rehabilitative ideology's compassionate-sounding rhetoric has cloaked a punitive logic reliant on distinguishing corrigibility from incorrigibility throughout mass incarceration's genesis. As a result, those looking to challenge mass incarceration must understand that rehabilitative language will never dismantle harsh sentencing regimes that have long been politically interpreted as consistent with the ideology of rehabilitation. That habitual offender laws and punitive components of the federal guidelines were interpreted as consistent with the systemic logics of rehabilitation reveals why core features of the carceral state cannot be dismantled by a politics of rehabilitation. Progressive applications of rehabilitative theory will simply lead us to recalculate the balance of corrigibility and incorrigibility in the prison population more favorably toward corrigibility, maintaining harsh justice for incorrigibles while laying the groundwork for a modern variant of Martinson's "nothing works" doctrine to materialize if recidivism rates do not promptly and permanently drop. Weaponizing rehabilitative language to challenge the sentencing practices driving mass incarceration misunderstands this history and will likely have adverse consequences if mobilized against the system it helped produce.

The Persistence of Regulation:
Regulatory Responses to Corporate Lawbreaking

I suppose there is no agency in the world that can prevent crookedness.
RICHARD WHITNEY, president, New York Stock Exchange (1933)

Three years after the 1929 Wall Street crash, the beleaguered president of the New York Stock Exchange (NYSE), Richard Whitney, was called to testify before the congressional committee investigating the implosion. Prodded by the committee chair, Ferdinand Pecora, about market oversight, an exasperated Whitney said, "I suppose there is no agency in the world that can prevent crookedness."[1] This chapter evaluates three moments in which public outrage over corporate "crookedness" sparked significant government responses—securities reforms during the Great Depression, changes to the FTC during the consumer rights movement of the 1970s, and the savings and loan (S&L) crisis of the 1980s. Each witnessed meaningful challenges to corporate power in which features of regulatory ideology shaped political change, but each also shows significant variations in the nature of regulatory development.

First, during the Great Depression, Ferdinand Pecora's congressional investigation into Wall Street's collapse ignited populist anger over the behavior of America's financiers. But there were limits to Pecora's politics. What financiers did to cause the Depression was unethical in retrospect but not illegal at the time, a common refrain that corporate America recites to avoid punishment during scandals. The pattern that was present in the ICC and FTC deliberations—first the proposal of criminalization in response to discoveries of wrongdoing, then a drift toward regulatory schemes over the course of debate—reappeared in this case. But during the Great Depression, when lawmakers were anxious to revive markets, regulation was seen as safer than Pecora's retributivism. Lawmakers viewed the independent regulatory commission as a well-known means of market control rather than a novel innovation, embracing it as a solution with a proven history to navigate extraordinary economic uncertainties. Although populist demands for law and order often emerge following corporate scandals, Pecora's story illustrates how the institutional entrenchment of regulatory ideological principles during the Progressive era solidified regulation as the state's tested and time-honored answer to corporate illegality. In the case of securities markets, surging retributive impulses were systematically subordinated to familiar regulatory remedies with established institutional precedents.

Second, the chapter explores the consumer rights movement of the 1970s, which notched many victories. The blistering rhetoric of activists like Ralph Nader depicted consumers as victims wronged by corporate forces, leading to major changes in civil and tort law while empowering agencies' capacities to secure equitable relief. But analysis of the movement's attempts to remake the FTC illustrates limitations on its operations. Nader and his allies vocally condemned the FTC for neglecting to refer criminal cases to the Department of Justice (DOJ) or seek enhanced criminal sanction powers from Congress. But for several reasons they did not secure changes to the institution's criminal enforcement powers. The FTC's established patterns of practice did not treat criminal punishment as core to the agency's mission, and consumer activists were able to increase DOJ referrals at the FTC only temporarily via staffing changes that were undone by subsequent administrations. The case illustrates that, while the enforcement of regulatory law can be variable in different administrative hands, the ideas embedded in agency design can pose challenges to structural reform.

Finally, while observers often lament that rich offenders always have the resources to avoid conviction, over one thousand bankers were prosecuted after the S&L crisis. Some observers view this as a celebratory story in which the state signaled that it can prosecute serious and complex cases of corporate lawbreaking when it wants to. Alternatively, critical perspectives dismiss the case as a historical oddity or emphasize that the government prosecuted only a fraction of the fraud behind the crisis. But careful analysis leads to the measured conclusion that the S&L prosecutions were neither an unqualified success nor a complete charade. That this story belies claims that the state is totally incapable of securing corporate prosecutions and that the one thousand prosecutions constituted only a small portion of the fraud behind the crisis are both true. However, it is critical to recognize that political decisions to reduce market regulations fueled the crisis in the first place and rendered prosecution the state's sole weapon for handling the unmanageably massive fallout. This is a reminder that while regulatory ideology has produced condemnable inequalities, regulation is a valuable crime-prevention mechanism, and that while corporate prosecution has a role to play in keeping markets healthy, it is a purely reactive instrument that cannot do all the work involved in managing complex economic behavior. Had policymakers maintained muscular New Deal era banking regulations, they could have prevented or mitigated the crisis by intervening earlier in its development and quelling dangerous misconduct via administrative tools.

Despite their differences, these cases share some themes. First, they show-case the adaptability of regulatory ideology. In the New Deal era, regulatory ideology was presented as a familiar and reliable governing solution for navi-gating the economy. During the FTC reforms of the 1960s, it was a force for stability as consumer coalitions struggled to reform an institution built on its premises. And the deregulatory zeal of the 1970s and 1980s made the S&L case unique, but the ideas of regulatory ideology were not abandoned—they were repackaged for new purposes. Even as the Carter and Reagan adminis-trations championed deregulation, they remained committed to the idea that for people running businesses gentler interventions were more appropriate than stern ones. When the banking sector later faced overwhelming criticism following the industry's collapse, Congress's statutory response was to dissolve agencies that failed to spot the crisis and consolidate their mandates in a new agency with the same structure as its predecessors, an outcome that cannot be interpreted as rejecting the regulatory approach to managing corporate crime.

Second, each case highlights variability in regulatory practice as different individuals have shifted agency norms over time. For instance, the Securities and Exchange Commission (SEC) has been nonpunitive for most of its his-tory, but it experienced a rise in enforcement in the 1970s under the leader-ship of Stanley Sporkin. Similarly, the 1970s FTC witnessed an enforcement shift facilitated by several proconsumer chairmen. But these changes were temporary functions of individual agency; the ideas underpinning the insti-tutions' designs were never dislodged in favor of structural reforms. Both the FTC and the SEC promptly returned to their norms of emphasizing admin-istration over enforcement on their exits. The S&L crisis was propelled by a change in regulatory practice in the opposite direction—deregulatory fervor left agencies underequipped to detect misconduct, while the appointment of agency leaders with conservative agendas made enforcement a low priority. Individuals retain authority to bend agencies' modes of practice even if the principles undergirding agencies' institutional structures prove stable and difficult to change. Each story showcases the varied ways regulatory ideology was mobilized and adapted as a logic of governance through moments of busi-ness vulnerability in the twentieth century.

Regulating Securities

Scholars disagree on the place of the New Deal in American political development. Some present it as a fundamental restructuring of American capitalism, while others contend that Roosevelt worked with capital-intensive industries to reinforce the capitalist order.[2] In reality, Roosevelt accommodated powerful industries in some ways while asserting control over them in others. The 1933 Securities Act (SA) and the 1934 Securities Exchange Act (SEA) illuminate this tension. Senate hearings led by Ferdinand Pecora generated populist demands to restructure markets and put financiers behind bars, but concerns about restoring market stability militated against these impulses. Anxious the state would enact a law-and-order agenda, financial interests insisted that criminal controls in securities markets would prolong the crisis by keeping markets depressed. When the White House proposed criminalizing a list of market actions, financial sector interests proposed creating the SEC to regulate securities markets with broadened discretion. Eager to resuscitate the economy, members of Congress heeded their input. Regulatory governance offered policymakers a familiar alternative for monitoring struggling markets in comparison to law-and-order tactics.

The SEC's construction was shaped by multiple forces. In part, it reflected the legacy of Progressive era ideas on New Deal politics.[3] New Deal Democrats embraced programmatic liberalism, a governing strategy relying on the public administration of economic programs to solve social problems.[4] They frequently tied themselves to Progressive ideas about economic regulation. In his Commonwealth Club Address, Roosevelt praised Woodrow Wilson for checking the financial sector through enlightened administration.[5] Pecora, who became an SEC commissioner after leading the congressional inquiry, was a stalwart of Teddy Roosevelt's Bull Moose Party.[6]

There were also structural economic forces driving lawmakers to regulatory solutions as 1930s politicians faced simultaneous demands to rein in and to rescue markets after reckless behavior in the financial sector prompted an economic crisis of unprecedented severity. In such grim circumstances, lawmakers sought cautious strategies for reviving the economy and viewed regulation via independent commission as a reliable and time-tested response to market abuses. These economic realities were substantial, and some lawmakers likely used the language of regulatory ideology to rationalize choices rooted in economic considerations and anxieties. But dismissing regulatory ideology as merely camouflage for economic decisions oversimplifies the multifaceted role that regulatory bodies play in the economy. It disregards the importance of regulators' crime control functions as incidental and subordinate to their economic management powers, failing to fully grasp the significant array of regulators' responsibilities. Attention to the full range of regulators' powers and functions beyond their economic mandates underscores that regulatory governance is also a branch of social control constituting one strategy among many for managing undesirable and illicit conduct. Understanding how the SEC fits within an institutional network in which regulatory and criminal justice institutions operate as related systems requires an analysis of how lawmakers explained, conceptualized, and treated illegal conduct in securities markets.

This analytic lens draws attention to how New Deal liberalism remained consistent with the approach of emphasizing administration over punishment in market spheres. While regulatory ideology offered a language behind which some lawmakers sought cover to explain and defend their decisions, its mobilization had real consequences. These ideas relegated criminal controls to the margins of administrative governance on the grounds that criminality was an exceedingly small piece of what happens in securities markets. References to the respectability and vigor of market actors as reasons for sidelining criminal sanction brought regulatory ideology's familiar overlap of racial and class assumptions into the conversation about securities reform, making the favorable racialization of the entrepreneur an important idea coloring debate. This directed questions of punishment onto the identity of business leaders rather than their actions, marginalizing criminal sanctions as viable options. This illustrates how the history of white-collar penality has been integrated with the racial arc of American criminal justice, deepening our understanding of how the regulatory state works with the carceral state to sustain the inequalities of punishment.

THE PECORA COMMITTEE

The securities reforms of the 1930s were a major victory for Roosevelt's early New Deal agenda. But the New Deal unfolded in stages, not as a monolithic program. In its earliest days, Roosevelt moved conservatively to save capitalism.[7] As one historian has written, the New Deal's securities packages constituted "a conservative revolution which nonetheless horrified a great many conservatives," referring to the tension between Roosevelt's populist posturing and the desire to preserve capitalism underpinning the era's securities packages.[8] Roosevelt's coalition moved to the left in the mid-1930s until the 1937 recession, when conservative opposition to the New Deal pushed Roosevelt toward moderated Keynesianism.[9] Writers including Lawrence Friedman,

Jennifer Taub, and Jesse Eisinger suggest that following his 1932 electoral landslide, Roosevelt demonstrated a willingness to prosecute corporate law-breakers. Friedman writes that in the early twentieth century "the business of America was business" and that "there was a certain lack of zeal for punishing business behavior" until Roosevelt's administration changed course.[10] These perspectives pinpoint Ferdinand Pecora as the man who took down America's criminal financiers.

A New York district attorney, Pecora was appointed by President Hoover to be chief counsel to the US Senate Banking and Commerce Committee during its investigation into the 1929 stock market crash. The investigation was something that Wall Street could have avoided entirely. After the collapse, Hoover told the NYSE to strengthen its self-regulation or face federal intervention, but NYSE president Richard Whitney refused. Then, under Pecora's leadership, the committee subjected the financial and banking sectors to intense scrutiny and helped shape the Glass-Steagall Act (GSA), the SA, and the SEA.[11] Pecora's stewardship of the investigation and interrogation of powerful financiers uncovered egregious behavior on Wall Street and earned him mythic status among historians of American finance.[12]

Despite Pecora's combative stance, the indictments he brought typically ended in acquittal, which angered the sociologist Edwin Sutherland so much that he was prompted to develop his famous theory of white-collar crime.[13] As is the case with many corporate crime scandals, the financiers of the 1920s engaged in practices that were reckless and unethical in retrospect but not illegal at the time.[14] Still, corporate crime historians depict Pecora as the gold standard for punishing corporate misconduct.[15] Senator Burton Wheeler (D-MT) famously called executives "banksters" who should be treated "the same way we treated Al Capone" after Pecora's investigation.[16]

Pecora's committee uncovered multiple scandals. One of its early revelations involved the Radio Corporation of America (RCA). Preceding the 1929 crash, a group of investors known as the "Radio Pool" orchestrated trades to skyrocket RCA's share values before selling their stock, turning a profit while leaving unsuspecting investors on the hook when trading ceased.[17] With Whitney's support, pool participants insisted that this was healthy market behavior.[18] Other executives admitted engaging in similar conduct. William Fox of the Fox Film Corporation was cited as saying that he "manipulated" his company's stock prices, was "proud of it," and would "continue to do it."[19] The RCA pool is one of the earliest examples of a pump-and-dump scheme, a practice that was not outlawed until Pecora publicly shamed RCA.[20] This highlights a unique challenge to managing corporate crime—the government often has to play catch-up. New techniques are always emerging in spheres of corporate action that may be unethical or dangerous but go unnoticed until crisis strikes, putting the government in a position to create legal boundaries only after the damage is done.

Some of the inquiry's most explosive findings were unearthed when Pecora pilloried Charles Mitchell, the president of the National City Company. National City traded its own stock to inflate share values and made several multimillion-dollar loans to negligent borrowers in Latin America, then unloaded securities backed by these loans on investors.[21] When Pecora said that this should have been publicly disclosed, Mitchell replied, "I can not yet conceive myself that the American practice has been wrong," reasoning that institutions should not be required to disclose details about the financial instruments they sell since the public would not understand them.[22] He insisted it was his "duty" to sell products customers deemed worthy investments even if he knew they were unsound.[23] But he made exceptions for corporate officers because insulating them from the company's vulnerabilities while allowing them to reap its earnings encouraged a healthy "esprit de corps."[24] Pecora revealed that Mitchell and his corporate officers took out millions from National City in interest-free personal loans while the bank's stock plummeted and that Mitchell himself paid no taxes in 1929 by claiming fraudulent losses through coordinated stock transactions with his wife.[25] Mitchell was indicted and acquitted and then settled on a $1 million civil fine for tax evasion.[26]

Pecora's biggest target was J. P. Morgan Jr. Pecora exposed Morgan's use of a "preferred list" of friends who received stocks at discounted prices, including President Calvin Coolidge and the Supreme Court justice Owen Roberts, and showed that Morgan went years without paying taxes (a result of genuine stock losses, though that did little to earn him public sympathy). Morgan detested Pecora's prosecutorial posture. He grumbled that "Pecora has the manners of a prosecuting attorney who is trying to convict a horse thief" and was a "sharp little criminal lawyer."[27] Other critics shared this sentiment. Raymond Moley, an initial Roosevelt aide turned conservative critic by his second term, fretted that "Pecora was like a police chief who rounds up all the suspicious characters in town to solve a jewel robbery."[28]

Not everyone proffered defenses of industry as some industry insiders pleaded for new government regulations before the Pecora Committee. One prominent example was the Chase National Bank president, Winthrop Aldrich. Aldrich succeeded Albert Wiggin, who resigned in 1930 and was chastised by Pecora for shorting his personal Chase shares during the crash while the bank bought stock.[29] Aldrich condemned institutions that combined investment and commercial banking, heaped criticism on executives whose concentrated power he viewed as a threat to market health and safety, and expressed a preference for "prohibit[ing] market practices which are clearly injurious," all of which sharply broke from the prevailing views of many other industrial leaders who sought to minimize state oversight of the economy.[30] Some of his claims were strong enough to unnerve Senator Carter Glass (D-VA), who remarked that Aldrich was "proposing now to put the whole banking community into a straight-jacket," although he had already put his name on the GSA, which enacted many of Aldrich's other wishes, such as mandating the separation of investment and commercial banking.[31] While lawmakers were eager to heed firms' input to ensure that their policy responses did not aggravate the dire economic situation, that some of Aldrich's core preferences had taken root over Morgan's indicates that fully restoring the political economic status quo as some powerful firms hoped would happen was not a politically tenable course of action.

The Pecora Committee's final report said that the SEC—under consideration by Congress—would "materially abate, if not eradicate, abuses that have caused much economic distress."[32] But despite taking a position on the SEC, Pecora remained skeptical of it. He wrote in 1939 that "[u]nder the surface of the governmental regulation . . . the same forces that produced the riotous speculative excesses of the 'wild bull market' of 1929 still give evidences of their existence and influence. Though repressed for the present, it cannot be doubted that, given a suitable opportunity, they would spring back into pernicious activity."[33] Pecora showed that what happened in boardrooms preceding 1929 was willful, reckless, and dangerous. He understood that regulation was a risk-prevention tool that could stop crime from becoming endemic but feared that the instincts fueling misconduct could break through regulatory constraints. His willingness to bring indictments made clear that he believed punishment had a role to play in suppressing those impulses. But lawmakers eager to revive struggling markets structured the New Deal's securities packages in ways that sidestepped Pecora's belief in the importance of prosecution.

THE SECURITIES EXCHANGE ACT

The SEC was the Roosevelt administration's core attempt at fixing securities markets and one of the most significant New Deal innovations, but it did not originate out of a desire to rebuke Wall Street. It reflected the programmatic liberalism of New Deal Democrats and was a stabilizing force aimed at resuscitating capitalism rather than a battering ram intended to destroy it. Just as David Vogel finds to be the case in the latter years of the twentieth century, midcentury political elites eager to revive floundering markets were receptive to the input of struggling industries during debate over regulatory design.[34] Warning that criminal restrictions would hamper recovery, major banking and financial sector interests convinced lawmakers that criminalization was not the answer. This recast what Pecora saw as criminal wrongs deserving punishment as simple economic missteps requiring gentle course corrections. While populist Democrats remained committed to fundamental market restructuring and punishment, programmatic liberals designed the SEC to humanize capitalism and resolve market problems on business's terms through administration. Although securities reform was motivated by Pecora's populism, regulatory ideology became the organizing framework for the legislative packages Roosevelt signed.

The SEC became a global model of regulatory governance and highlights the promise of regulation—that administrative tools can keep economic conditions healthy and render prosecution rarely necessary. This analysis does not reject the SEC's significant role in corporate governance, but it does advance a twofold critique of its design and operation. First, the utility of regulation does not warrant dismissing criminal sanctions for corporate lawbreaking. The credible threat of escalating sanctions, including prosecution, is necessary for regulatory controls to be effective, and regulatory ideology should not be used to render criminal law an empty threat. Second, the case again shows the state extending the regulatory approach only to corporate forms of misconduct. As John Braithwaite has written, the political influences that fueled the SEC's design "were not mediated by punishment" but geared toward managing market conditions to mitigate undesirable behavior—rendering the SEC "a non-punitive regulatory agency"—which constituted a "different trajectory from the responsibilization . . . of individuals" promoted by traditional criminal law at the time.[35]

To understand the SEC's design, it is necessary to look at both New Deal securities laws—the SA (1933) and the SEA (1934). The SA, the administration's first attempt at regulating securities, empowered the FTC to bring enforcement actions against companies, underwriters, and other signatories for falsehoods on securities registration statements.[36] There was support for it from the financial community, including the Investment Bankers Association of America (IBA). William Breed, legal counsel for the IBA, even endorsed "broadened" penalties for fraud before the House Commerce Committee.[37] However, the IBA also critiqued the initial bill's most stringent provisions subjecting violations of FTC rules to prosecution and imposing strict liability for negligence.[38] Many feared that this would disrupt markets, prompting the Associated Gas and Electric executive H. C. Hopson to warn Senator Duncan Fletcher (D-FL) that it would make honest businessmen risk averse and allow the "clever crook or weakly dishonest person" to dominate.[39] In an analysis of the bill, the law firm Sullivan and Cromwell, which specialized in securities law, cautioned that "popular dislike of investment bankers" was facilitating the "hasty adoption of legislation which may superficially appear to be punishing the investment bankers but . . . is in fact injuring the country as a whole."[40]

This input was not ignored. The Senate Banking Committee rewrote the law "to protect honest enterprise" and revive the economy.[41] It protected business through one notable mechanism—information provision requirements rendering sellers of securities liable only for fraud. As James Mott (R-OR) noted, "the average investor cannot read and interpret a balance sheet," and a fraud-free statement could still be written to "convey to the untutored investor the idea that an unsound company is sound."[42] But as long as there was no deliberate fraud, the law reflected the principle of caveat emptor—buyers were responsible for assessing the quality of their purchases. This made the bill less stringent than state blue-sky laws, which subjected securities to merit reviews by state agents who evaluated whether their quality made them fair public offerings, ensuring that unsound securities never made it to markets behind technically accurate but misleading statements.[43] Charles Wolverton (R-NJ) explained that "the theory that underlies [the SA] is different . . . from that which forms the basis of many of the so-called 'blue-sky' laws" because merit reviews risked "hampering developments" in the economy.[44] Lawmakers thus centered their efforts on revamping markets even if their solutions exhibited leniency toward ethically questionable practices.

The SA was rushed to passage via voice vote in both chambers, but not because the bill pleased everyone.[45] Everyone knew action was needed, but those favoring market oversight bemoaned business's fingerprints on the law, while conservatives condemned it as a knee-jerk response to Pecora.[46] One year later, the SEA constituted a more deliberate attempt to reform securities markets.[47] The initial SEA bill was proposed by the White House and empowered the FTC to regulate actions like wash sales and matched orders, among a catalog of others. The White House adviser Thomas Corcoran was its chief advocate, and he defended including statutory criminal sanctions for violating the statute or FTC rules. He protested that Wall Street's proposal to create a new commission to regulate securities amounted to putting "a baby into a cage with a tiger to regulate the tiger."[48] However, the law Roosevelt signed replaced Corcoran's statutory prohibitions with a five-person SEC. This reflected industry demands to bring order to markets with minimal punitive threats and the administration's general shift from a populist stance, which Roosevelt exhibited in public statements, toward a programmatic strategy of handling complex problems through order-maintaining administration.

Key to changing the bill's design were assertions that securities offenses should be understood as economic mistakes, not moral wrongs. Framing securities regulation as an empirical economic question without moral stakes dampened retributive urges, although the implication that morality can be severed from economics was disingenuous—economists since the Progressive era infused their work with strong moral dimensions. But it proved politically useful for those opposed to punishment to separate the two rhetorically. For instance, Woodlief Thomas of the Federal Reserve said that he understood the law through the lens of "economic matters rather than morals" and that "[f]rom an economic standpoint, gambling is not bad."[49] This framing had crucial political value; removing moral considerations from economic questions depicted regulation as preferable to moralizing prosecutions by excusing behaviors some might consider unethical as acceptable market norms.

Many lawmakers who thought that the law should address the immorality of corporate actors conceded that calculable economics should remain the focus. Edward Kenney (D-NJ) granted that while exchange regulation "presents a moral problem," questions about the economy's health "should be brought prominently to the front" of debate.[50] Even Corcoran conceded that his bill was "not at all a moral proposal" but rather "the result of the economic judgment of the community."[51] Once the moral frame was minimized in favor of an economic one, regulatory ideology emerged as the guiding principle of the law's design.

Richard Whitney exemplified how this rhetorical move was linked to the notion that regulation was preferable to a punitive approach. Whitney informed the Senate Banking Committee that he was "in entire agreement with the proponents of the bill" on the need for oversight but feared that punishment "would seriously disrupt our organized security markets and American business." This was a recognizable feature of regulatory ideology—excessive state intervention would hurt markets—but Whitney amplified it to alarmist levels during the Depression. He warned that the law's strictest provisions would "throttle industry . . . and postpone the return of prosperity."[52] He defended a separate commission as more "flexible and mobile" than Corcoran's bill. Other NYSE agents insisted that a commission would be effective "without in any way hampering ordinary and legitimate business transactions."[53]

Whitney's concerns were broadly shared. Even Paul Shields, a prominent broker who supported enhanced market regulations and led Wall Street moderates opposed to Whitney, agreed that Corcoran's bill went "way too far" and failed to "recognize that there are honest, decent people in this business, and that such people should not be destroyed."[54] Frank Hope, the president of the Association of Stock Exchange Firms, warned that the proposal would "regulate [the financial system] out of existence." Hope told the Senate that a new commission would have the "elasticity and discretion" necessary to solve the industry's problems.[55]

Howard Butcher, vice president of the Philadelphia Stock Exchange, eviscerated Corcoran's pitch. He told the Senate Committee: "It seems to me that the bill does not take into consideration what President Roosevelt has repeatedly said, that we must go forward in a united group, that we must fight the depression, that we must make a united effort towards recovery. And I do not believe there has been any group of men who have responded more readily and more thoroughly than stockbrokers to that desire expressed by the president."[56] Butcher lamented that in the bill "we are to be treated as a bunch of criminals" because Congress has focused on "one or two men," paying no attention to the "250 of 253 other men who have rendered outstanding service."[57] He maintained that it is "unfair to take a group of men who have had an honorable existence" and punish them for behavior previously considered a "routine matter of business . . . that is not adverse to the public interest . . . individual morals . . . [or] the law."[58]

The Corcoran proposal was ushered through the House by Commerce Committee chair Sam Rayburn (D-TX), who removed some statutory specifics in favor of granting broader discretion to the FTC. A House report said that this choice reflected "the pleas of the representatives of the stock exchanges," who "insisted that the complicated nature of the problems justified leaving much greater latitude of discretion with the administrative agencies than would otherwise be the case."[59] Rayburn claimed he took "much of this so-called 'fright' out of the bill" by reducing penalties and expanding FTC discretion, framing the law as protection for "the man who wants to conduct a straightforward and honest business" since "the vast majority of business in this country is high-minded and honest."[60]

The bill passed the House, but several members thought it remained too stringent. John Cooper (R-OH) of the Commerce Committee emphasized how "honest and sincere men" in business "suffered tremendous loss during the last 3 years of economic depression." He claimed that businesses "want to be let alone for a little while" because "they are trying to recover" and asserted that the law "will retard economic recovery and not assist it." He worried that it would harm the honest businessman and "destroy his standing and reputation," lamenting that the "mere indictment of a prominent citizen is a sad thing" for a community. Moderate Democrats shared Cooper's fears. Representative Elmer Studley (D-NY) cautioned that the men working on exchanges were not "just a lot of bad boys" but "the most resolute and resourceful element of our people." He warned that "Wall Street will go to

Canada" should Corcoran's proposal pass, suggesting that the nation's "most prolific source of revenue will be dried up and our business structure reduced to ashes."[61]

Once it passed the House, the bill faced the more moderate Senate. It is necessary to acknowledge that congressional Democrats rode Roosevelt's 1932 landslide to secure major gains, but institutional variables generated different dynamics in the House and the Senate. The impact of the electoral rout was pronounced in the House, where Republicans went from a two-seat majority to a triple-digit deficit as Democrats seized a nearly three-to-one advantage, quickly rendering the chamber a site of aversion for big business. But the staggered nature of senatorial elections spread the effect of the Democratic realignment across multiple cycles. By 1939 Democrats secured seventy-seven of ninety-six Senate seats, but in 1932 they held only fifty-eight, keeping the Senate more moderate than the House.

Statements across party lines illustrate the cautious stances senators took on securities reform. Millard Tydings (D-MD) argued that the Corcoran bill would contribute to an "atmosphere of insecurity" that was "stopping the revival of many businesses."[62] Frederic Walcott (R-CT) described the bill as "a black eye to business" that would inflict "great injury" on the economy and said that creating a new commission was "important and vital to the recovery of business."[63] The Senate's proposed bill created a separate commission. In conference, Rayburn kept criminal sanctions in the bill, including five years imprisonment and/or a $25,000 fine for certain violations, but the Senate secured the creation of the SEC.[64] Like previous regulatory reforms, the law granted the SEC discretion to respond to behavior defined as criminal via a variety of administrative interventions.[65]

The SEA sailed through Congress, with marginal opposition coming from GOP legislators. While a significant achievement, the SEC's creation was a concession from the Roosevelt administration to industries pleading for the restoration of market order via commission governance and minimal recourse to criminal enforcement.

LEADERSHIP AND ENFORCEMENT AT THE SECURITIES
AND EXCHANGE COMMISSION

Roosevelt's earliest SEC appointments viewed the commission as committed to handling corporate wrongdoing through technocratic management. The SEC's first chair, Joseph Kennedy, was a Wall Street insider before the 1929 crash and orchestrated a controversial stock-pooling scheme just one year before the SEC's creation (Pecora called Kennedy's appointment "a sardonic anticlimax").[66] While Kennedy eventually won over many liberal skeptics, he linked his vision for the SEC to an affirmative effort to save capitalism and a rejection of the appropriateness of criminal remedies. In a 1934 National Press Club speech, he promised that the commission "shall not sit as a prosecutor" but instead "seek to help all proper enterprises" by establishing "positive standards" to control market structures that might deteriorate in ways that permit misconduct. He pledged that the SEC commissioners "believe in affirmation, not negation," and promised that the SEC would not "start off with the belief that every enterprise is crooked and that those behind it are crooks."[67] The speech was so well received that Kennedy promptly received a letter from the Roosevelt adviser A. A. Berle thanking him for disregarding popular impulses to penalize exchanges through "fire and sword."[68]

Subsequent SEC chairs shared Kennedy's logic. The second chair, James Landis, differentiated between regulatory agencies and law enforcement, claiming that agencies should conceive their purposes "in terms of management rather than of police."[69] Rather than understanding them as linked, Landis represented managerial administration and enforcement as mutually exclusive, positioning himself in the managerial camp. His successor, William O. Douglas, described the SEC as designed "to meet business on business terms." Douglas insisted that markets were capable of self-regulation since businessmen had "sufficient brains, courage, and integrity" to monitor themselves with the state playing a "residual" role.[70] In a 1938 speech, he claimed that regulatory agencies "have become more and more the outposts of capitalism . . . [and] have been given increasingly larger patrol duties, lest capitalism by its own greed, avarice or myopia destroy itself."[71]

These statements exhibit the entrenched inequalities of American legal practice, but they also illuminate the promise of regulatory control. While early SEC leaders shunned the harsh justice often meted out to other types of lawbreaking, applying their words to street-level infractions would highlight regulatory logic's merit of deploying nonpunitive risk-prevention strategies to control crime. This could be overshadowed by seeing only the inequalities. Nonetheless, these statements foreshadowed deeper problems that emerged at the SEC. Many have shown that the commission has historically been loathe to resort to enforcement sanctions, which is likely due to both the attitudes of agency leaders and the commission's institutional design, which minimized the importance of prosecution—the SEC did not even have an enforcement division to coordinate its legal actions until 1972.[72] While a regulatory approach to managing misconduct has value, stronger sanctions should not be abandoned in markets. A deeper commitment to law enforcement may have been valuable at the SEC given the ample research indicating that the consistent use of criminal sanctions against serious corporate lawbreaking gives administrative tools more deterrent force.[73]

Despite the SEC's historic inclination toward nonpunitive administration, regulatory practice is not static. From 1974 to 1981, the SEC experienced what Jesse Eisinger described as a "silver age" of prosecutions—not quite a golden age, but more than normal. When Stanley Sporkin became the director of the SEC Enforcement Division in 1974, he adopted a strong enforcement mentality that earned him the nickname "the father of enforcement." Sporkin lacked resources to prosecute every case of wrongdoing and was saddled with institutional obstacles that sometimes impeded his prosecutorial ventures, like needing the approval of all five commissioners before legal action could be taken, but he took steps to enforce securities law more robustly via civil and criminal prosecution. He especially made use of SEC Rule 10b-5, which prohibited market manipulation, to initiate enforcement actions. This made prosecution a credible threat backing up lighter interventions in the SEC's arsenal as business leaders knew Sporkin was not afraid to escalate to prosecution should gentler interventions be disobeyed.[74]

Sporkin's tenure draws attention to two realities about regulation and law. First, Sporkin made use of criminal and civil prosecutions. Scholars disagree on whether corporate interests prefer facing civil or criminal suits—some suggest that they prefer criminal enforcement owing to the higher burdens of proof and robust procedural protections of criminal law, whereas others conclude that they prefer to pay seemingly enormous civil fines that wealthy firms can afford without confronting the specter of incarceration or a reputation-killing indictment.[75] However, both strategies have value. Civil suits provide quicker paths to securing fines and monetary damages, while criminal prosecutions can deter wrongdoing through prison time and reputational injury. Debates over which strategy is better or preferred by corporations are to some extent misguided since those strategies serve distinct purposes. Sporkin made effective use of both. Second, Sporkin illuminated the possibilities and pitfalls of personal agency as a means of shaping regulatory strategy. He showed how bold leadership could challenge an agency's norms and stretch its institutional warrants, even if only for a brief "silver age." However, not only did the SEC return to its customary practices after his departure since the rise in enforcement was a function of his choices rather than of institutional reform, but backlash to his strategies also facilitated structural changes that hampered the SEC's long-term prosecutorial capacities. In 1976, the Supreme Court undercut Sporkin by ruling that the SEC must prove "scienter," or knowledge of wrongdoing, in Rule 10b-5 cases, requiring proof that violators were consciously violating or disregarding the law in securities manipulation suits. This provided corporate actors an easy basis for claiming plausible deniability and made securities violations harder to prove, further differentiating the state's institutional approaches to handling corporate and street criminality.[76]

The story of the SEC shows how the ideas of regulatory ideology shaped the agency's design and became features of its institutional structure even as the commission experienced fluctuations in its leadership and patterns of practice. In many senses, the New Deal Democrats built on the Progressive legacy of managing corporate misconduct through administration by treating regulation as the state's proven and established method for managing corporate wrongdoing. Consequently, anticorporate outrage was ideologically and institutionally subordinated to familiar regulatory strategies that lawmakers believed would save capitalism from itself, thus blazing the trail for the agency's subsequent development.

The Consumer Rights Movement and the Federal Trade Commission

Prosecuting corporate crime was a low priority from the 1940s through the 1970s, at which point a newfound state commitment to punishing corporate malfeasants materialized.[77] This coincided with the rise of the consumer rights movement. While consumer activists were not solely responsible for this shift, they revived Pecora's tough-on-corporate-crime instincts. The movement compiled a slate of victories in areas such as environmental protection, transportation safety, and more, but this section focuses on its attempts to remake the FTC into a consumer advocate. In the 1970s, the FTC was one of many agencies staffed by new leaders who embraced proconsumer mentalities and took corporate illegality seriously. But while the movement secured some changes to the FTC, institutional reforms did not remake its criminal enforcement powers despite activists' demands that it embrace a greater commitment to prosecution. This case illustrates both the role that individual agency can play in challenging the ideological and institutional constraints on administrative action and the limits that political actors face in remaking existing institutions as the regulatory ideological premises undergirding the FTC's design proved difficult to dislodge.

CONSUMER ADVOCACY AND THE FEDERAL
TRADE COMMISSION

The proximate origins of the consumer rights movement lay in the 1930s, when activists like Frederick Schlink and Robert Lynd championed consumers' issues.[78] This lobby won some victories, including the Wheeler-Lea Act (WLA) of 1938, which enhanced the FTC's power to monitor unfair trade practices harming consumers. Before the WLA, the FTC's only constituency was businesses hurt by unfair competition, not injured consumers. The WLA was not an unambiguous win for consumer advocates, who preferred placing responsibility for consumer protection in the stronger Food and Drug Administration (FDA). Nonetheless, the WLA gave the FTC the potential to become a force for consumers, although without changing the agency's criminal enforcement tools.[79]

During the WLA's construction, it was widely understood that broadening the FTC's criminal powers cut against its designated role. Since the commission was designed to coexist with the DOJ's antitrust authority, debates over the WLA were wrapped into antitrust questions, and New Deal administrators expressed reluctance to use criminal prosecution in antitrust cases. A central site of these debates was the Temporary National Economic Committee (TNEC), a body consisting of six Roosevelt appointees and six congressmen created by Congress in 1938 to investigate economic concentration.[80] When discussing regulation, TNEC commissioner William O. Douglas lamented that most agencies had become too eager to "take every violator by the back of his neck and rub his nose in the sand, regardless of the effect upon the innocent." But Douglas praised the FTC for uniquely "cooperat[ing] with business by not making the corrective activity too severe." In testimony before the TNEC, FTC commissioner Ewin Davis stated that he and his colleagues "are glad [they] don't" have the authority to impose criminal sanctions because the issues the FTC monitored "generally do not pertain to criminal matters in the ordinary acceptation of that term."[81] That the WLA declined to expand the FTC's criminal enforcement powers on behalf of consumer interests was consistent with these prevailing views.

Resistance to handling antitrust cases as criminal was especially clear in the statements of Thurman Arnold. A TNEC commissioner, Arnold ran the DOJ Antitrust Division from 1938 to 1943 and won more antitrust suits than the DOJ had initiated in its prior history.[82] However, during TNEC hearings, Arnold said that antitrust cases largely dealt, not with "the criminal class," but with "ordinary law-abiding citizens," rendering criminal prosecution typically inappropriate.[83] This mirrored the argument of his *The Bottlenecks of Business* (1940), in which he wrote that "an antitrust violation is not an ordinary crime" because antitrust laws are "violated by respectable people." Such violations constitute "economic offense[s], the seriousness of which is not related to the moral turpitude of the offender," rendering antitrust law "different from ordinary criminal law."[84] TNEC reports shared these conclusions, noting that "[t]he connection between the idea of criminality and . . . moral obloquy is deeply rooted both in the law and the national psychology," rendering it misguided to prosecute actions that "have a pernicious economic effect" but are committed "by responsible and reasonably well-intentioned men." Prosecution made it "difficult to keep clearly before the public, the business community, and the courts the all-important fact that the antitrust laws must be regarded primarily as an economic instrument and not as a moral tract."[85]

The TNEC considered it a category error to equate market offenses like antitrust violations with criminality by interpreting antitrust infractions through the framework of economic performance and a favorable interpretation of corporate lawbreakers as decent citizens distinct from the criminal class. Consequently, it insisted that technocratic approaches were preferable to prosecutorial ones for the kinds of people targeted by antitrust law. This observation is not intended to imply that the inverse was true and that every antitrust offense warranted criminal treatment. Rather, it is to note that there are various legal weapons that the government can use to keep market actors in check with different degrees of compulsion and that dismissing criminal penalties as inappropriate for such respectable people removed a crucial weapon from the state's toolbox—criminal and administrative controls should be complementary, not mutually exclusive. This deeper history indicates that when the WLA assigned consumer advocacy responsibilities to the FTC, few understood wronged consumers as victims of corporate criminality.

Edwin Sutherland took a different perspective. When he published *White-Collar Crime* in 1949, he provided a theory of victimization identifying consumers as uniquely vulnerable to corporate crime. He explained that "[t]he persons injured [by white-collar crime] may be divided into two groups: first, a relatively small number of persons engaged in the same occupation as the offenders or in related occupations, and, second, the general public either as consumers or as constituents of the social institutions which are affected by the violations of the laws." He worried that consumers are "seldom in a position to fight" because "[they] are scattered [and] unorganized."[86] He thus depicted consumers as mired in a policymaking situation that James Wilson later described as "entrepreneurial politics"—because individual consumers are unlikely to take initiative on their own behalf, they require a "policy entrepreneur" to facilitate mobilization by galvanizing public sentiment and providing organizational means for political action.[87]

Ralph Nader may or may not have read Sutherland, but he and his allies similarly framed consumers as victims of corporate abuse. By the 1960s, when Nader emerged as the chief policy entrepreneur of the consumer rights movement, it had become a compelling force dominated by large public in-terest organizations drawing membership from educated professionals and the middle class as it posed challenges to corporate power.[88] Consumer ac-tivists pushed for change by altering standing doctrine to make it easier for consumers to sue corporations and securing the appointment of public in-terest advocates to regulatory bodies. Building new regulatory institutions and restructuring old ones were not always the movement's chosen tactics, as in many cases activists thought that existing regulatory statutes could be reformed or existing bureaucracies stacked with consumer allies.[89] But the movement pushed for some new agencies and singled out others for over-hauls in the name of consumer protection, and the FTC was an early target.[90]

In 1969, Nader and a team of law students (dubbed "Nader's Raiders" by the press) conducted observations of the FTC before publishing a scathing report on the institution. The report highlighted the FTC's historically re-strained approach to criminal enforcement. In the preface, Nader excoriated FTC chair Paul Rand Dixon—an appointment of the perceived consumer ally John F. Kennedy, who as president articulated a "consumers' bill of rights" in 1962—for relying almost entirely on administrative action over criminal charges. He condemned the FTC for historically "not actively seek[ing] from Congress powers of . . . criminal penalty." He accused the commissioners of endorsing "the myths that most large businesses are honest and law-abiding [and] that the problem is the few unscrupulous hucksters who give industry and commerce a bad image." The report emphasized that the FTC "can do more than slap the hand of a violator," including "recommend[ing] criminal action to the Justice Department." It criticized the FTC for relying on "the as-surance of voluntary compliance"—informal promises from corporate actors to cease illegal activity—which Nader's team alleged were used to "mollify growing consumer indignation without having to punish the guilty." The re-port expressed that regulatory interventions secure compliance only if vio-lations are met with enforcement, emphasizing that cease-and-desist orders (CDOs) could be "the FTC's most potent general enforcement weapon" but that if they are "to be at all effective . . . [market actors] must believe that the FTC will deal severely with violations."[91] Nader's Raiders essentially advocated for what contemporary research indicates deters corporate crime—an escalat-ing sanctions approach initially reliant on administrative tools to manage mis-conduct that are backed by stern interventions in cases of repeated violations.

Importantly, the WLA reformed the FTC's CDO powers. Under the WLA, administrative CDOs were rendered final after sixty days if the targeted party did not appeal the order, at which point violations became subject to civil penalties. This expedited the "three bites" procedure outlined in chapter 4 to two—an administrative CDO could be secured after a first violation, and civil contempt charges could be brought against a second violation once the order became final. But these changes applied only to administrative orders backed by civil penalties. Criminal contempt still required getting a judicial enforcement order from an Article III judge after a second violation, which could lead to criminal contempt charges on a third infraction. This expedited path to civil contempt provided the commission a useful means of quick intervention, but the comparative ease of the process had the secondary effect of rendering it a de facto substitute for criminal contempt.[92] Nader's team raised this issue, lamenting that the potential value of the CDO was undercut by administrators who "refused to recommend criminal action" by giving violators "not just the one free bite provided by the cease and desist order procedure but many more."[93]

Chairman Dixon dismissed the Nader Report as a "smear" project and a manifestation of the "extreme anti-business bias of these young zealots," who believed that "corporation executives [engaged] in much more reprehensible behavior than rapists, robbers, muggers, etc." He proclaimed, "I believe that the American businessman is basically honest and they believe he is basically dishonest." He was also dismissive of the team's claims about criminal punishment. The group published a rejoinder highlighting that many of the behaviors that the FTC regulated were already defined as criminal in statutory text, explaining that " 'criminal' provisions are *already* found in most of the statutes enforced by the FTC." It thus concluded that "the Critique's recommendations—that the Commission begin to make substantial use of its existing criminal powers and seek such powers in limited new areas—are not novel suggestions of violently anti-business 'zealots' but rather examples of responsible administrative and legislative recommendations."[94] This was a direct critique of how the criminalization of corporate misconduct gets lost under layers of administrative discretion, fostering institutional cultures reliant on regulation in the face of recurrent lawbreaking.

Despite resistance from the commission, some reforms were made to the FTC following the movement's push. The Alaska Pipeline Act of 1973 subjected violations of the agency's CDOs to a $10,000 fine, empowered federal courts to grant mandatory injunctions to enforce certain FTC orders, and expanded the FTC's information-gathering capacities. Highly significant was the Magnuson Moss Act of 1975 (MMA), a cornerstone of lemon law governing product warranties. The MMA empowered the FTC to sue on behalf of consumers injured by unfair or deceptive practices, expanded the agency's rulemaking authority, and instituted new civil penalties of up to $10,000.[95] These statutes strengthened the FTC's power to pursue civil enforcement and equitable relief.

After Dixon, several commission chairs endorsed more enforcement-driven proconsumer mindsets. From 1970 to 1973, the FTC chair, Caspar Weinberger, oversaw an internal reorganization of the commission via new operating bureaus—the Bureau of Economics, the Bureau of Consumer Protection, and the Bureau of Competition, the latter of which became the agency's enforcement division.[96] But as an internal reorganization, Weinberger's efforts did not expand the FTC's criminal enforcement powers as much as they consolidated the agency's existing enforcement resources. Other consumer advocates who endorsed enforcement logics followed Weinberger. For instance, Lewis Engman—the FTC chair from 1973 to 1976—described the commission as a "tough but fair policeman walking the economic beat."[97] This logic was shared by Michael Pertschuk, who headed the agency from 1977 to 1981 and encouraged staff to use stronger enforcement tools to complement their arsenal of administrative interventions. His robust understanding of the agency's mission prompted conservative backlash for the FTC's perceived excesses, earning it the denigrating moniker "national nanny." Weinberger, Engman, and Pertschuk all embraced the two faces of enforcement—criminal and civil—to stretch the institution's regulatory operations without major institutional reforms.

LIMITATIONS AND HURDLES TO REFORMING THE FEDERAL TRADE COMMISSION

To borrow Eisinger's term, perhaps the 1970s were also a "silver age" of enforcement at the FTC.[98] But the longer history of the commission shows that its institutional boundaries were only temporarily stretched and snapped back into place once new leadership took the helm. The most substantial structural change to the FTC was the internal reorganization under Weinberger, but the institutional powers of the FTC were not changed in relation to criminal enforcement. The most significant institutional change that could have substantially invigorated enforcement mentalities—the WLA reforms to the CDO—encouraged civil prosecutions in lieu of criminal ones. Subsequent chairs reverted to the commission's norm of eschewing criminal enforcement. This history highlights how this case differs from the other stories of regulatory development examined in this text by illuminating the challenges reformers faced working within a preexisting institution. Consumer activists failed to durably change the FTC's criminal powers or to permanently adjust its patterns of enforcement for several reasons—limitations to the consumers-as-victims frame, business community backlash, a changing political environment, and the forces of institutional inertia combined with an economistic shift in the nature of American regulation.

First, when consumers were politicized by the consumer rights movement as victims of corporate abuse, outrage was stoked that fueled standing doctrine reforms enabling consumers to initiate suits seeking compensatory damages.[99] Given the kind of injury caused by corporate wrongdoing, this was a valuable accomplishment. But the victimization frame was less successful in changing the FTC's criminal enforcement powers. It was not for lack of trying. The Nader Report claimed, "It is particularly important to apply criminal sanctions to dishonest corporate behavior, for it is far more damaging in contemporary America than all the depredations of street crime." For this reason, the committee wrote that "law and order must not stop at the doorstep of these massive and influential institutions."[100]

However, deep-seated institutional and ideological forces have long militated against recognizing the casualties of corporate abuse as victims of criminal action. Generations of corporate crime scholars have argued that popular understandings of crime victimization are conditioned to exclude the victims of white-collar crime owing to research in victimology, a subfield of criminology studying the experiences of crime victims that has systematically excluded the victims of corporate and white-collar crime. The National White-Collar Crime Center has found that about 25 percent of all US households have been victimized by white-collar crime, often repeatedly, but almost all major victimization research neglects to measure any type of corporate or white-collar criminality. Scholars explain the deficiencies of victimology with reference to the fact that most charges brought against corporations for criminal activity are handled through administrative, civil, or equity actions without recourse to criminal prosecution, meaning that corporate criminal activity rarely registers as crime in official data sets.[101]

This skewed conception of victimhood is essential for understanding 1960s and 1970s politics. While the consumer rights movement developed into a force for those victimized by corporations, a crime victims' movement emerged at roughly the same time. Marie Gottschalk has unearthed this history, showing how the crime victims' movement fueled state-building initiatives that centralized victims' interests in criminal justice institutions, laying foundations for the carceral state in the process. She illustrates how the movement harnessed federally funded victimology research to secure the allocation of state resources to champion victims' interests, such as funding victims' rights programs in prosecutors' offices or block grants for states providing aid to victims.[102] The biases inherent in common understandings of victimhood had consequences for how these institutionalized resources empowered victims by directing them to state and local prosecutors and law enforcement agencies handling street crime. Alternatively, victimized consumers were protected through regulatory bodies and secured new abilities to defend their interests through legislation like the MMA. These were laudable achievements, but comparing them to the victims' movement's accomplishments throws into relief how the institutional separation of street crime and corporate crime legitimated a politically constructed understanding of criminal victimhood. Having long been defined as an administrative problem rather than a criminal one, consumer victimization was handled by lawmakers through civil and equitable relief while crime victims' issues were being politicized to reform criminal justice institutions.

The point of this comparison is not to suggest that there was cooperation between the consumer rights and crime victims' movements or that the movements consciously chose to remain distinct, as by all indications they emerged as discrete phenomena. It is also not to suggest that laws like the MMA were insignificant; given the nature of consumer victimization, enhancing consumers' prospects for securing civil and equity remedies was meaningful. Rather, this juxtaposition is intended to highlight the fact that despite the potential of the consumer-as-victim framework to promote change in certain areas of law, the systematic exclusion of corporate and white-collar crime victims from common understandings of criminal victimhood left the consumer victimization framework separated from the political currents driving criminal justice reform. Consumer activists relied on victimization components to demand commendable reforms to civil law, torts, and standing, as did Weinberger, Engman, and Pertschuk when they brought civil suits and tort cases. But the politics of *criminal* victimization were different. Because existing institutions structurally separated corporate illegality from the traditional criminal process, public understandings of crime victimhood excluded victims of corporate wrongdoing, isolating the movement's consumer victimization rhetoric from broader conversations about criminal justice reform unfolding at the same time.

A second reason the consumer rights movement failed to reform the FTC's criminal powers was because its efforts prompted organized backlash from the business community. The seeds of this response were sown in a 1971 Chamber of Commerce (COC) memorandum written by former American Bar Association president and eventual Supreme Court justice Lewis Powell that outlined a strategy for industries to consolidate against the consumer rights movement. Powell expressed particular concern about Nader's views on corporate criminality. He quoted a profile of Nader from *Fortune* magazine, writing that "[Nader] thinks, and says quite bluntly, that a great many corporate executives belong in prison." He warned that CEOs needed to mount a counterattack. He depicted corporate leaders as victims of slander, claiming that "businessmen have not been trained or equipped to conduct guerilla warfare with those who propagandize the system" because "the traditional role of business executives has been to manage, to produce, to sell, to create jobs, to make profits, to improve the standard of living, to be community leaders, to serve on charitable and educational boards, and generally to be good citizens."[103]

Noting how consumer organizations used the judiciary to pursue their ends by relying on groups like the American Civil Liberties Union to lead litigation, Powell claimed that the COC had "a vast area of opportunity" to take on a similar role as "spokesperson for American business."[104] Through the 1970s Powell's recommendations helped promote a revival of business's political power. Business interests began coordinating through groups like the COC, the National Association of Manufacturers, and the National Federation of Independent Business. These organizations committed resources to challenging consumer activists while facilitating collective action among businesses whose political activities were previously fractured. As Kim Phillips-Fein writes, the COC morphed into "a social movement for capitalism."[105] David Vogel claims that backlash against the consumer rights movement helped the business community "turn the tide" through the 1970s.[106]

Third, while firms' successful counteroffensive was partially a result of effective coordinational and organizational strategies, it was also a consequence of changing political and intellectual environments in which neoliberal governing philosophies gained traction. In other words, public opinion, the political context, and the intellectual climate were already swinging against the consumer rights movement by the end of the 1970s. Although Vogel acknowledges that business coordination changed American politics, he also emphasizes that "on balance, business did not so much reshape the climate of intellectual debate as it benefited from and, in turn, helped promote a shift that was already occurring."[107] In this context, familiar constructs of corporate wrongdoers as well-intentioned entrepreneurs whose harmful actions were justifiable in markets dominated over negative frames.

When Reagan was elected president in 1980, his administration's hostility to regulation capitalized on developments that had been unfolding for years. Phillips-Fein has shown how free market intellectualism had been amassing influence for decades preceding Reagan's election, beginning in response to the New Deal and becoming mainstream by 1980.[108] In his acclaimed book *Wealth and Poverty*, George Gilder notably recalled favorable constructs of corporate criminality embedded within regulatory ideology. He described capitalism as "an inherently moral economic order" in which business leaders were motivated not by self-interest, but by "a spirit closely akin to altruism,

[and] a regard for the needs of others." He condemned excessive state over-sight of markets for disrupting the moral codes of competition and inhibiting entrepreneurs from bettering humankind.[109] Reagan valued *Wealth and Poverty* so deeply that he gave a copy to each member of his cabinet.[110]

Reagan's hostility to regulation was also preceded by the politics of his predecessor, Jimmy Carter. Carter signed off on Congress's assertion of control over the FTC through the FTC Improvement Act of 1980, which restricted trade ruling proceedings and other activities at the FTC and eliminated criminal penalties for failure to comply with orders from the commission.[111] Further, while Carter appointed public interest advocates to many agencies, he also signed major banking deregulation through the Depository Institutions Deregulation and Monetary Control Act (DIDA) of 1980, laying the groundwork for the S&L crisis.[112]

It is important to acknowledge that regulatory ideology has been wedded to both the politics of regulation and the politics of deregulation. Reagan framed himself as committed to "regulatory relief," suggesting the reduction of regulatory supervision over markets.[113] Within this framework, less regulation implied not more prosecution, but the minimization of state supervision of markets in general, leaving it consistent with an approach prioritizing mild sanctions over stringent ones. This mentality began taking shape in the 1970s, creating a political context hostile to state oversight of markets well before Reagan's election. The S&L case and the next chapter address in detail how political actors promoting "deregulation" are rarely seeking outright elimination of regulatory controls; rather, they are seeking the reduction and optimization of regulatory supervision in order to achieve cost-efficient market administration. In this context, the principles of regulatory ideology have been repackaged to further an agenda of scaling back the regulatory state in the name of cost efficiency.

Fourth, efforts to encourage enforcement by consumer-oriented agency leaders were counteracted by a subsequent shift in the nature of American regulation combined with the forces of institutional inertia—the stability that comes from an institution's established practices and culture that leaves it resistant to change.[114] The forces of institutional inertia were strong at an institution with a lengthy history like the FTC. As shown, the commission long eschewed strengthened criminal enforcement powers, and the legislative fixes to the agency in the 1970s focused on civil and equitable relief. Shifts in criminal enforcement at the FTC in the 1970s could be achieved only through the appointment of staff willing to use and reorganize the FTC's existing tools, rendering such a reorientation a temporary consequence of individual choice. Agency leadership appointed by Reagan embraced an economistic approach that revived the FTC's historic enforcement norms.

Reagan appointed James Miller, an opponent of consumer activists who eschewed an adversarial mentality, to lead the FTC. Miller believed that the FTC's purpose was to promote economic efficiency, and he thought that FTC decisions should be calculated within the frame of cost-benefit analytics.[115] The FTC Transition Report published when Miller assumed the chairmanship explained this philosophy in stark terms. Miller identified "two strongly-held views" about the FTC's role—one understanding the FTC as a "'cop on the beat'" and another viewing it as an "economic agency," drawing a sharp divide between law enforcement and economic regulation. He was dismissive of the law enforcement perspective, writing that "a decision to take issue with a particular business practice transcends the question of legality" because the FTC should always ask whether an intervention would "improve the functioning of the economy." In short, even if commissioners discovered activity warranting an enforcement action, the decision to intervene hinged on cost-benefit calculations forecasting whether the proposed FTC action was projected to impose measurable costs or gains on the market's economic performance. If the expected costs of enforcement outweighed the economic benefits, Miller would not intervene. He relied heavily on the FTC's Bureau of Economics, which conducted cost-benefit calculations that would sometimes override enforcement staff recommendations to take legal action.[116]

Miller's approach was consistent with what Marc Eisner calls the regulatory "efficiency regime" that emerged in the 1970s and 1980s, a mode of regulatory governance in which decisions about proposed rules and administrative actions are evaluated through cost-benefit analysis of their economic impact. This was a trend across agencies; before Reagan required all regulatory rules to go through cost-benefit analysis and secure approval from the Office of Information and Regulatory Affairs, agencies like the Environmental Protection Agency (EPA) began using their economic offices to perform such analyses. Even the DOJ Antitrust Division created an economic policy office in 1973 to make cost-benefit calculations, leading attorneys to shelve prosecutable cases owing to the potentially negative economic impacts of prosecution.[117] This led to slashing regulations deemed cost-inefficient and, as was the case at Miller's FTC, refraining from enforcement actions that could have negative economic effects.

This shift had clear consequences. Narrow cost-benefit frames emphasized immediately quantifiable costs and benefits, overlooking regulation's precautionary purposes. Regulations may impose short-term costs on markets, but they prevent long-term deteriorations in economic conditions that could eventually inflict larger costs on the public. Years of slashing cost-inefficient regulations in the 1980s may have enhanced short-term market performance at the expense of enabling the S&L crisis, which ended with what was at the time the largest taxpayer bailout in US history. Miller's cost-benefit strategy was critiqued by his predecessors for producing agency paralysis in the face of lawbreaking, disregarding the noneconomic harms of corporate abuse, and weakening the deterrent force of the law. In 1982, Pertschuk critiqued Miller's policies by stating that "the marketplace creates incentives which produce innovation and efficiency and productivity, but those incentives are so strong that they often lead to pressures to undermine the standards of a civilized society, to lie, to coerce, to cheat, to overreach." He cautioned, "That has been the experience of the human beings in the market system."[118] Pertschuk has been quoted as accusing Miller of "crippl[ing] the Commission's law enforcement mission."[119] But this claim is debatable, only because it is unclear that law enforcement was ever permanently defined as core to the FTC's institutional mission. It was Pertschuk's philosophy that constituted a deviation from the norm, not Miller's.

CHANGING STRUCTURES OF REGULATION

It is worth noting that the story of the consumer rights movement directs attention to two dynamics of regulatory development that are understudied in this book and warrant discussion. First, beginning in the 1960s, federal regulation increasingly reached into spheres of corporate action beyond strict economics. This "new social regulation" extended into health, safety, and noneconomic features of the production process and its negative externalities.[120] Examples of social regulation agencies created during this era included the Occupational Safety and Health Administration (OSHA), the EPA, and the National Highway Traffic and Safety Administration (NHTSA). Second, following the New Deal, agencies housed within executive branch departments became building blocks for the administrative state. Many social regulatory agencies took this form—for instance, OSHA was located within the Department of Labor and NHTSA within the Department of Transportation. This constituted a different institutional form of regulation than that of the ICC, the FTC, and the SEC, which were independent commissions operating outside executive branch supervision.

Despite being executive branch delegations or bodies committed to social regulation, many agencies built in the 1960s and 1970s adopted schemes similar to the independent commissions overseeing financial markets by emphasizing administrative tools over criminal ones. This raises the question of what role—if any—regulatory ideology played in the design of socially oriented regulatory bodies and executive branch agencies. While both developments had roots in the structural demands of the economy and the political environment, that does not mean that this book's arguments cannot add anything to their histories.

First, this book has emphasized the FTC's authority to regulate competitive practices, and that should not obscure the social regulatory role the commission gradually took on as a consumer advocate from the passage of the WLA in 1938 through the reforms of the 1970s. After all, Pertschuk's FTC earned the nickname "national nanny" after it attempted to regulate television ads targeting children, an unambiguous social regulatory action. When regulatory ideological ideas surfaced in these debates about reforming the FTC, it is worth remembering that these were major developments enhancing the commission's social regulatory authority.

Existing research also suggests that the recurring pattern of regulatory development narrated in this book—in which proposals aimed at curbing corporate malfeasance contemplate criminal controls, only to be ratcheted back during debate to produce regulatory structures reliant on administrative tools—is present in other debates over social regulation. For instance, initial bills governing the EPA's operations emphasized grave penalties, only to be rewritten during legislative deliberation to emphasize administrative schemes.[121] This indicates that during some of the most significant social regulatory debates of the era, lawmakers shifted from initially punitive designs toward institutional forms rooted in administrative regulation of illegality.

Second, that executive branch agencies have adopted similar regulatory schemes to control criminal conduct highlights an overlap in the institutional features of the independent commission and executive branch models of administration. Existing scholarship shows how arguments against criminalizing corporate misconduct appeared throughout debates about executive branch agencies. For instance, early business criticism of OSHA was rooted in concerns that businesspeople were being "treated like criminals" and that the agency's enforcement tactics were little different from those of criminal justice agencies.[122] The director of Reagan's Task Force on Regulatory Relief promised in 1982 that under Reagan's tenure, "at the level of inspection and enforcement, businessmen today are much less likely to mistake a visit from EPA or OSHA for a visit from the FBI." Thorne Auchter, OSHA director from 1981 to 1984, informed the *Washington Post* that "[o]ur philosophy is one of safety and health and not one of crime and punishment."[123] These statements reflected a reaction against the public interest movement in a way that depicted executive branch regulators as allies of business and not stern law enforcers.

Notably, regulatory history reveals that these distinctions—financial versus social regulation and the independent commission versus executive branch

regulatory models—are far from clear in the first place. For one, social regulation expanded in the 1960s, but it was not new. The FDA took on social regulatory responsibilities from its origins in 1906, and the WLA imbued the FTC
with enhanced social regulatory authority in 1938. Additionally, in 1887, the
ICC was initially housed within the Interior Department. It secured independence from the executive branch in 1889 only because Democrats feared that
incoming Republican president Benjamin Harrison, a former railroad attorney, would undermine its mission.[124] That it became an independent commission rather than an executive branch agency was a quirk of history informed
by late nineteenth-century political idiosyncrasies, not principled philosophical reasoning differentiating the two institutional forms. These details indicate
that regulatory ideology has long influenced the nature of regulation regardless of an agency's institutional configuration or mandate to regulate financial
or social matters, underscoring how the ideas embedded in regulatory design
shape an agency's warrants and operations independently of other aspects of
its structure.

The Savings and Loan Crisis

The consumer rights movement secured an impressive array of policy victories, but in the 1970s and 1980s its popularity gave way to the deregulatory zeal of the Carter and Reagan administrations. This led to one of the
most significant financial catastrophes in American history—the S&L crisis
of the 1980s. During the crisis, over one thousand S&L institutions (thrifts)
shut down during a collapse precipitated by widespread industry fraud and
recklessness, and over one thousand felony convictions of bankers followed.
While irresponsible lending and speculation helped ignite the crisis, it was
also prompted by flagrant crimes, including rampant securities and appraisal
fraud. Some scholars understand this as an unusually meaningful moment of
criminal accountability for corporate malfeasants.[125] Others treat the government's prosecutorial offensive as a farce that disguised the state's failure to
punish the worst S&L malefactors.[126] This division misleadingly presents a
sharp binary; both perspectives reveal partial truths and miss others. After
discussing the crisis's genesis, this section details what each perspective gets
right and wrong. While the S&L crisis shows that the state has the capabil-
ity to prosecute powerful business actors, prosecution also cannot do everything. Regulatory controls are valuable crime-prevention tools that should
complement the state's prosecutorial powers, and excessively reducing regulatory oversight can impose unreasonable expectations on prosecutors.[127]

The roots of the S&L crisis lay in political challenges to regulation in the 1970s and 1980s. With a robust deregulatory politics taking shape under Carter and flourishing under Reagan, the 1980s witnessed the consolidation of American neoliberalism—the governing ideology that markets know best in all domains of life.[128] Reagan's commitment to shrinking the regulatory state built on Carter's record of banking deregulation in the DIDA through the Garn–St. Germain Depository Institutions Act (GSGA) of 1982, which deregulated federally insured S&L institutions created during the Great Depression to promote mortgage lending and home ownership.[129] The DIDA and the GSGA laid the groundwork for the S&L industry's crash, but they were symptoms of a much broader downsizing of regulation across the marketplace. Scaling back regulation drove the broader economy's "financialization" by encouraging businesses to invest in financial ventures over product quality, sometimes even by legalizing previously prohibited activities like share buybacks.[130] Firms across sectors of the economy became reliant on risky financial maneuvering to make money as the profit motive was glorified and businesses focused on growing shareholder value over their companies. Many observers depict these developments as pouring gasoline onto markets by creating corporate cultures conducive to lawbreaking through crafting an economic environment amplifying the idea that activities with potentially harmful consequences were acceptable if they stimulated growth and profits.[131]

Scholars have offered varied descriptions of Reagan's deregulatory agenda. Richard Harris and Sidney Milkis stress that Reagan employed the language of "regulatory relief," implying the reduction of onerous regulations, while Marc Eisner describes the 1980s as a regime of "regulatory efficiency" glorifying cost-benefit analyses to justify slashing rules.[132] These commitments to relief and efficiency facilitated agency budget cuts, economistic analyses of regulatory rules and actions, and the appointment of agency heads hostile to their agency's missions. These changes kept regulators crippled while the number of rules in the *Federal Register* plummeted.[133] But institutionally entrenched agencies did not disappear or entirely cease working. Rather, they were forced to process the increasingly large workloads that came with the era's private sector expansion while navigating a hostile political environment.[134] These deregulatory initiatives were committed to reducing the regulatory state's reach in order to decrease the odds that market participants would face any state monitoring. The languages of deregulation, regulatory relief, and efficiency never suggested entirely abandoning regulation, remaining consistent with the idea of relying on minimal and mild interventions to manage illegality. Both administrative supervision and criminal oversight of economic actors were rolled back by these political impulses.

Anyone favoring reinstating regulatory authority was derided as an advocate of "reregulation"—like Edwin Gray, chair of the Federal Home Loan Bank Board (FHLBB) from 1983 to 1987. Gray was politically ostracized for repeatedly warning of the S&L industry's impending collapse. He protested to the House Banking Committee that "[i]ndustry leaders say they want to get rid of incompetent managers and crooks, but they don't want to give the regulators enough power to do that."[135] Despite knowing that S&L markets were careening toward disaster, he was denied the authority to intervene. He claimed that Donald Regan, Reagan's treasury secretary and later chief of staff, tried to "drive [him] from office" because he had "repeatedly committed the unpardonable sin of being a reregulator." Gray said that he was admonished for warning the White House of the coming crisis because identifying risk "was not [his] role." Rather, it was indicated to him that "[his] job was to be the chief advocate of the industry and the cheerleader." He was not imagining the target on his back. The former California Department of Savings and Loans commissioner, Larry Taggart, was later interrogated by the House Banking Committee about a controversial letter he wrote to Regan in 1986 in which he complained that "actions being done" by Gray "are likely to have a very adverse impact on the ability of our party to raise needed funds in the upcoming elections."[136]

The subsequent collapse of the industry was followed by the prosecution of over one thousand bankers. This illustrates that the American state can prosecute powerful corporate actors when it wants to, especially when confronted with clear paper trails showing unambiguous fraud. But while this is sometimes celebrated as an instance of corporate criminal accountability, exploring *why* the state responded this way muddies this rosy picture. Considering this a prosecutorial success overlooks three unique features of the S&L crisis that distinguished it from most corporate scandals and created specific conditions that prompted elected leaders to respond with a stern hand. Closely examining these features gives reason for pause before overly glorifying the prosecutorial assault.

First, the S&L crisis was historically unusual in that it was fueled by paring back the power of institutions to enforce existing regulations. The deregulatory initiatives of Carter and Reagan trusted corporate actors to behave well without monitoring; when they did not, it was easy to condemn them. In this context, the S&L industry's allies had few effective defenses after the crash, and dubious claims that the state prompted the crisis by overregulating S&Ls were roundly dismissed by a chorus of voices blaming deregulation for enabling criminal conditions to fester in the marketplace.[137] Representative Henry Gonzalez (D-TX) protested that it was unfair to opine that regulators "should have been able to catch the crooks" when lawmakers "cut [their] legs off without giving [them] the proper level of auditors, accountants, and those that would be able to catch that."[138] The former chair of the Resolution Trust Corporation, L. William Seidman, was so frustrated with deregulatory fanaticism that he said, "[I]f I were asked to defend the S&L gang in court, I'd use the defense of entrapment."[139] The argument often presented after corporate scandals that "the things they did were bad, but not illegal," was irrelevant under circumstances in which industrywide misconduct was prompted by years of removing regulatory checks. It was the state's own policy choices that gave it an unusually strong basis for responding severely. In this sense, mass prosecutions gave the state a means of claiming credit for responding to the crisis while obscuring its role in causing it.

Second, the crisis involved "control fraud," in which corporate leaders exploit an organization for personal gain. The victims in this framework are not the public, but financial institutions. While debates over corporate crime have often focused on protecting markets, during the neoliberal revolution, lawmakers were eager to avenge victimized banks holding federally insured deposits by punishing executives who abused their institutions. For instance, Attorney General Dick Thornburgh claimed that prison time for executives would "go some part of the way toward restoring the integrity of the institutions that they have ripped off."[140] Danny Wall, FHLBB chair after Gray left in 1987, was "heartened" to see prosecutions for those who committed "crimes against financial institutions."[141] The banking commissioner of Texas called what S&L fraudsters did "raping a bank." Largely missing from this rhetoric was concern for members of the public whose savings were wiped out, prompting Representative Steve Bartlett (R-TX) to lament that "the borrowers or the bank customers . . . have been . . . the forgotten segment for all of this."[142] This framing was consequential for the political response—the Financial Institutions Reform, Recovery, and Enforcement Act (FIRREA) of 1989 created tools to pursue financial fraud by increasing penalties for financial institution crimes, defined as offenses against financial institutions.[143] Meanwhile, the FIRREA covered the industry's losses via a $50 billion taxpayer-financed bailout, the largest bailout in US history to that point. While the significant number of S&L convictions gave their punitive rhetoric some credibility, the impetus driving lawmakers to respond was a concern to avenge victimized banks, not the public stuck paying the bill.[144]

Third, discourses of respectability have historically insulated executives from punishment, but lawmakers and executives at surviving thrifts impugned the respectability of executives at failed thrifts. While arguments about punishing the "bad apples" in business date back a century but failed to occasion prosecutions, this rhetoric had unique applicability during a crisis prompted by explicitly fraudulent transactions rather than new forms of misconduct. But this rhetoric scapegoated individuals who ruined banks as the source of the problem without acknowledging the fraud committed by executives at surviving institutions.

Deregulation turned thrifts into attractive enrichment vehicles by loosening the restrictions on behavior known to be risky, making it easy for policymakers to lambaste failed S&L executives as self-serving schemers. As one senior federal investigator said of thrift executives prior to the 1980s, "They dressed in blue suits, they had polished shoes, they were very honest people. They may have come from a family of banking of tradition [sic]. The people who came in and bought the S&Ls in the early 1980s have none of these [qualities]."[145] Herbert Sandler of World Savings and Loan said that the deregulatory climate enticed "crooks and high rollers" who "of course raped and looted the system."[146] Without the respectability defense, fraudulent executives were deemed greedy gamblers by an army of federal officials.[147] Executives who weathered the storm like Charles Koch of the National Council of Savings Institutions explained the crisis as the result of a few "sickies" who destroyed the reputations of prudent executives by "doing really dumb things."[148] Barney Beeksma of the US League of Savings Institutions gave an impassioned speech to the Senate lamenting "the pain the honest manager of a healthy institution suffers when he or she is lumped together with the handful of crooks and highrollers who looted their companies," warning that a "lynch-mob mentality" was "unjustly threatening the innocent majority along with the handful of scoundrels."[149]

This framing created space for prosecuting the decisions of the bad actors while qualifying that criminality was not a systemic industry problem. Frank Annunzio (D-TX), chair of the House Subcommittee on Financial Institutions Supervision, said that "nowhere is the saying 'A few rotten apples can spoil the whole barrel' more true than in the S&L industry."[150] Representative Chuck Schumer (D-NY) similarly stated that "it's more important than ever that we ferret out these few bad apples that threaten to drag down an entire industry."[151] But an irony of this logic is that a bad apple can run a surviving institution as easily as a failing one; FHLBB officials found that "many institutions having a superficially healthy appearance" showed evidence of fraud on inspection, undercutting the idea that the "bad apples" at failed banks bore sole responsibility for the industry's demise.[152] This suggests that the response to the crisis was less about punishing crime—in which case fraud would have been prosecuted regardless of a bank's well-being—and more about political and economic damage control.[153] The bad apple rhetoric gave lawmakers license for a one-off prosecutorial crackdown without abandoning their commitment to deregulatory governance for the good guys, leaving fraud-ridden surviving banks unscathed.

This analysis seems disheartening. The state resorted to prosecution only because of the political fallout caused by state-sponsored deregulation, sympathy was directed toward victimized banks rather than the public, and prosecutors left fraud unpunished as long as it did not torpedo an institution. At this point, it is worth examining the criticisms of the S&L prosecutorial response as an inadequate endeavor. In *Big Money Crime* (1997), Kitty Calavita, Henry Pontell, and Robert Tillman show how the over one thousand S&L prosecutions constituted a fraction of the criminal referrals sent to the DOJ. Congress's choice to allocate $75 million annually for three years to the DOJ to prosecute financial institutions fraud cases was paltry in comparison to the $50 billion bailout handed to the banks, and the authors conclude that it was not enough to process the heap of criminal referrals prompted by the crisis. As of 1990, the FBI had 28,150 unaddressed criminal referrals for financial fraud—a number that only grew—dwarfing the roughly one thousand prosecutions brought throughout the crisis. The authors' scrutiny of criminal referral data leads them to claim that the DOJ and the FBI were "highly selective," pursuing only cases with enormous losses and irrefutable evidence of wrongdoing while neglecting thousands of credible cases without those traits.[154]

Other work corroborates this narrative. In 1993, the Commission on Financial Institution Reform, Recovery, and Enforcement published a report assessing the response to the S&L crisis. The resources of white-collar defendants and case complexity made prosecutions challenging, but, "because the perpetrators were not 'criminal-like,'" the report emphasized that prosecutors faced an uphill battle before juries.[155] This is consistent with research from the 1980s indicating that favorable impressions of white-collar offenders typically checked judges' and juries' impulses to punish wealthy offenders viewed as unlikely to recidivate.[156] S&L looters may not have looked respectable to industry insiders, but as US Attorney Robert Bonner said, the average S&L offender read to juries as "an intelligent, well-educated and relatively sophisticated person" deterrable through mild sanctions.[157] Even after the undeniable fraud behind the S&L crisis, leniency for executives remained tied to the impression that executives were not part of an inherently problematic criminal class. And despite hefty sentences for a few executives, relative leniency for S&L defendants was the norm. In 1990, then senator Joe Biden (D-DE) noted that while S&L fraudsters received 1.9 years on average, the average bank robber received 9.4 years, a trend that scholars found persisted through the remainder of the S&L prosecutions.[158]

This presents a formidable case that the success of the S&L prosecutorial blitz has been overstated, but careful consideration gives reason to resist dismissing it as a total charade. It would be rash to regard the prosecution of over one thousand bankers—including some at the top of their corporations like Charles Keating, David Paul, and Michael Milken, who received multiyear prison sentences—as wholly insignificant. Rather than oscillating between whether it was significant or inadequate, a more complicated but fulfilling answer is that the prosecutorial surge was both significant and inadequate. It was significant because this shows that the state *can* prosecute corporate crime. Over one thousand prosecutions and several multiyear sentences for high-powered executives was a striking achievement proving that the state has the capacity to punish corporate malfeasants when it commits the time, energy, and resources to doing so. However, it is true that the prosecutorial onslaught addressed only a small segment of the most flagrant criminal cases. But the state's response was not inadequate because prosecution did not do enough; it was inadequate because prosecution should not have to do everything. The atrophying of the state's regulatory muscle under the Carter and Reagan administrations was a necessary precursor to the S&L crisis. Structural changes deregulating the economy laid the groundwork for the crash by leaving dangerous conduct unchecked and allowing harmful market incentives to flourish. Regulatory governance does important work preventing criminal conduct from becoming commonplace and preserving robust banking regulations might have prevented the S&L crisis or at least rendered it smaller.

Criminogenic conditions thrived in the S&L industry as bipartisan zeal for deregulation facilitated dangerous structural shifts in the banking and financial sectors.[159] Rolling back banking regulations, combined with increasing the federal insurance backing deposits, enabled S&Ls to engage in high-risk, high-reward ventures without exposure to consequences. This created market conditions governed by perverse incentives through what economists call *moral hazard*—a situation in which financial actors can engage in extreme risk-taking to earn profits while trusting that taxpayers will cover any losses by bankrolling federal insurance or bailouts should their operations collapse.[160] Combined with resource, staffing, and budget cuts at agencies and the rejection of rules, regulations, and enforcement actions deemed cost-inefficient, regulators were hard-pressed to monitor the financial sector for red flags or intervene to discourage dangerous misconduct early in the crisis's formation.

Prosecution is an individual-level reactive tool, rendering it insufficient for single-handedly managing a crisis characterized by thousands of complex fraud cases with powerful defendants. This book has repeatedly argued that criminal punishment is an important weapon for the state to employ in cases of serious corporate wrongdoing; if administrative controls are to have deterrent power, business malefactors must know that repeated and serious violations will face escalating sanctions. But this book has also repeatedly argued that while regulatory ideology has promoted infuriating inequalities, regulation is a beneficial crime-prevention mechanism. The S&L crisis showcases how emaciating regulations can negatively affect prosecutors. Deregulation created conditions for a crisis that could have been avoided or mitigated had regulators been able to intercede earlier at lower cost to the industry, the state, and the taxpayer. Praising or critiquing the state's prosecutorial response should not eclipse how a decade of deregulation paved the way for an unmanageably large economic catastrophe to unfold that could not realistically be resolved by prosecutors alone.

There are several other troubling features of this case. First, when prosecution becomes the state's only response to corporate wrongdoing, it allows lawmakers to remain committed to deregulation by blaming individuals rather than structural economic dynamics as the cause of criminal activity. The neoliberal deregulatory drive trusted market actors to do the right thing without state referees. The result was the collapse of a fifty-year-old federally insured sector of the banking industry. Criminal prosecution was never going to clean up the entire mess, but its aggressive use obscured how deregulation fueled the crisis in favor of blaming individuals. Second, critics of the carceral state should not want prosecution to have cleaned up the entire mess. The astronomical investment necessary to process tens of thousands of banking prosecutions would have massively expanded America's carceral state, which already has a long history of being wielded against the poor and marginalized more often than against the wealthy and powerful.

Notably, Congress's primary legislative answer to the crisis in the FIRREA did little to signal a meaningful change in how the economy is governed. The law walked back some deregulations, but mostly it emphasized a reshuffling of administrative governance. It centralized and consolidated the powers formerly held by the Federal Savings and Loan Insurance Corporation (FSLIC) and the FHLBB, which were dissolved and discredited after allegedly failing to spot the crisis (an unfair claim given that FHLBB Chair Gray's warnings went ignored), within the new Office of Thrift Supervision (OTS). The OTS was designed little differently from other depository institution regulators, with the banks it regulated paying assessments and fees that funded the agency's budget. It earned a reputation as a relatively lax regulator in the 1990s and operated for only twenty-two years before being absorbed into another regulatory body, the Consumer Financial Protection Bureau, after it failed to foresee the financial crisis of 2007–8.[161] Along with other banking agencies (like the Office of the Comptroller of the Currency), the FSLIC, the FHLBB, and the OTS were granted administrative cease-and-desist powers comparable to those of the FTC and the SEC and shared a similar institutional design that elevated administrative controls as the primary mechanism for controlling criminal conduct.[162] Given that these banking regulators were all executive branch delegations within the Treasury Department, this provides further evidence that modern executive branch agencies continue to utilize schemes to control criminal behavior via administration.

Despite its intentions, the FIRREA had a limited impact. Rearranging the powers of dissolved agencies among new ones bearing similar structural designs hardly constituted a departure from how regulatory ideology had long been practiced. But when coupled to long-term investments in regulation and enforcement, the FIRREA had potential to provide an institutional foundation for a stronger approach to managing financial crime. This is because Congress shored up the DOJ's prosecutorial powers in Title XXV of the 1990 Crime Control Act by establishing the DOJ Financial Institutions Fraud Unit to coordinate and prosecute financial institution fraud cases.[163] However, a 1993 Government Accounting Office report revealed inadequacies in its mandates and design, finding that the unit had limited capabilities to promote coordination among decentralized US attorneys' offices and that it was unable to build a caseload without regulatory support. With agencies managing ongoing budgetary and resource constraints through the 1990s, the unit lacked the necessary assistance to build a robust caseload and was unable to fulfill its functions.[164] Because prosecution and regulation should serve as complementary controls on markets, controlling financial crime required substantial reforms and investments across multiple institutions of government. The persistence of neoliberal commitments to minimal regulation and fiscal austerity left the FIRREA and the Financial Institutions Fraud Unit unable to realize their potential.

The political shifts of the 1970s and 1980s unleashed America's financial institutions and resulted in crisis. Subsequent prosecutorial zeal was driven by lawmakers' desire to curb economic and political fallout by stanching the financial hemorrhaging at victimized banks that were rapidly losing federally insured money.[165] But while some executives landed long sentences, years of regulatory cuts left the state able to pursue only a fraction of the cases referred to the DOJ while securing average sentences far lower than the average punishments for street-level property crimes. This unique moment of criminal accountability for some executives should not obscure how the case also highlights deeper inadequacies in lawmakers' approach to managing the economy and the important role effective regulation plays in keeping markets safe.

Regulation in the Twentieth Century

The Great Depression, the consumer rights movement, and the S&L crisis each involved serious challenges to the regulatory model of managing corporate wrongdoing. Roosevelt's securities packages imposed significant constraints on markets in the wake of the riveting Pecora hearings, but those reforms were designed to stabilize capitalism, and the SEC has historically been reluctant to resort to criminal charges.[166] Consumer activists secured meaningful changes to the FTC by empowering consumers to seek compensatory damages, but the institution's criminal enforcement powers remained untouched. The S&L crisis showed that there are conditions under which the state can pursue major corporate prosecutions, but those circumstances were unique, and we should not let prosecutorial enthusiasm overshadow how deregulation allowed the crisis to take shape. Each case offers lessons for how corporate power can be challenged, but each also shows the durability of the state's commitments to elevating regulation over prosecution of corporate wrongdoing in changing contexts.

From Keynesians in Roosevelt's Brain Trust to outraged lawmakers from both parties in the S&L era, principles of the ideology of regulation were endorsed, modified, and repackaged across the political spectrum as the proper organizing logic for the state's response to corporate lawbreaking. By the time these debates unfolded, American institutions were already firmly structured on these principles, which had become established as the state's tried-and-true approach to dealing with corporate crime. As it was modified and adapted by political actors, and as it interacted with evolving arrangements of political and legal institutions, the ideology of regulation proved durable in the face of repeated scandals involving egregious and widely condemned instances of corporate misconduct.

7

Reunifying Rehabilitative and Regulatory Ideologies in the Twenty-First Century

> It always amazes me in America that we can lock up a single mother for stealing a can of spaghetti sauce at the convenience store, but we allow this kind of stuff to go on.
> REPRESENTATIVE CHARLES WILSON (D-OH) on the
> Madoff Ponzi scheme

Rehabilitative and regulatory ideologies are not historical relics, but entrenched features of American politics. When critics of the carceral state argue that we should resurrect the rehabilitative prison and opponents of corporate power advocate for more regulation to control corporate crime, they reinforce established assumptions about race, class, and social control that keep rehabilitative and regulatory ideologies alive.

This chapter addresses the tenacity and adaptability of these ideologies today. The first section explores how, after operating on separate tracks following their emergence, rehabilitative and regulatory ideologies are being reunified by an ensemble of conservative voices in the modern era. Their political development followed unpredictable and nonparallel paths through the twentieth century, but today conservative actors are reconfiguring their social control logics to support neoliberal cost-efficiency goals. While biological understandings of human behavior are quieted in but not gone from these conversations, myths of natural difference and incorrigibility remain in operation without eugenic politics as the ideologies have been repurposed in pursuit of lean and waste-free governance. The second section traces the influence of these modified rehabilitative ideas in the 2018 First Step Act (FSA), while the final section explores the mobilization of regulatory ideas in cases spanning from the accounting scandals of the early twenty-first century through the Dodd-Frank Act of 2010 and ongoing conservative efforts to undermine it.

Neoliberalism and Governing Efficiencies

Conservative lawmakers and right-wing knowledge-producing institutions have been pivotal in advocating rehabilitative and regulatory mentalities in

the modern era as means to streamline governance and achieve policy efficiencies in criminal justice and market regulation.[1] This section explores key
institutional players in this network, including the Manhattan Institute, the
Heritage Foundation, the Hudson Institute, the Cato Institute, the American
Enterprise Institute, and the Right on Crime Association. Supported by dark
money from the Koch brothers, this collection of think tanks has revived,
adapted, and modified these ideologies by linking their core tenets to the
goals of neoliberal cost efficiency instead of eugenic principles.[2]

As a political ideology, neoliberalism emphasizes market mechanisms as
the appropriate means for organizing all aspects of life, conceptualizing citizens
as the entrepreneurs of their own human capital and as entirely responsible
for their own success or failure. This mentality discards the role that structural
forces play in producing inequality by explaining every individual's circumstances as a function of personal choices, portraying welfare and regulation as
disruptions to processes that produce a natural social order. Despite neoliberalism's philosophical commitments to smaller government, neoliberal policies
often manifest as forceful state interventions that foist competitive dynamics
into nonmarket contexts, repurposing the state rather than reducing its role.[3]

Rehabilitative discourse aligns with neoliberalism by proposing techniques
to equip individuals with the skills necessary to survive in middle-class settings as means of reducing crime. This overlooks the consequences of returning individuals to marginalized communities with scarce opportunities to use
those skills. Rehabilitative thinking serves as an appealing justification for
the neoliberal order by emphasizing the enhancement of individuals' human
capital as the solution to crime, prioritizing fixing individuals before sending
them home without fixing the issues in their home communities. However,
it seems harder to reconcile regulatory ideology with neoliberal commitments to deregulation. But, in a way that is similar to the cases presented in
the previous chapter, contemporary conservatives understand "deregulation"
as entailing the implementation of trimmed-down regulation rather than its
wholesale elimination. This mentality squares regulatory ideology with a
neoliberal framework by assuming that disciplined, market-incentivized executives will behave conscientiously and produce social benefits if they are
permitted to pursue their own interests with less stringent oversight. In a
neoliberal climate, rehabilitative and regulatory ideologies consequently become self-fulfilling logics. Rehabilitative ideology portrays criminality as a
function of individual-level forces, rationalizing slashing social safety nets
and expanding carceral institutions for irredeemable economically disadvantaged offenders, while regulatory ideology assumes that disciplined executives can be efficiently controlled with less supervision.

REHABILITATIVE-CARCERAL EFFICIENCY

The rehabilitative ideal's sorting logic is one of its most persistent ideological features in contemporary discourse. Rehabilitative strategies that accurately sort redeemable from irredeemable inmates are increasingly being framed as cost-effective practices that efficiently direct the allocation of limited public funding. This is particularly clear in the modernization of risk assessments. While this reframing of the rehabilitative approach justifies harsh justice for presumed incorrigibles without an explicitly eugenic grounding, the surging popularity of biocriminology risks complementing these trends by providing new scientific bases for linking inherent criminality to the variables of class and race.

Conservative think tanks' embrace of rehabilitative cost-efficiency logics becomes clear in the next section's analysis of the FSA, but conservative thought leaders endorsed this framework for streamlining prison spending prior to the act's passage. For instance, consider the 2015 testimony of the Heritage Foundation's John Malcolm before the House Oversight Committee, in which he advocated for rehabilitative reforms to the justice system. He began by articulating the duality of the rehabilitative ideal: "While some hardened and violent offenders will likely always pose a threat to public safety and should remain incarcerated, many offenders, particularly those with only a modest prior record who take advantage of prison rehabilitation and skills training programs, could end up becoming productive, law-abiding members of society." But he then explained that he saw "each prison cell as very valuable real estate" that should be preserved for those posing "the greatest threat." He expressed concern about the inefficient expenditure of "billions of dollars" on imprisoning inmates "at a time when we actually have control over them and can provide incentives, both positive (in the case of prisoners) and negative (in the case of probationers), to participate in and complete such programs."[4] His statement tailored the rehabilitative ideal's duality to economize prison space and correctional operations, underscoring that rehabilitation's benevolent and punitive prongs both employ coercive state action to yield positive outcomes by simultaneously detaining the incorrigible inmates while reshaping the behavior and mindset of others. Another longtime advocate of rehabilitation as a path to cost savings has been the conservative activist Grover Norquist.[5] His Right on Crime initiative defends expanding probation for adult offenders on the grounds that "probation is significantly cheaper than incarceration" and "can be a cost-effective form of rehabilitation." Right on Crime proposes that the state "institute performance-based funding for probation departments," directing spending only to successful departments.[6]

These statements may appear to present an opportunity to pursue bipartisan prison reform, but many scholars persuasively caution against rooting a prison reform agenda in the language of cost efficiency. Fiscal arguments have proved ineffective in reducing incarceration, only generating spending cuts that create bleaker prison conditions and diminished oversight and accountability for penal institutions.[7] Framing probation as a net taxpayer benefit also disregards the myriad economic consequences of imposing invasive probation requirements on more citizens.[8] Finally, tying probation departments' budgets to their performance is self-defeating as evaluating rehabilitative interventions against the slippery metric of recidivism regularly rebounds to law-and-order impulses. Imposing punitive fiscal austerity measures on underperforming departments would reduce their resources and lead to poorer-quality services, undermining their prospects for improvement and increasing the likelihood that their probationers would earn designations of incorrigibility.

Modern rehabilitative discourse has also shifted by abandoning the explicit identification of incorrigibles on the basis of racial and class traits. However, these biases have been subtly integrated into growingly popular actuarial risk-assessment technologies. Through these tools, which counties and states typically purchase from private companies, the racial and class biases of the rehabilitative model have been transformed into mathematical calculations that use an offender's personal traits—including familiar variables like criminal history, employment status, and educational history as well as nebulous factors like "antisocial personality pattern[s]" and "procriminal attitudes"—to estimate the rate at which individuals with comparable profiles recidivate. Assessment metrics are used by sentencing judges and prison administrators to forecast individuals' likelihood of recidivism, determine their prison term, and consider their potential release and access to reformative programming behind bars.[9] Risk assessments reflect a simultaneous commitment to punishment and rehabilitation by sorting inmates into categories of criminal risk with varying degrees of access to rehabilitative interventions and early release.[10] Even in jurisdictions lacking actuarial tools, the concept of risk assessment still permeates criminal justice as many states incorporate assessment principles into sentencing guidelines via criminal history scores.[11]

Risk assessments are sometimes framed as "risk/needs assessments," with a focus on needs allegedly fortifying their rehabilitative character by emphasizing an individual's changeable traits as the flip side to static risks requiring a punitive hand. But there is little reason to think the inclusion of needs variables—typically a catalog of arguably transformable personality traits—is anything more than a strategic reformulation meant to defend risk assessments under the cover of rehabilitative rhetoric. Rather than leading to benevolent prisons, risk/needs dichotomies have fueled a punitive culture in which populations compete for access to limited resources.[12] This risk/needs binary is not a new innovation; it is an established facet of the rehabilitative model that reframes diverse traits and inequalities as individual faults. Like rehabilitation, risk/needs logics assume that people can navigate socioeconomic deprivation if they are individually empowered with the tools needed to overcome those structural barriers and that those who fail to get on the right path after treatment must be irredeemable. This adaptation in phraseology deploys rehabilitative language to buy more credibility for metrics that are just putting another brick in the wall of the carceral state.

Risk assessments make penal determinations technical, allowing their advocates to assert that they efficiently cleanse bias from decision-making. Conservative supporters of risk assessments, like Rafael Mangual of the Manhattan Institute, defend their technical predictivity by citing evidence that risk assessments have little impact on the demographic profile of inmate populations, a logic that necessarily ignores the racial and class skews that already exist in prisons and jails.[13] Similarly, Hudson Institute scholars have defended risk assessments as empirically sound by emphasizing that "[a] large body of research suggests that actuarial systems based on large data pools—especially if they incorporate 'dynamic' factors (like age and psychological profile) into their otherwise 'linear' or 'static' predictive algorithms—provide more accurate risk assessments than are generally possible using the judgments of experienced, professional individuals alone."[14]

Despite their scientific character, risk assessments have become subjects of criticism because of their predictive inaccuracies and their legitimation of racial and class inequalities.[15] Bernard Harcourt has shown that this is not new; since the early twentieth century, actuarial assessments of criminal risk have been infused with racial bias. But in the modern age, a heavy emphasis on criminal history in risk assessments serves "as a proxy for race," and the inclusion of class characteristics like financial circumstances cements additional prejudices into assessments.[16] Some jurisdictions also code by geographic variables, generating biases against citizens in urban communities.[17] A sizable body of scholarship has attacked the flawed assumptions underlying these assessments, particularly by accentuating their reliance on arrest and conviction data to determine risk. Arrest and prosecution rates vary significantly across race, class, zip code, and more because they are influenced by the discretionary choices of law enforcement and different local budgetary priorities.[18] Such measures do not reliably gauge genuine behavioral trends, but the use of these data to calculate risk produces higher risk estimates for those prone to criminal justice encounters, whether that be for racial, class, or regional reasons, laundering the biases of law enforcement into individual-level risks.[19]

Risk assessments are consistent with rehabilitative ideology. The indeterminate sentence originated as a means of separating low-risk reformable inmates from high-risk incorrigibles, and Elmira's "marks system" graded inmates into tiers of corrigibility dictating access to certain resources and opportunities.[20] Judges and penal administrators have long attempted to assess defendants' risk, often through racial and class variables, when implementing the indeterminate sentence. As the rehabilitative ideal has long done, modern risk assessments offer a framework for turning structural inequalities into individual-level risks.[21] But notably, modern risk assessments achieve this without the eugenic flavor of older rehabilitative techniques by replacing clinical judgment and determinist assumptions with calculations and cost-efficacy mentalities to sort the prison population, justifying racial and class biases through the use of mathematical language.

While rehabilitative politics is distanced from its eugenic foundation, it is worth acknowledging that biological theories of crime have gained prominence in recent years. This discourse is consistent with neoliberalism's emphasis on individual responsibility and merit.[22] As Stephen Jay Gould aptly notes, "Resurgences of biological determinism correlate with periods of political retrenchment and destruction of social generosity."[23] Biocriminological theory and neoliberalism together attribute criminality and inequality to a shared set of inherent deficiencies, creating a political context ripe for racial and economically determinist notions of incorrigibility to flourish and justify harsh policies against marginalized groups.

The contemporary revival of such ideas stems from 1970s and 1980s genetics research that, despite being strenuously disputed and criticized, legitimized genetics as an analytic framework in criminology.[24] Determinist arguments appeared in the research of James Wilson, Richard Herrnstein, and Charles Murray through the 1980s and the 1990s via theories that IQ was genetically predetermined and explained social ills like crime.[25] Some recent scholarship is even more explicitly determinist. Adrian Raine's *The Anatomy of Violence* (2013) claims that Lombroso "was on the path towards a sublime truth," connects violent crime to genetic and neurological factors, and proposes a future in which risk assessments are based on genetic and neurological screening to segregate high-risk offenders for indefinite detention and partial-risk offenders for enhanced police surveillance.[26]

Some may suggest that this scholarship need not be taken seriously given that criminal justice reform is a popular social cause in the modern moment.

That is mistaken. Biocriminology is a growing academic field, with the American Society of Criminology establishing its Biopsychosocial Criminology Division in 2017.[27] The general public is also receptive to these ideas. Raine's book so effectively tapped into the public's lurid fascination with the criminal mind that it was adapted as a CBS pilot.[28] This is not simply morbid curiosity, but a sign that the public is open to these concepts. And while technically they are not compulsory, programs in at least nine states permit chemical or surgical castration for sex offenders, although the policies are more coercive in practice than is suggested, while illegal inmate sterilizations have been conducted in several other states.[29] Meanwhile, growing authoritarian and White-supremacist groups are increasingly embracing genetic explanations of human difference to rationalize their agendas.[30] And importantly, biocriminology aligns with rehabilitative ideology by sorting individuals as reformable or incorrigible. For example, Raine supports solutions ranging from inclusive social interventions like early childhood education or rehabilitative strategies like meditation training to surgical and chemical castration for sex offenders and issuing state licenses to would-be parents to curtail the spread of criminal genetics.[31] Similarly, the neuroscientist David Eagleman defends "a more biologically informed jurisprudence" that "customize[s] sentencing [and] leverage[s] new opportunities for rehabilitation." In a sentence that could have been written by Boies or Brockway, he suggests that "deeper biological insight into behavior will foster a better understanding of recidivism," meaning that "some people will need to be taken off the streets for a longer time (even a lifetime), because their likelihood of reoffense is high; others, because of differences in neural constitution, are less likely to recidivate, and so can be released sooner." This, he concludes, will "parlay biological understanding into customized rehabilitation."[32]

Modern biocriminologists insist that their work is rooted in cutting-edge techniques, distinguishing it from the crude and prejudiced methods of earlier generations. This logic sounds persuasive, but it eschews the humility of historical perspective. Progressive era eugenicists genuinely believed that they were employing objective methods as true scientists. Nevertheless, the flaws in their approaches became apparent over time. This history serves as a reminder that overzealous scientific certainty has often reinforced the punitive aspect of the rehabilitative ideal. Genetics is a young intellectual enterprise, and while it has made significant contributions in medical treatment and testing, the alleged heritability of crime is not comparable to the heritability of disease, as some biocriminologists suggest.[33] Crime is a social construct that evolves across time and place and is subject to contestation and change; it is not an organic phenomenon like a malignant tumor. As a result, new medical treatments and proactive screening for diseases like cancer prompted by genetic research do not raise the same ethical, due process, and human rights concerns as the proactive punishment and surveillance of presupposed criminals. Relying on contested knowledge to make such recommendations is perilous, but as was the case with earlier generations, the disputable empirics of an emergent science are veiled behind complex language that allows scholars to overreach without criticism.[34]

Although modern conservatives have effectively distanced rehabilitative rhetoric from eugenics, some still promote determinist views of crime. For example, a 2022 Manhattan Institute report linked the psychological state of "entitlement," understood as "a frame of mind that prioritizes the whims, wants, and needs of the individual above the rights, desires, and needs of others," to crime, suggesting that "the prevalence of entitlement among criminal offenders" explains the failure of correctional interventions to reduce recidivism.[35] Other Manhattan Institute publications defend the work of Wilson, Murray, and Herrnstein, highlighting factors like "IQ [and] brain chemistry" as shaping the "predisposition to offend."[36] The American Enterprise Institute has been especially active in championing determinist ideas, facilitated by Charles Murray's position there (he holds an endowed chair), from which he regularly defends his controversial 1994 book *The Bell Curve*. He insists that "the relationship of IQ to criminality is especially pronounced in the small fraction of . . . chronic criminals that account for a disproportionate amount of crime," who he states dominate the bottom of the class hierarchy.[37] Biocriminology may not be necessary for modern rehabilitative politics to have harmful consequences, but it is a growing field that validates neoliberal impulses and could contribute to a political climate inclined toward punitive innovations for incorrigibles.

REGULATORY EFFICIENCY

Right-wing politicians and think tanks have similarly been revitalizing regulatory ideology to advance a neoliberal cost-efficiency agenda. Again, they claim that *deregulation* is a misunderstood word. They advocate for easing, not eliminating, regulations. According to Jason Gattuso of the Heritage Foundation, *deregulation* is a "shorthand to describe the repeal or easing of particular rules."[38] Norbert Michel, also of the Heritage Foundation, similarly embraces this mindset, claiming that the Trump administration focused on "finely tailoring" regulations to achieve cost-effective oversight rather than pursuing "massive deregulation," as his critics assert.[39] Within this framework, beliefs in the inherent market-disciplined tendencies of economic actors persist, justifying minimal regulations rather than stern prohibitions on economic infractions.

A good case illustrating how conservative forces are repurposing regulatory ideology comes from a 2016 piece by Michel in which he argues that the Reagan and Bush administrations provided regulatory relief by easing rules without engaging in full deregulation. He contends that the two presidents actually "cemented an ever-expanding financial regulatory framework" by "allow[ing] financial firms to engage in activities that were previously prohibited . . . under the watchful eye of regulators."[40] Repurposing regulation to allow previously prohibited actions to occur under administrative supervision certainly does not reject regulatory ideology. Scaling back state oversight by replacing strict prohibitions with administrative supervision reflects the very essence of the regulatory ideological approach, showing how conservative forces are molding regulatory ideological ideas to suit new goals.

One year later, Michel and his colleague Gerald Dwyer proposed reforms that would allow financial institutions to apply for Office of the Comptroller of the Currency (OCC) approval to be subjected to "lower federal regulatory restrictions" and earn exemptions from a litany of federal regulations, including rules intended to spot signs of money laundering that the authors claim are "clearly not cost-effective." Their proposal would restrict the OCC to considering only "the character of management and directors through standard background checks and verifying that the firm meets a relatively high equity ratio" in approving applications.[41] Loosening oversight of potentially criminal activity in pursuit of cost savings on the basis of positive character assessments of corporate leadership remains entirely consistent with the regulatory ideological mentality of relaxing supervision for respectable corporate actors.

Some argue that regulation must be further reduced because the deregulatory agendas of recent conservatives never actually diminished regulation, but these perspectives rely on deceptive reasoning. David Henderson of the Cato Institute employs a common tactic to rationalize this view by citing the number of rules in the *Federal Register*, noting that despite promises of deregulation from recent conservative presidents, there were approximately seventy-five thousand rules in 2009, compared to about seventy-two thousand in 1981. This, Henderson states, shows that concerns about deregulation are overstated and that regulations require reduction. But rule counting is a superficial measure of regulatory power that does not consider agency enforcement cultures, the priorities and agendas of agency leadership, staffing and budgetary cuts to regulatory bodies, or the need for new rules in growing sectors (a 4 percent increase in the number of rules from 1981 to 2009 seems inadequate when considered against the tremendous growth of the private sector in that time).[42] Despite this, Henderson uses the argument to position himself as an advocate of leaner regulation.[43]

Demands for smarter regulation sync with neoliberal preoccupations over cost efficiency. Casey Mulligan, the former chief economist for President Trump's Council of Economic Advisers, defended the administration's regulatory reforms in a Manhattan Institute piece highlighting their "considerable cost savings."[44] Likewise, the Hudson Institute's Christopher DeMuth commended the Trump administration's regulatory budgeting approach, which required new rules to be accompanied by the withdrawal of enough existing rules to offset the estimated costs of new regulations.[45] Relatedly, Heritage Foundation authors have raised familiar concerns about excessive regulatory penalties compromising natural market efficiencies. In an essay in the Heritage Foundation volume *Prosperity Unleashed: Smarter Financial Regulation*, Amanda Rose asserts that negative consequences follow overzealous regulatory enforcement, like firms withholding information from investors or inundating them with excessive information as protective measures against prosecution, rendering market interactions less efficient. She concludes that "criminal penalties raise serious over-deterrence concerns."[46]

As is the case with rehabilitative discourse, cost-efficiency rhetoric has made it unnecessary for conservative forces to invoke eugenic assumptions about the inherent qualities of the capitalist class in these conversations about regulation and corporate punishment. However, this language perseveres, with Charles Murray again being a prominent voice. In American Enterprise Institute pieces reiterating *The Bell Curve*'s conclusions, Murray contends that a "cognitive elite" is emerging, which he defines as a social class consisting of individuals with naturally high IQs who are channeled into "lucrative and influential careers." He associates this social stratum with the capitalist class, stating that IQ is particularly "important for business executives," and concluding that executive suites have been "filled with bright people" from this group owing to their superior genetic inheritance.[47] But he goes beyond naturalizing class inequality and capitalist meritocracy. After asserting that criminality is naturally concentrated among the lower classes, he claims that "high intelligence also provides some protection against lapsing into criminality," providing arguments that jointly reinforce beliefs that the poor are perpetually incorrigible while the "cognitive elite" in corner offices naturally respect the law.[48] This logic disregards myriad explanations of white-collar criminality through differential association, psychological distancing, and more by suggesting that the natural traits of capitalist elites insulate them from criminal temptations.[49]

Scholarship examining the biology of corporate lawbreakers is limited but reinforces popular assumptions about class differences and crime. A 2011 study comparing a group of white-collar offenders with matched controls concluded that "white-collar criminals have better executive functioning, enhanced information processing, and structural brain superiorities." The authors did not necessarily intend to present white-collar criminals favorably, but they drew a sharp and familiar contrast between white-collar criminality and street criminality.[50] Given the growing popularity of biocriminological ideas, such work could exacerbate the inclination of justice officials to mitigate sentences for elite wrongdoers on the basis of positive beliefs about their transformability. Scholars have demonstrated how assumptions regarding the intellectual and social intelligence of executives continue to sway judges and prosecutors to seek lenient sentences for elite offenders as they are perceived as rational and sufficiently deterrable via minimal sanctions following the distress of arrest and trial.[51]

The reunification of rehabilitative and regulatory ideologies by modern conservative forces seeking neoliberal governing efficiencies highlights their dynamic nature. With their eugenic foundations suppressed, they have been reformulated to serve the goals of cost-effective governance and fiscal austerity. This showcases both ideologies' adaptability, exhibiting how they have evolved in the hands of policy-driven governing elites and political interests putting them into practice in pursuit of specific policy objectives.

Risk, Rehabilitation, and the First Step Act

Enacted in 2018 with bipartisan support, the FSA reformed federal prisons and sentencing and increased rehabilitative opportunities for those in federal custody. A central component of the law was a risk-assessment tool for the Federal Bureau of Prisons (BOP) to use when making judgments about inmates' recidivism risk that dictated their access to rehabilitative opportunities and potential for early release. Lawmakers built the FSA and its risk and needs assessment on the assumption that reformable inmates should be transformed into productive citizens while incorrigibles are kept incarcerated. Once more, the language of rehabilitation cloaked a policy's harsh features, and conservative forces have kept public discussion of the law rooted in a rehabilitative framework dressed in considerations of cost efficiency and risk.

In the FSA debates, lawmakers routinely defended the law's risk assessment using the language of rehabilitation. Representative Bob Goodlatte (R-VA), chair of the House Judiciary Committee and cosponsor of the bill, defended the FSA when it first reached the chamber floor by stating that it "places a new focus on rehabilitation." But he qualified that a new "risk and needs assessment" ensured that the law would take "a practical, intelligent approach to rehabilitation" by rehabilitating the prison population to "the greatest extent practicable" through limiting interventions to those likely to succeed. Some House Democrats expressed concern. Jerry Nadler (D-NY) worried that the "problematic risk-assessment tool" could "exacerbate racial and socioeconomic disparities already present in the criminal justice system," while Pramila Jayapal (D-WA) lamented that it could be used to "[fight] attempts to advance racial justice" if administered by the wrong hands, such as then attorney general Jeff Sessions.[52] The House Judiciary Committee's report on the bill reflected this tension. A group of liberal dissenters claimed that the assessment "could exacerbate racial biases in our criminal justice system," while the Republican majority framed the tool as a cost-saving measure that would enable administrators to "[improve] the effectiveness and efficiency of the federal prison system in order to control corrections spending, manage the prison population, and reduce recidivism."[53] The alleged fiscal benefits of the bill earned it support from conservative institutions, which wedded its rehabilitative orientation to promises of cost efficiency. Michael Tanner of the Cato Institute defended the FSA by writing that, "[o]ver the long run, most experts believe the legislation would save money" and explaining that "since nearly all prisoners will eventually be released, programs to reduce recidivism are also likely to prove cost-effective."[54]

Democrats in the Senate gave the bill a chilly reception. Senators Cory Booker (D-NJ) and Kamala Harris (D-CA) opposed the bill's risk assessment, lack of sentencing reforms, and long list of offenses triggering exclusion from rehabilitative programming. The bill was also opposed by the Leadership Conference on Civil and Human Rights (LCCHR), which published a scathing critique of the bill signed by over one hundred criminal justice reform and civil rights groups. The letter condemned the risk algorithm for creating a means of legitimizing the racial biases in the prison system.[55] However, the Senate passed the bill after Booker and others introduced a version including modest sentencing reforms and creating an independent review committee (IRC) that would be staffed by an independent organization that would oversee the design and implementation of the risk assessment. Booker justified his change of heart through a commitment to rehabilitation, saying, "None of us should ever be judged by the least of what we have done but, instead, by our ability and our capacity to find redemption."[56] Booker's conservative colleagues shared his enthusiasm but emphasized the risk assessment's cost-effective nature as the bill limited rehabilitative opportunities only to those deemed low risk. Senator Chuck Grassley (R-IA), one of the cosponsors of the Senate bill, defended the risk assessment by connecting the individualizing language of rehabilitative ideology to the bill's anticipated cost effectiveness:

Today, taxpayers pay more than $7 billion a year on our federal prison popu-
lation. However, despite that high cost, nearly half of the inmates released
today are re-arrested. . . . I consider myself a law and order Republican. I'm
also a taxpayer watchdog. And I believe in the redemptive power of rehabilitation. . . . We needed to make the system work better for the taxpayer, help law
enforcement fight crime, and put a stopper in the revolving prison door. . . .
The First Step Act is carefully crafted to provide opportunities at redemption
for low-risk inmates while ensuring that dangerous and career criminals stay
behind bars. It does this through a multi-layer system that filters out dangerous criminals and those likely to commit new crimes.[57]

The Senate bill also enjoyed support from groups like the International Association of Chiefs of Police and the National District Attorneys Association,
among others.[58]

The Senate version received approval from House Democrats. Nadler
moved to support the bill in part because the inclusion of an IRC would
help "make this new system more fair." Sheila Jackson Lee (D-TX) similarly
changed her position on the basis of these changes. Even the LCCHR and
the American Civil Liberties Union (ACLU) switched sides, urging Congress
to pass the revised FSA and noting that the IRC would "ensure the risk and
needs assessment system is evidence based" and thus "mitigate any harms"
the law might otherwise inflict. They also praised the reformed bill for expanding opportunities to use earned credits to receive supervised community
release, checking prison administrators' discretion to deny early release, and
providing funding for traditional rehabilitative techniques like drug treatment and vocational training.[59]

This shift by the ACLU and the LCCHR highlights a significant obstacle
in contemporary prison reform. Many critics of the carceral state sincerely
champion rehabilitation on the basis of the word's plain meaning, believing
that a *rehabilitative* criminal justice system should operate on the assumption
that everyone has the capacity for redemption. Their advocacy for expanding
traditional rehabilitative methods is not tied to a promise of merciless punishment for incorrigibles. Rather, their politics are geared toward genuinely
trying to dislodge the logics that have powered mass incarceration by securing humane improvements to the justice system via compassionate rehabilitative solutions. The problem is that despite their virtuous intentions, they do
not see how America's network of criminal justice institutions is steeped in
premises and practices designed to operate on the assumption that reformable offenders can be identified only in contrast to the incorrigibles requiring
punishment. When such actors promote a benevolent understanding of the
rehabilitative ideal in an attempt to extend its compassionate hand, they do

so at the cost of unintentionally enabling the extension of its clenched fist for incorrigibles. In other words, because the two prongs of rehabilitative ideology operate in tandem, earnestly appealing to a humane understanding of rehabilitation cannot resolve America's carceral crisis.

These difficulties and the punitive duality of the FSA's rehabilitative logic became apparent soon after the law went into effect. The FSA's rehabilitative programs have consistently been left unavailable to large swaths of federal inmates, largely because of the law's risk-assessment PATTERN (Prisoner Assessment Tool Targeting Estimated Risk and Needs).[60] PATTERN calculates risk utilizing variables like employment history, criminal record, education, offense severity, and myriad other factors. In a defense of PATTERN, Heritage Foundation fellow Charles Stimson praised the DOJ for relying on experts to design a "sophisticated" assessment tool incorporating "eight main dynamic risk factors," including "anti-social attitudes . . . peers . . . personality . . . substance abuse . . . marital/family issues . . . employment . . . education, and . . . use of leisure time." These variables constitute the potentially malleable "needs" of an offender, though it is unclear how factors like "personality" or "anti-social attitudes" can reliably be empirically valued for risk calculation. Stimson said that the success of PATTERN hinged on the success of its recidivism reduction programs and that PATTERN would sort eligible prisoners into programs suited to their unique needs. But he adopted a narrow lens to assess its efficacy that echoed assumptions of incorrigibility and embraced the ethic of individual responsibility. He wrote that "[t]he success or failure for any federal prisoner, once PATTERN is fully operational and funded, falls on the shoulders of the prisoner" because "[i]t is the convicted prisoner who must decide whether to fully participate in custom-designed programs in prison created to help him re-enter society with the skills to succeed, and then stay out of trouble once free from custody."[61] The Manhattan Institute's Rafael Mangual has called for evaluating PATTERN through an economistic lens, proposing that funding for FSA antirecidivism programs should be tied to measures of "offender behavior during and after their terms of incarceration" so that funding can be allocated only to programs that proved cost-effective at achieving rehabilitative outcomes.[62]

PATTERN is an example of how easily assessment tools built in the name of rehabilitation can exacerbate punitive inequalities. The first version of PATTERN, released in 2019, was widely condemned for narrowly limiting the availability of rehabilitative programming credits while demonstrating racial disparities in assessing risk.[63] A July 2019 report from the DOJ indicated that to that date PATTERN had classified 53 percent of Black men in federal custody as high risk, compared to 29 percent of White men, while 7 percent of

Black men earned the minimum-risk classification, compared to 30 percent of White men.[64] The DOJ conducted another analysis of PATTERN in early 2020, with Heritage's Stimson praising the report for proving that PATTERN was race neutral through an "Area under the Curve Analysis," a conclusion that overlooked the "layers of bias" embedded in the arrest and conviction data feeding the assessment metric.[65] Then, in May 2020, ProPublica published a report showing that the BOP secretly wrote an internal policy document modifying PATTERN's algorithm to render it harder for inmates to qualify as low risk, violating the FSA's transparency requirements.[66] In June, the DOJ published a response publicizing the reformed calculations but did not refute concerns over PATTERN's racial and class biases. The DOJ had also previously stated that federal prisons would release more low-risk inmates to home confinement given the spread of COVID-19 behind bars, but while the DOJ's June report indicated that about 20 percent of inmates earned a minimum-risk classification, only 1.8 percent of people under BOP control were released by that time.[67] The DOJ's manipulation of PATTERN reflects a familiar legacy of rehabilitative politics—rehabilitative language can be used to rationalize punitiveness simply by altering the balance of how many inmates are deemed incorrigible.

The IRC has done little to fix these problems. Normally, an organization serving in such a capacity would be selected by the National Institute of Justice (NIJ) through a competitive process. But faced with an expedited timeline, the NIJ issued a noncompetitive award to the Hudson Institute to act as the IRC. Hudson has a lengthy history of advancing tough-on-crime arguments, with its website running articles describing mass incarceration as a "myth" and arguing that President Trump should oppose criminal justice reform.[68] Lawmakers on both sides of the aisle viewed the choice as nothing less than an attempt to undermine the FSA. Senator Dick Durbin (D-IL) compared the selection to "let[ting] a fox in the chicken coop," and after learning of Hudson's selection, Senator Mike Lee (R-UT) said, "I don't see a lot of good faith in implementing this law."[69] Hudson's initial report on the risk assessment emphasized that "recidivism is a serious issue," warning that nearly half of those released from federal prison are rearrested within two years. Despite acknowledging its mandate to "incrementally reduce the federal prison population," Hudson claimed that "a not insignificant percentage" of inmates would be disqualified from rehabilitative programming and early release because of their risk estimates.[70]

The story of the IRC is partially a failure of implementation and partially one of design. Rehabilitative interventions have long been evaluated in terms of their ability to produce measurable reductions in recidivism. The IRC's failures were expedited by Bill Barr's DOJ and the selection of Hudson, but even an administration committed to a compassionate rehabilitative approach would have prompted a punitive backlash in the absence of any immediate reduction in recidivism. This is a deeper problem with rehabilitative logic. By attempting to rehabilitate individuals without addressing the structural inequalities that drive behavior, rehabilitative ideology justifies punitive outcomes for those who recommit crimes by assuming that they personally are the sole cause of their behavior. Had a different DOJ made a genuinely magnanimous attempt to rehabilitate more inmates under the FSA and then released them to decaying communities with limited opportunities to succeed, it likely would have ended in a revival of Martinson's "nothing works" doctrine.

Rehabilitative ideology has long been connected to the logic of risk assessment. In the FSA, soft-sounding rehabilitative language once again concealed the state's unforgiving evaluation of risk to justify harsh justice.

Contemporary Responses to Corporate Crime

During a banking committee hearing in 2014, Senator Elizabeth Warren (D-MA) grilled federal regulators for regularly settling conflicts with major banks without criminal charges. She said, "Without criminal prosecution, the message to every Wall Street banker is loud and clear. If you break the law, you are not going to jail; but you might end up with a much bigger paycheck."[71] But these practices are not markedly different from those evident in America's historical record. The nation has suffered multiple corporate scandals since the S&L crisis, and while politicians have repeatedly condemned the transgressors with law-and-order rhetoric, their policy responses have consistently been couched in the register of regulation.

Notably, Congress has been aware of the justice system's systematized leniency toward white-collar offenders throughout the modern era. When drafting the Sentencing Reform Act of 1984, the Senate Judiciary Committee explicitly blamed rehabilitation-oriented sentencing for this disparity. It explained in a report that "[t]he Committee is of the view that in the past there have been many cases, particularly in instances of major white collar crime, in which probation has been granted because the offender required little or nothing in the way of institutionalized rehabilitative measures and because society required no insulation from the offender, without due consideration being given to the fact that the heightened deterrent effect of incarceration and the readily perceivable receipt of just punishment accorded by incarceration were of critical importance."[72] In 1991 the US Sentencing Commission promulgated the Chapter 8 organizational guidelines, which dictated revised white-collar sentencing practices and specified methods for calculating criminal fines that were intended to check judges' tendencies to lower sentences for wealthier offenders who seemingly required no correction.[73] The guidelines have not met these aims and systematically advantage white-collar defendants in several ways, such as by mitigating sentences for an individual's community contributions or enhancing punishments only under unusual circumstances.[74] Guidelines for financial crimes are also driven by imprecise variables like "reasonable estimate[s] of the loss" made by sentencing judges. Judicial loss estimates can vary by billions of dollars, giving judges a flexible standard to reach the end they want.[75] The guidelines' emphasis on criminal history also favors corporate offenders, given that corporate crime is undercounted in official crime statistics.[76] The organizational guidelines also mandate judicial consideration of "any collateral consequences of conviction" of an organization.[77] Consequently, they have not durably reformed white-collar sentencing.

Through the 1990s and the first decade of the twenty-first century, several corporate scandals showcased the guidelines' minimal deterrent impact. A prominent one involved the energy-trading company Enron. In 2001, Enron perpetrated one of the biggest accounting frauds in history with help from the accounting firm Arthur Andersen by hiding the company's financial losses in order to project a misleading image of profitability. Enron's was not the only case of accounting fraud to surface during this time, but it was the subject of a high-profile DOJ investigation in which thirty-two Enron officers faced legal charges and several ranking executives were criminally convicted. The Andersen firm was also convicted for enabling the fraud.[78] Like the S&L crisis, this demonstrated that the federal government has the capacity to prosecute major corporate frauds, but the case had damaging long-term consequences for the DOJ's reputation as the public and the legal community became convinced that federal prosecutors abused their power by putting Andersen out of business and costing thousands their jobs.[79] However, this perspective fails to acknowledge Andersen's troubled history—the firm was experiencing a client exodus before Enron's collapse as its reputation deteriorated under the 175 shareholder suits and 13 government investigations it was already facing before its indictment related to the Enron scandal.[80] Furthermore, Andersen had paid more than $500 million in regulatory settlements in the years immediately preceding Enron's crash, never facing criminal charges. Despite this, prosecutors still offered the firm a safe landing—it could have avoided trial by signing a deferred prosecution agreement subjecting the company to internal monitoring in exchange for an admission of wrongdoing with no guilty plea. Andersen gambled on trial, but the belief still persists that the government's prosecutorial zeal prompted the firm's demise, not the company's own record.[81]

Brandon Garrett has shown that following the Andersen prosecution, federal prosecutors have become increasingly reliant on deferred prosecution agreements (DPAs) and nonprosecution agreements (NPAs) to manage corporate lawbreaking. In these agreements, prosecutors promise to forgo criminal charges if corporations meet certain conditions within a specified time (usually implementing internal compliance reforms and paying an accompanying fine). DPAs and NPAs enable prosecutors to secure settlements swiftly, impose seemingly substantial fines and sanctions, and score public relations victories without risking courtroom defeats, but the agreements often lack effective compliance monitoring, and the apparently hefty fines amount to trivial fees for large wealthy firms.[82]

The Sarbanes-Oxley Act (SOA) of 2002 was lawmakers' law-and-order answer to Enron and Andersen. Among other things, the SOA put in place rules monitoring corporate accounting, auditing, and financial disclosures, mandated that the US Sentencing Commission enhance the guidelines for white-collar offenses, created the Public Company Accounting Oversight Board (PCAOB) to oversee the accounting profession, and increased the penalties for securities offenses and falsifying or tampering with records.[83] The SOA was heralded as putting teeth into corporate sentencing, but some have questioned its impact because of the political climate surrounding its passage. Weeks before signing the law, President Bush promised a mild approach to its enforcement, explaining, "I think by far the vast majority of C.E.O.s in America are good, honorable, honest people who have nothing to hide."[84] But a more substantial structural reason for the law's limited enforcement was rooted in circumstances following the September 11 attacks as the Bush administration slashed funding for the FBI's criminal investigative arms in order to prioritize its counterterrorism and national security operations. Several officials warned that this funding shift left the bureau undersupported in its efforts to track white-collar crime, and it was followed by a 50 percent decrease in white-collar prosecutions across the board from 2000 to 2007.[85] David Skeel and William Stuntz therefore suggest that despite its potential to grow the state's prosecutorial muscle in the corporate sphere, the SOA reflected the familiar historical pattern of get-tough corporate crime legislation being enforced "rarely and idiosyncratically," resulting in a few symbolic moralizing prosecutions to create an appearance of prosecutorial strength.[86]

One notable symbolic prosecution following the SOA targeted Bernie Madoff. Following the act's passage, the SEC exempted privately held

brokerage firms like Madoff Securities from an SOA rule requiring brokerage firms to undergo audits conducted by accounting firms registered with
the PCAOB, which the SOA specifically created to supervise the legality and
quality of accounting operations. Consequently, the unregistered firm Friehling and Horowitz audited Madoff's company without PCAOB oversight.
Friehling and Horowitz failed to recognize that Madoff was coordinating the
largest Ponzi scheme in history—exceeding $50 billion—until his company
collapsed.[87] Madoff was the most prominent white-collar conviction following the financial crisis of 2007–8, but despite the gravity of his offenses,
Madoff was a solo con artist rather than an executive who triggered the collapse.[88] The institutions that financed Madoff faced lesser consequences;
his banker JP Morgan received a DPA after the crisis.[89] Madoff's prosecution also followed a regulatory failure. Following Madoff's arrest, the independent fraud examiner Harry Markopolos testified before Congress that
he repeatedly "gift-wrapped and delivered" the case to the SEC by alerting
the agency to Madoff's activities on five occasions but that the SEC intervened only after his scheme collapsed. The SEC was severely criticized during
House hearings, with Representative Gary Ackerman (D-NY) calling it "deaf,
dumb, and blind."[90] But the end result was not institutional reform; it was a
150-year sentence for Madoff that fostered a misleading sense of confidence
in the state's capacity to prosecute fraudsters, obscured how the SEC's inac-
tion and exemptions in the SOA's regulatory scheme enabled his operation to
persist undetected, and diverted attention away from the lack of prosecutions
against the executives most involved in the crisis.

The lead-up to the financial crisis was fueled by financial institutions extending subprime mortgage loans to low- and limited-credit borrowers and
pooling those loans into mortgage-backed securities sold to investors, creating a housing bubble and metastasizing risk throughout the financial system.
Like the S&L crisis, the financial crisis was precipitated by moral hazard; too-
big-to-fail financial institutions engaged in extreme risk-taking knowing that
any consequences would be borne by taxpayers. This reality eventually played
out through bailouts, the temporary nationalization of troubled institutions,
and the federal purchasing of toxic assets after the financial system plunged
into crisis.[91] But the Great Recession significantly differed from the S&L crisis. William Black, a highly reputed banking regulator during the S&L crisis,
determined that the S&L crisis was roughly one-seventieth the size of the
financial crisis. Further, regulators made tens of thousands of criminal referrals during the S&L scandal. There were zero regulatory criminal referrals
during the financial crisis, a difference that Black attributes to agency staffing
deficiencies.[92] After the financial crisis, there was also no political appetite for

prosecution. Attempts to revive the Bush-era Corporate Fraud Task Force or create a meaningful alternative within President Obama's DOJ floundered as tepid DOJ leadership was unwilling to risk potential trial losses.[93]

The legislative solution to the crisis—the Dodd-Frank Wall Street Reform and Consumer Protection Act (DFA) of 2010—attempted to solve the financial sector's problems through precise interventions requiring the creation of hundreds of regulatory rules. Fundamental structural overhauls to the financial sector, like breaking up too-big-to-fail institutions, were eschewed in favor of technocratic specificity. Given the DFA's twenty-three hundred pages of statutory text and mandated involvement of eleven agencies, only two-thirds of its required regulations were in place by 2015.[94]

Familiar debates over balancing criminalization and regulation resurfaced during the DFA debates. Senator Chris Dodd (D-CT) repeatedly said that regulators should be "cops on the beat" to enforce the rules of the marketplace.[95] Senator Mike Crapo (R-ID) and Sandor Samuels of Countrywide Financial, respectively, countered with warnings of "swing[ing] the pendulum too far back" and leading to "an over correction" if the law was too punitive.[96] When Senator Richard Blumenthal (D-CT) described the proposed Consumer Financial Protection Bureau (CFPB) as a "Federal Consumer Financial Super Cop," Edward Yingling, the president of the American Bankers Association, cautioned that "healthy, well-regulated banks have already been hurt deeply by unscrupulous players and regulatory failures" and would unfairly suffer under the CFPB.[97] The terms of this debate were not radically different from previous instances of regulatory state building in response to corporate scandals, but in the neoliberal era, there was resistance to costly regulations on both sides of the aisle. Senator Richard Shelby (R-AL) warned that "we must be careful not to regulate for regulation's sake."[98] Representative Barney Frank (D-MA), one of the sponsors of the law, emphasized that while "there is a consensus" that "regulation is required," it must be "market sensitive." He noted that "we don't want to do anything that would interfere with our wonderful financial system."[99]

President Obama signed the DFA in July 2010 after it passed on a party-line congressional vote. The law's list of reforms is too lengthy to unpack here in full, but it is worth highlighting some of its core components. It created the CFPB, the brainchild of the then Harvard professor Elizabeth Warren, to be a consumer protection watchdog. It established the Financial Stability Oversight Council (FSOC), chaired by the secretary of the Treasury with membership spanning ten federal agencies so that regulators could work together to identify emerging systemic risks in the financial system. It also mandated the creation of the Volcker Rule, which banned proprietary trading by commercial banks and required large companies to create "funeral plans" outlining how they could be shut down should they go bankrupt, holding them to strict rules and capital requirements if they did not produce an acceptable plan. It also imposed penalties for irresponsible mortgage lending, established an SEC whistleblowing program, and more.[100]

While bold in its aims, the law left in place too-big-to-fail taxpayer-backed financial institutions driven by the incentives of moral hazard. Although the Volcker Rule offered some promise to check these dynamics, 93 percent of input on the rule's design came from financial institutions and industry trade groups, keeping it reflective of industry preferences.[101] The rule did not go into full effect until 2015 and was radically scaled back in June 2020, existing in force for a mere five years.[102] Corporations still often receive DPAs and NPAs rather than criminal charges since Dodd-Frank's passage.[103] Meanwhile, the fines authorized by the DFA are understood as the cost of doing business. In 2013, when Elizabeth Warren warned J. P. Morgan CEO Jamie Dimon that his institution could face DFA fines, he retorted, "So hit me with a fine. We can afford it."[104]

Importantly, the DFA concealed that the lead-up to the crisis involved clear cases of prosecutable fraud. The refrain that what Wall Street did was bad but not illegal resurfaced after the crash to explain the lack of prosecutions. In 2011, Obama claimed that "one of the biggest problems . . . is that a lot of that stuff wasn't necessarily illegal" even though "it was immoral or inappropriate or reckless." He went on to conclude, "That's exactly why we needed to pass Dodd-Frank."[105] But while some practices involving complex financial instruments were not illegal before the DFA, others like incomplete disclosures and fraud in real estate sales, securities, and mortgages clearly were.[106] The lack of prosecution prior to the DFA was a choice, not a necessity, and rhetoric surrounding its passage hid this reality.

The argument that nothing preceding the crash was technically illegal was undermined in several contexts. The Financial Crisis Inquiry Commission, a bipartisan ten-member commission appointed by Congress in 2009, found widespread evidence of mortgage and securities fraud, predatory lending, and fraudulent home appraisals. Its report noted that FBI assistant director Chris Swecker repeatedly warned lawmakers over several years that criminal fraud was becoming endemic in the market, but his claims were ignored by regulators who preferred to offer nonbinding guidance to industry rather than intervening with prosecution.[107] Other regulators explicitly promised criminal enforcement before Dodd-Frank was passed. SEC chair Christopher Cox told Congress in 2008 that "law enforcement is now needed more than ever" because "there's no question that somewhere in this terrible mess many laws were broken."[108] For instance, the SEC opened a high-profile investigation into Goldman Sachs for working with the hedge fund Paulson and Company to structure a bad securities investment it offloaded onto unsuspecting investors and shorted for profit on the basis of their predictions of the impending subprime mortgage crisis. But Jesse Eisinger has shown how the SEC's leadership resisted charging higher-ups and focused on one low-level Goldman employee, Fabrice Tourre, who had an email record overtly describing and joking about the fraud. After Tourre's conviction, the SEC's lead investigator warned staffers to not be punitive with other Goldman employees given that most were "good people who have done one bad thing." Eisinger shows that SEC leadership directed staffers to "keep in mind that the vast majority of the losses suffered had nothing to do with fraud and the like, and are more fairly attributable to lesser human failings of greed, arrogance, and stupidity, of which we are all guilty from time to time," and that executives "will strike most jurors as nice, likable, [and] down-to-earth." The SEC eventually sued the Goldman corporation, but Tourre served as the sole individual prosecution.[109]

Elizabeth Warren, who rose to public prominence when she served on a panel monitoring the Troubled Asset Relief Program (TARP) and turned it into an outlet for populist outrage, similarly undermined the bad-but-not-illegal narrative. She resurrected the idea that the regulatory state needed a cop on the beat to enforce consumer protection laws and framed the CFPB as a means of enforcing laws already on the books that went unenforced prior to the crash. But her progressive bona fides prompted enough conservative and industrial ire that Obama, with whom she already had a contentious relationship given her unforgiving treatment of his administration during the TARP hearings, appointed the more palatable moderate Richard Cordray to head the CFPB.[110]

The passage of the DFA has sparked conservative criticism that it hinders market efficiencies. The Heritage Foundation scholars Mark Calabria, Norbert Michel, and Hester Peirce have condemned the regulatory bodies created by the DFA, including the CFPB, the FSOC, and the Office of Financial Research for impairing the efficiency of the financial system.[111] The CFPB is a particular point of contention for conservatives. Alden Abbott and Todd Zywicki, also from the Heritage Foundation, assert that the CFPB "intervenes in financial market consumer-related practices in a heavy-handed arbitrary fashion that ignores sound economics" and "reduces market efficiency." They express concern that the CFPB has used its broad discretion to sanction conduct deemed "abusive" to capriciously penalize anything it dislikes "without regard to its merits." But they suggest a solution formulated within the framework of regulatory ideology, proposing that the powers of the CFPB be consolidated in the FTC. They reason that the FTC's Bureau of Economics has experience weighing enforcement actions against cost efficiency and economic considerations "to which the CFPB has paid no heed." They believe that the FTC would be more inclined to refrain from legal action if cost-benefit analyses suggest that intervention would impose net costs.[112] While these recommendations were never implemented, they underscore how conservatives have repurposed regulatory ideology to demand minimized and cost-efficient regulatory governance.

The DFA and the CFPB have faced a number of challenges from conservatives. In October 2023, the Supreme Court heard a case challenging the constitutionality of the CFPB's funding structure, which relies on subgrants derived from the revenues accumulated by the Federal Reserve via assessment fees on regulated institutions.[113] The Trump administration also reformed several components of the DFA. A 2018 law modified DFA rules that subjected bank holding companies with over $50 billion in assets to greater Federal Reserve supervision and stricter debt and liquidity requirements, raising that threshold to $250 billion. Many institutions lobbied for these changes and subsequently faced lessened regulations, one of which was Silicon Valley Bank (SVB).[114] SVB was a California-based institution that primarily served technology start-ups and held tremendous deposits from corporate investors, and the San Francisco Fed had planned to move it to this higher level of regulatory scrutiny until the 2018 reforms delayed that transition. Years later, when the SVB met the new threshold warranting heightened supervision, it was already exhibiting worrisome indicators like holding a high number of uninsured deposits exceeding the $250,000 Federal Deposit Insurance Corporation guarantee and having significant investments in US bonds declining in value as interest rates rose. Deposit withdrawals at the bank spiked as economic conditions worsened in the tech sector, prompting SVB to sell its bonds at significant losses.[115] These circumstances triggered a bank run culminating in SVB's collapse within forty-eight hours. But amid claims from conservatives like the American Enterprise Institute fellow Paul Kupiec that federal regulators were "asleep at the wheel" as the SVB collapse developed, it is important to remember that reforms implemented during the Trump administration delayed the stricter oversight SVB would have encountered under the original DFA.[116] The Trump administration diminished regulatory oversight, illustrating how regulatory ideological principles have been reoriented to leave regulators underequipped to manage corporate conduct and then subject to criticism when they fail to fulfill their duties.

In contrast to actors weaponizing regulatory ideology to push for deregulation, some market players have deployed it to alternative ends, highlighting its malleability in the current moment. Consider the entrepreneur Sam Bankman-Fried, whose cryptocurrency exchange FTX collapsed in 2022. Bankman-Fried built his public reputation around effective altruism, a philosophy of dedicating oneself to a high-paying career with the intention of donating one's fortune to charity. He publicly discussed business ethics and corporate social responsibility in sophisticated and nuanced ways while supporting particular regulatory systems for cryptocurrency markets. But his critics questioned whether his advocacy for specific regulatory reforms was a strategic public relations move geared toward serving his own interests and buttressing his public persona rather than promoting real oversight—he aimed to have the Commodity Futures Trading Commission (CFTC) regulate cryptocurrency markets rather than the better-funded SEC and sought to revise CFTC rules to allow customers to borrow money from FTX to speculate large sums on cryptocurrency futures. But his benevolent public image distinguished him from other billionaires in the industry, largely earning him public trust and support.[117]

That all changed when a run on FTX deposits in November 2022 left the company with an $8 billion shortfall, prompting bankruptcy and a federal investigation revealing that Bankman-Fried improperly used FTX funds to prop up his trading firm Alameda Research, rendering his charitable contributions susceptible to recovery by creditors in bankruptcy court.[118] In an exchange with a *Vox* reporter shortly following FTX's collapse, Bankman-Fried starkly laid bare his true views in unambiguous terms, validating his critics' concerns that his support for regulation was a front. He confessed to never having genuinely supported regulations that would have meaningfully constrained the industry, casually dismissing his public statements favoring regulation as "just PR," following with "fuck regulators . . . they make everything worse" before brushing off his prior comments about business ethics as "not true," "dumb shit," and "mostly a front."[119] Bankman-Fried used his public persona to deploy regulatory ideology toward building new regulatory architecture—a sharp contrast to modern conservatives that highlights the ideology's pliability—but in disingenuous and strategic ways that he believed would secure public favor without imposing significant safeguards on the industry.

Such startlingly transparent admissions later proved useful to prosecutors. In November 2023, Bankman-Fried was convicted on seven counts of fraud, conspiracy, and money laundering. During the trial, prosecutors persuaded the judge to allow the jury to see the messages cited above, among others, as pieces of evidence, arguing that they were revealing of Bankman-Fried's true intentions and state of mind when he operated his business and engaged with regulators. Bankman-Fried's story ended with the rare conviction of a corporate lawbreaker after he made these unusually candid and public confessions of his intentions, handing prosecutors strong pieces of evidence to make their case.[120]

Bankman-Fried's favorable image has been discredited, but other contemporary corporate felons have experienced public image restorations. Consider a May 2023 *New York Times* article on Elizabeth Holmes, the disgraced founder of Theranos. The piece explains how Holmes, now going by "Liz" rather than "Elizabeth," is crafting a new image as a devoted mother while she prepares to serve an eleven-year prison sentence for defrauding Theranos investors via false claims about the company's blood-testing technology. The author wrote about her interviews with Holmes at her family's home, saying, "I didn't expect her to be so . . . normal." She stated that she sees "Elizabeth," the convicted criminal, and "Liz," the devoted mother, as two different people and found herself "swept up in Liz as an authentic and genuine person." She wrote that Holmes "didn't seem like a hero or a villain" but, "like most people, somewhere in between." The reporter acknowledged her skepticism of Holmes, but asked herself, "[H]ow could I ask someone who was nursing her 11-day-old baby on a white sofa two feet away if she was actually conning me?"[121]

This is just one article, and while it is potentially interpretable as subtly capturing Holmes's manipulation skills, it generally reads as sanitizing her image. But either interpretation illustrates a deeper reality. Whether a reader comes away seeing Holmes as a sympathetic and reformed person or as a con artist using her family life to rescue her reputation, the article prompts nuanced thought about wrongdoing and encourages readers to connect with and find humanity in its subject. Millions of incarcerated poor and minority mothers and fathers who are guilty of far less would do anything for a public profile expressing surprise that they are "normal" and "somewhere in between" the poles of the ethical spectrum. That Holmes received this treatment is a testament to the cultural tendency to look for nuance, context, and relatability in the behavior of white-collar lawbreakers, considerations rarely extended to lower-class offenders.

In recent decades, America has experienced several high-profile corporate criminal scandals. But despite punitive posturing from lawmakers and a few symbolic prosecutions, the core ideas of the regulatory ideological framework have continued to color not only how political actors construct policy, but how the public understands and evaluates corporate criminality.

Modernized Ideologies

The ideologies of rehabilitation and regulation remain alive in the modern era. We still take their basic premises for granted, and their persistence is a result of how they have proved malleable for political actors seeking to shape American political and legal institutions. As American politics has evolved in the twenty-first century, conservative forces have effectively restyled both ideologies to serve the neoliberal imperatives of governing efficiency, cost efficacy, and fiscal austerity.

The adaptability and utility of rehabilitative and regulatory ideologies have rendered them tenacious forces in American political life. Understanding and challenging their influence on American politics requires treating them as moving targets that have been adjusted and repurposed over time to validate shifting policy goals. In the neoliberal era, conservative interests and policymakers are mobilizing them in novel ways to inscribe their logics onto new features of America's carceral and regulatory apparatuses behind the rhetoric of scientific neutrality, optimized governance, and cost efficiency. These political tactics must be challenged and rejected to avoid perpetuating and legitimating the inequalities of American criminal justice behind practices rooted in these modernized forms of rehabilitative and regulatory ideological frameworks.

8

Deconstructing Ideology and Criminality:
Possibilities for a Different Future

I learned early that class is universally admired. Almost any fault, sin or crime is considered more leniently if there's a touch of class involved.

FRANK ABAGNALE AND STAN REDDING, *Catch Me If You Can* (2002)

In February 2020, President Trump pardoned several high-profile white-collar felons, praising their characters during his public statement. Most notable were his words about Michael Milken, whose junk bond schemes during the S&L crisis led to criminal convictions for securities and reporting violations. Trump described Milken as "one of America's greatest financiers," emphasizing that he "pioneered the use of high-yield bonds in corporate finance." He then characterized what happened to Milken in the following terms: "In 1989, at the height of his finance career, Mr. Milken was charged in an indictment alleging that some of his innovative financing mechanisms were in fact criminal schemes. The charges filed against Mr. Milken were truly novel. In fact, one of the lead prosecutors later admitted that Mr. Milken had been charged with numerous technical offenses and regulatory violations that had never before been charged as crimes."[1] By invoking words like *greatest*, *pioneered*, and *innovated*, Trump presented Milken's crimes as extensions of his entrepreneurial spirit, and the fact that Milken's actions had previously only been regulated and never prosecuted was all Trump needed to conclude that prosecutors mistook capitalist vigor for criminality. But in the general election that fall, Trump took different positions on criminal justice. He repeatedly emphasized the need for "law and order" in his first debate with Joe Biden as he promised to restore order in American cities but reversed course in the final debate by championing his leadership on criminal justice reform in the First Step Act.[2] These shifts in Trump's rhetoric can be fully comprehended only in light of the history detailed in this book.

Rehabilitative and regulatory ideologies emerged and evolved as related visions for governing misconduct, and they have been critical features of American political development (APD) reinforcing racially and class-skewed understandings about what causes crime and who should be punished. Rehabilitative ideology expresses the idea that incarceration should transform inmates into law-abiding citizens via programming and incentives designed to reduce their likelihood of offending and tasks judges and penal administrators with the duty to tailor offenders' carceral experiences to their perceived rehabilitative potential. It thus advocates a two-pronged solution of rehabilitating the corrigible and punishing the incorrigible. Meanwhile, regulatory ideology treats corporate misconduct as an inevitable secondary effect of letting corporate elites' competitive and innovative tendencies thrive in market spheres. It prescribes regulatory tools for handling corporate lawbreaking, often by managing market conditions to discourage illicit activity, so as to not suppress these desirable traits under prosecutorial threat. While both ideologies have evolved over time, this book illustrates how their individualizing orientations, eugenic underpinnings, and racial and class biases have contributed to a fundamentally unfair legal system.

This could give readers a sense of fatalism. Opponents of mass incarceration may fear that this comparison justifies sizing up the carceral state to punish corporate offenders or that abandoning the rehabilitative ideal might further dehumanize prisons, while observers of finance might lament that neither regulatory nor prosecutorial solutions are capable of managing the enormous institutions dominating the economy. This chapter offers reform proposals that address these concerns. The entrenchment of rehabilitative and regulatory ideologies within institutions hampers our political imagination from envisioning new solutions to the pathologies of American law, and abandoning their legacies requires a balanced combination of institutional fixes and radical solutions.

This chapter unfolds in three sections. The first reviews the book's contributions to scholarly literatures. The second outlines strategies for reforming institutions to ameliorate the dysfunctions of rehabilitative and regulatory ideologies. The final section acknowledges that rehabilitative and regulatory ideologies sustain deeper inequalities that no amount of institutional change will fix. It argues that the best way to control crime—on the streets and in the suites—is to directly challenge the economic conditions that produce it.

Punishment, Regulation, and American Political Development

The book has presented its primary scholarly interventions across three categories: race, class, and the carceral state; corporate crime and the regulatory state; and ideas and institutions in APD. This chapter begins by briefly reviewing the book's most important conclusions and scholarly contributions, which have been discussed in detail in the introductory and substantive chapters.

Most significantly, this analysis distinctively argues that the carceral and the regulatory states are related institutions warranting joint analysis. Scholars typically overlook the interrelated nature and intertwined developmental paths of these two ostensibly distinct constellations of institutions.[3] But an incomplete image emerges when we try to solve the puzzle of American penality only by assembling the pieces involving punitive crime control. Consequently, scholars researching the sociology of punishment offer myriad theories attempting to describe the big picture of American penality on the basis of a half-finished puzzle. We must put together the pieces involving regulatory control to see the full picture. This perspective challenges the entire idea of what we should study when examining the political development of crime, law, and social control by shedding light on essential political decisions missed in analyses of the justice system that examine only punitive policies. Exploring which behaviors have been channeled toward and which have been channeled away from the prison—and which get punitive or alternative controls—provides a holistic view of how legal institutions express and reinforce particular ideas about who deserves punishment and who does not.

In providing this analysis, the book offers a new alternative to prevailing genealogies of mass incarceration. It counters the story that the repudiation of rehabilitation in the 1970s was the prison boom's proximate trigger.[4] It excavates a lengthier and more sinister history behind the rehabilitative model than is provided in existing scholarship by unearthing its roots in a punitive determinist ideology of the Progressive era that has shaped political development in insidious ways. This reveals deep and unexplored biopolitical roots to American law by illuminating how racially and economically determinist assumptions about incorrigibility have long infected the legal system through practices inherited from the rehabilitative model, keeping American criminal justice infused with a eugenic undercurrent.

Combined with the book's class-driven framework, this biopolitical perspective offers nuanced insights into how the dynamics of class and race have fueled the carceral state's construction, complicating narratives about mass incarceration's racial and class roots. Rehabilitative ideology has recurrently facilitated racial injustices by providing lawmakers with a cosmic rationale for linking race to incorrigibility, but the book illustrates how the idea of natural incorrigibility is a malleable concept that has also been used to justify diverse forms of class control throughout the carceral state's rise. Its combination of critical criminological, biopolitical, and historical institutionalist lenses reveals how political actors have repeatedly deployed and adjusted rehabilitative ideology in different settings to politicize economic inequality, racial inequality, and criminal behavior as results of a common set of inherent individual failings requiring strict controls. We cannot understand how rehabilitative ideology shaped innovations in the Progressive era South without considering its mobilization in service of postbellum White-supremacist agendas, but we also cannot understand how notions of incorrigibility were weaponized to repress organized labor at the same time without recognizing the idea's utility for elites seeking to structure the economic order on behalf of capitalist interests. This underscores the ideology's elasticity as a cudgel that politicians have molded into different shapes to help build and uphold myriad repressive legal systems.

Ideologically informed scientific research about criminality has regularly validated the rehabilitative ideal's harsh justice mindset by denoting shifting undesirable populations, including diverse racial and class groups, as incorrigible. The book's case studies show meaningful variations in how determinist understandings of incorrigibility linked to class and race interacted as they were politicized by actors with diverse motives across different regions and historical contexts. For instance, chapter 5 illustrates that similarities and differences in the developmental routes of habitual offender statutes in New York and California could in part be attributed to differences in how racial and class issues were politicized in relation to concerns about incorrigibility in each state. This illuminates how racial inequalities are related to the economic dynamics of modern capitalism and how both racial and class control imperatives are served by the state's broader biopolitical framework for governing crime through rehabilitative logics, painting a textured portrait of the history behind the carceral state's racial and class injustices.

CORPORATE CRIME AND
THE REGULATORY STATE

Studying economic regulation as one piece of the state's larger governing system for controlling undesirable conduct reorients understandings of the regulatory state. Examining regulation as a relative of and alternative to punitive crime control helps us gain not only a fuller picture of the sociology of punishment, but also a deeper appreciation of the nature and politics of regulatory governance. Clarifying the regulatory state's dynamic relationship to the criminal justice system forges a clearer understanding of its foundational principles as a system for controlling illicit conduct, shedding new light on often-overlooked ways in which the regulatory state affects American life.

The arguments presented in this book recalibrate scholarly accounts of the regulatory state's political origins, which emphasize how administrators, political elites, judges, and business interests facilitated the development of the regulatory state during the Progressive era.[5] This book makes a novel intervention in this conversation by arguing that the nature of the regulatory state's design and development can be fully grasped only on recognizing its relationship to the politics of crime. Regulatory bodies' crime control functions should not be brushed aside as minor secondary errands that regulators perform while carrying out their economic management mandates. They warrant analysis as significant and consequential responsibilities of regulatory operations. This impels us to pay heed to how concerns about crime and punishment have conditioned the political debates that have fueled regulatory state development.

This leads to a unique perspective on the rarity of corporate prosecutions in the United States. Research on this issue often pinpoints the disproportionate power of business interests, structural economic variables, or relatively recent shifts in legal practice as the primary reasons for the state's limited prosecution of corporate wrongdoing.[6] Some scholars offer longer-term structural explanations for the disparity among the state's approaches to punishing street and corporate crime via reference to historic shifts in criminological theory, the durable influence of libertarian free market governing logics, or Marxist explanations of the legal system as a tool of the capitalist class.[7] Alternatively, this book offers a deeper institutionally and ideologically grounded explanation for this trend rooted in the influence of the Progressive era governing ideologies of rehabilitation and regulation. Existing scholarship emphasizes diverse and valid reasons for the state's lenient treatment of corporate crime in comparison to street crime, but this book shines a wider light on the entire institutional system that perpetuates this inequality.

The book's biopolitical framework also underscores why regulatory governance must be situated within the broader racial arc of American legal development. Regulatory and rehabilitative ideology are polar ends of a governing logic rooted in racial terms. The regulatory and criminal justice systems should consequently not be studied as evolving on entirely separate planes of development. Rather, they must be understood as parts of an integrated governing arrangement designed to differentiate racialized bodies that require punishment from racialized bodies that do not, helping maintain the power relations and social and class hierarchies of American racial capitalism.

IDEAS, INSTITUTIONS, AND AMERICAN
POLITICAL DEVELOPMENT

The book's ideational argument also speaks to literature on ideas and institutions in APD. By presenting a nuanced view of how rehabilitative and regulatory ideologies have been mobilized and adjusted in shifting political contexts, the case studies demonstrate how ideas can condition the use of political power and the direction of political change. Political actors have regularly found value in rehabilitative and regulatory ideologies as frameworks for communicating their preferences and championing their favored policies. This underscores how ideas can shape the ways in which political actors wield their influence. For instance, this book has claimed that we cannot fully understand the outcomes of regulatory policy debates without looking to how shifting groups of powerful industrial interests have adjusted and mobilized regulatory ideology to pursue particular goals. Writing off the outcomes of these debates as consequences of powerful firms ordering politicians around as they pleased overlooks subtleties and nuances in the exercise of political power. Industrial interests have often disagreed on major policy questions, and firms have had varying degrees of political leverage in different political economic climates. Understanding how shifting groups of industrial interests have adjusted the principles of regulatory ideology to shape policy in different environments illuminates the significant role ideas can play in influencing how political actors employ their power. The ideologies have shaped the terms on which powerful political forces have engaged in political debate and discourse, thus transmitting the ideologies' premises and properties into conflicts that have produced significant institutional and policy changes.

This history shows that ideas are not static forces in political development. Rehabilitative and regulatory ideologies have been pliable tools that lawmakers have adjusted under different circumstances and deployed to varied effects. As chapter 7 demonstrated, lawmakers and conservative political interests are bringing the same basic assumptions and mentalities of rehabilitative and regulatory ideologies into the twenty-first century behind new promises that they will bring cost-effective and streamlined governance. The significance and consequences of this move can be perceived and understood only by examining the longer history of rehabilitative and regulatory ideologies and their influence on APD. Attention to their malleability highlights the dynamic effects ideas can have on political change and how an idea can be carried into new political contests in modified forms.

Examining the impact of rehabilitative and regulatory ideologies on political development showcases how institutions express and maintain the ideas entrenched within them. Carceral and regulatory institutions have hardened and sustained the underlying ideological premises on which they rest. Myths about incorrigibility among street-level offenders and the redeemability of corporate elites are kept alive through contemporary legal norms inherited from rehabilitative and regulatory ideological frameworks. Modern risk-assessment tools and the severe punishment of individuals with extensive criminal records are practices that stem from the rehabilitative model and carry a fixation on identifying incorrigibles into the twenty-first century. Similarly, subsuming corporate crime under administrative governance continues to leave it underdocumented in crime statistics, reinforcing popular conceptions that white-collar offenders are more law-abiding and redeemable than the average street offender. When political actors mobilized rehabilitative and regulatory ideologies in political conflicts, they did more than justify their preferred policies rhetorically. Regardless of their intentions when speaking within these frameworks—whether political actors genuinely thought the ideologies promoted good policy or simply saw them as tools for pursuing some other policy end—they consequently built self-rationalizing institutional systems that rest on and reinforce the ideologies' central tenets in the modern era.

Ideas play dynamic and often mercurial roles in shaping political development. Political actors have mobilized rehabilitative and regulatory ideologies to differential effects and varying degrees of success in shifting contexts, producing intentional and predictable outcomes in some instances and unintentional and unpredictable outcomes in others. Examining the history of these ideologies and their roles in shaping political development reveals a complicated story about the ways in which ideas can condition the nature and direction of political change.

Institutional Solutions

Reforming the pathologies of American law requires institutional remedies to undo the damage of rehabilitative and regulatory ideologies. The subsequent sections detail reforms that would help reverse this damage and should be central to any comprehensive agenda aimed at reforming criminal justice and regulatory institutions.

RETHINKING REHABILITATION AND CRIMINAL JUSTICE

Rehabilitation must be abandoned as an aspiration of the justice system, but that will not be enough to resolve America's carceral crisis without sweeping changes to criminal punishment. Many scholars have detailed the diverse and comprehensive reforms required to undo mass incarceration, including reducing the time served for large swaths of inmates and drastically cutting down the number of people incarcerated in the first place—changes that would effectively reserve imprisonment only for individuals posing unambiguous and grave public safety threats.[8] However, this book has shown that rehabilitative ideology helped build the carceral state and will not help undo it. Excising the harmful legacies of rehabilitative ideology must be central to any criminal justice reform agenda, and four steps can be taken in this direction.

The first step requires discarding the myth of natural incorrigibility by recognizing the reemergence of biocriminology as a genuine danger given the disturbing history of the scientific metaphor in penology. The historical record indicates that rehabilitative politics would not only fail to counter racialized and class-skewed biases about natural criminality, but also reinforce them. The myth of natural criminality has persisted ever since nineteenth-century race scientists incorporated terms like *incorrigible* or *born criminal* into their racial taxonomies, offering policymakers a convenient label to stick onto any undesirable population. Scientific analyses of race, class, and crime have since worked together to justify oppression based on these labels, and modern biocriminology puts impoverished citizens and communities of color already disproportionately affected by the justice system at further risk. As chapter 7 discussed, these ideas hold meaningful public and political appeal today. Well-intentioned voices championing rehabilitation could inadvertently create opportunities for the racialized and class-skewed specter of the incorrigible to resurface in new determinist forms if these ideas are not soundly rejected.

Second, the assumption that a criminal record signifies incorrigibility must be abandoned as a guiding principle of the justice system. For over a century, lawmakers and criminal justice practitioners have rationalized harsh treatment for those with lengthy records as consistent with their allegiance to the rehabilitative ideal. Challenging rehabilitative ideology's legacy requires dislodging the justice system's fixation on using criminal history to forecast defendants' rehabilitative prospects in penal decisions.

Notably, criminal history is a deeply misinterpreted metric. Criminal records are not impartial reflections of citizens' behavioral histories, but indicators of their likelihood of interacting with the justice system, and the aggressive policing of poor Black and Hispanic citizens in urban neighborhoods produces extensive criminal records among populations with limited access to adequate legal representation. In contrast, citizens in wealthier and predominantly White neighborhoods experience less policing, can afford better lawyers when they do, and are less likely to accumulate criminal records even if their behavior is comparable. Nonetheless, criminal history has become a one-size-fits-all proxy for incorrigibility, and racially and class-skewed penal outcomes are justified through sentencing and risk-assessment practices treating criminal records as objective reflections of individuals' behavioral tendencies. Discrediting the notion of incorrigibility requires dismantling practices that maintain that eugenic myth by interpreting criminal history as an indicator of limited rehabilitative potential.

Reducing the weight put on criminal history in sentencing seems like a big demand, but it bears repeating that America is exceptional in how significantly it allows prior convictions to augment the severity of punishment. In the United States, people's criminal histories often increase their sentences more than the offenses they committed do.[9] Other countries assign far more limited and precisely defined roles to criminal history in sentencing. In Scandinavian nations, opportunities for sentencing enhancements based on prior offenses are statutorily authorized only under narrow circumstances. Scandinavian legal norms typically treat previous crimes as irrelevant in sentencing on the grounds that defendants should not be penalized again for past offenses. In England, statutory language permits the consideration of prior convictions only if they are "recent" and "relevant" to the offense at hand, meaning that the offenses are similar and occurred without much time between them. English case law confines how much a sentence can increase under these conditions. Australia adopts a common approach dictating that criminal history cannot enhance a sentence above what a serious instance of the offense would earn by itself.[10] Dismantling the carceral state will require comprehensive sentencing reform, and reducing the emphasis on criminal history in sentencing must be part of this agenda. These international standards could be useful for reconsidering the American approach of using criminal history to ratchet up punishment substantially on the basis of assumptions about incorrigibility.

Third, recidivism reduction needs to be rejected as the goal of in-prison programming. Lawmakers treat recidivism reduction as a critical measure of effectiveness for all criminal justice policies, especially rehabilitative interventions. But measuring the efficacy of in-prison treatments on the basis of recidivism reduction is a self-defeating practice that must be discarded.

Rehabilitative programs like in-prison education, cognitive therapy, and professional training largely do not correlate with robust changes in recidivism.[11] But negatively interpreting this research as evidence of incorrigibility rests on the individualizing assumptions of rehabilitative ideology. Studies indicate that the economic circumstances under which offenders live after their release, like labor markets and income levels in their home communities, bear far more on their likelihood of recidivism than do the rehabilitative programs they complete behind bars.[12] In other words, there is little reason to think that rehabilitation will change people's behavior if they return to communities systematically denying them the chance to build a better life. Looking to recidivism to evaluate the efficacy of rehabilitative interventions myopically assumes that empowering individuals will change their conduct without recognizing how rehabilitative benefits are often offset by the chronic marginality most offenders live under on release.

Recidivism is also a misleading empirical measure. The majority of recidivists do not return to prison for serious crimes. However, even slight missteps, like missed meetings with a parole officer or failed drug tests, can land people back in prison, significantly driving up recidivism rates for minor violations and mistakes.[13] The practice in many municipalities of criminalizing behaviors associated with homelessness on the assumption that poverty is indicative of criminality—behaviors such as sleeping on sidewalks or in public spaces—can give the poor inflated criminal records for trivial quality-of-life infractions that are unavoidable when living in extreme poverty.[14] For these reasons, some scholars oppose the use of recidivism as a measure of policy effectiveness.[15]

Notably, studying rehabilitative efficacy through recidivism rates was one of Robert Martinson's mistakes. When he published his findings that rehabilitative programs failed to reduce recidivism, he failed to realize that his work would be interpreted as validating ideas about incorrigibility rather than suggesting that prisons were failing in their correctional mission and should be closed. But his argument took seriously the idea that rehabilitation should be evaluated in terms of recidivism reduction, missing the chance to advance the deeper critique that we should never have expected such programming to reduce recidivism. To avoid harsh justice and truly abandon rehabilitation as a goal of the justice system, we must refrain from evaluating in-prison programming on the basis of recidivism rates that have long been read to justify notions of incorrigibility.

Fourth, what we call *rehabilitative* measures should be not eliminated behind bars, but reconceptualized in different terms. This book's arguments might spark concerns that forsaking rehabilitation and recidivism reduction as objectives of the prison effectively abandons the entire rationale for offering in-prison programs, which could facilitate their total elimination and render prisons even less humane. But self-improvement and treatment programs have inherent value in creating healthy and supportive living environments for inmates, regardless of their effectiveness in reducing recidivism.[16] While reform should cleanse the penal system of rehabilitative ideology's problematic assumptions, in-prison programming should be detached from rehabilitative aims rather than discarded. To avoid this outcome, in-prison treatment and programming must be reframed as means of respecting human rights and dignity rather than as correctional tools used to correct broken people in the service of recidivism reduction.

Several scholars have explored how many Western European nations operate their prisons in accord with ideals of human rights and dignity to ensure that inmates live under humane conditions with access to therapeutic and self-improvement programs, prompting suggestions that similar strategies in America could challenge mass incarceration.[17] Some countries concretize these commitments by embedding language from international human rights instruments—such as the Universal Declaration of Human Rights—into their national constitutions.[18] But notably, jurisprudential concepts of dignity come with risks. It is questionable whether these ideals could feasibly be embraced at all in America, much less to egalitarian ends, without legitimizing mass incarceration and its racial and class injustices behind rhetorical promises that inmates are well treated.[19] These are legitimate reservations, but access to education, vocational training, and employment is guaranteed in many European prisons through dignity- and human rights–based protections.[20] Such language could reformulate rehabilitative interventions as elements of humane treatment disconnected from rehabilitative and recidivism reduction goals. This would constitute progress toward maintaining dignified treatment behind bars without the harmful assumptions of rehabilitative ideology, but it is not enough. To avoid legitimizing mass incarceration by civilizing the prison, dignity-based reforms must be coupled with far-reaching sentencing reforms and the other changes detailed in this chapter.

Mass incarceration cannot be eradicated through these reforms alone, but forsaking faith in rehabilitative ideology has to be part of any political effort aiming to dismantle the carceral state. The proposals detailed above represent tangible steps in that direction. Any other major reforms to the justice system risk being undermined if institutional practices and legacies of rehabilitative ideology justifying punitive treatment toward incorrigibles are left intact.

RETHINKING REGULATION AND CORPORATE PROSECUTION

It is necessary to reconsider how the state balances its responsibilities to regulate and prosecute corporate misconduct. This book endorses the responsive regulation model of Braithwaite and Ayres, which suggests regulators use a "sanctions pyramid" emphasizing lighter sanctions as responses to minor offenses and more severe sanctions for serious and repeated infractions, ensuring that criminal punishment serves as a credible deterrent threat reinforcing administrative measures.[21] But to implement this model meaningfully, agencies would need to clearly define the circumstances under which they would escalate to prosecution, such as by clarifying that specific repeated offenses or actions inflicting certain degrees or types of harm would result in criminal referrals, and receive increased funding to secure the staff and resources needed to carry out those promises and send strong deterrent signals. Realizing the sanctions pyramid by increasing the certainty of prosecution in severe cases thus seems like a daunting task entailing substantial changes to regulatory norms and operations. Enforcement mentalities shift under different agency leaders, creating inconsistencies in regulatory practice, and demanding greater public investment in regulation seems politically implausible in a neoliberal landscape. This section proposes three means of overcoming these obstacles and moving toward a governing model that more effectively balances prosecutorial and regulatory controls.

First, there are real advantages to prosecuting corporate misconduct that political challengers of corporate power should emphasize in order to discredit too-big-to-jail logics and justify greater investment in corporate law enforcement. The assumption that revenge-motivated prosecutions of corporate crime end up levying economic costs outweighing their benefits is central to the too-big-to-jail philosophy.[22] However, corporate crime research shows the opposite, concluding that consistently prosecuting corporate crime enhances market health by deterring abusive practices, a point that opponents of corporate power must bring to the public's attention to counter too-big-to-jail thinking.[23] Further, failing to prosecute severe corporate infractions does more than compromise the economy's safety and stability. It also risks undercutting the legitimacy of the entire legal system, both in the eyes of the public, which sees boardrooms as insulated from the law's reach, and in the eyes of executives, who lack cause to fear accountability. Still, the persistent appeal of the presumption that prosecuting corporate lawbreakers would constitute economic self-sabotage illustrates how dominant regulatory ideology's grasp is over the body politic, and the faulty reasoning behind this belief must be laid bare by those challenging corporate power.

Less appreciated is the fact that commonly held beliefs about the expense of regulation and corporate prosecution are misconceptions founded on misleading information. As chapter 7 discussed, lawmakers often justify cutting regulators' funding via familiar arguments that regulatory oversight is cost-inefficient. But the Revolving Door Project, a branch of the Center for Economic and Policy Research, has analyzed enforcement data from the DOJ Antitrust Division and the SEC Enforcement Division and found that both secure annual criminal penalties that outpace their annual budgets several times over. Simply put, they bring in more money than they cost. However, the Congressional Budget Office (CBO) is prohibited from considering these secondary effects of regulatory enforcement when analyzing legislative proposals, generating misconceptions about the real cost of agency operations.[24] The CBO must be allowed to consider these realities, which could and should be harnessed to rationalize meaningful investment in regulatory institutions.

Lawmakers routinely advance a litany of arguments to keep the regulatory state chronically underfunded that could be undermined by emphasizing these benefits. Beyond anxieties about cost inefficiency, regulators are often lampooned by stereotypes depicting them as intellectually inferior to Wall Street professionals who effortlessly outwit them while regulatory complexity is often condemned as producing messy overlaps in regulatory authority that impair agency cooperation.[25] However, agency dysfunctionality is typically a consequence of resource deficiencies. For example, despite a tripling of reported mergers since 2010, budgets for the FTC and the DOJ Antitrust Division have been stagnant when accounting for inflation.[26] Such mismatches between budgets and responsibilities unsurprisingly generate operational challenges. Financially strained agencies may adopt risk-averse strategies focused on easy cases to bolster their statistics and stave off claims of ineffectiveness while bodies established to coordinate agency operations, like the Financial Stability Oversight Council (FSOC), are plagued by structural hurdles that inhibit communication among underresourced agencies. As Graham Wilson explains, the underfunded agencies constituting the FSOC have to "compete with each other in persuading financial institutions to choose them as their regulator—and pay them the associated fees," thus keeping powerful business forces pitted against "weak and divided regulators."[27] Attempts to enhance the state's ability to prosecute corporate crime will be limited without accompanying investment in agencies, and emphasizing the benefits of regulatory enforcement provides a route to securing support for such investment.

A reasonable concern is that emphasizing enforcement's profitability could be weaponized to hollow out institutions in the name of cost savings. Particularly, lawmakers could try to invert this logic to cut funding for agencies not generating more money than they cost even if they provide critical benefits not readily measurable in terms of revenue. Agencies could then become hyperaggressive in seeking financial penalties to avoid the budgetary chopping block. As a result, this framing must be employed carefully. Notably, money generated by enforcement actions flows to the general Treasury, not agencies directly. Not only does this inhibit the development of incentives for agencies to impose penalties for self-gain, but it also means that this revenue could fund critical agencies that provide nonmonetary benefits. An emphasis on the financial gains of enforcement must be coupled with the qualification that agencies providing essential nonmonetary benefits could be funded with the revenues brought in by others.[28] Lawmakers insisting on slashing agency budgets already do so on the basis of misleadingly inflated cost estimates, so allowing the CBO to consider these gains simply forces these debates onto more accurate terms that could spark broader conversations about how such gains could better fund all forms of regulation, not just those that are revenue producing. Fully informed discourse about regulation and corporate law requires a complete understanding of the benefits provided by corporate accountability, and highlighting these realities could secure financial support for agencies while catalyzing more knowledgeable public discussions about the many benefits of corporate regulation and prosecution.

Second, effectively prosecuting financial crime requires reforms to the Justice Department. Jennifer Taub proposes creating an "elite crime division" (ECD) within the DOJ that would exist separately from the Fraud Section and focus on prosecuting large, complex varieties of financial crime rather than securing NPAs and DPAs. Annual funding for specialized attorneys, FBI agents, and support staff would enable the division to tackle crimes committed by and through large firms. The ECD should also possess the authority to actively monitor markets for repeat offenders, ensuring that it is not entirely dependent on regulatory criminal referrals to build its caseload.[29]

This book seconds that proposal, but recent history shows that such institutional reform must be coupled with comprehensive institutional changes. After the S&L debacle, the Financial Institutions Reform, Recovery, and Enforcement Act created the DOJ Financial Institutions Fraud Unit, which could have served a similar function but floundered owing to its limited coordinational capacities and the lack of accompanying changes strengthening regulatory institutions. Regulators play critical roles not only in referring cases but also in assisting federal prosecutors in white-collar cases, so even if the ECD was endowed with independent investigation and enforcement powers, agencies would still require expanded staff to provide expert assistance to federal prosecutors in complex cases. Further, the ECD would require new funding that could initially be provided by the fines secured by the Antitrust Division. There is every reason to believe that increasing the Antitrust Division's long-stagnant budget would only bring in more revenue to support an ECD that could eventually fund itself. Additionally, ensuring that the ECD is not reliant on regulatory referrals to build its caseload would require workable means for tracking the behavior of large corporations operating across diverse market sectors, an issue addressed in the next proposal.

Third, a concern first raised by Edwin Sutherland involves the lack of reliable statistics tracking corporate crime.[30] Regulators possess considerable discretion in responding to illegal conduct with regulatory sanctions, allowing corporate actors to maintain ostensibly clean criminal records. This hampers regulators from obtaining complete pictures of markets. An agency may opt for a gentle persuasive sanction against a firm it believed committed a first-time offense, but it might choose differently had it known that several other agencies also applied mild sanctions against the firm for illicit activities in recent years. The coordination challenges plaguing agencies' operations are well-known, but the systematic absence of reliable, accessible, and comprehensive agency enforcement data compounds these problems.[31]

The DFA created regulatory bodies like the FSOC and the Office of Financial Research with the aim of building a more comprehensive view of the financial system's health, and to achieve this goal one of these institutions or another preexisting body like the Government Accounting Office should be empowered to collect and centralize data cataloging regulatory activity across agencies. This system would function as a statistical clearinghouse logging all administrative actions taken by federal regulators ranging from informal measures to cease-and-desist orders, civil suits, criminal referrals, and all other sanctions. The platform would provide a single picture of federal regulatory activity that could be used to track patterns in administrative scrutiny of major firms. If regulators encounter what appears to be a first offense warranting an administrative sanction, such a system could illuminate a firm's track record of repeatedly facing light interventions from other agencies, which could justify a different approach. It would likely not be overly challenging to create; the American Bankers Association's Enforcement Action Database already serves a similar function for bank members.[32]

This may seem unnecessary since agencies often have a general knowledge of each other's doings as major regulatory interventions are often publicized and regulators release their own data, but methods of data collection and presentation can vary substantially across agencies.[33] Consequently, using one resource to obtain a holistic picture of a firm's interactions with federal regulators would be more efficient and practical than scouring diversely written reports from separate agencies. This would enable regulators to more easily make decisions based on fuller understandings of economic and regulatory dynamics while empowering the ECD to operate more effectively without criminal referrals by offering it an efficient means for tracking firms with records of scrutiny from various agencies. Additionally, critical observers studying agency enforcement trends would likely find such a system to be a valuable resource. Journalistic or academic analyses of agency enforcement activity could publicly expose agencies that regularly overlook repeat offending or target only minor offenders to bolster their statistics without monitoring the market's most powerful and dangerous actors, generating pressure on agencies to take their enforcement mandates seriously and carry them out with care.

The political economy is ruled by huge institutions driven by problematic incentives to prioritize profit making above all else, a problem that institutional rejiggering cannot fully resolve on its own.[34] However, the solutions detailed above are necessary steps toward achieving a better balance of state regulatory and prosecutorial oversight over corporations. Even should the political economy be structurally reformed, maintaining the faults of the regulatory approach could undermine those changes by perpetuating the same problems and inequalities examined in this book.

Political Economic Solutions

Rehabilitative and regulatory ideologies emerged from and have upheld deeper pathologies in the political economy. Undoing their influence requires challenging that economic system head-on. The following sections provide routes for directly confronting and ameliorating maladies in the political economy that risk being sustained even by reformed versions of criminal justice and regulatory institutions.

RETHINKING REGULATORY IDEOLOGY AND STREET CRIME

Instead of resolving penal inequalities by subjecting corporate offenders to the punitive impulse of American politics, this book has argued that a more constructive solution is to expand the regulatory approach. The promise of the regulatory approach is that it treats its targets as universally rational and capable of being guided via gentler interventions and the management of economic conditions, contradicting rehabilitative notions that certain people are innately criminal and others can be fixed via individualized treatment. Regulatory ideology can serve as a blueprint for managing street-level misconduct by marrying political efforts to rein in capitalism's most egregious abuses to a preventative crime control mentality emphasizing economic management. The following analysis provides examples of how this could work—it is not an exhaustive listing—with the intention of spurring broader conversations about how regulatory controls could promote a different approach to governing street crime.

However, two considerations should be emphasized. First, in discussing political economic reform, it is important to distinguish the "crime crisis" from the "carceral crisis."[35] Serious problems of crime and violence plague poor and predominantly Black urban communities in the United States, where persistent structural economic disadvantages sustain alarmingly high rates of criminal violence.[36] However, this simply does not rationalize the harsh punishment of so many Americans. It is well-documented that punitive governing strategies not only fail to meaningfully reduce crime, but also make life much harder for vulnerable populations in the process.[37] While the crime crisis in marginalized communities must be taken seriously, it is distinct from the carceral crisis of unnecessarily imprisoning so many of those communities' residents for so long. This book shows how rehabilitative ideology has operated at the nexus of the crime and carceral crises to pernicious effects. Rehabilitation is often pitched as a solution to the crime crisis by promising crime reduction via individual empowerment. But when supposedly rehabilitated offenders return to communities plagued by profound inequalities and state neglect and later find themselves back in prison, rehabilitative mentalities interpret their recidivism as proof of incorrigibility. This creates a self-fulfilling cycle contributing to the carceral crisis by justifying draconian punishment for incorrigibles. Using regulatory governance to control crime via economic management is grounded in the belief that alleviating the economic inequalities of American life is the only true long-term solution to the crime crisis, but importantly, it also rejects rehabilitative ideology's individualizing logic that has contributed to the carceral crisis.

Second, it is crucial to eschew a Pollyannaish view of regulation while acknowledging its potential. Administrative law can significantly affect average citizens via surveillance requirements and monetary sanctions that constitute enormous impositions on those without wealth.[38] States and municipalities sometimes combine administrative measures with criminal and civil law, blurring their distinctions and obscuring punitive consequences behind the facade of administrative law.[39] And light-handed techniques of administrative oversight could be enforced to punitive effects on street-level offenders. For instance, deferred prosecution agreements, discussed in chapter 7 as federal prosecutors' chosen tactic for managing corporate crime, were originally created in 1936 to handle first-time juvenile offenders without criminal charges.[40] Restoring the original purpose of DPAs could facilitate the application of a more administrative and less punitive approach to juvenile offending, but it is easy to imagine that DPAs could be imposed more sternly on juveniles than on executives. While juvenile DPAs could have positive effects if implemented carefully, this concern illustrates why applying the regulatory model to street criminality must do more than replace individualized punitive controls with individualized administrative controls. The greatest appeal of regulatory ideology is its emphasis on controlling economic conditions to discourage undesirable behavior, and it should be applied to street crime in ways that restructure how America governs the relationship between the political economy and criminal conduct.

This may sound unrealistic, but there are historical examples of the American state applying regulatory techniques to contexts that we manage punitively today. For instance, few scholars have compared America's ineffective record of punitive drug governance to its more successful record of regulating drugs. Early twentieth-century law managed drugs by regulating businesses putting opiates and cocaine in their products and doctors prescribing such substances.[41] Contemporary antitobacco campaigns have slashed smoking rates not via punitive sanctions and criminal law, but through advertising regulations, rules dictating where and when smoking is permitted, and agency-led public education initiatives discouraging tobacco use.[42] More recently, states that have legalized marijuana have opted for a variety of regulatory schemes to govern its production, distribution, and purchase.[43] As a result, not only is governing drug use via regulatory measures an alternative to punitive techniques; it is also a strategy with a record of success.

While drug control is one area where this approach could take root, this book advocates bolder applications of regulatory ideology aimed at protecting access to public goods and economic welfare as forms of administrative crime prevention. It is well established that the material conditions under which returning offenders live—including job availability, average wages, residential stability, and unemployment rates in their home neighborhoods—are among the strongest predictors of criminal behavior.[44] The regulatory framework offers a means for managing the real problems of crime in desperately poor communities via a crime-preventative politics focused on social spending and economic management. Rehabilitative politics embraces the proposition that equipping vulnerable populations with new skills will help them succeed under bleak circumstances of marginality, but the regulatory approach could be mobilized to tether criminal justice to structural economic controls instead.

Just as regulatory controls on pricing, advertising, and other features of market activity can prevent markets from becoming criminogenic, macroeconomic policies providing economic stability can be reconceptualized as administrative measures that prevent marginalized communities from

becoming criminogenic. Violence, drug markets, and property crime flourish in communities entrenched in poverty. These realities are consequences
of unregulated dimensions of modern capitalism's most extreme abuses, not
of individual residents' incorrigibility. Instead of reducing crime by trying to
rehabilitate individuals with GED classes during their incarceration, a regulatory perspective would compel the Department of Education to expand access
to and improve the quality of public schooling in state-neglected high-crime
communities so that residents can get a good education outside prison walls.
While rehabilitative strategies rely on vocational training behind bars to help
felons find work after release, a regulatory approach would channel public
spending toward igniting job growth in depressed labor markets so that populations in high-crime areas can find reliable and meaningful work opportunities. Rather than denying public housing to felons, regulatory interventions
from the Department of Housing and Urban Development should enhance
the quality and accessibility of public housing—and open doors to convicted
felons—in order to provide those living in criminogenic communities with
an assured residence while they seek to build stable livelihoods. And instead
of leaving marginalized populations to fend for themselves to find dignified
work, state regulations guaranteeing everyone a livable wage and more robust
workplace protections vigorously enforced by the Department of Labor could
prevent exploitative pay and abusive working conditions from driving people
into criminal activity. These questions of welfare and public goods are critical issues of economic justice, but framing them as proactive regulations of
criminogenic economic conditions could garner broader support by situating
them within a crime-preventative lens.

Similarly, given the documented connection between unemployment and
crime, jobs programs have been presented as routes to crime reduction.[45] In
the United States, New Deal era initiatives like the Works Progress Administration and the Civilian Conservation Corps have been credited with keeping crime rates down by creating federally regulated public works programs
that kept millions of people susceptible to criminogenic economic pressures
employed during the Great Depression.[46] Bold federal jobs proposals of the
past have also highlighted their crime-prevention benefits. In their "Freedom
Budget" of 1967, the civil rights leaders A. Philip Randolph and Bayard Rustin presented an economic proposal including a federal jobs guarantee and a
livable wage, among other policies. Their plan, which became a cornerstone
of the Poor People's Campaign, stated that through these provisions "the
breeding grounds of crime and discontent will be diminished."[47] Federal jobs
proposals ranging from moderate to bold retain bipartisan popularity with
the working class.[48] Federally regulated jobs initiatives investing in urban

redevelopment, public housing and school construction, green energy, and the care economy would have additional effects beyond providing economic stability by serving the goals of crime prevention.

Reconceptualizing street crime as something to be controlled via economic regulatory measures creates space to reconceptualize parole and probation. In other developed nations, parole and probation officers typically assist released inmates by helping them secure resources enabling them to navigate reentry smoothly. In contrast, American parole and probation officers are tasked with the punitive responsibility of scrutinizing released felons for future crimes and mistakes warranting a return to prison.[49] This is because the American models of parole and probation remain mired in the rehabilitative mindset, keeping officers focused on surveilling released offenders for signs of incorrigibility. A regulatory approach could reconceptualize parole and probation officers as forms of administrative assistance designed to help inmates get what they need to readjust successfully, reimagining them as something closer to social workers by no longer defining the power to punish and surveil for incorrigibility as central to their institutional mission.[50]

Many of these policies champion a radically reformed understanding of economic citizenship that would carry crime-prevention benefits. They should be incorporated into criminal justice reform conversations via framings presenting them as administrative measures aimed at remedying the economic conditions that produce crime, moving away from the self-defeating rehabilitative strategy of emphasizing individual empowerment to reduce crime. Stressing these policies' crime-prevention benefits would cultivate deepened public understandings of how investing in public goods and economic justice can provide sweeping social benefits improving our collective welfare.

RETHINKING THE FINANCIAL ECONOMY

That corporate frauds can now devastate the global economy is not simply a function of poor regulation and enforcement—it is a function of an economic system that gave birth to dangerously powerful institutions. Regulation will do little to improve American life if it sustains an economic system that gave rise to such corporate behemoths. All options should be on the table to make the economy more equitable, manageable, and stable if we are to ensure that regulators and prosecutors uphold an economic system that is truly fair and functional.

This section surveys three radical options for remaking the political economy. However, they vary in how much they depart from our current economic system and coexist in some tension. The section thus discusses their advantages, disadvantages, and potential to work in concert in an effort to encourage broadened and more enlightened conversations about fixing the financial economy. Further, it should be clarified that these ideas are radical, complex, and unlikely to take root in the current political climate given that America lacks the political willpower to impose even minor regulations on the financial sector, not to mention drastically restructure it. But truly fixing the economy requires substantial changes and bold ideas, and given Wall Street's repeated missteps, radical solutions should be considered now to ignite more informed discussions that could lead to change under the right conditions. As Thomas Hanna writes, this would leave us better prepared for "the crisis next time."[51]

First, some have suggested breaking up banks to disrupt criminogenic markets. The rise of too-big-to-fail institutions has made it difficult for lawmakers and regulators to control the financial economy in any meaningful way and punish wrongdoers within giant corporations. As chapter 6 explored, financial institutions are often driven by the adverse incentives of moral hazard. Corporate leaders feel free to engage in imprudent high-risk, high-reward activities when they believe that their institution's demise would devastate the economy and thus anticipate that they would receive a taxpayer bailout to prevent economic catastrophe should they fail. But a 2018 congressional bill detailed a plan for breaking up financial institutions, capping their total exposure at 3 percent of national GDP ($584 billion in 2018, when J. P. Morgan held $2.4 trillion in liabilities). This would compel institutions to shrink to sizes that pose fewer risks to economic stability should they go under, eliminating the need for bailouts to steady markets following an institution's failure and curbing the incentives of moral hazard.[52]

A component of this strategy should be the reenactment of the Glass-Steagall separation of investment and commercial banking. This would not only prevent institutions from mixing risky investment activities with deposit-taking operations, but also compel financial institutions to shrink by divesting either the investment banking or the commercial banking components of their business. This would complement the broader goal of breaking up the banks by reducing the likelihood that any single institution would be so large as to require a bailout to buoy the economy.[53] These techniques would thus directly alter current incentive structures enabling big corporations to participate in risky or fraudulent activities without concern that they may eventually have to face the consequences, something hard to do only via reforms to regulatory oversight, making the financial system safer and more manageable for the state to monitor.

As an idea that has received significant public attention in recent years, breaking up the banks is the most feasible solution advanced here. There would be substantial challenges in disentangling the complex financial operations performed by large banks, but the idea has garnered surprising bipartisan support ranging from the Democratic Party's most progressive flanks to conservative economists like Alan Greenspan and George W. Bush's Council of Economic Advisers chair R. Glenn Hubbard.[54] The idea's conservative proponents typically view it as consistent with capitalist principles by promoting healthy competition, while its left-leaning supporters understand it as expanding state management over the market. This consensus clearly has room for disagreement as conservatives and progressives will split over the details of such a strategy and the state's precise role in implementing it, but this is indicative of the plan's potential to secure broad appeal as a realistic path to restructuring the economy.

A second proposal is a federal corporate chartering system. The Accountable Capitalism Act, introduced in Congress in 2018, required corporations with over $1 billion in annual revenue to secure a federal charter from the Department of Commerce. The charter would tie company directors to a range of stakeholder interests beyond just those of shareholders—including employees, customers, and communities in which the company operates. The bill was based on the belief that profit-maximization incentives encourage firms to disregard social welfare and that, since state chartering systems failed to rectify this misalignment, federal intervention became necessary to compel directors and executives to consider goals beyond profit making. The bill granted state attorneys general the ability to petition the government to revoke a corporate charter if a company engaged in illegal conduct.[55]

There are potential limits to this form of stakeholder capitalism. The bill is based on largely successful state-level "benefit corporation" systems, which are voluntary chartering schemes firms can opt into in order to be legally tasked with a dual mission of pursuing profits and providing a stated public benefit.[56] But the federal proposal departs from those systems by requiring large corporations to comply with its rules rather than making doing so voluntary, rendering it an untested approach leaving some observers concerned that it will lack the value of the benefit corporation model.[57] Moreover, binding corporate leaders to the interests of a wider collection of stakeholders would create obstacles to swift decision-making by requiring them to balance the often-conflicting interests of employees, customers, communities, and shareholders. Some critics thus express concern that this would hamper firms' capacity to act with speed and decisiveness.[58] The strategy could also grant legitimacy to too-big-to-fail institutions by ostensibly aligning them with social welfare considerations.

The idea's potential value offsets these concerns. Importantly, despite their shared emphasis on expanding stakeholder input and promoting corporate social responsibility, the federal bill serves a different purpose than do state-level benefit corporation frameworks. The federal bill's compulsory nature serves the goal of mandating accountability for large firms with over $1 billion in revenue, whereas state benefit corporation systems are designed to give firms of all sizes optional legal protection to serve public interest goals and make decisions that might contradict shareholder interests in value maximization. In other words, the federal proposal is different because it is uniquely focused on promoting accountability for big corporations. This is particularly evident in the bill's enforcement mechanism enabling state attorneys general to petition for charter revocation in cases of illegality.

The law also outlines specific requirements for corporate governance that are not necessarily included in state-level systems. One of the idea's core proposals is that rank-and-file workers elect 40 percent of the membership on corporate boards of directors. This is a popular idea that could rearrange corporate incentive structures revering profit maximization above all else while restoring an ethic of social responsibility to business culture.[59] And while it is certainly true that the input of opposing stakeholders will impede firms' decisiveness, that is a reasonable cost to pay for more inclusive corporate deliberation over choices that can carry sweeping social consequences. Additionally, it is worth noting that the strategy could avoid legitimizing too-big-to-fail institutions if implemented along with a breaking-up-the-banks approach. It is imaginable that institutions with over $1 billion in revenue could be required to secure a federal charter while their maximum exposure is also capped at 3 percent of GDP, concomitantly diminishing moral hazard while forcing corporate decision-making processes to rely on deeper understandings of the diverse interests affected by firms' choices.

The most radical idea—and the one that warrants the most circumspection—is nationalizing portions of the banking sector. This proposal exists in tension with the previous strategies that keep institutions in private ownership and would face distinctively enormous political resistance, implementation challenges, and low prospects for passage, but careful consideration of the idea unearths surprising truths that should inform public discourse about American finance.

Historical and comparative analysis reveals ample precedent for nationalized banks, and the political economies of many nations consist of a mix of state-owned and privatized banks. Since the 1980s, several countries have moved toward nationalizing portions of their banking sectors, and hundreds of public and semipublic banks operate in Europe, South America, and Asia.[60]

The American federal government had ownership stakes in the First and Second Banks of the United States in the early republic and ran a successful postal banking system for fifty years in the twentieth century. North Dakota currently operates a one-hundred-year-old publicly owned bank, the Bank of North Dakota (BND), which holds $7.3 billion in assets and a loan portfolio of $4.3 billion. The BND kept the state's foreclosure rate among the lowest in the country during the subprime mortgage crisis while contributing revenues to the state. Nationalization has also enjoyed support from unexpected corners; the early Chicago school economists Henry Simons and Frank Knight entertained ideas ranging from transforming banks into semipublic institutions to their "outright socialization," and in 2008 the Citigroup chief economist, Willem Buiter, acknowledged the case for keeping banks "in permanent public ownership" since they cannot exist without a taxpayer-underwritten deposit guarantee.[61]

There are benefits to a financial system with a mix of state- and privately owned banks. By diversifying risk across the public and the private sectors, a mixed banking system with a public presence could provide greater stability during economic crises by minimizing the need to bail out failed private institutions to rescue a faltering economy, thus further breaking the incentives of moral hazard that encourage financial crime. Public banks are capable of lessening the impact of economic downturns by extending financial services and credit to individuals, businesses, and communities in need when private institutions are apt to adopt more stringent lending criteria.[62] Public banks could also enhance and improve market standards since private institutions with records of engaging in unduly risky behavior or predatory practices might struggle to survive in competition with public options that customers view as safer, thus preventing the normalization of undesirable misconduct.[63] Further, public banks could invest in ventures serving the public interest that private actors may be quick to deem too costly or risky to be worthy investments, such as renewable energy infrastructure, or commit themselves to social functions such as the provision of financial services to underserved populations or the construction of low-income housing.[64] Increasing the availability of public goods, financial services, and economic opportunities for marginalized groups would consequently render public banks useful tools for ameliorating the economic conditions that fuel street crime in structurally disadvantaged communities via regulatory-economic interventions.

This is not to ignore the risks that such a radical measure could pose by introducing new dynamics into the financial system. Public banks are often assumed to be less productive, efficient, and innovative than private ones, although research suggests that this concern is overstated and that public and

private banks perform comparably.[65] Nevertheless, a public foothold in banking would have broader systemic benefits. Public banks could help steady
fluctuations in the economic cycle, maintain equitable access to financial
services through recessions, and ensure the consistent availability of public
goods to all, all of which are inherently valuable services regardless of their
profitability.[66] Additionally, there are valid questions about whether public
banks would be dangerously susceptible to shifting political pressures. However, government-run institutions are subject to unique transparency requirements and oversight. Given the opacity of what happens behind the private
doors of America's boardrooms, public banks would likely receive heightened
scrutiny in comparison to private ones and as a result would likely be far
more vulnerable to public inspection and criticism if they became problem-
atically politicized.

Notably, nationalizing failed banks exists in tension with the underlying
principles of corporate chartering and breaking up the banks, which promote
financial stability and corporate responsibility while keeping institutions in
private ownership. But this section does not insist that all three solutions
be fully implemented together. Rather, it aims to facilitate greater discourse
about them as options that could be adopted in isolation or carefully balanced
combinations. For instance, only institutions failing to stay under a 3 percent
cap on bank size in a breaking-up-the-banks strategy could be exposed to
potential nationalization, creating a powerful motivation for institutions to
maintain their size. Under a regulatory regime reinstituting Glass-Steagall-
style rules separating commercial and investment banking, only failed commercial banks could be considered for possible permanent public ownership,
while investment banking could remain in the private sector.[67] The conditions warranting nationalization, such as severe fraud or crime, could even be
delineated within a chartering framework—a move that would create enormous incentives for institutions to stay within the law's bounds just by putting such plans on paper.

It goes without saying that enacting these proposals would require tec-
tonic realignments in American politics and protracted political struggles.
Nonetheless, if we are to remake the political economy and lessen the frequency and harm of corporate crime, they should be placed on the public
agenda and taken into consideration immediately. Even an effective combination of prosecution and regulation risks sustaining rather than restructuring a political economy characterized by profound power imbalances and
inequalities. Introducing these ideas into political discourse would allow us
to engage with them seriously and prepare more thought-out solutions to

propose in the future should political conditions change and become more favorable to radical ideas.

Conclusion

Undoing the dysfunctions and inequalities of rehabilitative and regulatory ideologies within American law will require hard work. The solutions provided in this chapter are not the only answers to solving the problems this book has studied—countless others have detailed the need for changes to sentencing, regulation, the Justice Department, and more—but they are necessary if we are to move toward a better and more equitable future in American law.

Both institutional reforms and deep political economic changes are needed to resolve these problems. Like much research on the sociology of crime and on corporate offending, this book argues that long-term structural economic reform is necessary to ameliorate the underlying causes of both street and corporate criminality. But importantly, that perspective overlooks immediate and pressing problems. Vulnerable populations are being targeted by the carceral state right now, and institutional solutions must abandon the rehabilitative ideal and its punitive assumptions to immediately reduce the damage being inflicted on American citizens. Meanwhile, swiftly restoring some meaningful measure of deterrence and criminal accountability in America's boardrooms requires clear, consistent, and strengthened enforcement of corporate law. But these institutional fixes will have little durable effects unless the fundamental dysfunctions in the political economy are addressed. Both approaches—the institutional and the economic—must be advocated together.

It is a testament to the prejudices inherent in our political understanding of criminality that someone can get a life sentence for three shoplifting offenses but that CEOs can commit crimes that cause global economic crises without facing serious consequences. We must recognize how carceral and regulatory institutions internalize, reproduce, and legitimize a common politically constructed understanding of criminality if we are to address the deep inequalities of American law and engage in the hard work necessary to pave a path toward a different future.

Acknowledgments

I am fortunate to have benefited from the support of so many people as I navigated the long and challenging path of writing this book. I owe many thanks to those who have provided me with guidance, support, and encouragement over the course of its development.

It has been a privilege to work with Marie Gottschalk. Marie was an exceptional graduate adviser from my first day at Penn, and I am deeply grateful for the remarkable amount of time, energy, and effort she put into helping me conduct the project I envisioned. I am fortunate to have worked with someone who is so genuinely committed to her students and who set an ideal example of what it means to be a teacher and a scholar.

I am lucky to have had the support of Rogers Smith. Rogers has always offered sharp and insightful feedback that spoke directly to the core of my work while providing clear and actionable paths for its improvement. His ability to make time for students while juggling his many professional commitments is a testament to his dedication to mentorship, and I am indebted to him for the kindness and guidance he has extended to me.

The conversations I have had with Adolph Reed have been some of the most formative of my career. Adolph's thoughts always left the project improved, and his excitement about it always left me encouraged. He has profoundly shaped not just this book, but how I fundamentally understand the political world, and his work and guidance are constant reminders that politics is something worth being passionate about.

My interest in research was sparked by the outstanding scholars I learned from at Rutgers University. My experience as a research assistant for Andrew Murphy exposed me to academic research and helped me discover my passion for it. No one is more responsible for my choosing this career than

Milton Heumann. From advising my undergraduate thesis to offering me advice through graduate school and my professional career, he has always been an ally and a friend, and I am fortunate to have had him as my first academic mentor.

I am grateful to have received input on this project from an exceptional group of scholars. Thanks to Sarah Cate, Mackenzie Colella, Farah Godrej, Loren Goldman, Bill Laufer, Howard Levinson, Hugh Liebert, Daniel Moak, Spencer Piston, Katie Rader, Stephan Stohler, Robinson Woodward-Burns, and Joanna Wuest for reading and providing feedback on excerpts and chapter drafts. Special thanks to Naomi Murakawa, Jonathan Simon, and Stephen Skowronek for reading the full manuscript and offering feedback that made it immeasurably better. Richard Harris and Lisa Miller deserve particular thanks for reading and critiquing the full manuscript, offering thoughts on multiple iterations of chapter drafts, and providing valuable guidance on the publishing process and the profession more generally. I am also grateful to those who read chapters at meetings of the American Political Science Association, the Northeast Political Science Association, the Western Political Science Association, the Law and Society Association, and the American Society of Criminology for helping refine and hone my arguments.

During my time at the University of Pennsylvania, I was lucky to become friends with many kind, smart, and gifted people in the political science graduate program. Their friendship has made me a better teacher, scholar, and person. For this I owe thanks to Sarah Cate, Danielle Hanley, Max Margulies, Daniel Moak, James Morone, Katie Rader, Gabe Salgado, Nate Shils, Robinson Woodward-Burns, and Joanna Wuest.

I am grateful for the professional support I have received from Rutgers and West Point. Thanks to my colleagues at West Point, especially Heidi Demarest, Hugh Liebert, Scott Limbocker, and Suzanne Nielsen. I also thank my colleagues and the staff at Rutgers-Camden, including Lisa Alston, Mike Boyle, Sheila Diggs, Kelly Dittmar, Maureen Donaghy, Kelly Esterly, Tim Knievel, Beth Rabinowitz, Shauna Shames, and Wojtek Wolfe, for their advice and guidance. Additional thanks are due to my talented research assistants, Andrew Bongiovanni, Adam Colgate, and Benjamin Harvey, who provided crucial assistance at key points in the process. Thanks to Penn's School of Arts and Sciences, Political Science Department, Robert A. Fox Leadership Program, and Zicklin Center for Business Ethics Research for providing me with institutional support during the dissertation stage. West Point and Rutgers also provided support and resources for which I am grateful. Additionally, I thank the New York State Archives for granting me a Larry J. Hackman Residency Award to expand my archival research.

Thanks to my editor, Sara Doskow, for seeing value in my manuscript and ushering it to publication. I am also indebted to Rosemary Frehe, Michaela Luckey, Christine Schwab, and the team at the University of Chicago Press for their patience and guidance. Many thanks to Joseph Brown for his thorough copyediting and to Theresa Wolner for her diligent work in creating the index. Thanks as well to the anonymous reviewers at Chicago and other presses for providing constructive input and critiques. I also express my gratitude to John Conley, Charles Epp, and Lynn Mather for publishing this book as part of the Chicago Series in Law and Society.

Finally, I would like to thank my family. One of the most intelligent and positive people I know, my sister Christine has always been an ideal role model as a critical thinker and person. She deserves particular thanks for her thoughtful proofreading of the full manuscript at multiple stages. I could ask for no better model of perseverance than my father, Tony, who taught me what it means to be committed in every sense. My mother, Beth, did not get to see me complete the project, but she always gave me the encouragement I needed to finish it. My in-laws, Joyce and Paul, have always provided support for which I am grateful. I am also grateful to my longtime friend Benjamin Lapidus and brother-in-law Peter Talarico for their help in the book's final stages. The greatest thanks are for my wife, Kelly, whose encouragement and love made this book possible. And special thanks to Cecily, who reminds me what really matters and makes me smile even when things are particularly stressful.

I apologize to anyone I failed to mention. Despite the influence of so many throughout these pages, all errors and omissions are my own.

Notes

Chapter One

1. "Full Transcript: First 2016 Presidential Debate."

2. Laufer, *Corporate Bodies and Guilty Minds*, 69; Tillman, Pontell, and Black, *Financial Crime and Crises*, 2; Eisinger, *The Chickenshit Club*, xv–xvi.

3. Gramlich, "America's Incarceration Rate."

4. Simon, *Poor Discipline*; Garland, *The Culture of Control*; Rothman, *The Discovery of the Asylum*; Pisciotta, *Benevolent Repression*; Stuntz, *The Collapse of American Criminal Justice*.

5. On local economic regulations in early nineteenth-century America, see Novak, *The People's Welfare*. The few empirical analyses of class and punishment before the late nineteenth century find that states fostered a relative equality in punishment compared to Europe. See Spindel, *Crime and Society in North Carolina*, 130–31; Greenberg, *Crime and Law Enforcement*, 114; and Whitman, *Harsh Justice*, 165–70.

6. Lombroso, *Criminal Man*.

7. Knight, "Transformations"; Van Dijk, "Ideology and Discourse Analysis"; Larner, "Neo-Liberalism"; Reed, "Marx, Race, and Neoliberalism."

8. Foucault, *The Birth of Biopolitics*; Foucault and Ewald, *"Society Must Be Defended."*

9. Foucault and Ewald, *"Society Must Be Defended,"* 61. For more on Foucault's general views on race and biopolitics, see ibid., 61–62, 241–60; and Foucault, *The Birth of Biopolitics*, 239–66.

10. Skowronek, "The Reassociation of Ideas and Purposes"; Lieberman, "Ideas, Institutions, and Political Order"; Orren and Skowronek, *The Search for American Political Development*; Blyth, Helgadottir, and Kring, "Ideas and Historical Institutionalism"; Smith, "Ideas and the Spiral of Politics"; Pierson, "Increasing Returns."

11. Browning and Gerassi, *The American Way of Crime*, 20–23, 130–33; Gottschalk, *The Prison and the Gallows*; McLennan, *The Crisis of Imprisonment*, 19; Morone, *Hellfire Nation*, 455–77.

12. Resources used to develop a starting point for studying prominent thinkers in these fields include Rafter, *Creating Born Criminals*; Pisciotta, *Benevolent Repression*; Black, *War against the Weak*; Cohen, *Imbeciles*; and Leonard, *Illiberal Reformers*.

13. Lieberman, "Ideas, Institutions, and Political Order," 700.

14. Schmidt, "Reconciling Ideas"; Smith, "Which Comes First"; Béland and Cox, "Introduction: Ideas and Politics."

15. Skowronek, "The Reassociation of Ideas and Purposes"; Smith, "Ideas and the Spiral of Politics"; Béland and Cox, "Introduction: Ideas and Politics"; Berman, "Ideology, History, and Politics."

16. Béland and Cox, "Introduction: Ideas and Politics," 8–9.

17. Knight, "Transformations," 619.

18. Tonry, *Sentencing Fragments*, 50–63 (esp. 57–62), and "Equality and Human Dignity."

19. Wheeler, Mann, and Sarat, "Sentencing the White-Collar Criminal"; Galvin and Simpson, "Prosecuting and Sentencing."

20. Karmen, *Crime Victims*; Taub, *Big Dirty Money*, 65–90; Croall, "What Is Known"; Barak, *Theft of a Nation*, 117–20; Sutherland, *White-Collar Crime*, 22, 218–23.

21. O'Malley, "Volatile and Contradictory Punishment."

22. Braithwaite, "What's Wrong."

23. Garland, *The Culture of Control*; Tonry, *Sentencing Fragments*, and *Punishing Race*; Beckett, *Making Crime Pay*; Simon, *Governing through Crime*; Hinton, *From the War on Poverty to the War on Crime*.

24. Grasso, "Broken beyond Repair"; Goodman, Page, and Phelps, *Breaking the Pendulum*; Hannah-Moffat, "Criminogenic Needs and the Transformative Risk Subject"; Godrej, "Yoga, Meditation, and Neoliberal Penality," and *Freedom Inside?*

25. Murakawa, *The First Civil Right*; Muhammad, *The Condemnation of Blackness*; Goodman, Page, and Phelps, *Breaking the Pendulum*; Gottschalk, *The Prison and the Gallows*, and *Caught*; Weaver, "Frontlash"; Hinton, *From the War on Poverty to the War on Crime*.

26. Alexander, *The New Jim Crow*; Oshinsky, *"Worse Than Slavery"*; Muhammad, *The Condemnation of Blackness*.

27. Reed, "Marx, Race, and Neoliberalism," 49.

28. Fields and Fields, *Racecraft*, 101, 266.

29. Reed and Chowkwanyun, "Race, Class, Crisis."

30. Wacquant, *Punishing the Poor*, and "Deadly Symbiosis"; Quinney, *Critique of Legal Order*; Chambliss, "The Saints and the Rough-Necks"; Reiman and Leighton, *The Rich Get Richer and the Poor Get Prison*.

31. Stocking, *Race, Culture, and Evolution*.

32. One other notable work not discussed here is Taibbi's *The Divide*, which is more journalistic and descriptive than social scientific.

33. Reiman and Leighton, *The Rich Get Richer and the Poor Get Prison*.

34. Hagan, *Who Are the Criminals?*

35. Harcourt, *The Illusion of Free Markets*.

36. Braithwaite, "What's Wrong."

37. Braithwaite, "What's Wrong."

38. Sutherland, *White-Collar Crime*.

39. Katz, "United States," 838. On Sutherland, see Taub, *Big Dirty Money*, 1–18; Hagan, *Who Are the Criminals?*, 44, 198; and Cressey, foreword to *White-Collar Crime*.

40. Shapiro, *Wayward Capitalists*; Mann, *Defending White-Collar Crime*; Wheeler, Mann, and Sarat, *Sitting in Judgment*; Weisburd, Wheeler, Waring, and Bode, *Crimes of the Middle Class*; Taibbi, *The Divide*; Friedrichs, *Trusted Criminals*.

41. On economic consequences, see Garrett, *Too Big to Jail*. On deregulation and financialization, see Tillman, Pontell, and Black, *Financial Crime and Crises*; Foroohar, *Makers and Takers*; and Hagan, *Who Are the Criminals?* On political access, see Morgenson, *Reckless Endangerment*.

42. Vogel, *Trading Up*, and "Why Businessmen Distrust Their State"; Moran, "The Rise of the Regulatory State"; Dobbin, *Forging Industrial Policy*.

43. Kolko, *Railroads and Regulation*; Berk, *Alternative Tracks*; Bensel, *The Political Economy of American Industrialization*; Skowronek, *Building a New American State*; DeCanio, *Democracy and the Origins of the American Regulatory State*; Eisner, *Regulatory Politics in Transition*.

44. On competing perspectives about the regulatory state's character, see Coen, Grant, and Wilson, "Political Science," 21; and Bardach and Kagan, *Going by the Book*. On nuanced realities about regulatory oversight missed in such debates, see Galanter, "Why the 'Haves' Come Out Ahead"; and Albiston, "The Rule of Law"; Shaffer, "Law and Business."

45. Bernstein, *Regulating Business*; Schattschneider, *The Semisovereign People*; Lindblom, *Politics and Markets*; Werner and Wilson, "Business Representation in Washington, DC"; Baumgartner, Berry, Hojnacki, Leech, and Kimball, *Lobbying and Policy Change*.

46. Vogel, *Fluctuating Fortunes*.

47. Harvey, *A Brief History of Neoliberalism*, 31–36.

48. Wilson and Grant, "Business and Political Parties"; Werner and Wilson, "Business Representation in Washington, DC."

49. Sklar, *The Corporate Reconstruction of American Capitalism*; Novak, *The People's Welfare*; Grasso, "'No Bodies to Kick or Souls to Damn.'"

50. Whitman, *Harsh Justice*.

51. Sampson, *Great American City*; Western, "The Penal System and the Labor Market"; Bushway, "Labor Markets and Crime"; Savage, Bennett, and Danner, "Economic Assistance and Crime."

52. Tcherneva, "The Federal Jobs Guarantee"; Raphael and Winter-Ebmer, "The Effect of Unemployment"; Falk and Zweimüller, "Unemployment and Right-Wing Extremist Crime"; Freeman, "Crime and the Employment of Disadvantaged Youths"; Western, "The Penal System and the Labor Market."

53. Pandiani, "The Crime Control Corps"; Johnson, Kantor, and Fishback, "Striking at the Roots of Crime."

54. Schell-Busey, Simpson, Rorie, and Alper, "What Works?," 388, 406–7. For more on deterrence, also see Paternoster, "Deterring Corporate Crime"; Simpson, *Corporate Crime*; Hawkins, "Compliance Strategy"; and Croall, *Understanding White Collar Crime*.

55. Braithwaite and Ayres, *Responsive Regulation*, 19–53.

56. Schell-Busey, Simpson, Rorie, and Alper, "What Works?," 408; Yeager, "The Elusive Deterrence of Corporate Crime," 447; Braithwaite, "In Search of Donald Campbell"; Haugh, "Exactly Wrong."

57. Yeager, "The Elusive Deterrence of Corporate Crime"; Foroohar, *Makers and Takers*; Tillman, Pontell, and Black, *Financial Crime and Crises*; Schell-Busey, Simpson, Rorie, and Alper, "What Works?"; Haugh, "Exactly Wrong."

Chapter Two

1. For overviews of this history, see Hattam, *Labor Visions*; Bensel, *Yankee Leviathan*, and *The Political Economy of American Industrialization*; Wiebe, *The Search for Order*; Sklar, *The Corporate Reconstruction of American Capitalism*; Orren, *Belated Feudalism*; Trachtenberg, *The Incorporation of America*; Fraser, *The Age of Acquiescence*; and Smith, *Civic Ideals*, 347–409.

2. Fraser, *The Age of Acquiescence*, chap. 4; McGerr, *A Fierce Discontent*; Postel, "The American Populist and Anti-Populist Legacy," and "TR, Wilson, and the Origins of the Progressive

Tradition"; Cowie, *The Great Exception*, 54–61; Shefter, "Trade Unions and Political Machines"; Kolko, *Railroads and Regulation*.

3. Chandler, *The Visible Hand*, 13–14, 76–87, 121–24, 244–45, 316. Also see Carosso, *Investment Banking*, 29–50.

4. Smith, *Civic Ideals*, 351 (quote), 409.

5. Hofstadter, *The Age of Reform*.

6. Frank, *The People, No*, 153–68. For a similar critique of Hofstadter, see Leonard, "Origins of the Myth of Social Darwinism."

7. On the broad appeal of Social Darwinism and eugenics, see Leonard, *Illiberal Reformers*; and Black, *War against the Weak*. On the broad appeal of race science, see Muhammad, *The Condemnation of Blackness*; and Fabian, *The Skull Collectors*.

8. Claeys, "The 'Survival of the Fittest.'"

9. Postel, "The American Populist and Anti-Populist Legacy," and "TR, Wilson, and the Origins of the Progressive Tradition."

10. Fraser, *The Age of Acquiescence*, 102; Leonard, *Illiberal Reformers*, 97–105; Smith, *Civic Ideals*, 351–57.

11. For an overview of the history of these ideological currents, see Hofstadter, *Social Darwinism in American Thought*, 31–66; and Smith, *Civic Ideals*, 351–53.

12. Sumner, *What Social Classes Owe to Each Other*, 119–20.

13. Sumner, *What Social Classes Owe to Each Other*, 8–10, 55–58, 107, 114–16, 126.

14. Hofstadter, *Social Darwinism in American Thought*, 3–30.

15. Postel, "The American Populist and Anti-Populist Legacy," and "TR, Wilson, and the Origins of the Progressive Tradition."

16. Skowronek and Engel, "The Progressives' Century"; Mellow, "The Democratic Fit."

17. Rodgers, "In Search of Progressivism"; Smith, "The Progressive Seedbed"; Skowronek and Engel, "The Progressives' Century."

18. Leonard, *Illiberal Reformers*; McGerr, *A Fierce Discontent*; Stern, *Eugenic Nation*; Muhammad, *The Condemnation of Blackness*.

19. Rodgers, *Contested Truths*, 182. For more on similar ideas, see Rodgers, "In Search of Progressivism."

20. Skowronek and Engel, "The Progressives' Century."

21. Rafter, *Creating Born Criminals*; Black, *War against the Weak*.

22. Leonard, *Illiberal Reformers*, 8.

23. Leonard, *Illiberal Reformers*.

24. Bernstein, "A Brief History of the American Economic Association."

25. Ely, *Studies*, 456. Also see Leonard, *Illiberal Reformers*, 34.

26. Ripley, *The Races of Europe*; Veblen, *The Theory of the Leisure Class*, 215–20.

27. Attaining political autonomy was more easily said than done. On how bureaucracies achieve autonomy by building relationships and reputations among a diverse range of interests, see Carpenter, *The Forging of Bureaucratic Autonomy*.

28. Gould, *The Mismeasure of Man*; Lancaster, *The Trouble with Nature*; Muhammad, *The Condemnation of Blackness*; Stern, *Eugenic Nation*.

29. Beccaria, *On Crimes and Punishments*; Browning and Gerassi, *The American Way of Crime*, 122–23; Whitman, *Harsh Justice*, 51–52; Maestro, *Cesare Beccaria*; Conrad, "Correctional Treatment."

30. See Lombroso, *Criminal Man*.

31. Lombroso, *Criminal Man*, 224, 348. Also see Rafter, *Creating Born Criminals*.

32. Lombroso, "Illustrative Studies in Criminal Anthropology." Also see Lombroso, *Criminal Man*, 300, 352–55.

33. Lombroso, "Why Homicide Has Increased in the United States," 647.

34. Dugdale, *The Jukes*, 15, 28–30, 66, 92–94, 105–15. *Juke* was a pseudonym for the real family name.

35. Conrad, "Correctional Treatment," 269–70.

36. Wines, "Declaration of Principles," 541–47 (see esp. principles 2, 3, 4, 8, 10, 15, 16, and 31).

37. Beccaria, *On Crimes and Punishments*, 68.

38. Wines, "Declaration of Principles," 541.

39. Pisciotta, *Benevolent Repression*, 4, 14–27, 81–126; McLennan, *The Crisis of Imprisonment*, 177–86 (on prison labor).

40. Allen, *The Decline of the Rehabilitative Ideal*; Pisciotta, *Benevolent Repression*; Garland, *The Culture of Control*; Goodman, Page, and Phelps, *Breaking the Pendulum*. On the presence of multiple conflicting penological influences in American penality, see O'Malley, "Volatile and Contradictory Punishment."

41. Pisciotta, *Benevolent Repression*.

42. Brockway, "Crime," 73, 78.

43. Brockway, "Prisoners and Their Reformation," 615. For similar ideas, see Brockway, "The Ideal," 39.

44. Brockway, *Fifty Years of Prison Service*, 214–22.

45. Brockway, "Crime," 96, and "Prisoners and Their Reformation," 613.

46. Brockway, "The Ideal," 42.

47. Brockway, "Crime," 79–80, 89–91, 96, "An Absolute Indeterminate Sentence," "The Ideal," 42, 52–56, "Reformatory Prison Discipline," 206–7, and "The Incorrigible Criminal," 105–7.

48. Brockway, *Fifty Years of Prison Service*, 265.

49. For the methodology in selecting these authors, see Rafter, *Creating Born Criminals*, 129 nn. 29 and 30.

50. On Boies's work with the Pennsylvania Board of Charities, see Odell, *Henry Martyn Boies*.

51. MacDonald, *Criminology*, i, 22, 204, 219, 228, 271.

52. Boies, *Prisoners and Paupers*, 171–72.

53. Boies, *Prisoners and Paupers*, 179; Henderson, *An Introduction*, 15–16.

54. MacDonald, *Criminology*, 271; Boies, *Prisoners and Paupers*, 189–90; Drahms, *The Criminal*, 365–70; Henderson, *An Introduction*, 288–93; Lydston, *The Diseases of Society*, 605; McKim, *Heredity and Human Progress*, 20–26; Parsons, *Responsibility for Crime*, 177–81.

55. Boies, *The Science of Penology*, 147–57; Henderson, *An Introduction*, 288–93; MacDonald, *Criminology*, 271; McKim, *Heredity and Human Progress*, 23–26.

56. MacDonald, *Criminology*, 271.

57. Drahms, *The Criminal*, 365–70; Boies, *Prisoners and Paupers*, 179, 186–90.

58. Boies, *The Science of Penology*, 188–89.

59. Parsons, *Responsibility for Crime*; McKim, *Heredity and Human Progress*; Lydston, *The Diseases of Society*; Drahms, *The Criminal*.

60. McKim, *Heredity and Human Progress*, 159 (also see 162–64).

61. Lydston, *The Diseases of Society*, 88 (quote), 517–55 (on criminal crania).

62. Drahms, *The Criminal*, 365–70; McKim, *Heredity and Human Progress*, 20–26, 146, 188–93; Lydston, *The Diseases of Society*, 562–68, 605; Parsons, *Responsibility for Crime*, 65, 149–59, 177–81.

63. Muhammad, *The Condemnation of Blackness*, esp. 35–88; Hoffman, *Race Traits*, 225 (also see 217–28, 234, 236).

64. Boies, *Prisoners and Paupers*, 69–70.

65. Henderson, *An Introduction*, 247.

66. Brockway, "Prisoners and Their Reformation," 614.

67. Lydston, *The Diseases of Society*, 145–47, 517–55. For analysis of "the skull of a tramp and petty thief," see ibid., 528–29.

68. Boies, *Prisoners and Paupers*, 206–10.

69. Sumner, *What Social Classes Owe to Each Other*, 138.

70. Sumner, *The Challenge of Facts*, 422.

71. Boas, *The Mind of Primitive Man*. Also see Stocking, *Race, Culture, and Evolution*, 230–33.

72. Muhammad, *The Condemnation of Blackness*, 101–11. For additional analyses of how cultural theorists often rely on essentialist racial narratives, see Stocking, *Race, Culture, and Evolution*, 195–223; Michaels, "Race into Culture"; and Reed, "Revolution as 'National Liberation.'"

73. Leonard, *Illiberal Reformers*, 70.

74. Du Bois, *The Souls of Black Folk*, 59.

75. For this argument, see Muhammad, *The Condemnation of Blackness*. Also see Du Bois, *The Philadelphia Negro*, 242, 255.

76. Gould, *The Mismeasure of Man*, 178–87.

77. Goddard, *The Kallikak Family*, 59.

78. Goddard, *Feeble-Mindedness*, 6–7.

79. Terman, *The Measurement of Intelligence*, 7.

80. Terman, *The Measurement of Intelligence*, 132–33.

81. Henderson, *An Introduction*, 153, 286–88; MacDonald, *Criminology*, 269–70; Lydston, *The Diseases of Society*, 562–68; Boies, *The Science of Penology*, 311–31, and *Prisoners and Paupers*, 269–71; Parsons, *Responsibility for Crime*, 65, 137, 148–49; McKim, *Heredity and Human Progress*, 146, 188–93.

82. Davenport, *Heredity*, 261 (also see 83–92, 266). Also see Black, *War against the Weak*, 39–60; and MacDonald, *Criminology*, 269–70.

83. Estabrook and Davenport, *The Nam Family*. For another similar "degenerate family" study about a mixed-race family, see Estabrook, *Mongrel Virginians*.

84. Estabrook, *The Jukes in 1915*, 66–67, 85.

85. Goddard, *The Kallikak Family*, 59.

86. Grant, *The Passing of the Great Race*, 49, 51.

87. Davenport, *Heredity*, 261–62.

88. Davenport, *Eugenics*, 33–34.

89. Roosevelt, "Twisted Eugenics," 32. For similar statements, see Roosevelt, "T. Roosevelt Letter to C. Davenport," and *The Foes of Our Own Household*, 258.

90. Ripley, *The Races of Europe*. For instance, Ripley wrote that the Teuton was predisposed to property crime and that the Celt and the "Alpine type" were both prone to violent crime. Ibid., 523.

91. On delays in southern eugenics, Cohen, *Imbeciles*, 58, 71–76. Also see Bean, "The Negro Brain"; Shufeldt, *The Negro*, 124, 129, 134; McCord, *The American Negro*, 189, 217–21, 282, 293. For a general discussion of this intellectual history, see Muhammad, *The Condemnation of Blackness*, 78–80.

92. Leonard, *Illiberal Reformers*.

93. Ely, *Introduction to Political Economy*, 120.

94. Ely, "Pauperism," 395, 407.

95. Taussig, *Principles of Economics*, 300.

96. Ross, *Social Control*, 110.

97. Ross, "Social Control," 518, 521.

98. Ross, *Social Control*, 118–19.

99. Leonard, *Illiberal Reformers*; Commons, *Races and Immigrants in America*; US Industrial Commission, *Report of the US Industrial Commission on the Relations and Conditions of Capital and Labor* (Commons's testimony 38–45).

100. Ross, "Recent Tendencies," 447.

101. Ross quoted in Vecoli, "Sterilization: A Progressive Measure?," 196.

102. Commons, *Social Reform and the Church*, 6.

103. Ely, *Studies*, 141. For similar statements, see Ely, *Introduction to Political Economy*, 62.

104. Sumner, *The Challenge of Facts*, 90.

105. Henderson, "Business Men and Social Theorists," 385–86, 394.

106. Lydston, *The Diseases of Society*, 56, 116.

107. Leland, "What Mr. Leland Got No Chance to Say," 82–83.

108. Rockefeller quoted in Hofstadter, *Social Darwinism in American Thought*, 45.

109. Carnegie, "Wealth," 654, 655 (emphasis added), 656.

110. Ely, *Introduction to Political Economy*, 74.

111. Ross, "Recent Tendencies," 447.

112. See Leonard, *Illiberal Reformers*, esp. chaps. 6–7.

113. Ely, *Introduction to Political Economy*, 50, 88.

114. Commons quoted in Gonce, "John R. Commons," 765.

115. Ely, *Introduction to Political Economy*, 62–63.

116. Ely, "Social Progress," 64.

117. Berk, *Louis D. Brandeis*.

118. Brandeis, "Competition," 6, 8.

119. US House Committee on Interstate and Foreign Commerce, *Interstate Trade Commission: Hearings*, 89–91.

120. Beccaria, *On Crimes and Punishments*, 68.

121. For a thorough analysis of Beccaria's philosophy of regulation and punishment, see Harcourt, *The Illusion of Free Markets*.

122. Ross discussed in Taub, *Big Dirty Money*, 11–12.

123. Ross, *Sin and Society*, 46–51, 58–59.

124. Roosevelt, "Letter to Edward Alsworth Ross," September 19, 1907.

Chapter Three

1. Lombroso-Ferrero, *Criminal Man*, xix (quote), xi–xx (generally). Lombroso also cites America's juvenile courts, probation systems, and the George Junior Republic as implementing his ideas, with Elmira being the first place he cites.

2. Garland, *The Culture of Control*; Tonry, *Sentencing Fragments*.

3. Goodman, Page, and Phelps, *Breaking the Pendulum*; Pisciotta, *Benevolent Repression*; Grasso, "Broken beyond Repair."

4. On labor and religious alternatives, see Graber, *The Furnace of Affliction*; Erzen, *God in Captivity*; and McLennan, *The Crisis of Imprisonment*.

5. For more on extralegal forms of punishment in the South, see Stuntz, *The Collapse of American Criminal Justice*; Oshinsky, *"Worse Than Slavery"*; Garland, *Peculiar Institution*.

6. See Pisciotta, *Benevolent Repression*; and Rafter, *Creating Born Criminals*.

7. "Crime and Its Cure."

8. Ohio State Board of Charities, *Fifteenth Annual Report*, 36–37, 43–44, and *Sixteenth Annual Report*, 424.

9. Ohio State Board of Charities, *Twenty-Fourth Annual Report*, 9.

10. The board's 1903 report indicated that the statute had been in operation for six years. See Indiana State Board of Charities, *Fourteenth Annual Report*, 61.

11. Indiana State Board of Charities, *Third Report*, 43.

12. Indiana State Board of Charities, *Fourth Annual Report*, 33–34.

13. Illinois Board of Commissioners of Public Charities, *Eighth Biennial Report*, 168–69.

14. Illinois Board of Commissioners of Public Charities, *Tenth Biennial Report*, 177.

15. Illinois Board of Commissioners of Public Charities, *Sixteenth Biennial Report*, 363.

16. Illinois Board of Charities, *Seventeenth Biennial Report*, 253, and *Biennial Report* (1909), 38, 206, 539–40, 634–39, 646.

17. Pennsylvania Board of Commissioners of Public Charities, *Twentieth Annual Report*, 7, *Twenty-Third Annual Report*, 13, and *Thirty-First Annual Report*, 5.

18. New York State Board of Public Charities, *Annual Report of the State Board of Charities for the Year 1905*, 795. For similar statements, also see *Annual Report of the State Board of Charities for the Year 1907*, 435, 850.

19. New York State Board of Public Charities, *Annual Report of the State Board of Charities for the Year 1905*, 805.

20. Illinois Board of Commissioners of Public Charities, *Tenth Biennial Report*, 181.

21. New York State Board of Public Charities, *Annual Report of the State Board of Charities for the Year 1905*, 795, 798, 804, and *Annual Report of the State Board of Charities for the Year 1907*, 647.

22. Chambliss, "A Sociological Analysis of the Law of Vagrancy."

23. DePastino, *Citizen Hobo*, 12; Ringenbach, *Tramps and Reformers*, 10 (on "revolvers" who rotated between precincts, spending each night in a different station house).

24. See Mitrani, *The Rise of the Chicago Police Department*, 28; Monkonnen, *Police in Urban America*; Lane, "Urban Police," 20; Monkonnen, "History of Urban Police," 553–59; and Reisig, "Community and Problem-Oriented Policing," 13.

25. Ringenbach, *Tramps and Reformers*, 11; Goldstein, *Political Repression*, 27.

26. Dugdale, "Hereditary Pauperism," 81; Ringenbach, *Tramps and Reformers*, 19.

27. Ringenbach, *Tramps and Reformers*, 4; DePastino, *Citizen Hobo*, 4–7, 91; Kusmer, *Down and Out, on the Road*. While many tramps lived this life by necessity, others intentionally chose it to challenge industrial capitalism and the wage labor system.

28. Dugdale, "Hereditary Pauperism," 81–95.

29. Brockway, "Prisoners and Their Reformation," 614.

30. Boies, *Prisoners and Paupers*, 206–10.

31. Lydston notes the comparatively similar "defective frontal and temporal development" in tramps and petty thieves. See Lydston, *The Diseases of Society*, 528.

32. Parsons, *Responsibility for Crime*, 145 (quotes); Henderson, *An Introduction*, 278.

33. SBCs had close relationships with the American Social Science Association. This produced a symbiotic relationship between social science reformers and SBCs. See Haskell, *The Emergence of Professional Social Science*, 55, 86, 91–121, 135–37.

34. Wayland, "The Tramp Question," 118–19; Conference of Boards of Public Charities, *Proceedings*, 95–134; Brace, "Mendicity," 410 (cited in Ringenbach, *Tramps and Reformers*, 17).

35. Wayland, "The Tramp Question," 112 (also see 115, 118).

36. Gault, "Pathologic Vagrancy," 321.

37. Lisle, "Vagrancy Law," 500.

38. Lindsey, "The Bill"; Albrecht, "Cesare Lombroso."

39. Ely, "Pauperism," 400.

40. Taussig, *Principles of Economics*, 300.

41. US Industrial Commission, *Report of the Industrial Commission on Prison Labor*, 57–58.

42. US Industrial Commission, *Report of the Industrial Commission on the Relations and Conditions of Capital and Labor*, ccxxxi.

43. US Industrial Commission, *Report of the Industrial Commission on Labor Legislation*, 178, 187–89, 194, 197–99.

44. "The Question of 'Tramps,'" 4.

45. "Vagrancy Laws."

46. "Protection against Tramps."

47. Bentwick, "Street Begging as a Fine Art."

48. On Chaplin, see Kusmer, *Down and Out, on the Road*, 183–84. On the tramp's evolving public image, see ibid., 169–92. For a similar analysis, see DePastino, *Citizen Hobo*, 152–67.

49. "Ball and Chain for Tramps."

50. "Crime and Vagrancy."

51. "What Tramps Cost the Nation."

52. Ohio State Board of Charities, *Sixteenth Annual Report*, 37–38, 48–49 (quotes). For similar language, see ibid., 404.

53. Indiana State Board of Charities, *Second Annual Report*, 33, 57.

54. Pennsylvania Board of Commissioners of Public Charities, *Twenty-Seventh Annual Report*, 111.

55. "Perpetual Imprisonment." Also see Wayland and Sanborn, "Report on Tramp Laws and Indeterminate Sentence," 278.

56. "Vagrancy Laws"; "The Convict Camps of Alabama and the Vagrancy Laws of Michigan"; "A Stringent Anti-Vagrant Act Passed"; "The Tramp Problem."

57. Millis, "The Law Affecting Immigrants and Tramps."

58. DePastino, *Citizen Hobo*, 22; Montgomery, *Citizen Worker*, 86–87.

59. "Notes: Industrial Armies."

60. Bristow, "Statement Before the American Bar Association," 100–102; New Jersey State Legislature, "An Act to Define and Suppress Tramps," chap. 126, General Public Laws, 218–20, sec. 1876; "The Public Statutes of the Commonwealth of Massachusetts, Enacted Nov. 19, 1880, to Take Effect Feb. 1, 1882" (Boston, 1883), chap. 207, pp. 1169–70, cited in Keyssar, *Out of Work*, 135–37. Also see Millis, "The Law Affecting Immigrants and Tramps."

61. Tabulated from *Laws of the Various States Relating to Vagrancy*. Only West Virginia did not have a vagrancy law.

62. *Laws of the Various States Relating to Vagrancy*.

63. Millis, "The Law Affecting Immigrants and Tramps."

64. Montgomery, *Citizen Worker*, 70; Harring, *Policing a Class Society*, 34–75; Monkonnen, "Cop History to Social History"; Mitrani, *The Rise of the Chicago Police Department*, 136.

65. Monkonnen, *Police in Urban America*; Lane, "Urban Police," and *Policing the City*.

66. Millis, "The Law Affecting Immigrants and Tramps."

67. Brockway, "The Ideal," 42–43.

68. US Industrial Commission, *Reports of the Industrial Commission on Immigration*, ix–x, xlvii, xliv, xxi–xxii.

69. US Industrial Commission, *Report of the Industrial Commission on the Relations and Conditions of Capital and Labor*, 45 (also see 38–40).

70. Brace, *The Dangerous Classes*, 25–73 ("dangerous classes" generally, but esp. 27, 29); George, *Social Problems*, 6 ("barbarians").

71. Brinton, "The Aims of Anthropology," 249. Brinton's article is discussed in Smith, *Civic Ideals*, 356.

72. Cabot Lodge, "Lynch Law and Unrestricted Immigration," 604, 609 (quote).

73. Cited in Gambino, *Blood of My Blood*, 109.

74. See, e.g., *Laws of the Various States Relating to Vagrancy*, 57 ("North Carolina").

75. For good historical reviews of convict leasing, see Oshinsky, *"Worse Than Slavery"*; Mancini, *One Dies, Get Another*, 98–116; and Lichtenstein, *Twice the Work*. On Florida, see Carper, "Martin Tabert."

76. Muhammad, *The Condemnation of Blackness*; Hoffman, *Race Traits*, 217–25, 234–36.

77. Boies, *Prisoners and Paupers*, 69–70; Henderson, *An Introduction*, 29, 247.

78. "Remarks of Mr. Henley of Alabama, and P. D. Sims," 120–21. These statements are also discussed in Oshinsky, *"Worse Than Slavery,"* 83–84.

79. Oshinsky, *"Worse Than Slavery,"* 47.

80. Powell, *The American Siberia*, 5.

81. DePastino, *Citizen Hobo*, 32–35, 95–119; Darlington, *Syndicalism and the Transition to Communism*, 97; Smith, "The Floater and the Iconoclast."

82. DePastino, *Citizen Hobo*, chap. 1, esp. 16–17; Harris, *The Man Who Tramps*, 21.

83. Brockway, "Crime," 43 (also see 40, 60–61).

84. Boies, *Prisoners and Paupers*, 239.

85. Lydston, *The Diseases of Society*, 53.

86. Goldstein, *Political Repression*, 31; Foner, *The Great Labor Uprising of 1877*.

87. DePastino, *Citizen Hobo*, 24–25.

88. Wayland, "The Tramp Question," 112, 117.

89. Ringenbach, *Tramps and Reformers*, 13. Ringenbach takes the quotations from "Once More the Tramp," 883; Brewer, "What Shall We Do with Our Tramps," 532; and "From Another Point of View," 444. He does not specify which comes from which source.

90. "Tramps Who Are Criminals." Also see Ringenbach, *Tramps and Reformers*, 12–13; Bruce, *1877*, 226–27; and Pinkerton, *Strikers, Communists, Tramps, and Detectives*, 67.

91. Goldstein, *Political Repression*, 14–15.

92. Goldstein, *Political Repression*, 13–18, 32.

93. Harring, *Policing a Class Society*, 144–47; DePastino, *Citizen Hobo*, 105 n. 34; "Execution of Anarchists"; Goldstein, *Political Repression*, 11–16, 68–80, 108–10, 139–53. Four states passed laws criminalizing anarchism, indicative of public receptivity to a greater state role in handling political repression that foreshadowed the robust federal interventions that came during World War I. For an example of the convergence of business and state interests, see Aurand, *From the Molly Maguires to the United Mine Workers*. The Molly Macguire investigation—in which strikers on the Philadelphia and Reading Railroad were prosecuted for violence against mineowners—relied entirely on private detectives, private police, and private prosecuting

attorneys hired by the corporation, leading to six executions and twenty convictions with almost no state involvement.

94. Gottschalk, *The Prison and the Gallows*, 53–55.

95. Goldstein, *Political Repression*, 50–53; Paul, *Conservative Crisis*, 129.

96. Goldstein, *Political Repression*, 53–57; Paul, *Conservative Crisis*, 113–46.

97. Hattam, *Labor Visions*.

98. Cowie, *The Great Exception*, 56–61; Shefter, "Trade Unions and Political Machines," esp. 230; Goldstein, *Political Repression*, 42–43, 56–60.

99. US Senate Committee on the Judiciary, *Charges of Illegal Practices*, 623.

100. Pisciotta, *Benevolent Repression*, 114–18, 125–31.

101. Christian, "The Irresponsible Social Offender," 2. Also see Christian, "Statistics and Comments," 7–9 ("damaged heredity" quote p. 9); and "The Management of Penal Institutions," 2, 9–10, 15 ("frequently afflicted" quote p. 2; "excellent results" quote p. 9; "custodial care" quote p. 15).

102. Oschner, "Surgical Treatment of Habitual Criminals," 867.

103. Makuen, "Some Measures," 2–7 (quotes on 5, 7). Also see McKim, *Heredity and Human Progress*, 188.

104. Risley, "Some of the Ethical and Sociological Relations," 584–86.

105. Barr, *Mental Defectives*, 191. For similar quotes from additional medical professionals, see Sharp, *Vasectomy*, 12–17.

106. Carrington, "Sterilization of Habitual Criminals," 175.

107. Phelan, "The Mental and Physical Characteristics of the Criminal and Degenerate," 223, 226, 228–29, 233, 253; Cooke, "The Advisability of Laws."

108. Black, *War against the Weak*, 65–66.

109. Sharp, *The Sterilization of Degenerates*, 1, 8 (see further 1–10).

110. Sharp, *Vasectomy*, 4–6.

111. On Barr, Sharp, and others, see Cohen, *Imbeciles*, 66–76. On Ross, see Leonard, *Illiberal Reformers*, 110.

112. Davenport, *Eugenics*, 33–34.

113. Jordan, "The Training of the Physician," 137.

114. Barr, *Mental Defectives*, 191.

115. Laughlin, *Eugenical Sterilization*, 100–101.

116. Laughlin, *Eugenical Sterilization*, 123, 152–54, 158–59.

117. Laughlin, *Eugenical Sterilization*, 159, vi (quote). For similar statements, see ibid., 327–28.

118. Willrich, "The Two Percent Solution," 66.

119. For the relationship between Laughlin and Olson, see Cohen, *Imbeciles*, chap. 5; and Laughlin, *Eugenical Sterilization*, introduction.

120. Lindsey, "The Bill." Olson quoted in Willrich, "Two Percent Solution," 85.

121. On Pound, see Willrich, "Two Percent Solution," 76–77.

122. Simon, "'The Criminal Is to Go Free.'"

123. Cardozo, *The Growth of the Law*, 11.

124. Cardozo, "What Medicine Can Do for Law," 589–92.

125. For the laws and their texts, see Laughlin, *Report of the Committee*, and *Eugenical Sterilization*. For the Wilson quote, see "Gov. Wilson Signs the Sterilization Bill."

126. *Buck v. Bell*, 274 U.S. 200 (1927).

127. Dudziak, "Oliver Wendell Holmes."

128. Holmes, "The Path of the Law," 470.

129. Leonard, *Illiberal Reformers*, 170–72, 178–79.

130. The estimate of two thousand is based on statistics provided in Black, *War against the Weak*, 122–23.

131. Hunter, "Sterilization of Criminals."

132. Black, *War against the Weak*, 398.

133. Walker, *Popular Justice*, 169–79.

134. American Bar Foundation, *The Administration of Criminal Justice in the United States*, 5–6.

135. Spillane and Wolcott, *A History of Modern American Criminal Justice*, 146; Walker, *Popular Justice*, 169–73.

136. Cleveland Crime Commission, *Criminal Justice in Cleveland*, 439–88.

137. Missouri Association for Criminal Justice and Thompson, *The Missouri Crime Survey*, 397–430.

138. Illinois Association for Criminal Justice and Chicago Crime Commission, *The Illinois Crime Survey*, 737–814, 430, 433, 448.

139. Missouri Association for Criminal Justice and Thompson, *The Missouri Crime Survey*, 406, 497.

140. Black, *War against the Weak*, 395–409; Spillane and Wolcott, *A History of Modern American Criminal Justice*, 73–74.

141. Black, *War against the Weak*, 396–98; Cohen, *Imbeciles*, 318–19. See *Oklahoma v. Skinner*, 316 U.S. 535 (1942).

142. Hansen and King, *Sterilized by the State*, 237–58; Stern, *Eugenic Nation*.

143. Cohen, *Imbeciles*, 319.

144. Gottschalk, *Caught*, 373. Also see Schwartz, "Following Reports of Forced Sterilization"; "Nashville Assistant DA Fired"; Jackson, "Tennessee County Inmates Offered Reduced Jail Time for Getting a Vasectomy"; and Park, "Using Chemical Castration to Punish Child Sex Crimes."

Chapter Four

1. Grant, review of *The First Tycoon*, 544.

2. Sutherland, "White-Collar Criminality," 2 (Vanderbilt quote), 6 (on regulatory agencies). Sutherland would flesh out his explanation of how regulatory agencies govern corporate crime in the 1949 *White-Collar Crime*.

3. Skowronek, *Building a New American State*; Berk, *Alternative Tracks*; Bensel, *The Political Economy of American Industrialization*; DeCanio, *Democracy and the Origins of the American Regulatory State*.

4. Dunlavy, *Politics and Industrialization*; Dobbin, *Forging Industrial Policy*; Dempsey, "The Rise and Fall of the Interstate Commerce Commission," 1160; Raper, *Railway Transportation*, 1–60.

5. Harris and Milkis, *The Politics of Regulatory Change*, 45–47. For a discussion of how national regulation insulated political elites from public pressure, see DeCanio, *Democracy and the Origins of the American Regulatory State*.

6. Novak, *The People's Welfare*, and "Law and the Social Control of American Capitalism." Also see Sklar, *The Corporate Reconstruction of American Capitalism*. Cook calls the shift from state to federal regulations a shift from the first to the second administrative state. See Cook, *The Fourth Branch*.

7. Novak, "Law and the Social Control of American Capitalism," 395.

8. Sklar, *The Corporate Reconstruction of American Capitalism*; Grasso, "'No Bodies to Kick or Souls to Damn'"; Marchand, *Creating the Corporate Soul*; Dewey, "The Historic Background of Corporate Legal Personality."

9. Novak, *The People's Welfare*, and "Law and the Social Control of American Capitalism"; Sklar, *The Corporate Reconstruction of American Capitalism*; Cook, *The Fourth Branch*; DeCanio, *Democracy and the Origins of the American Regulatory State*.

10. Proctor, *Not without Honor*; 6 Cong. Rec. 193 (1877) (Reagan's bill).

11. Skowronek, *Building a New American State*, 140–41; Proctor, *Not without Honor*.

12. Skowronek, *Building a New American State*, 5–8, 23; Chandler, *The Visible Hand*, 316; Bensel, *The Political Economy of American Industrialization*, 337–38; Kirkland, *Industry Comes of Age*, 278–305; Thorelli, *The Federal Antitrust Policy*, 42–53, 80–83, 259–67.

13. 8 Cong. Rec. 93–102 (1878), and 10 Cong. Rec. 1079–82 (1880); 10 Cong. Rec. 4018–32 (1880); Skowronek, *Building a New American State*, 28, 143–44.

14. James, *Presidents, Parties, and the State*, 36–122.

15. Quotes in Nielson, *Shelby M. Cullom*, 93–94. Also see Skowronek, *Building a New American State*, 144–45.

16. "A Bill to Regulate Commerce," S. 1093, 49th Cong. (1886); US Senate Select Committee on Interstate Commerce, "Report of the Senate Select Committee on Interstate Commerce, to Accompany Bill H.R. 1093," 5–6.

17. *Munn v. Illinois*, 94 U.S. 113 (1877); *Wabash, St. Louis & Pacific Railway v. Illinois*, 118 U.S. 557 (1886).

18. 17 Cong. Rec. 4423 (1886); 17 Cong. Rec. 7756 (1886).

19. Interstate Commerce Act of 1887, Pub. L. No. 49-104, 24 Stat. 379 (1887). Sutherland argues that this trend started with the Sherman Antitrust Act, but this book shows that its true origins lay with the Interstate Commerce Act. See Sutherland, *White-Collar Crime*, 32–48.

20. For an outline of more modern retributive theories of punishment, see Von Hirsch and Committee for the Study of Incarceration, *Doing Justice*.

21. Fraser, *The Age of Acquiescence*; McGerr, *A Fierce Discontent*.

22. US House Commerce Committee, "Views of the Minority," 5.

23. James, *Presidents, Parties, and the State*, 36–122.

24. 18 Cong. Rec. 481 (1887). Beck was quoting Hudson, *The Railways and the Republic*. For other discussions of Hudson, see 17 Cong. Rec. 7282 (1886); and 18 Cong. Rec. 570 (1887).

25. 16 Cong. Rec. 61 (1885).

26. 16 Cong. Rec. 751 (1885). Five years later, Van Wyck mounted an unsuccessful campaign for the governorship of Nebraska as the Populist Party candidate.

27. 17 Cong. Rec. 7293 (1886) (Caldwell quote); 16 Cong. Rec. 194 (1885) (Dunn quote). As evidence of his Populist bona fides, Dunn spoke fervently on behalf of the Populist candidate William Jennings Bryan in the 1896 election. See Harpine, *From the Front Porch to the Front Page*, 86–87.

28. 16 Cong. Rec. 199 (1885). McAdoo framed himself in the image of William Jennings Bryan during his run for the Democratic Party presidential nomination in 1924. See Schlesinger, *The Crisis of the Old Order*, 94–95.

29. 17 Cong. Rec. 7295 (1886). Also see Moger, *Virginia*, 161. O'Ferrall was one of a handful of Democrats who opposed Bryan's candidacy in 1896.

30. US House Committee on Commerce, *Arguments and Statements* (1882), 209. For MacVeagh's similar statements defending a "well-considered system of supervision and publicity" over "penal laws," see ibid., 16.

31. 16 Cong. Rec. 100 (1885).

32. 16 Cong. Rec. 165, 192–93 (1885).

33. "Populist Party Platform."

34. Berk, *Alternative Tracks*, 88–100.

35. US House Committee on Commerce, *Arguments and Statements* (1882), 209.

36. US House Committee on Commerce, *Arguments and Statements* (1884), 36.

37. US House Committee on Commerce, *Arguments and Statements* (1884), 95.

38. US House Committee on Commerce, *Arguments and Statements* (1882), 162, 185.

39. 16 Cong. Rec. 120 (1885).

40. 16 Cong. Rec. 47, app. (1885).

41. 16 Cong. Rec. 99 (1885).

42. 18 Cong. Rec. 869 (1887).

43. 18 Cong. Rec. 789 (1887).

44. 18 Cong. Rec. 657 (1887).

45. 17 Cong. Rec. 4307 (1886).

46. Rothman, "The Structure of State Politics," 84, 824; Murphy, *L. Q. C. Lamar*; Byrd, *The Senate*, 367.

47. US House Committee on Commerce, *Arguments and Statements* (1882), 4–5.

48. US House Committee on Commerce, *Arguments and Statements* (1882), 162.

49. US House Committee on Commerce, *Arguments and Statements* (1884), 61.

50. US Senate Select Committee on Interstate Commerce, *Report of the Senate Select Committee on Interstate Commerce: Testimony*, 9, 341–42.

51. 16 Cong. Rec. 371 (1885).

52. 18 Cong. Rec. 393 (1887).

53. 16 Cong. Rec. 41–42 (1885).

54. 16 Cong. Rec. 1084, 1086 (1885).

55. 16 Cong. Rec. 197 (1885).

56. Byrd, *The Senate*, 367; James, *Presidents, Parties, and the State*, 51–55, 93–98.

57. 16 Cong. Rec. 281 (1885).

58. Grasso, "'No Bodies to Kick or Souls to Damn.'"

59. Grasso, "'No Bodies to Kick or Souls to Damn'"; Khanna, "Corporate Criminal Liability"; Laufer, *Corporate Bodies and Guilty Minds*; Garrett, *Too Big to Jail*; Eisinger, *The Chickenshit Club*, 85–87.

60. US House Committee on Commerce, *Arguments and Statements* (1882), 53.

61. US House Committee on Commerce, *Arguments and Statements* (1882), 107.

62. US House Committee on Commerce, *Arguments and Statements* (1882), 192. For similar arguments, see US Senate Select Committee on Interstate Commerce, *Report of the Senate Select Committee on Interstate Commerce: Testimony*, 6–7, 20 (John Kernan's statements).

63. 16 Cong. Rec. 1084 (1885). Also see Rothman, "The Structure of State Politics," 824.

64. 18 Cong. Rec. 854 (1887).

65. 18 Cong. Rec. 572–73 (1887).

66. Frank, *The People, No*, 19–82.

67. US House Committee on Commerce, *Arguments and Statements* (1882), 49.

68. US House Committee on Commerce, *Arguments and Statements* (1882), 185, 191–92.

69. US House Committee on Commerce, *Arguments and Statements* (1882), 231.

70. US House Committee on Commerce, *Arguments and Statements* (1884), 100.

71. 16 Cong. Rec. 120 (1885).

72. 16 Cong. Rec. 45 (1885).

73. 18 Cong. Rec. 657 (1887).

74. 16 Cong. Rec. 201 (1885).

75. 18 Cong. Rec. 881 (1887).

76. James, *Presidents, Parties, and the State*, 101–6.

77. Berk, *Louis D. Brandeis*; Leonard, *Illiberal Reformers*, 58. For varying perspectives within Progressive circles, see Smith, "The Progressive Seedbed."

78. Sutherland famously posited that the SAA was the first real attempt to criminalize white-collar crime. See Sutherland, *White-Collar Crime*, 32–48, 62–69.

79. 21 Cong. Rec. 2644 (1890). John Sherman (R-OH), Orville Platt (R-CT), John Spooner (R-WI), and George Hoar (R-MA) were particularly forceful in pushing for this approach. For their statements, see 21 Cong. Rec. 2564, 2568, 2640, 2725, 3146 (1890).

80. Hazlett, "The Legislative History"; Paul, *Conservative Crisis*, 109–16, 227; *U.S. v. E.C. Knight Co.* 156 U.S. 1 (1895). For details on criminal prosecutions and the SAA's use as a weapon against organized labor, see Thorelli, *The Federal Antitrust Policy*, 369–405, 535–36, 587–97. During the "merger movement" from 1890 to 1903, the federal government initiated only twenty-three anti-trust cases, of which only seven were criminal and only one ended in conviction. See Lamoreaux, *The Great Merger Movement*; and Gould, *The Presidency of Theodore Roosevelt*, 100–101.

81. Roosevelt, *Autobiography*, 470. Also see Roosevelt, "Message Communicated to the Two Houses of Congress at the Beginning of the First Session of the Fifty-Seventh Congress, December 3, 1901," 292–94. On the "predatory capitalist" rhetoric, see Dorsey, "Theodore Roosevelt and Corporate America," 733.

82. Roosevelt, "Applied Idealism"; Dorsey, "Theodore Roosevelt and Corporate America"; McGerr, *A Fierce Discontent*, 158.

83. Thorelli, *The Federal Antitrust Policy*, 528–55; Skowronek, *Building a New American State*, 250; Kolko, *The Triumph of Conservatism*, 70–71.

84. Gould, *The Presidency of Theodore Roosevelt*, 204–25, 272.

85. For high-profile prosecutions and Roosevelt's preference for informal negotiations, see Thorelli, *The Federal Antitrust Policy*, 421; McGerr, *A Fierce Discontent*, 155–56; Kolko, *The Triumph of Conservatism*, 67; Gould, *The Presidency of Theodore Roosevelt*, 204–25, 272; Ruiz, "The Ideological Convergence"; Dorsey, "Theodore Roosevelt and Corporate America," 729–31; and *Northern Securities v. U.S.*, 193 U.S. 197 (1904).

86. Sklar, *The Corporate Reconstruction of American Capitalism*, 185; Mitchell, *The Speculation Economy*, 124–28; Urofsky, "Proposed Federal Incorporation in the Progressive Era," 166–67; Kim, "The Failure of Federal Incorporation Law."

87. US Bureau of Corporations, Department of Commerce and Labor, *Annual Report* (1906), 6. Also see Sklar, *The Corporate Reconstruction of American Capitalism*, 189–91.

88. Roosevelt, "State of the Union, 1907"; US Bureau of Corporations, Department of Commerce and Labor, *Report of the Commissioner* (1908), 5. Also see Sklar, *The Corporate Reconstruction of American Capitalism*, 193–94.

89. On business support for licensing, see Urofsky, "Proposed Federal Incorporation in the Progressive Era," 167, 175–76; Mitchell, *The Speculation Economy*, 171; and Sklar, *The Corporate Reconstruction of American Capitalism*, 252–53, 283.

90. Sklar, *The Corporate Reconstruction of American Capitalism*, 229–39, 283.

91. Sklar, *The Corporate Reconstruction of American Capitalism*, 181, 198–247, 268–76, 283.

92. *Standard Oil of New Jersey v. U.S.*, 221 U.S. 1 (1911). Also see *Addyston Pipe and Steel Co. v. U.S.*, 175 U.S. 211 (1899); Dickson and Wells, "The Dubious Origins of the Sherman Antitrust Act," 3–14; Clements and Cheezum, *Woodrow Wilson*, 111; Cressey, "The Poverty of Theory," 44–45 (on enforcement difficulties); and Burgason, "Wickersham, George." Critics lamented that the rule of reason gave judges the power to distinguish good from bad trusts on the basis of preference.

93. Taft, "Address at the Lincoln Birthday Banquet," 584.

94. Sidney Milkis described it as "the decisive battle of the Progressive Era." See Milkis, *Theodore Roosevelt*, 1.

95. For helpful primers on the role of antitrust in the 1912 election, see Crane, "All I Really Need to Know"; and Kolasky, "The Election of 1912" (82 for "regulating competition").

96. For a detailed analysis of these coalitions, see Sanders, *Roots of Reform*, 273–97.

97. Hoofnagle, *The Federal Trade Commission*, chap. 1; Bryan, "The Trusts Have Won"; Sanders, *Roots of Reform*, esp. 282–89.

98. Sanders, *Roots of Reform*, 282–83.

99. For a valuable history of the FTC, particularly during its early years, see Harris and Milkis, *The Politics of Regulatory Change*, 140–44.

100. The only criminal penalties in the CAA—a minimum fine of $100 or a prison sentence of one to ten years—were specified for embezzlement or misapplication of funds. No penalties were provided for actual restraints of trade. See An Act to Supplement Existing Laws against Unlawful Restraints and Monopolies, Pub. L. No. 63-212, chap. 323, 38 Stat. 730 (1914).

101. Hoofnagle, *The Federal Trade Commission*, 9; An Act to Establish the Department of Commerce and Labor, Pub. L. No. 57-87, 32 Stat. 825 (1903).

102. US House Subcommittee of the Committee on Banking and Currency, *Money Trust Investigation*, 812–13, 831.

103. "Lax Methods in Stock Exchange"; "Sturgis Gives Evidence in Money Trust Inquiry."

104. See US Senate Committee on Interstate Commerce, *Interstate Trade*, 1059–60 (quoting the New York Chamber of Commerce's "Report on Proposed Antitrust Legislation").

105. US House Subcommittee of the Committee on Banking and Currency, *Money Trust Investigation*, 163–65.

106. 51 Cong. Rec. 9653 (1914).

107. 51 Cong. Rec. 14205 (1914).

108. 51 Cong. Rec. 9411, 14039 (1914) (Moore and Stone quotes, respectively). For comparable statements from Senator Albert Cummins (R-IA), see 51 Cong. Rec. 14251 (1914).

109. US House Committee on the Judiciary, "Report from the Committee on the Judiciary to Accompany H.R. 15657," 29, 42–43.

110. Sanders, *Roots of Reform*, 281–97 (esp. 293–95).

111. US House Committee on Interstate and Foreign Commerce, "Interstate Trade Commission," 1–8.

112. Hoofnagle, *The Federal Trade Commission*, 10–13.

113. Brandeis, *Other People's Money*.

114. Brandeis, "Competition," 6.

115. Berk, *Louis D. Brandeis*, esp. chaps. 1, 2, and 4.

116. For a particularly close analysis of Brandeis's role in this debate, see Berk, *Louis D. Brandeis*, chap. 4. Berk's account challenges several prevailing narratives presenting this debate as being between a strong commission and a weak commission. On how the FTC was a victory for corporate liberals, see Sklar, *The Corporate Reconstruction of American Capitalism*. On how

the FTC's creation was about partisan compromises, see James, *Presidents, Parties, and the State*. On how the FTC was a compromise between sectional and economic interests, see Sanders, *Roots of Reform*.

117. US House Committee on Interstate and Foreign Commerce, *Interstate Trade Commission: Hearings*, 9, 89–90.

118. US House Committee on Interstate and Foreign Commerce, *Interstate Trade Commission: Hearings*, 89–91.

119. For similar statements Brandeis published before giving this testimony, see Brandeis, "Competition," 8–11, 14.

120. US Senate Committee on Interstate Commerce, "Federal Trade Commission," 6; US House Committee on Interstate and Foreign Commerce, "Interstate Trade Commission," 5.

121. US Senate Committee on Interstate Commerce, *Interstate Trade*, 874.

122. US Senate Committee on Interstate Commerce, *Interstate Trade*, 874, 1102, and 1114 (quotes).

123. 51 Cong. Rec. 9065 (1914).

124. 51 Cong. Rec. 11539 (1914).

125. 51 Cong. Rec. 13060–61 (1914).

126. By the 1920s, it became clear that Progressives overestimated the will of the state to regulate corporations as Presidents Harding, Coolidge, and Hoover revived laissez-faire. Appointments to the FTC favored informal compliance agreements, and William Ewart Humphrey's term as chair during the Coolidge administration earned the FTC the approval of big business. Even in his favorable account of the FTC, Gerald Berk noted that these were serious setbacks. See Berk, *Louis D. Brandeis*, chap. 8. While the regulated competition model was not destroyed, the FTC exhibited a reluctance to use its most robust enforcement powers. The Supreme Court also asserted authority to determine the scope of unfair competitive methods in a series of rulings, particularly *FTC v. Gratz*, limiting the commission to monitoring practices illegal under common law. See McGerr, *A Fierce Discontent*, 315; Hoofnagle, *The Federal Trade Commission*, 19; *FTC v. Gratz*, 253 U.S. 421 (1920); *FTC v. Beech-Nut Packing Co.*, 251 U.S. 441 (1922); and *FTC v. Raladam Co.*, 283 U.S. 643 (1931).

127. An Act to Create a Federal Trade Commission, Pub. L. No. 63-203, chap. 311, 38 Stat. 717 (1914).

128. On the Progressive reformer George Rublee's role in assigning such responsibility to the FTC, see Sanders, *Roots of Reform*, 295.

129. Kauper, "History, Effect, and Scope," 1098–1106.

130. 51 Cong. Rec. 11112 (1914), cited in Kauper, "History, Effect, and Scope," 1102–3.

131. Kauper, "History, Effect, and Scope," 1116 (see also 1119–23).

132. US House Committee on Interstate and Foreign Commerce, "Interstate Trade Commission," 3.

133. US Senate Committee on Interstate Commerce, "Federal Trade Commission," 12.

134. For sophisticated perspectives on regulatory change in this light, see Harris and Milkis, *The Politics of Regulatory Change*; and Eisner, *Regulatory Politics in Transition*.

135. The ICA was amended in 1889 to add imprisonment as a penalty for violation. Numerous legislators pointed out that this amendment was a disingenuous effort to redirect blame away from corporate leaders. Some senators said that the amendment served "the interest of the railroad corporations" because executives pushed it to convince the public that "their clerks and subordinates are the law-breakers, and that they are honest men and not responsible." 20 Cong.

Rec. 1477, 2699 (1889). ICC reports noted that the imprisonment amendments were designed to punish "unscrupulous shippers and weak or unreliable employees" who are "not [working] upon the highest plane of honorable conduct." US Interstate Commerce Commission, *Interstate Commerce Commission Reports*, 647. These amendments did not radically change the law, instead redirecting blame onto shippers and low-level employees instead of railroad executives. For general discussion of these changes, see 19 Cong. Rec. 5146 (1888); 20 Cong. Rec. 1475-78, 2667-69 (1889); and US Interstate Commerce Commission, *Interstate Commerce Commission Reports*, 647-56. On changes to the FTC, see Berk, *Alternative Tracks*; Hoofnagle, *The Federal Trade Commission*, 19; *FTC v. Gratz*, 253 U.S. 421 (1920); *FTC v. Beech-Nut Packing Co.*, 251 U.S. 441 (1922); and *FTC v. Raladam Co.*, 283 U.S. 643 (1931).

Chapter Five

1. Brief on the Merits of Amicus Curiae. California District Attorneys Association, 2002 WL 1378856, *Lockyer v. Andrade*, July 17, 2002; *Lockyer v. Andrade*, 538 U.S. 63 (2003).

2. Zimring, Hawkins, and Kamin, *Punishment and Democracy*; Tonry, *Sentencing Matters*, 3–5, 134–38, 191–92; Whitman, *Harsh Justice*, 53–57.

3. Boies, *Prisoners and Paupers*, 178.

4. Morone, *Hellfire Nation*, 281–349.

5. Tonry, *Punishing Race*; Weaver, "Frontlash"; Flamm, *Law and Order*; Beckett, *Making Crime Pay*.

6. *Michigan v. Harmelin*, 501 U.S. 957 (1991).

7. Gottschalk, *The Prison and the Gallows*, 60–62; Morone, *Hellfire Nation*, 281–349.

8. Calder, *The Origins and Development of Federal Crime Policy*, 5; Chambliss, *Power, Politics, and Crime*, 34; Walker, *Popular Justice*, 185–86.

9. Gottschalk, *The Prison and the Gallows*, 65–76; O'Reilly, "A New Deal for the FBI"; Denney, "'To Wage a War.'"

10. On Roosevelt's election as a regime change, see Skowronek, *The Politics Presidents Make*. For a different argument on the New Deal as the "great exception," see Cowie, *The Great Exception*. For arguments that the New Deal had a shorter impact on American politics than many accounts suggest, see Domhoff, *The Myth of Liberal Ascendancy*; Lichtenstein, "From Corporatism to Collective Bargaining"; and Katznelson, "Was the Great Society a Lost Opportunity?"

11. Hagan, *Who Are the Criminals?*; Tonry, *Sentencing Fragments*; Allen, *The Decline of the Rehabilitative Ideal*; Flamm, *Law and Order*; Garland, *The Culture of Control*.

12. Katznelson, *Fear Itself*; Mettler, *Dividing Citizens*; Fox, *Three Worlds of Relief*; Lieberman, *Shifting the Color Line*.

13. Gottschalk, *The Prison and the Gallows*, 63–76.

14. Murakawa, *The First Civil Right*, chap. 2. In important ways, this was facilitated by decades of Supreme Court rulings emphasizing procedural over substantive due process in criminal cases. See Stuntz, *The Collapse of American Criminal Justice*, 196–214.

15. Hagan, *Who Are the Criminals?*, 69–100. Hagan closely analyzes the history of criminological theory during this period, tracing the work of scholars like Merton, McKay, Shaw, and Sutherland to illustrate the concrete impact of their scholarly ideas on policy.

16. Garland, *The Culture of Control*, 27–28, 35.

17. Reitz, "Sentencing," 473.

18. *Williams v. New York*, 337 U.S. 241 (1949).

19. Hagan, *Who Are the Criminals?*, 69–100.

20. *Williams v. New York*, 337 U.S. 241 (1949).

21. Petersilia, Joan, "Community Corrections," 504; Allen, *The Decline of the Rehabilitative Ideal*, 41.

22. Chappell and Evjen, "The Presentence Investigation Report," 1.

23. Chappell and Evjen, "The Presentence Investigation Report," 2, 5.

24. Chappell and Evjen, "The Presentence Investigation Report," 7 (quote), 11.

25. Chappell and Evjen, "The Presentence Investigation Report," 9–12.

26. Administrative Office of the United States Courts, *The Presentence Investigation Report*, v, 1.

27. Modern risk assessments will be discussed further in chap. 7, but for useful critiques and historical overviews, see Eckhouse, Lum, Conti-Cook, and Ciccolini, "Layers of Bias"; Monahan and Skeem, "Risk Assessment"; and Starr, "Evidence-Based Sentencing."

28. Harcourt, "Risk as a Proxy."

29. On trends in proceduralization, see Walker, *Popular Justice*; Murakawa, *The First Civil Right*.

30. McLennan, *The Crisis of Imprisonment*, 448–62.

31. Baumes quoted in "Court Treatment of General Recidivist Statutes," 238.

32. New York State Crime Commission, *New York State Crime Commission Report*, 10, 13.

33. New York State Crime Commission, *New York State Crime Commission Report*, 13.

34. New York State Board of Public Charities, *Annual Report of the State Board of Charities for the Year 1905*, 795–96, 798–99, 804.

35. New York State Board of Public Charities, *Annual Report of the State Board of Charities for the Year 1907*, 659, 668. The board especially focused on implementing the "genuinely indeterminate sentence" for women, discussing how "Lombroso has said that the prostitute among women is the equivalent of the criminal among men." Ibid., 666.

36. "Gets Life Sentence."

37. "Baumes Talks to Bankers: New Criminal Laws Are for Society's Protection, He Says."

38. *People v. Gowasky*, 244 N.Y. 451 (1927).

39. *People v. Spellman*, 136 N.Y.S. 25 (1930) (emphasis added).

40. *Hogan v. Bohan*, 101 N.Y.S. 566 (1951). Also see *People v. Tramonti*, 275 N.Y.S. 517 (1934) for similar statements.

41. McLennan, *The Crisis of Imprisonment*, 458; Gibson, "Writing Crime into Race"; Muhammad, "Where Did All the White Criminals Go?"

42. Goodman, Page, and Phelps, *Breaking the Pendulum*, 17.

43. California Department of Corrections, Adult Authority, "Parole: Philosophy, Policies and Programs," 7.

44. On the important role California played as a leader in criminal justice reform from the 1940s through the 1960s, see Walker, *Popular Justice*, 208–15. For statistics on incarceration rates in California, see ibid., 214.

45. California Department of Corrections, "Progress Report," 4–5.

46. Glueck and Glueck, *500 Criminal Careers*. Also see Glueck and Glueck, *Unraveling Juvenile Delinquency*.

47. Coffee, "The Future of Sentencing Reform"; Walker, *Popular Justice*, 214.

48. Beverly, "Analysis of Base Expectancy Tables."

49. California Department of Corrections, "Policies, Organization, and Procedures," i, 2, 7, 25, 93.

50. California Department of Corrections, "Biennial Report of the Department of Corrections," 44.

51. *People v. Richardson*, 74 Cal. App. 2d 528 (1946).

52. *In re McVickers*, 29 Cal. 2d 264 (1946). Also see *In re Harincar*, 29 Cal. 2d 403 (1946); *In re Bramble*, 31 Cal. 2d 43 (1947); *In re Wolfson*, 30 Cal. 2d 20 (1947); *People v. Stein*, 52 Cal. 2d 250 (1948); *In re Tartar*, 52 Cal. 2d 250 (1959).

53. *Washington v. Edelstein*, 146 Wash. 221 (1927); *Washington v. Hensley*, 20 Wn. 2d 495 (1944); *Hansen v. Rigg*, 258 Minn. 388 (1960); *Davis v. O'Grady*, 137 Neb. 708 (1940); *Goodman v. Kunkle*, 72 F.2d 334 (1934); *New Jersey v. Tuddles*, 38 N.J. 565 (1962); *New Jersey v. Van Buren*, 29 N.J. 548 (1959).

54. *People v. Reed*, 249 Cal. App. 2d 468 (1967).

55. Goodman, Page, and Phelps, *Breaking the Pendulum*, 81–86.

56. The forty-two were traced and compiled from "Court Treatment of General Recidivist Statutes"; Tappan, "Habitual Offender Laws in the United States"; and Brown, "The Treatment of the Recidivist in the United States." These resources had a small number of discrepancies in how they characterized some laws (e.g., a given state's laws were presented as mandatory in one article but discretionary in another). This is likely due to a combination of errors by the authors and ongoing revisions to the laws. Figure 2 labels the states' laws on the basis of what could be validated by looking up the statutory and legal citations provided in each article to iron out any discrepancies.

57. Brown, "The Treatment of the Recidivist in the United States," 643. Those states were Oregon, Florida, North Dakota, Minnesota, and Vermont.

58. "Minnesota Has Its Baumes Law."

59. Brown, "The Treatment of the Recidivist in the United States," 644, 657, 672–73.

60. Michael Klarman, "Is the Supreme Court Sometimes Irrelevant?"

61. Garland, *Peculiar Institution*.

62. Hansen and King, *Sterilized by the State*, 237–58; Stern, *Eugenic Nation*.

63. Grasso, "Broken beyond Repair"; Goodman, Page, and Phelps, *Breaking the Pendulum*; Hannah-Moffat, "Criminogenic Needs and the Transformative Risk Subject"; Godrej, "Yoga, Meditation, and Neoliberal Penality," and *Freedom Inside?*

64. California Department of Corrections, "Biennial Report for the Period Ending December 1, 1948," 50.

65. President's Commission on Law Enforcement and Administration of Justice, *The Challenge of Crime in a Free Society*, 297.

66. Quoted in Von Hirsch and Committee for the Study of Incarceration, *Doing Justice*, 9.

67. Martinson, "What Works?," 22, 49.

68. Martinson, "New Findings, New Views."

69. Ruth and Reitz, *The Challenge of Crime*, 83–84.

70. Von Hirsch and Committee for the Study of Incarceration, *Doing Justice*, 6.

71. Ruth and Reitz, *The Challenge of Crime*, 81–91.

72. Wilson, *Thinking about Crime* (1975), 239.

73. Wilson, *Thinking about Crime* (1983), 162–77 (quote 175).

74. Wilson, "What to Do about Crime."

75. Dilulio, "The Coming of the Super-Predators."

76. Beckett, *Making Crime Pay*, chaps. 3–4.

77. Flamm, *Law and Order*; Tonry, *Punishing Race*.

78. Ruth and Reitz, *The Challenge of Crime*, 88.

79. Martinson, "Prison Notes of a Freedom Rider."

80. Quoted in Miller, "The Debate on Rehabilitating Criminals."

81. Tonry, *Sentencing Matters*, 12–13, 89.

82. Murakawa, *The First Civil Right*, 99–112.

83. Ruth and Reitz, *The Challenge of Crime*, 474–75; Mitchell, "State Sentencing Guidelines."

84. US House Committee on the Judiciary, *Federal Sentencing Revision: Hearings*, pt. 2, 810–11, 844.

85. US House Committee on the Judiciary, *Federal Sentencing Revision: Hearings*, pt. 2, 947.

86. US House Committee on the Judiciary, *Federal Sentencing Revision: Hearings*, pt. 1, 255.

87. US Senate Committee on the Judiciary, *Sentencing Reform Act of 1983*, 73.

88. US House Committee on the Judiciary, *Sentencing Revision Act of 1984*, 35–36.

89. US Senate Committee on the Judiciary, *Sentencing Reform Act of 1983*, 72–73, and US House Committee on the Judiciary, *Sentencing Revision Act of 1984*, 40.

90. *Mistretta v. U.S.*, 488 U.S. 361 (1989).

91. US Sentencing Commission, *Guidelines Manual* (1987), 1.1, 5.8–9, 5.23.

92. US Sentencing Commission, *Guidelines Manual* (1987), 4.1.

93. US House Committee on the Judiciary, *Sentencing Revision Act of 1984*, 99.

94. Shapiro, "Comity of Errors."

95. US Sentencing Commission, *Guidelines Manual* (1987), 4.8.

96. *U.S. v. Watts*, 519 U.S. 148 (1997). The irony was not lost on John Paul Stevens, who wrote in dissent that *Williams* was "decided in the context of a sentencing system that focuse[d] on subjective assessments of rehabilitative potential."

97. US Sentencing Commission, *Guidelines Manual* (1987), 4.1.

98. Von Hirsch and Committee for the Study of Incarceration, *Doing Justice*, 85–88; Morris, *The Future of Imprisonment*, 79–80.

99. Wilson, *Thinking about Crime* (1983), 135, 140–58. In his classic text, Beccaria wrote, "[I]t is essential that it [punishment] be public, prompt, necessary, the minimum possible under the given circumstances, [and] proportionate to the crimes." Beccaria, *On Crimes and Punishments*, 81. He believed that if all sentences were equally severe, there would be no incentive for criminals to cease engaging in more serious forms of crime and that they may even commit more serious (even violent) crimes following a trivial offense if it would decrease their odds of detection since the severity in punishment for the two offenses differed little. On the negative consequences of excessive severity, see ibid., 46–47.

100. Murakawa, *The First Civil Right*; Western, *Punishment and Inequality*; Tonry, *Sentencing Fragments*.

101. On career criminal criminology—which manifested in the Armed Career Criminal Act, passed as part of the Sentencing Reform Act of 1984—see Hagan, *Who Are the Criminals?*, 101–36.

102. Grasso, "Broken beyond Repair"; Goodman, Page, and Phelps, *Breaking the Pendulum*.

103. US House Committee on the Judiciary, *Federal Sentencing Revision: Hearings*, pt. 2, 1119.

104. US House Committee on the Judiciary, *Federal Sentencing Revision: Hearings*, pt. 1, 761.

105. Harcourt, "Risk as a Proxy."

Chapter Six

1. US Senate Committee on Banking and Currency, *Stock Exchange Practices* (1933), 6:2223.

2. For those who see the New Deal as a significant restructuring of American politics, see Block, "The Ruling Class Does Not Rule"; Leuchtenburg, *In the Shadow of FDR*; and Postel, "TR, Wilson, and the Origins of the Progressive Tradition." For those who see the New Deal as stabilizing capitalist interests, see Gordon, *New Deals*; Domhoff and Webber, *Class and Power in the New Deal*; and Swenson, "Arranged Alliance."

3. Postel, "TR, Wilson, and the Origins of the Progressive Tradition"; Brinkley and Woolner, "Franklin Roosevelt and the Progressive Tradition."

4. On programmatic liberalism, see Milkis, *The President and the Parties*.

5. Roosevelt, "Commonwealth Club Address."

6. "Ex-Justice Ferdinand Pecora."

7. Cowie, *The Great Exception*, 91-134; Ferguson, "Industrial Conflict," 14-15, 19-24; Domhoff and Webber, *Class and Power in the New Deal*, 24-26; Carosso, *Investment Banking*, 322-51.

8. Parrish, *Securities Regulation*, 4.

9. Phillips-Fein, *Invisible Hands*, chaps. 1-2, 77-78, 262-69; Vogel, *Fluctuating Fortunes*, 107-8; Cowie, *The Great Exception*, 115-18; Carosso, *Investment Banking*, 383-407; Collins, *The Business Response to Keynes*, chap. 1-3; Kazin, Edwards, and Rothman, *The Concise Princeton Encyclopedia of American Political History*, 46-47.

10. Friedman, *Crime and Punishment*, 290-91. Also see Taub, *Big Dirty Money*, 45; and Eisinger, *The Chickenshit Club*, 59-62.

11. Domhoff and Webber, *Class and Power in the New Deal*, 24-26; Carosso, *Investment Banking*, chap. 16.

12. Perino, *The Hellhound of Wall Street*; Taub, *Big Dirty Money*; Chernow, "Where Is Our Ferdinand Pecora?"

13. Pecora, *Wall Street under Oath*, 191, 240-49; Breslow, "Were Bankers Jailed"; Eisinger, *The Chickenshit Club*, 59-61.

14. Tillman, Pontell, and Black, *Financial Crime and Crises*, 1-4; Eisinger, *The Chickenshit Club*, 61-62.

15. Breslow, "Were Bankers Jailed"; Taub, *Big Dirty Money*, 45; Eisinger, *The Chickenshit Club*, 60-62; Hagan, *Who Are the Criminals?*, 177-80; Chernow, "Where Is Our Ferdinand Pecora?"

16. Hagan, *Who Are the Criminals?*, 178.

17. Carosso, *Investment Banking*, 324-25.

18. US Senate Committee on Banking and Currency, *Stock Exchange Practices* (1932), 2:418, 478, 560, and *Stock Exchange Practices* (1933), 6:2222-23.

19. US Senate Committee on Banking and Currency, *Stock Exchange Practices* (1932), 3:984 (statements of Counsel William Gray recalling the words of William Fox).

20. "Reveal Stock Pool."

21. US Senate Committee on Banking and Currency, *Stock Exchange Practices* (1933), 6:2082-87, 2137, and *Stock Exchange Practices: Report*, 166-73; Pecora, *Wall Street under Oath*, 92, 95-100, 110-12. These loans are also discussed in Carosso, *Investment Banking*, 330-31.

22. US Senate Committee on Banking and Currency, *Stock Exchange Practices* (1933), 6:1804. For similar statements from National City's former vice president Ronald Byrnes, see ibid., 2137.

23. Pecora, *Wall Street under Oath*, 95.

24. US Senate Committee on Banking and Currency, *Stock Exchange Practices: Report*, 206–8 (quote 207). Also see Carosso, *Investment Banking*, 333–34.

25. Carosso, *Investment Banking*, 334.

26. King, "The Man Who Busted the 'Banksters'"; Brinkley, "When Washington Took on Wall Street."

27. Morgan quoted in Hagan, *Who Are the Criminals?*, 178–79. Hagan notes that this was "the kind of criminal framing or stigma probably intended by Pecora as a former prosecutor from the criminal courtrooms of New York." Also see Brinkley, "When Washington Took on Wall Street."

28. Moley quoted in Perino, *The Hellhound of Wall Street*, 4.

29. Chernow, "Where Is Our Ferdinand Pecora?"

30. US Senate Committee on Banking and Currency, *Stock Exchange Practices* (1934), 8:3978–97 (quote 3990).

31. US Senate Committee on Banking and Currency, *Stock Exchange Practices* (1934), 8:4017.

32. US Senate Committee on Banking and Currency, *Stock Exchange Practices: Report*, 393.

33. Pecora, *Wall Street under Oath*, ix.

34. Vogel, *Fluctuating Fortunes*. Vogel's work goes back only to the 1960s, but these debates demonstrate comparable dynamics.

35. Braithwaite, "What's Wrong," 19–20. Also see Garland, *The Culture of Control*, which Braithwaite is discussing in this quoted passage.

36. For a good historical review of the law's passage, see Parrish, *Securities Regulation*, chap. 3.

37. US House Committee on Interstate and Foreign Commerce, *Federal Securities Act*, 173–74. For more on the IBA, see Carosso, *Investment Banking*, chap. 8.

38. US House Committee on Interstate and Foreign Commerce, *Federal Securities Act*, 174–93.

39. US Senate Committee on Banking and Currency, *Securities Act*, 92–93.

40. US Senate Committee on Banking and Currency, *Securities Act*, 282–84 (full summary), 284 (quote).

41. US Senate Committee on Banking and Currency, *Regulation of Securities: Report*, 1. For similar arguments, see US House Committee on Banking and Currency, *Federal Supervision of Traffic in Investment Securities*, 2.

42. 77 Cong. Rec. 2948 (1933).

43. Carosso, *Investment Banking*, chap. 7.

44. 77 Cong. Rec. 2931 (1933). For similar commentary, see 77 Cong. Rec. 2935, 2949–51 (1933).

45. 77 Cong. Rec. 2954, 2995 (1933).

46. Eisinger, *The Chickenshit Club*, 60–61.

47. Parrish, *Securities Regulation*, chaps. 3–5.

48. US Senate Committee on Banking and Currency, *Stock Exchange Practices* (1934), 15:6467 for quote. For a more general perspective on Corcoran's views, see 6508–10, 6463–67, 6506–9, 6576–77.

49. US House Committee on Interstate and Foreign Commerce, *Stock Exchange Regulation*, 64.

50. US House Committee on Interstate and Foreign Commerce, *Stock Exchange Regulation*, 731.

51. US Senate Committee on Banking and Currency, *Stock Exchange Practices* (1934), 15:6552.

52. US Senate Committee on Banking and Currency, *Stock Exchange Practices* (1934), 16:7484–85, 7538.

53. US Senate Committee on Banking and Currency, *Stock Exchange Practices* (1934), 15:6512, 6734. For similar statements from Whitney, see ibid., 6582–86.

54. Parrish, *Securities Regulation*, 122, 129 (quoting Shields's personal correspondence).

55. US Senate Committee on Banking and Currency, *Stock Exchange Practices* (1934), 15:6901, 6916. For additional statements by Hope, see ibid., 6904, 6907, 6910–13.

56. US Senate Committee on Banking and Currency, *Stock Exchange Practices* (1934), 15:6965.

57. US Senate Committee on Banking and Currency, *Stock Exchange Practices* (1934), 16:7459, 7463. For similar arguments from Harold Stuart of Halsey, Stuart and Co., see US Senate Committee on Banking and Currency, *Stock Exchange Practices* (1933), 5:1615–16.

58. US Senate Committee on Banking and Currency, *Stock Exchange Practices* (1934), 16: 7456.

59. US House Committee on Interstate and Foreign Commerce, *Securities Exchange Bill of 1934*, 6–7.

60. 78 Cong. Rec. 770 (1934).

61. For the Cooper quotes, see 78 Cong. Rec. 7690, 7930 (1934). For the Studley quotes, see 78 Cong. Rec. 7943 (1934).

62. 78 Cong. Rec. 8709 (1934).

63. 78 Cong. Rec. 8700–8701 (1934).

64. US Congress Committee of Conference, *Securities Exchange Act of 1934: Conference Report*, 30; Parrish, *Securities Regulation*, 139–43.

65. US Congress Committee of Conference, *Securities Exchange Act of 1934: Conference Report*, esp. 6, 18, 20–25, 38 (for details on penalties and enforcement).

66. De Bedts, "The First Chairmen," 167–68 (quote); Norris, "She's a Candidate for a Job She Devised."

67. Kennedy, *Address of Hon. Joseph P. Kennedy*.

68. Berle, "Letter from A. A. Berle Jr. to Joseph Kennedy."

69. Landis, *The Administrative Process*, 13.

70. Douglas, *Democracy and Finance*, 130, 264. For more on the state's "residual role," see ibid., 64, 78, 82, 232, 252–58.

71. Douglas, "Administrative Government," 2.

72. Eisinger, *The Chickenshit Club*, 63; Braithwaite, "What's Wrong," 19–20; Shapiro, *Wayward Capitalists*; Wyatt, "Promises Made."

73. For a discussion of the corporate crime deterrence literature, see chap. 1.

74. Eisinger, *The Chickenshit Club*, 59–82.

75. On preferring criminal penalties, see Khanna, "Corporate Crime Legislation," and "Corporate Criminal Liability." On preferring civil penalties, see Uhlmann, "The Pendulum Swings."

76. Eisinger, *The Chickenshit Club*, 67.

77. Pleyte, "White Collar Crime in the Twenty-First Century"; Taub, *Big Dirty Money*, 46–49; Eisinger, *The Chickenshit Club*, 62–63.

78. Harris and Milkis, *The Politics of Regulatory Change*, 148–49. For background on the consumers movement, see Cohen, *A Consumers' Republic*; and Glickman, *Buying Power*.

79. Harris and Milkis, *The Politics of Regulatory Change*, 140–53. Harris and Milkis note that protecting businesses and protecting consumers are not incompatible goals, but they emphasize that the FTC's overbroad mandate made it difficult to serve either goal well.

80. For a summary of the TNEC, see Brinkley, "The New Deal and the Idea of the State," 89–92.

81. US Temporary National Economic Committee, *Investigation*, 5:1756–57, 1850.

82. Brinkley, "The New Deal and the Idea of the State," 90–91.

83. US Temporary National Economic Committee, *Investigation*, 21:11314.

84. Arnold, *The Bottlenecks of Business*, 135.

85. US Temporary National Economic Committee, *Preliminary Report*, 19.

86. Sutherland, *White-Collar Crime*, 32, 230–31.

87. Wilson, *Political Organizations*, and *Bureaucracy*.

88. Vogel, *Fluctuating Fortunes*, 10–12, 26, 37–58 (chap. 3), 99; Phillips-Fein, *Invisible Hands*, 128, 139–41; Smith, "The Progressive Seedbed."

89. Vogel, *Fluctuating Fortunes*, 93–111. McCann says that Carter appointed over sixty public interest advocates to powerful administrative positions. See McCann, *Taking Reform Seriously*, 63.

90. Harris and Milkis, *The Politics of Regulatory Change*, 158–62.

91. Cox, Fellmeth, and Schulz, *"The Nader Report*," viii–xii, 58–59, 61–64, 68.

92. Kauper, "History, Effect, and Scope," 1106–10.

93. Cox, Fellmeth, and Schulz, *"The Nader Report*," 64.

94. Cox, Fellmeth, and Schulz, *"The Nader Report*," 180–84, 194.

95. Harris and Milkis, *The Politics of Regulatory Change*, 172–74.

96. "Federal Trade Commission—Drafting in a Regulatory Agency," 828–29.

97. US Senate Committee on Commerce, *Federal Trade Commission Oversight*, 150, 154. Also see Harris and Milkis, *The Politics of Regulatory Change*, 168–70.

98. Eisinger, *The Chickenshit Club*, 59–82.

99. Vogel, *Fluctuating Fortunes*, 108.

100. Cox, Fellmeth, and Schulz, *"The Nader Report*," 90–91.

101. Karmen, *Crime Victims*; Taub, *Big Dirty Money*, 65–90; Croall, "What Is Known"; Barak, *Theft of a Nation*, 117–20; Sutherland, *White-Collar Crime*, 22, 218–23.

102. For an overview of the victims' rights movement and institution building, see Gottschalk, *The Prison and the Gallows*, 77–114.

103. Powell, "Confidential Memorandum," 6, 8.

104. Powell, "Confidential Memorandum," 27.

105. Phillips-Fein, *Invisible Hands*, 150–212 (quote 202).

106. Vogel, *Fluctuating Fortunes*, 148–239.

107. Vogel, *Fluctuating Fortunes*, 227.

108. Phillips-Fein, *Invisible Hands*.

109. Gilder quoted in Phillips-Fein, *Invisible Hands*, 177–78. On the resurgence of free market intellectualism, see ibid., chaps. 2–8.

110. Vogel, *Fluctuating Fortunes*, 227.

111. Congressional Research Service, "Bill Summary: H.R. 2313." Criminal penalties were retained for noncompliance with judicial orders.

112. Calavita, Pontell, and Tillman, *Big Money Crime*, 10, 89–90; Barak, *Theft of a Nation*, 48–51; Harris and Milkis, *The Politics of Regulatory Change*, 103–5, 191–92; Hagan, *Who Are the Criminals?*, 170–73.

113. Harris and Milkis, *The Politics of Regulatory Change*, 8.

114. On institutional inertia and regulatory change, see Harris and Milkis, *The Politics of Regulatory Change*, esp. chap. 2.

115. Harris and Milkis, *The Politics of Regulatory Change*, 186–206.

116. For a reprint of the 1981 Transition Report, see 127 Cong. Rec. 21349–56 (1981) (quotes 21349). For information on the FTC Bureau of Economics, see Harris and Milkis, *The Politics of Regulatory Change*, 168–70, 202–6.

117. Eisner, *Regulatory Politics in Transition*, chap. 8, esp. 194–95.

118. Harris and Milkis, *The Politics of Regulatory Change*, 221 (quoting congressional hearings).

119. Harris and Milkis, *The Politics of Regulatory Change*, 189 (quoting Pertschuk).

120. Vogel, "The 'New' Social Regulation."

121. Eisner, *Regulatory Politics in Transition*, 135–39; Marcus, *Promise and Performance*, 141–49.

122. Vogel, *Fluctuating Fortunes*, 140. Also see Harris and Milkis, *The Politics of Regulatory Change*, 249–51.

123. Both cited in Vogel, *Fluctuating Fortunes*, 249–51.

124. Eisner, *Regulatory Politics in Transition*, 48, 120.

125. Holland, "Hundreds of Wall Street Execs"; Rakoff, "The Financial Crisis."

126. Calavita, Pontell, and Tillman, *Big Money Crime*; Green, "After the Fall"; Tillman and Pontell, "Organizations and Fraud."

127. For another scholarly perspective acknowledging both the prosecutorial significance of the S&L crisis and its roots in deregulatory policy, see Taub, *Big Dirty Money*, 51–52.

128. On neoliberalism, see Brown, *Undoing the Demos*; Larner, "Neo-Liberalism"; and Harvey, *A Brief History of Neoliberalism*.

129. Hagan, *Who Are the Criminals?*, 70, 170–73; Hacker and Pierson, *Winner-Take-All Politics*, 185.

130. In 1982, the SEC legalized previously prohibited share buybacks, through which companies repurchased their own stock to manipulate share prices. See Foroohar, *Makers and Takers*, 52, 125–28, 293–94. For an overview of "financialization," see Krippner, "The Financialization of the American Economy."

131. Barak, *Theft of a Nation*; Tillman, Pontell, and Black, *Financial Crime and Crises*; Taibbi, *The Divide*; Hagan, *Who Are the Criminals?*; Krippner, "The Financialization of the American Economy"; Foroohar, *Makers and Takers*.

132. Harris and Milkis, *The Politics of Regulatory Change*, 8; Eisner, *Regulatory Politics in Transition*, chap. 8.

133. Vogel, *Fluctuating Fortunes*, 247–87.

134. Some suggest that as a result real regulatory spending increased 10 percent under Reagan. See Braithwaite, "What's Wrong," 11. Braithwaite cites Tramontozzi and Chilton, "US Regulatory Agencies under Reagan."

135. US House Committee on Banking, Finance, and Urban Affairs, *Findings of Booz Allen and Hamilton Study*, 41–42.

136. US House Committee on Banking and Urban Affairs, *The Savings and Loan Crisis*, 112, 115, 158–59.

137. James Turner of the Kansas League of Savings Institutions called the FHLBB "the Gestapo," and Representative Fernand St. Germain (D-RI) said that regulators created "a police state." See US House Committee on Banking, Finance, and Urban Affairs, *Federal Savings and Loan Insurance Corporation Recapitalization Act of 1987*, 521, and *Federal Asset Disposition Association*, 48.

138. US House Committee on Banking, Finance, and Urban Affairs, *Findings of Booz Allen and Hamilton Study*, 30.

139. Calavita, Pontell, and Tillman, *Big Money Crime*, 15.

140. US Senate Committee on Banking, Housing, and Urban Affairs, *Problems of the Federal Savings and Loan Insurance Corporation (FSLIC)*, pt. 1, 320.

141. US Senate Committee on Banking, Housing, and Urban Affairs, *Problems of the Federal Savings and Loan Insurance Corporation (FSLIC)*, pt. 2, 772.

142. US House Committee on Banking, Finance, and Urban Affairs, *Financial Condition*, 683, 218.

143. US Department of Justice, "Criminal Resource Manual Archives, Section 958."

144. Calavita, Pontell, and Tillman, *Big Money Crime*, 126–32.

145. Calavita, Pontell, and Tillman, *Big Money Crime*, 124 (quoting a personal interview conducted by the authors).

146. US Senate Committee on the Budget, *Current Conditions*, 141.

147. These included Gray, Wall, Thornburgh, Comptroller Robert Clarke, and Frederick Wolf of the General Accounting Office. See US Senate Committee on Banking, Housing, and Urban Affairs, *Oversight on the Condition of the Financial Services Industry*, 360, 439; US House Committee on Banking and Urban Affairs, *The Savings and Loan Crisis*, 37; and US Senate Committee on Banking, Housing, and Urban Affairs, *Problems of the Federal Savings and Loan Insurance Corporation (FSLIC)*, pt. 1, 295–305.

148. US Senate Committee on Banking, Housing, and Urban Affairs, *Thrift Charter Enhancement Act of 1988*, 78.

149. US Senate Committee on Banking, Housing, and Urban Affairs, *Problems of the Federal Savings and Loan Insurance Corporation (FSLIC)*, pt. 3, 148–49.

150. US House Committee on Banking, Finance, and Urban Affairs, *The Other Side of the Savings and Loan Industry*, 1.

151. US House Committee on the Judiciary, *Prosecuting Fraud in the Thrift Industry*, 2.

152. US House Committee on Government Operations, *Fraud and Abuse*, 122, 132–33.

153. Calavita, Pontell, and Tillman, *Big Money Crime*, 135–36.

154. Calavita, Pontell, and Tillman, *Big Money Crime*, 126–29, 132 (quote). For the full argument explaining the response as "damage control," see ibid., 130–68.

155. National Commission on Financial Institution Reform, Recovery, and Enforcement, *Origins and Causes*, 70.

156. Wheeler, Mann, and Sarat, "Sentencing the White-Collar Criminal."

157. US House Committee on Government Operations, *Fraud and Abuse*, 373.

158. Green, "After the Fall," S175 (n. 142). Years later, Calavita, Pontell, and Tillman found that the median S&L fraud sentence was twenty-two months, with only 4 percent of offenders getting more than ten years. See Calavita, Pontell, and Tillman, *Big Money Crime*, 156–57.

159. Hagan, *Who Are the Criminals?*, 168–76; Barak, *Theft of a Nation*, 48–51; Foroohar, *Makers and Takers*, 52, 125–28, 293–94.

160. On moral hazard, see Hagan, *Who Are the Criminals?*, 166, 190. For more general related historical context on the S&L crisis, see ibid., 170–83.

161. Barak, *Theft of a Nation*, 42–43.

162. Smith, "SEC Cease-and-Desist Orders," 1210.

163. The specific statute's name was the Comprehensive Thrift and Bank Fraud Prosecution and Taxpayer Recovery Act.

164. US Government Accounting Office, "Bank and Thrift Criminal Fraud," esp. 3–7, 15–23, 44–57. On the persistence of deregulation since the 1980s, see Hagan, *Who Are the Criminals?*, 168–212, 257–68; Eisinger, *The Chickenshit Club*; and Barak, *Theft of a Nation*, 133–50.

165. Calavita, Pontell, and Tillman, *Big Money Crime*, 130–36.

166. Wyatt, "Promises Made"; Shapiro, *Wayward Capitalists*.

Chapter Seven

1. On knowledge-producing institutions and "knowledge regimes," see Campbell and Pedersen, "Policy Ideas," 167–73.

2. Kopan, "Report."

3. Brown, *Undoing the Demos*, 1–74; Soss, Fording, and Schram, *Disciplining the Poor*; Spence, *Knocking the Hustle*.

4. Malcolm, "Testimony."

5. Norquist, "Conservative Principles and Prison."

6. "Adult Probation."

7. Gottschalk, *Caught*, 7–10, chaps. 2–3; Cate, *The Myth of the Community Fix*, 94–97, 130–33, 192–94.

8. Butts and Schiraldi, "Recidivism Reconsidered"; Petersilia, "Community Corrections"; Western, *Punishment and Inequality*.

9. "Risk/Needs Assessment 101," 3.

10. Eckhouse, Lum, Conti-Cook, and Ciccolini, "Layers of Bias," 186.

11. Monahan and Skeem, "Risk Assessment," 494–96; Starr, "Evidence-Based Sentencing," 805.

12. Hannah-Moffat, "Criminogenic Needs and the Transformative Risk Subject."

13. Mangual, "New York." Mangual favorably cites evidence that New Jersey's risk assessments "don't seem to have changed the racial composition of that state's pretrial jail population."

14. Walters and Tell, "Criminal Justice Reform."

15. For example, consider the company NorthPointe's scandal with New York's COMPAS risk assessment. See Angwin, Larson, Mattu, and Kirchner, "Machine Bias."

16. Harcourt, "Risk as a Proxy."

17. Pennsylvania's guidelines score risk higher in urban counties than they do in rural counties for the same offenses. See Monahan and Skeem, "Risk Assessment," 495.

18. Starr, "Evidence-Based Sentencing"; "The Hidden Discrimination in Criminal Risk-Assessment Scores"; Eckhouse, Lum, Conti-Cook, and Ciccolini, "Layers of Bias"; Harcourt, "Risk as a Proxy"; Hannah-Moffat, "Criminogenic Needs and the Transformative Risk Subject."

19. Eckhouse, Lum, Conti-Cook, and Ciccolini, "Layers of Bias."

20. Pisciotta, *Benevolent Repression*, 19–21.

21. Cate, *The Myth of the Community Fix*, 133–36; Starr, "Evidence-Based Sentencing"; Goddard and Myers, "Against Evidence-Based Oppression."

22. Criminologists have demonstrated that trends in criminological research often reflect shifts in prevailing governing ideologies. See Hagan, *Who Are the Criminals?*; and Savelsberg, "Knowledge."

23. Gould, *The Mismeasure of Man*, 28.

24. Mednick, Gabrielli, and Hutching, "Genetic Influences in Criminal Convictions"; Van Dusen, Teilmann, Mednick, Gabrielli, and Hutching, "Social Class and Crime in an Adoption Court"; Harpending and Draper, "Antisocial Behavior and the Other Side of Cultural Evolution."

25. Herrnstein and Murray, *The Bell Curve*; Wilson and Herrnstein, *Crime and Human Nature*.

26. Raine, *The Anatomy of Violence*, 13 (quote), 329–74 (on policy prescriptions).

27. "Biopsychosocial Criminology."

28. Fallon, "Penn Professor's Book Inspires TV Show." For another example of the popular appeal of these ideas, see "Inside the Criminal Mind."

29. Gottschalk, *Caught*, 373; "Nashville Assistant DA Fired"; Schwartz, "Following Reports of Forced Sterilization."

30. Murphy, "White Nationalists."

31. Raine, *The Anatomy of Violence*, 249–50, 260–64, 273–87, 299–300, 344–51, 369–72.

32. Eagleman, "The Brain on Trial."

33. Raine explicitly equates the heritability of crime and cancer. See Raine, *The Anatomy of Violence*, 339–40, 340, 345.

34. Crossley, "The Genetic Defense."

35. DeLisi, Wright, and Mangual, "Psychology, Not Circumstances."

36. Lehman, "Contra 'Root Causes.'"

37. Murray, "'The Bell Curve', Explained: Part II." Also see Murray, "'The Bell Curve', Explained: Introduction," and "'The Bell Curve', Explained: Part I."

38. Gattuso, "Meltdowns and Myths."

39. Michel, "Profit and Deregulation."

40. Michel, "The Myth."

41. Dwyer and Michel, "A New Federal Charter," 350, 352, 354–56.

42. For an overview of private sector (especially financial sector) growth, see Foroohar, *Makers and Takers*.

43. Henderson, "Are We Ailing."

44. Mulligan, "Trump's Vast Deregulatory Landscape."

45. DeMuth, "Trump vs. the Deep Regulatory State."

46. Rose, "Designing," 256.

47. Murray, "'The Bell Curve', Explained: Part I."

48. Murray, "'The Bell Curve', Explained: Part II."

49. For overviews of some of these ideas, see Tillman, Pontell, and Black, *Financial Crime and Crises*, chap. 6.

50. Raine, Laufer, Yang, Narr, Thompson, and Toga, "Increased Executive Functioning," 2932.

51. Galvin and Simpson, "Prosecuting and Sentencing"; Wheeler, Mann, and Sarat, "Sentencing the White-Collar Criminal"; Benson and Cullen, *Combating Corporate Crime*; Henning, "Is Deterrence Relevant"; Levi, "Sentencing Respectable Offenders."

52. 164 Cong. Rec. H4310, H4311, H4314 (daily ed., May 22, 2018) (statements of Representatives Goodlatte, Nadler, and Jayapal, respectively).

53. US House Committee on the Judiciary, *Formerly Incarcerated Reenter Society Transformed Safely Transitioning Every Person Act*, 22, 100.

54. Tanner, "A Prison-Reform Bill."

55. Gottschalk, "Kamala Harris' Disturbing Brand"; Leadership Conference on Civil and Human Rights, "Vote 'No.'"

56. 164 Cong. Rec. S7764 (daily ed., December 18, 2018).

57. 164 Cong. Rec. S7838 (daily ed., December 19, 2018).

58. 164 Cong. Rec. S7916–S7917 (daily ed., December 19, 2018).

59. 164 Cong. Rec. H10361, H10364–H10365, H10399 (daily ed., December 19, 2018) (statements of Representatives Nadler and Lee and letter from the ACLU and the LCCHR submitted

into the record, respectively). Also see Leadership Conference on Civil and Human Rights, "Support S. 756," 3.

60. Grawert, "What Is the First Step Act?"

61. Stimson, "The First Step Act's Risk and Needs Assessment Program," 6–10.

62. Mangual, "Ideas," 3–4.

63. Grawert, "What Is the First Step Act?," and "Public Comment."

64. US Department of Justice, "The First Step Act of 2018," 62.

65. US Department of Justice, "Department of Justice Announces"; Stimson, "The First Step Act's Risk and Needs Assessment Program," 17; Eckhouse, Lum, Conti-Cook, and Ciccolini, "Layers of Bias."

66. MacDougall, "Bill Barr Promised."

67. US Department of Justice, "First Step Act Implementation"; MacDougall, "Bill Barr Promised."

68. Anderson, "Why Trump Should Oppose"; Walters, "The 'Mass Incarceration' Myth."

69. Michaels, "Trump Keeps Celebrating."

70. Walters and Tell, "Criminal Justice Reform."

71. Petroni, "VIDEO: Sen. Warren Asks."

72. US Senate Committee on the Judiciary, *Sentencing Reform Act of 1983*, 88.

73. Richman, "Federal White Collar Sentencing."

74. Taub, *Big Dirty Money*, xvii, 120–24. Taub gives the particular example of wire fraud.

75. Henning, "Is Deterrence Relevant," 5–7; Richman, "Federal White Collar Sentencing."

76. The same trend is visible in risk assessments. See Harbinson, Benson, and Latessa, "Assessing Risk."

77. US Sentencing Commission, *Guidelines Manual* (1991), 369–70; Eisinger, *The Chickenshit Club*, 94.

78. For histories of Enron and Andersen, see Eisinger, *The Chickenshit Club*, 1–59; and Garrett, *Too Big to Jail*, 19–44.

79. Garrett, *Too Big to Jail*, 41–44; Eisinger, *The Chickenshit Club*, 54–58. The Supreme Court later reversed Andersen's conviction on procedural grounds.

80. Markoff, "Arthur Andersen"; Eisinger, *The Chickenshit Club*, 38, 54.

81. Eisinger, *The Chickenshit Club*, 36–40, 45–50, 54–58; Garrett, *Too Big to Jail*, 25–26, 40–44; Taibbi, *The Divide*, 21–23; Markoff, "Arthur Andersen."

82. Garrett, *Too Big to Jail*, 5–7, 12–17, 67–70, 148–50, 292–94.

83. Richman, "Federal White Collar Sentencing," 56–57; Eisinger, *The Chickenshit Club*, 51; Skeel and Stuntz, "Christianity," 826.

84. "President Bush's Comments."

85. Lichtblau, Johnston, and Nixon, "F.B.I. Struggles"; Pontell, Black, and Geis, "Too Big to Fail," 1–2.

86. Skeel and Stuntz, "Christianity," 826–27.

87. Norris, "Oversight for Auditor of Madoff."

88. Pontell, Black, and Geis cite Madoff as an example of the state choosing its corporate prosecutions for strategic public relations purposes. See Pontell, Black, and Geis, "Too Big to Fail," 3.

89. Eisinger, *The Chickenshit Club*, 233–36.

90. US House Committee on Financial Services, *Assessing the Madoff Ponzi Scheme*, 8, 65.

91. Hagan, *Who Are the Criminals?*, 180–99.

92. Holland, "Hundreds of Wall Street Execs."

93. Eisinger, *The Chickenshit Club*, 167–85, esp. 172–74 (on the Corporate Fraud Task Force).

94. Grant and Wilson, "Preface"; Barak, *Theft of a Nation*, 133–36; Ydstie, "5 Years Later."

95. Dodd used this language recurrently. See US Senate Committee on Banking, Housing, and Urban Affairs, *Mortgage Market Turmoil*, 1, *Recent Developments*, 22, *Modernizing*, 2, and *Consumer Protections*, 4.

96. US Senate Committee on Banking, Housing, and Urban Affairs, *Mortgage Market Turmoil*, 8 (Crapo quote), 42 (Samuels quote).

97. US Senate Committee on Banking, Housing, and Urban Affairs, *Creating a Consumer Financial Protection Agency*, 69 (Blumenthal quote), 79 (Yingling quote).

98. US Senate Committee on Banking, Housing, and Urban Affairs, *The State of the Securities Markets*, 4.

99. US House Committee on Financial Services, *Systemic Risk*, 1, 13.

100. For an outstanding summary of the law and major critiques of it that shapes the analysis in this chapter, see Barak, *Theft of a Nation*, 139–50.

101. Krawiec, "Don't 'Screw Joe the Plummer,'" 59, 63, 67.

102. Hamilton, "Banks Get Easier Volcker Rule."

103. Holland, "Hundreds of Wall Street Execs"; Hennelly, "Dodd-Frank at 5"; Garrett, *Too Big to Jail*, 37, 82, 267–80. For an overview of deferred prosecution agreements, see Garrett, *Too Big to Jail*, 45–80.

104. Dimon quoted in Foroohar, *Makers and Takers*, 304.

105. "Transcript of Obama's Press Conference."

106. Barak, *Theft of a Nation*, 154–55 (discussing Obama's statements).

107. Financial Crisis Inquiry Commission, "Financial Crisis Inquiry Report," 12–15, 160–64, 170–74, 291–92.

108. US House Committee on Oversight and Government Reform, *The Financial Crisis*, 55, 64.

109. Eisinger, *The Chickenshit Club*, 252, 259, 262 for quotes. For a full summary and an analysis of this story, see ibid., 244–68.

110. Thompson, "Why Are You Pissing in Our Face"; Norris, "She's a Candidate for a Job She Devised."

111. Calabria, Michel, and Peirce, "Reforming the Financial Regulators," 135–39.

112. Abbott and Zywicki, "How Congress Should Protect Consumers' Finances," 288, 290, 292.

113. Gyauch-Lewis, "An Overview"; Liptak, "Supreme Court Skeptical."

114. Taub, "Bank Bailouts"; Rugaber, "Federal Reserve."

115. Eisinger, "Regulatory Failure 101"; Smialek, "Trump-Era Rollback."

116. Kupiec, "Bank Regulators."

117. Yaffe-Bellany, "A Crypto Emperor's Vision"; Brewster, "A Young Crypto."

118. Yaffe-Bellany, "How Sam Bankman-Fried's Crypto Empire Collapsed"; Hyatt, "Sam Bankman-Fried's Donations."

119. Piper, "Sam Bankman-Fried."

120. Cohen, "Sam Bankman-Fried Trial Jury"; Yaffe-Bellany, Goldstein, and Moreno, "Sam Bankman-Fried Is Found Guilty."

121. Chozick, "Liz Holmes."

Chapter Eight

1. "Statement from the Press Secretary Regarding Executive Grants of Clemency."

2. "Read the Full Transcript"; "Debate Transcript."

3. Chapter 1 discusses the few exceptions to this trend, though none of those exceptions address this relationship with the lens and historical scope adopted here. See Braithwaite, "What's Wrong"; Hagan, *Who Are the Criminals?*; Harcourt, *The Illusion of Free Markets*; and Reiman and Leighton, *The Rich Get Richer and the Poor Get Prison*.

4. Garland, *The Culture of Control*; Tonry, *Sentencing Fragments*, and *Punishing Race*; Beckett, *Making Crime Pay*.

5. Skowronek, *Building a New American State*; Kolko, *Railroads and Regulation*; Berk, *Alternative Tracks*; Bensel, *The Political Economy of American Industrialization*; DeCanio, *Democracy and the Origins of the American Regulatory State*.

6. Shapiro, *Wayward Capitalists*; Mann, *Defending White-Collar Crime*; Wheeler, Mann, and Sarat, *Sitting in Judgment*; Friedrichs, *Trusted Criminals*; Garrett, *Too Big to Jail*; Tillman, Pontell, and Black, *Financial Crime and Crises*; Foroohar, *Makers and Takers*.

7. Hagan, *Who Are the Criminals?*; Harcourt, *The Illusion of Free Markets*; Reiman and Leighton, *The Rich Get Richer and the Poor Get Prison*.

8. For a sample of books arguing for such sweeping and comprehensive reforms, see Tonry, *Punishing Race*, and *Sentencing Fragments*; Gottschalk, *Caught*; Alexander, *The New Jim Crow*; Simon, *Governing through Crime*; Murakawa, *The First Civil Right*; and Pfaff, *Locked In*.

9. Tonry, *Sentencing Fragments*, 50–63, esp. 57–62.

10. For a worldwide overview of these techniques, see Tonry, *Sentencing Fragments*, 60–61, and "Equality and Human Dignity," 487.

11. Austin et al., *Unlocking America*; Aos, Miller, and Drake, *Evidence Based Adult Corrections Programs*; Gottschalk, *Caught*, 83–85.

12. Gottschalk, *Caught*, 84; Western, "The Penal System and the Labor Market"; Bushway, "Labor Markets and Crime"; Raphael and Weiman, "The Impact of Local Labor-Market Conditions."

13. Gottschalk, *Caught*, 94–97; Butts and Schiraldi, "Recidivism Reconsidered," esp. 11–12; Petteruti and Fenster, "Finding Direction," especially 33–35.

14. Beckett and Herbert, *Banished*; National Law Center on Homelessness and Poverty, "No Safe Place."

15. Gottschalk, *Caught*, 94–97; Butts and Schiraldi, "Recidivism Reconsidered."

16. Gottschalk, *Caught*, 95; Cullen and Johnson, "Rehabilitation and Treatment Programs"; Austin et al., *Unlocking America*.

17. Tonry, "Equality and Human Dignity," 464–65; Van Zyl Smit and Snacken, *Principles of European Prison Law and Policy*; Whitman, *Harsh Justice*; Simon, "Dignity and Its Discontents," and "The Second Coming of Dignity"; Henry, "The Jurisprudence of Dignity."

18. Logan, *The Ex Post Facto Clause*, 180–81; Gallant, *The Principle of Legality*, 59–60, 241–43.

19. For analyses of these risks from scholars sympathetic to dignity, see Simon, "The Second Coming of Dignity"; and Whitman, *Harsh Justice*.

20. Simon, "The Second Coming of Dignity," and "Dignity and Its Discontents"; Tonry, "Equality and Human Dignity."

21. Braithwaite and Ayres, *Responsive Regulation*, chap. 2. Also see Paternoster, "Deterring Corporate Crime"; and Schell-Busey, Simpson, Rorie, and Alper, "What Works?"

22. Garrett, *Too Big to Jail*; Pontell, Black, and Geis, "Too Big to Fail."

23. Yeager, "The Elusive Deterrence of Corporate Crime"; Schell-Busey, Simpson, Rorie, and Alper, "What Works?"; Haugh, "Exactly Wrong"; Foroohar, *Makers and Takers*; Tillman, Pontell, and Black, *Financial Crime and Crises*.

24. Eagan and Brown, "Enforcement"; Levy, "Spending Money to Make Money."

25. Barak, *Theft of a Nation*, 158–59.

26. Boyle, Beaty, and Marsano, "To Reverse Decades of Neglect."

27. Wilson, "The United States," 56.

28. Eagan and Brown, "Enforcement."

29. Taub, *Big Dirty Money*, 218–19.

30. Sutherland repeatedly makes this point in *White-Collar Crime*.

31. Barak, *Theft of a Nation*, 158–59; Wilson, "The United States," 53–57.

32. American Bankers Association, "Enforcement Action Database."

33. Eagan and Brown note this, explaining that not all agencies' enforcement data are clear and easily interpreted. See Eagan and Brown, "Enforcement."

34. On the "pathological" nature of the profit driven corporation, see Bakan, *The Corporation*.

35. Gottschalk powerfully makes this distinction. See Gottschalk, *Caught*, 258–82, esp. 276–79.

36. Miller, *The Myth of Mob Rule*; Forman, *Locking Up Our Own*; Fortner, *Black Silent Majority*; McCall, Land, and Parker, "An Empirical Assessment"; Sampson, Wilson, and Katz, "Reassessing."

37. Gottschalk, *Caught*; Western, *Punishment and Inequality*; Alexander, *The New Jim Crow*; Weaver and Lerman, *Arresting Citizenship*.

38. Beckett and Murakawa, "Mapping the Shadow Carceral State"; Kohler-Hausmann, *Misdemeanorland*.

39. Beckett and Herbert, *Banished*; Beckett and Murakawa, "Mapping the Shadow Carceral State"; Logan, *The Ex Post Facto Clause*.

40. Rackhill, "Printzlein's Legacy."

41. Braithwaite, "What's Wrong," 17–18; Stuntz, *The Collapse of American Criminal Justice*, 176–81.

42. US Food and Drug Administration, "Family Smoking Prevention," and "The Real Cost Campaign"; US Center for Disease Control and Prevention, "Regulation"; Bonnie, Stratton, and Wallace, *Ending the Tobacco Problem*.

43. Kamin, "Marijuana Regulation in the United States."

44. Gottschalk, *Caught*, 84; Western, "The Penal System and the Labor Market"; Bushway, "Labor Markets and Crime"; Raphael and Weiman, "The Impact of Local Labor-Market Conditions."

45. On unemployment and crime, see Raphael and Winter-Ebmer, "The Effect of Unemployment"; Falk and Zweimüller, "Unemployment and Right-Wing Extremist Crime"; and Freeman, "Crime and the Employment of Disadvantaged Youths." On jobs programs, see Tcherneva, "The Federal Jobs Guarantee," esp. 62–68 (on crime and the preventative benefits of jobs programs).

46. Pandiani, "The Crime Control Corps"; Johnson, Kantor, and Fishback, "Striking at the Roots of Crime."

47. Randolph and Rustin, "A 'Freedom Budget,'" 8–15 (quote 14).

48. Pressley and Stein, "A Federal Job Guarantee"; Rader and Guadron, "Running on a Jobs Guarantee."

49. Gottschalk, *Caught*, 96; Petteruti and Fenster, "Finding Direction," esp. 33–39; Butts and Schiraldi, "Recidivism Reconsidered."

50. On looking to European models to reconceive American parole and probation as forms of social work rather than as techniques of surveillance and punishment, see Petteruti and Fenster, "Finding Direction," esp. 33–35.

51. Hanna, "The Crisis Next Time."

52. Kress, "Solving Banking's 'Too Big to Manage' Problem," esp. 202–6.

53. Hanna, "The Crisis Next Time," 28–29. For more background on reinstating Glass-Steagall, see Kress, "Solving Banking's 'Too Big to Manage' Problem," 206–9.

54. Allen, "Too Big to Fail"; Hubbard, Scott, and Zingales, "Banks Need Fewer Carrots and More Sticks"; "MIT's Johnson Says Too-Big-to-Fail Banks Will Spark New Crisis."

55. Bartley, "The Accountable Capitalism Act."

56. Clark and Babson, "How Benefit Corporations."

57. Bartley, "The Accountable Capitalism Act."

58. Laufer and Caulfield, "Wall Street and Progressivism," esp. 47–50.

59. Yglesias, "Elizabeth Warren."

60. Hanna, "The Crisis Next Time," 33–34, 39–40; European Bank for Reconstruction and Development, *Transition Report*, 68–89.

61. For quotes, see Hanna, "The Crisis Next Time," 33, 44. On the BND and the argument for long-term public banking in the United States, see ibid., 39–45. For more arguments for public banking, see Alperovitz, "Wall Street Is Too Big to Regulate"; and Day, "The Case for a State-Owned Bank."

62. One how public banks can provide enhanced financial stability, see European Bank for Reconstruction and Development, *Transition Report*, 76–77; Marshall and Rochon, "Public Banking"; and Hanna, "The Crisis Next Time."

63. Herndon and Paul, "A Public Banking Option"; European Bank for Reconstruction and Development, *Transition Report*, 71–74.

64. Hanna, "The Crisis Next Time," 41–44, 48; Gowan, "Permanently Nationalize the Banks during the Next Crisis."

65. European Bank for Reconstruction and Development, *Transition Report*, 75–76; Hanna, "The Crisis Next Time," 41–43.

66. Hanna discusses this point about the socioeconomic benefits of public banks that cannot be measured as profits. See Hanna, "The Crisis Next Time," 41.

67. Hanna proposes that during public takeovers nationalized banks' commercial and investing activities could be separated, with the former staying under permanent public ownership and the latter being returned to the private sector under strict regulations. See Hanna, "The Crisis Next Time," 47–48.

Works Cited

Abbott, Alden, and Todd Zywicki. "How Congress Should Protect Consumers' Finances." In *Prosperity Unleashed: Smarter Financial Regulation*, ed. Norbert J. Michel, 287–94. Washington, DC: Heritage Foundation, 2017. https://thf-reports.s3.amazonaws.com/2017/Pros perityUnleashed.pdf.

Administrative Office of the United States Courts. *The Presentence Investigation Report*. Washington, DC: US Government Printing Office, 1965.

"Adult Probation." Right on Crime, n.d. https://rightoncrime.com/initiatives/adult-probation.

Albiston, Catherine. "The Rule of Law and the Litigation Process: The Paradox of Losing by Winning." *Law and Society Review* 33, no. 4 (1999): 869–910.

Albrecht, Adalbert. "Cesare Lombroso: A Glance at His Life Work." *Journal of the American Institute of Criminal Law and Criminology* 1, no. 2 (1910): 71–83.

Alexander, Michelle. *The New Jim Crow: Mass Incarceration in the Age of Colorblindness*. New York: New Press, 2012.

Allen, Francis. *The Decline of the Rehabilitative Ideal: Penal Policy and Social Purpose*. New Haven, CT: Yale University Press, 1981.

Allen, Karma. "'Too Big to Fail, Too Big to Exist': Bernie Sanders Takes Aim at Banks with New Bill." *ABC News*, October 4, 2018. https://abcnews.go.com/Politics/big-fail-big-exist-bernie -sanders-takes-aim/story?id=58276622.

Alperovitz, Gar. "Wall Street Is Too Big to Regulate." *New York Times*, July 22, 2012. https://www .nytimes.com/2012/07/23/opinion/banks-that-are-too-big-to-regulate-should-be-national ized.html.

American Bankers Association. "Enforcement Action Database." n.d. https://www.aba.com /banking-topics/compliance/enforcement-action-database.

American Bar Foundation. *The Administration of Criminal Justice in the United States: Plan for a Survey*. Chicago: American Bar Foundation, 1955.

Anderson, Jeffrey H. "Why Trump Should Oppose 'Criminal-Justice Reform.'" Hudson Institute, May 18, 2016. https://www.hudson.org/research/12506-why-trump-should-oppose-crimi nal-justice-reform.

Angwin, Julia, Julia Larson, Surya Mattu, and Lauren Kirchner. "Machine Bias." *ProPublica*,

May 23, 2016. https://www.propublica.org/article/machine-bias-risk-assessments-in-criminal -sentencing.

Aos, Steve, Marna Miller, and Elizabeth Drake. *Evidence Based Adult Corrections Programs: What Works and What Does Not*. Olympia: Washington State Institute for Public Policy, 2006.

Arnold, Thurman. *The Bottlenecks of Business*. New York: Reynal & Hitchcock, 1940.

Associated Press. "Nashville Assistant DA Fired amid Reports of Sterilization in Plea Deals." *CBS News*, April 1, 2015. http://www.cbsnews.com/news/nashville-prosecutor-fired-amid-reports -of-sterilization-in-plea-deals.

Aurand, Harold W. *From the Molly Maguires to the United Mine Workers: The Social Ecology of an Industrial Union, 1869–1897*. Philadelphia: Temple University Press, 1971.

Austin, James, Todd Clear, Troy Duster, David Greenberg, John Irwin, Candace McCoy, Alan Mobley, Barbara Owen, and Joshua Page. *Unlocking America: Why and How to Reduce America's Prison Population*. JFA Institute, 2007. https://www.prisonpolicy.org/scans/jfa /UnlockingAmerica.pdf.

Bakan, Joel. *The Corporation: The Pathological Pursuit of Profit and Power*. London: Constable, 2005.

"Ball and Chain for Tramps: Women Vagrants to Get Same Treatment as the Males." *Los Angeles Times*, January 28, 1901.

Barak, Gregg. *Theft of a Nation: Wall Street Looting and Federal Regulatory Colluding*. Lanham, MD: Rowman & Littlefield, 2012.

Bardach, Eugene, and Robert A. Kagan. *Going by the Book: The Problem of Regulatory Unreason-ableness*. New Brunswick, NJ: Transaction, 2002.

Barr, Martin. *Mental Defectives: Their History, Treatment and Training*. Philadelphia: P. Blakis-ton's Son, 1904.

Bartley, Carew S. "The Accountable Capitalism Act in Context and Its Implications for Legal Ethics." *Georgetown Journal of Legal Ethics* 33, no. 3 (2020): 373–96.

"Baumes Talks to Bankers: New Criminal Laws Are for Society's Protection, He Says." *New York Times*, January 18, 1928.

Baumgartner, Frank R., Jeffrey M. Berry, Marie Hojnacki, Beth L. Leech, and David C. Kimball. *Lobbying and Policy Change: Who Wins, Who Loses, and Why*. Chicago: University of Chicago Press, 2009.

Bean, Robert. "The Negro Brain." *Century Magazine*, September 1906, 778–84.

Beccaria, Cesare. *On Crimes and Punishments*. 1764. Translated by David Young. Indianapolis: Hackett, 1986.

Beckett, Katherine. *Making Crime Pay: Law and Order in Contemporary American Politics*. New York: Oxford University Press, 1997.

Beckett, Katherine, and Steve Herbert. *Banished: The New Social Control in Urban America*. New York: Oxford University Press, 2009.

Beckett, Katherine, and Naomi Murakawa. "Mapping the Shadow Carceral State: Toward an In-stitutionally Capacious Approach to Punishment." *Theoretical Criminology* 16, no. 2 (2012): 221–44.

Béland, Daniel, and Robert Henry Cox. "Introduction: Ideas and Politics." In *Ideas and Politics in Social Science Research*, ed. Daniel Béland and Robert Henry Cox, 3–20. New York: Ox-ford University Press, 2011.

Bensel, Richard Franklin. *The Political Economy of American Industrialization, 1877–1900*. New York: Cambridge University Press, 2000.

———. *Yankee Leviathan: The Origins of Central State Authority in America, 1859–1877*. New York: Cambridge University Press, 1990.

Benson, Michael L., and Francis T. Cullen. *Combating Corporate Crime: Local Prosecutors at Work*. Boston: Northeastern University Press, 1998.

Bentwick, K. K. "Street Begging as a Fine Art." *North American Review* 158 (1894): 125–28.

Berk, Gerald. *Alternative Tracks: The Constitution of American Industrial Order, 1865–1917*. Baltimore: Johns Hopkins University Press, 1994.

———. *Louis D. Brandeis and the Making of Regulated Competition, 1900–1932*. New York: Cambridge University Press, 2009.

Berle, A. A. "Letter from A. A. Berle Jr. to Joseph Kennedy." July 30, 1934. https://www.sechistorical.org/collection/papers/1930/1934_07_30_Berle_to_JPK.pdf.

Berman, Sheri. "Ideology, History, and Politics." In *Ideas and Politics in Social Science Research*, ed. Daniel Béland and Robert Henry Cox, 105–26. New York: Oxford University Press, 2011.

Bernstein, Marver H. *Regulating Business by Independent Commission*. Princeton, NJ: Princeton University Press, 1955.

Bernstein, Michael. "A Brief History of the American Economic Association." *American Journal of Economics and Sociology* 67, no. 5 (2008): 1007–23.

Beverly, Robert. "A Comparative Analysis of Base Expectancy Tables for Selected Subpopulations of California Youth Authority Wards." Research Report. Sacramento: California State Department of the Youth Authority, 1968.

"Biopsychosocial Criminology." n.d. https://bpscrim.org.

Black, Edwin. *War against the Weak: Eugenics and America's Campaign to Create a Master Race*. New York: Four Walls Eight Windows, 2003.

Block, Fred. "The Ruling Class Does Not Rule: Notes on the Marxist Theory of the State." *Socialist Revolution* 33 (1977): 6–28.

Blyth, Mark, Oddny Helgadottir, and William Kring. "Ideas and Historical Institutionalism." In *The Oxford Handbook of Historical Institutionalism*, ed. Orfeo Fioretos, Tulia Falleti, and Adam Sheingate, 142–62. New York: Oxford University Press, 2016.

Boas, Franz. *The Mind of Primitive Man*. New York: Macmillan, 1911.

Boies, Henry M. *Prisoners and Paupers: A Study of the Abnormal Increase of Criminals, and the Public Burden of Pauperism in the United States: The Causes and Remedies*. New York: Putnam, 1893.

———. *The Science of Penology: The Defence of Society against Crime*. New York: G. P. Putnam's Sons, 1901.

Bonnie, Richard, Kathleen Stratton, and Robert Wallace, eds. *Ending the Tobacco Problem: A Blueprint for the Nation*. Washington, DC: National Academies Press, 2007.

Boyle, K. J., Andrea Beaty, and Emma Marsano. "To Reverse Decades of Neglect, Antitrust Agencies Need Robust Budgets." *Revolving Door Project* (blog), April 19, 2023. https://therevolvingdoorproject.org/to-reverse-decades-of-neglect-antitrust-agencies-need-robust-budgets.

Brace, Charles Loring. *The Dangerous Classes of New York, and Twenty Years' Work among Them*. New York: Wynkoop & Hallenbeck, 1880.

———. "Mendicity." In *Johnson's New Illustrated Universal Cyclopedia*, 3:410–11. New York, 1877.

Braithwaite, John. "In Search of Donald Campbell: Mix and Multimethods." *Criminology and Public Policy* 15, no. 2 (2016): 417–37.

———. "What's Wrong with the Sociology of Punishment?" *Theoretical Criminology* 7, no. 1 (2003): 5–28.

Braithwaite, John, and Ian Ayres. *Responsive Regulation: Transcending the Deregulation Debate.* Oxford: Oxford University Press, 1992.

Brandeis, Louis D. "Competition." *American Legal News* 24 (1913): 5–14.

———. *Other People's Money: And How the Bankers Use It.* New York: F. A. Stokes, 1914.

Breslow, Jason. "Were Bankers Jailed in Past Financial Crises?" *PBS Frontline*, January 22, 2013. https://www.pbs.org/wgbh/frontline/article/were-bankers-jailed-in-past-financial-crises.

Brewer, W. H. "What Shall We Do with Our Tramps." *New Englander and Yale Review* 37 (July 1878): 521–32.

Brewster, Freddy. "A Young Crypto Billionaire's Political Agenda Goes Well beyond Pandemic Preparedness." *Los Angeles Times*, August 12, 2022. https://www.latimes.com/politics/story/2022-08-12/sam-bankman-fried-ftx-political-donations.

Brinkley, Alan. "The New Deal and the Idea of the State." In *The Rise and Fall of the New Deal Order, 1930–1980*, ed. Steve Fraser and Gary Gerstle, 85–121. Princeton, NJ: Princeton University Press, 1989.

———. "When Washington Took on Wall Street." *Vanity Fair*, June 2010. https://www.vanityfair.com/news/2010/06/pecora-201006.

Brinkley, Alan, and David Woolner. "Franklin Roosevelt and the Progressive Tradition." In *Progressivism in America: Past, Present, and Future*, ed. David Woolner and Jack Thompson, 17–29. New York: Oxford University Press, 2015.

Brinton, Daniel. "The Aims of Anthropology." *Science* 2, no. 35 (1895): 241–52.

Bristow, Benjamin H. "Statement Before the American Bar Association." In *Annual Report: Including Proceedings of the Annual Meeting*, 3:81–107. Philadelphia: E. C. Markley & Son, 1880.

Brockway, Zebulon. "An Absolute Indeterminate Sentence." In *Fifty-Ninth Annual Report of the Prison Association of New York for the Year 1903*. Albany, NY: Oliver A. Quayle State Legislative Printer, 1904.

———. "Crime: Annual Address Before the National Prison Congress, 1898." In *Papers on Penology*, 4:76–96. Elmira: New York State Reformatory at Elmira, 1899.

———. *Fifty Years of Prison Service: An Autobiography.* New York: Charities Publication Committee, 1912.

———. "The Ideal of a True Prison System for a State." In *Transactions of the National Congress on Penitentiary and Reformatory Discipline: Held at Cincinnati, Ohio, October 12–18, 1870*, ed. E. C. Wines, 38–66. Albany, NY: Weed Parsons, 1871.

———. "The Incorrigible Criminal: What Is He, and How Should He Be Treated?" In *The National Prison Association of the United States of America, 5th and 6th Report of Proceedings*, 105–7. Boston: Geo. E. Crosby, 1886.

———. "Prisoners and Their Reformation." In *Prisoners and Reformatories at Home and Abroad, Being the Transactions of the International Penitentiary Congress, Held in London, July 3–13 1872*, ed. Edwin Pears, 612–62. London: Longman, Greens, 1872.

———. "Reformatory Prison Discipline—What Is It, and by What Agencies to Be Attained?" In *Transactions of the Third National Prison Reform Congress*, ed. E. C. Wines, 205–16. New York: Office of the Association, 1874.

Brown, George. "The Treatment of the Recidivist in the United States." *Canadian Bar Review* 23 (1945): 640–83.

Brown, Wendy. *Undoing the Demos: Neoliberalism's Stealth Revolution.* New York: Zone, 2015.

Browning, Frank, and John Gerassi. *The American Way of Crime.* New York: G. P. Putnam's Sons, 1980.

Bruce, Robert V. *1877: Year of Violence*. Indianapolis: Bobbs-Merrill, 1959.

Bryan, William Jennings. "The Trusts Have Won." *The Commoner* (Lincoln, NE), May 26, 1911.

Burgason, Kyle. "Wickersham, George." In *The Social History of Crime and Punishment in America: An Encyclopedia*, 1937–39. Thousand Oaks, CA: Sage Reference, 2012.

Bushway, Shawn. "Labor Markets and Crime." In *Crime and Public Policy*, ed. James Wilson and Joan Petersilia, 183–209. New York: Oxford University Press, 2011.

Butts, Jeffrey A., and Vincent Schiraldi. "Recidivism Reconsidered: Preserving the Community Justice Mission of Community Corrections." Cambridge, MA: Program in Criminal Justice Policy and Management, Harvard Kennedy School, 2018. https://www.hks.harvard.edu/sites/default/files/centers/wiener/programs/pcj/files/recidivism_reconsidered.pdf.

Byrd, Robert. *The Senate, 1789–1989: Addresses on the History of the United States Senate*. Edited by Mary Sharon Hall. Vol. 1. Washington, DC: US Government Printing Office, 1988.

Cabot Lodge, Henry. "Lynch Law and Unrestricted Immigration." *North American Review* 152, no. 414 (May 1891): 602–12.

Calabria, Mark A., Norbert J. Michel, and Hester Peirce. "Reforming the Financial Regulators." In *Prosperity Unleashed: Smarter Financial Regulation*, ed. Norbert J. Michel, 129–54. Washington, DC: Heritage Foundation, 2017. https://thf-reports.s3.amazonaws.com/2017/ProsperityUnleashed.pdf.

Calavita, Kitty, Henry Pontell, and Robert Tillman. *Big Money Crime: Fraud and Politics in the Savings and Loan Crisis*. Berkeley: University of California Press, 1997.

Calder, James D. *The Origins and Development of Federal Crime Policy: Herbert Hoover's Initiatives*. Westport, CT: Praeger, 1993.

California Department of Corrections. "Biennial Report for the Period Ending December 1, 1948." Sacramento, CA, 1948.

———. "Biennial Report of the Department of Corrections." Sacramento, CA, December 1, 1946.

———. "The Policies, Organization, and Procedures for Classification in the Department of Corrections in the State of California." Sacramento, CA, 1951.

———. "Progress Report of the Department of Corrections, May 1, 1944–December 1, 1944." Sacramento, CA, 1944.

California Department of Corrections. Adult Authority. "Parole: Philosophy, Policies and Programs." Sacramento, CA, 1961.

Campbell, John L., and Ove K. Pedersen. "Policy Ideas, Knowledge Regimes and Comparative Political Economy." *Socio-Economic Review* 13, no. 4 (2015): 167–90.

Cardozo, Benjamin. *The Growth of the Law*. New Haven, CT: Yale University Press, 1924.

———. "What Medicine Can Do for Law." *Bulletin of the New York Academy of Medicine* 5, no. 7 (1929): 581–607.

Carnegie, Andrew. "Wealth." *North American Review* 148, no. 391 (June 1889): 653–64.

Carosso, Vincent P. *Investment Banking in America: A History*. Cambridge, MA: Harvard University Press, 1970.

Carpenter, Daniel. *The Forging of Bureaucratic Autonomy: Reputations, Networks, and Policy Innovation in Executive Agencies, 1862–1928*. Princeton, NJ: Princeton University Press, 2001.

Carper, N. Gordon. "Martin Tabert: Martyr of an Era." *Florida Historical Quarterly* 52, no. 2 (1973): 115–31.

Carrington, Charles. "Sterilization of Habitual Criminals." In *Proceedings of the Annual Congress of the American Prison Association*, 174–77. Indianapolis: Wm. B. Burford, 1908.

Cate, Sarah. *The Myth of the Community Fix: Inequality and the Politics of Youth Punishment.* New York: Oxford University Press, 2023.

Chambliss, William J. *Power, Politics, and Crime.* Boulder, CO: Westview, 1999.

———. "The Saints and the Rough-Necks." *Society* 11 (1973): 24–31.

———. "A Sociological Analysis of the Law of Vagrancy." *Social Problems* 12, no. 1 (Summer 1964): 67–77.

Chandler, Alfred. *The Visible Hand: The Managerial Revolution in American Business.* Cambridge, MA: Harvard University Press, 1977.

Chappell, Richard, and Victor Evjen. "The Presentence Investigation Report." Publication 101. Washington, DC: Administrative Office of the United States Courts, 1943.

Chernow, Ron. "Where Is Our Ferdinand Pecora?" *New York Times*, January 5, 2009. https://www.nytimes.com/2009/01/06/opinion/06chernow.html.

Chozick, Amy. "Liz Holmes Wants You to Forget about Elizabeth." *New York Times*, May 7, 2023. https://www.nytimes.com/2023/05/07/business/elizabeth-holmes-theranos-interview.html.

Christian, Frank. "The Irresponsible Social Offender." Elmira: New York State Reformatory, 1920. A0636-78, box 1, New York State Archives.

———. "The Management of Penal Institutions." Elmira: New York State Reformatory, 1921. A0636-78, box 1, New York State Archives.

———. "Statistics and Comments." Elmira: New York State Reformatory, 1921. A0636-78, box 1, New York State Archives.

Claeys, Gregory. "The 'Survival of the Fittest' and the Origins of Social Darwinism." *Journal of the History of Ideas* 61, no. 2 (2000): 223–40.

Clark, William H., Jr, and Elizabeth K. Babson. "How Benefit Corporations Are Redefining the Purpose of Business Corporations." *William Mitchell Law Review* 38, no. 2 (2012): 817–51.

Clements, Kendrick, and William Cheezum. *Woodrow Wilson.* Washington, DC: CQ Press, 2003.

Cleveland Crime Commission. *Criminal Justice in Cleveland: Reports of the Cleveland Foundation Survey of the Administration of Criminal Justice in Cleveland, Ohio.* Cleveland, OH: Cleveland Foundation, 1922.

Coen, David, Wyn Grant, and Graham Wilson. "Political Science: Perspectives on Business and Government." In *The Oxford Handbook of Business and Government*, ed. David Coen, Wyn Grant, and Graham Wilson, 9–34. Oxford: Oxford University Press, 2010.

Coffee, John C., Jr. "The Future of Sentencing Reform: Emerging Legal Issues in the Individualization of Justice." *Michigan Law Review* 73, no. 8 (1974): 1361–1462.

Cohen, Adam. *Imbeciles: The Supreme Court, American Eugenics, and the Sterilization of Carrie Buck.* New York: Penguin, 2016.

Cohen, Lizbeth. *A Consumers' Republic: The Politics of Mass Consumption in Postwar America.* New York: Vintage, 2003.

Cohen, Luc. "Sam Bankman-Fried Trial Jury Sees His Profane Messages about Regulators." Reuters, October 18, 2023. https://www.reuters.com/legal/sam-bankman-fried-trial-jury-sees-his-profane-message-about-regulators-2023-10-18/.

Collins, Robert M. *The Business Response to Keynes, 1929–1964.* New York: Columbia University Press, 1981.

Commons, John. *Races and Immigrants in America.* New York: Macmillan, 1907.

———. *Social Reform and the Church.* New York: T. Y. Crowell, 1894.

Conference of Boards of Public Charities. *Proceedings of the Conference of Charities*. Boston: A. Williams, 1877.

Congressional Research Service. "Summary: H.R. 2313—An Act to Amend the Federal Trade Commission Act." May 1, 1980. https://www.congress.gov/bill/96th-congress/house-bill/2313.

Conrad, John Phillips. "Correctional Treatment." In *Encyclopedia of Crime and Justice*, ed. Sanford H. Kadish, 1:266–77. New York: Free Press, 1983.

"The Convict Camps of Alabama and the Vagrancy Laws of Michigan." *Chicago Daily Tribune*, February 8, 1883.

Cook, Brian. *The Fourth Branch: Reconstructing the Administrative State for the Commercial Republic*. Lawrence: University Press of Kansas, 2021.

Cooke, Theodore. "The Advisability of Laws Making It Compulsory That Every Prisoner Charged with Any Offense against the State in Any Court of Justice Be Examined Before Trial by a Physician." In *Proceedings of the Annual Congress of the American Prison Association*, 235–53. Indianapolis: Wm. B. Burford, 1909.

"Court Treatment of General Recidivist Statutes." *Columbia Law Review* 48 (1948): 238–53.

Cowie, Jefferson. *The Great Exception: The New Deal and the Limits of American Politics*. Princeton, NJ: Princeton University Press, 2017.

Cox, Edward, Robert Fellmeth, and John Schulz. *"The Nader Report" on the Federal Trade Commission*. New York: Richard W. Baron, 1969.

Crane, Daniel A. "All I Really Need to Know about Antitrust I Learned in 1912." *Iowa Law Review* 100 (2015): 2025–38.

Cressey, Donald. Foreword to *White-Collar Crime*, by Edwin Sutherland, iii–xii. New York: Holt, Rinehart & Winston, 1961.

———. "The Poverty of Theory in Corporate Crime Research." In *Advances in Criminological Theory*, ed. Williams S. Laufer and Freda Adler, 1:31–55. New Brunswick, NJ: Transaction, 1989.

"Crime and Its Cure: Z. R. Brockway on Methods of To-Day and the Future." *Washington Post*, April 20, 1901.

"Crime and Vagrancy." *New York Times*, May 2, 1907.

Croall, Hazel. *Understanding White Collar Crime*. Philadelphia: Open University Press, 2001.

———. "What Is Known and What Should Be Known about White-Collar Crime Victimization?" In *The Oxford Handbook of White-Collar Crime*, ed. Shanna R. Van Slyke, Michael L. Benson, and Francis T. Cullen, 59–77. New York: Oxford University Press, 2016.

Crossley, Mary. "The 'Genetics Defense': Hurdles and Pressures." In *Genetics and Criminality: The Potential Misuse of Scientific Information in Court*, ed. Jeffrey Botkin, William McMahon, and Leslie Pickering Francis, 174–81. Washington, DC: American Psychological Association, 1999.

Cullen, Francis, and Cheryl Lero Johnson. "Rehabilitation and Treatment Programs." In *Crime and Public Policy*, 293–344. New York: Oxford University Press, 2011.

Darlington, Ralph. *Syndicalism and the Transition to Communism: An International Comparative Analysis*. Burlington, VT: Ashgate, 2008.

Davenport, Charles. *Eugenics: The Science of Human Improvement by Better Breeding*. New York: Henry Holt, 1910.

———. *Heredity in Relation to Eugenics*. New York: Henry Holt, 1915.

Day, Meagan. "The Case for a State-Owned Bank." *Jacobin*, August 21, 2018. https://jacobinmag
.com/2018/08/public-state-owned-bank-finance-nationalized-banking.

"Debate Transcript: Trump, Biden Final Presidential Debate Moderated by Kristen Welker." *USA Today*, October 23, 2020. https://www.usatoday.com/story/news/politics/elections/2020/10/23
/debate-transcript-trump-biden-final-presidential-debate-nashville/3740152001.

De Bedts, Ralph. "The First Chairmen of the Securities and Exchange Commission: Successful
Ambassadors of the New Deal to Wall Street." *American Journal of Economics and Sociology*
23, no. 2 (1964): 165–78.

DeCanio, Samuel. *Democracy and the Origins of the American Regulatory State*. New Haven, CT:
Yale University Press, 2015.

DeLisi, Matt, John Wright, and Rafael A. Mangual. "Psychology, Not Circumstances: Understanding Crime as Entitlement." Manhattan Institute Issue Brief, June 2022. https://media4
.manhattan-institute.org/sites/default/files/DeLisi-Wright-Mangual-Understanding-Crime
-As-Entitlement-r11152022.pdf.

Dempsey, Paul Stephen. "The Rise and Fall of the Interstate Commerce Commission: The Tor-
tuous Path from Regulation to Deregulation of America's Infrastructure." *Marquette Law
Review* 95, no. 4 (2012): 1151–89.

DeMuth, Christopher. "Trump vs. the Deep Regulatory State." Hudson Institute, November 17,
2017. https://www.hudson.org/economics/trump-vs-the-deep-regulatory-state.

Denney, Matthew. "'To Wage a War': Crime, Race, and State Making in the Age of FDR." *Studies
in American Political Development* 35, no. 1 (2021): 16–56.

DePastino, Todd. *Citizen Hobo: How a Century of Homelessness Shaped America*. Chicago: University of Chicago Press, 2003.

Dewey, John. "The Historic Background of Corporate Legal Personality." *Yale Law Journal* 35,
no. 6 (1925): 655–73.

Dickson, Peter R., and Philippa K. Wells. "The Dubious Origins of the Sherman Antitrust Act:
The Mouse That Roared." *Journal of Public Policy and Marketing* 20, no. 1 (2001): 3–14.

DiIulio, John. "The Coming of the Super-Predators." *Washington Examiner*, November 27, 1995.
https://www.washingtonexaminer.com/weekly-standard/the-coming-of-the-super-predators.

Dobbin, Frank. *Forging Industrial Policy: The United States, Britain, and France in the Railway
Age*. Cambridge, MA: Cambridge University Press, 1994.

Domhoff, G. William. *The Myth of Liberal Ascendancy: Corporate Dominance from the Great
Depression to the Great Recession*. Boulder: Paradigm, 2013.

Domhoff, G. William, and Michael J. Webber. *Class and Power in the New Deal: Corporate Moderates, Southern Democrats, and the Liberal-Labor Coalition*. Stanford, CA: Stanford University Press, 2011.

Dorsey, Leroy. "Theodore Roosevelt and Corporate America, 1901–1909: A Reexamination."
Presidential Studies Quarterly 25, no. 4 (1995): 725–39.

Douglas, William O. "Administrative Government." Address of William O. Douglas, Chairman, Securities and Exchange Commission, Before the Eighth Annual Forum on Current
Problems, New York City, October 26, 1938. https://www.sec.gov/news/speech/1938/102638
douglas.pdf.

———. *Democracy and Finance: The Addresses and Public Statements of William O. Douglas as
Member and Chairman of the Securities and Exchange Commission*. New Haven, CT: Yale
University Press, 1940.

Drahms, August. *The Criminal, His Personnel and Environment*. New York: Macmillan, 1900.

Du Bois, W. E. B. *The Philadelphia Negro: A Social Study.* Philadelphia: University of Pennsylvania Press, 1899.

———. *The Souls of Black Folk.* 1903. New York: Oxford University Press, 2007.

Dudziak, Mary. "Oliver Wendell Holmes as Eugenic Reformer: Rhetoric in the Writing of Constitutional Law." *Iowa Law Review* 71, no. 3 (1986): 833–68.

Dugdale, Richard L. "Hereditary Pauperism, as Illustrated in the 'Juke' Family." In *Proceedings of the Conference of Charities, 1877,* 81–95. Boston: A. Williams, 1877.

———. *The Jukes: A Study in Crime, Pauperism, Disease, and Heredity.* New York: G. P. Putnam's Sons, 1877.

Dunlavy, Colleen. *Politics and Industrialization: Early Railroads in the United States and Prussia.* Princeton, NJ: Princeton University Press, 1994.

Dwyer, Gerald P., and Norbert J. Michel. "A New Federal Charter for Financial Institutions." In *Prosperity Unleashed: Smarter Financial Regulation,* ed. Norbert J. Michel, 349–61. Washington, DC: Heritage Foundation, 2017. https://thf-reports.s3.amazonaws.com/2017/ProsperityUnleashed.pdf.

Eagan, Eleanor, and Hannah Story Brown. "Enforcement: The Untapped Resource." *Revolving Door Project* (blog), August 25, 2022. https://therevolvingdoorproject.org/enforcement-the-untapped-resource.

Eagleman, David. "The Brain on Trial." *The Atlantic,* July/August 2011. https://www.theatlantic.com/magazine/archive/2011/07/the-brain-on-trial/308520.

Eckhouse, Laurel, Kristian Lum, Cynthia Conti-Cook, and Julie Ciccolini. "Layers of Bias: A Unified Approach for Understanding Problems with Risk Assessment." *Criminal Justice and Behavior* 46, no. 2 (2019): 185–219.

Eisinger, Jesse. *The Chickenshit Club: Why the Justice Department Fails to Prosecute Executives.* New York: Simon & Schuster, 2017.

———. "Regulatory Failure 101: What the Collapse of Silicon Valley Bank Reveals." *ProPublica,* March 17, 2023. https://www.propublica.org/article/silicon-valley-bank-failure-fdic-fed-failure.

Eisner, Marc Allen. *Regulatory Politics in Transition.* Baltimore: Johns Hopkins University Press, 1993.

Ely, Richard T. *An Introduction to Political Economy.* 1893. 2nd ed. New York: Eaton & Mains, 1901.

———. "Pauperism in the United States." *North American Review* 152, no. 413 (1891): 395–407.

———. "Social Progress." *Cosmopolitan* 31, no. 1 (1901): 61–64.

———. *Studies in the Evolution of Industrial Society.* New York: Chautauqua, 1903.

Erzen, Tanya. *God in Captivity: The Rise of Faith-Based Prison Ministries in the Age of Mass Incarceration.* Boston: Beacon, 2017.

Estabrook, Arthur. *The Jukes in 1915.* Washington, DC: Carnegie Institute of Washington, 1916.

———. *Mongrel Virginians: The Win Tribe.* Baltimore: Williams & Wilkins, 1926.

Estabrook, Arthur, and Charles Benedict Davenport. *The Nam Family: A Study in Cacogenics.* Cold Spring Harbor, NY: New Era Printing, 1912.

European Bank for Reconstruction and Development. *Transition Report, 2020–21: The State Strikes Back.* European Bank for Reconstruction and Development, 2020. https://www.ebrd.com/publications/transition-report-202021.

"Execution of Anarchists." *Washington Post,* February 25, 1908.

"Ex-Justice Ferdinand Pecora, 89, Dead." *New York Times,* December 8, 1971. https://www.nytimes.com/1971/12/08/archives/exjustice-ferdinand-pecora-89-deadi.html.

Fabian, Ann. *The Skull Collectors: Race, Science, and America's Unburied Dead.* Chicago: University of Chicago Press, 2010.

Falk, Armin, and Josef Zweimüller. "Unemployment and Right-Wing Extremist Crime." London: Centre for Economic Policy Research, 2005.

Fallon, Harrison. "Penn Professor's Book Inspires TV Show: Raine's Book Will Be Adapted for a Pilot Production on CBS." *Daily Pennsylvanian,* March 25, 2013. http://www.thedp.com/article/2013/03/penn-professors-book-inspires-tv-show.

"Federal Trade Commission—Drafting in a Regulatory Agency." *Catholic University Law Review* 21, no. 4 (1972): 816–47.

Ferguson, Thomas. "Industrial Conflict and the Coming of the New Deal: The Triumph of Multinational Liberalism in America." In *The Rise and Fall of the New Deal Order, 1930–1980,* ed. Steve Fraser and Gary Gerstle, 3–31. Princeton, NJ: Princeton University Press, 1989.

Fields, Karen, and Barbara Fields. *Racecraft: The Soul of Inequality in American Life.* New York: Verso, 2012.

Financial Crisis Inquiry Commission. "Financial Crisis Inquiry Report: Final Report of the National Commission on the Causes of the Financial and Economic Crisis in the United States." Washington, DC: US Government Printing Office, January 2011.

Flamm, Michael. *Law and Order: Street Crime, Civil Unrest, and the Crisis of Liberalism in the 1960s.* New York: Columbia University Press, 2005.

Foner, Philip S. *The Great Labor Uprising of 1877.* New York: Monad, 1977.

Forman, James. *Locking Up Our Own: Crime and Punishment in Black America.* New York: Farrar, Straus & Giroux, 2017.

Foroohar, Rana. *Makers and Takers: The Rise of Finance and the Fall of American Business.* New York: Crown Business, 2016.

Fortner, Michael Javen. *Black Silent Majority: The Rockefeller Drug Laws and the Politics of Punishment.* Cambridge, MA: Harvard University Press, 2015.

Foucault, Michel. *The Birth of Biopolitics: Lectures at the Collège de France, 1978–1979.* Edited by Arnold I. Davidson, Michel Senellart, Francois Ewald, and Alessandro Fontana. Translated by Graham Burchell. New York: Palgrave Macmillan, 2008.

Foucault, Michel, and François Ewald. *"Society Must Be Defended": Lectures at the Collège de France, 1975–1976.* Edited by Mauro Bertani, Alessandro Fontana, and Arnold Davidson. New York: Picador, 2003.

Fox, Cybelle. *Three Worlds of Relief: Race, Immigration, and the American Welfare State from the Progressive Era to the New Deal.* Princeton, NJ: Princeton University Press, 2012.

Frank, Thomas. *The People, No: A Brief History of Anti-Populism.* New York: Metropolitan, 2020.

Fraser, Steve. *The Age of Acquiescence: The Life and Death of American Resistance to Organized Wealth.* Boston: Little, Brown, 2015.

Freeman, Richard. "Crime and the Employment of Disadvantaged Youths." In *Urban Labor Markets and Job Opportunity,* ed. George Peterson and Wayne Vroman, 201–37. Washington, DC: Urban Institute Press, 1992.

Friedman, Lawrence. *Crime and Punishment in American History.* New York: Basic, 1993.

Friedrichs, David O. *Trusted Criminals: White Collar Crime in Contemporary Society.* Belmont, CA: Thomson Wadsworth, 1997.

"From Another Point of View." *Rural New Yorker* 37 (July 13, 1878): 444.

"Full Transcript: First 2016 Presidential Debate." *Politico*, September 27, 2016. https://www.po litico.com/story/2016/09/full-transcript-first-2016-presidential-debate-228761.

Galanter, Marc. "Why the 'Haves' Come Out Ahead: Speculations on the Limits of Legal Change." *Law and Society Review* 9, no. 1 (1974): 95–160.

Gallant, Kenneth. *The Principle of Legality in International and Comparative Law*. Cambridge University Press, 2009.

Galvin, Miranda, and Sally Simpson. "Prosecuting and Sentencing White-Collar Crime in US Federal Courts: Revisiting the Yale Findings." In *The Handbook of White-Collar Crime*, ed. Melissa Rorie, 381–97. Hoboken: John Wiley & Sons, 2020.

Gambino, Richard. *Blood of My Blood: The Dilemma of the Italian-Americans*. Garden City, NY: Doubleday, 1974.

Garland, David. *The Culture of Control: Crime and Social Order in Contemporary Society*. Chicago: University of Chicago Press, 2001.

———. *Peculiar Institution: America's Death Penalty in an Age of Abolition*. Cambridge, MA: Belknap Press of Harvard University Press, 2010.

Garrett, Brandon L. *Too Big to Jail: How Prosecutors Compromise with Corporations*. Cambridge, MA: Belknap Press of Harvard University Press, 2014.

Gattuso, James. "Meltdowns and Myths: Did Deregulation Cause the Financial Crisis?" Heritage Foundation Report, October 22, 2018. https://www.heritage.org/report/meltdowns-and -myths-did-deregulation-cause-the-financial-crisis.

Gault, Robert. "Pathologic Vagrancy." *Journal of the American Institute of Criminal Law and Criminology* 5, no. 3 (September 1914): 321–22.

George, Henry. *Social Problems*. 1883. New York: Doubleday Page, 1906.

"Gets Life Sentence under Baumes Law for a \$51 Hold-Up: Youth Who Robbed Brooklyn Store the First to Draw the Maximum Penalty." *New York Times*, August 21, 1926.

Gibson, Lydialyle. "Writing Crime into Race." *Harvard Magazine*, July/August 2018. https://har vardmagazine.com/2018/07/khalil-muhammad-condemnation-of-blackness.

Gilder, George. *Wealth and Poverty*. New York: Basic, 1981.

Glickman, Lawrence. *Buying Power: A History of Consumer Activism in America*. Chicago: University of Chicago Press, 2009.

Glueck, Sheldon, and Eleanor Glueck. *500 Criminal Careers*. New York: Knopf, 1930.

———. *Unraveling Juvenile Delinquency*. New York: Commonwealth, 1950.

Goddard, Henry Herbert. *Feeble-Mindedness: Its Causes and Consequences*. New York: Macmillan, 1914.

———. *The Kallikak Family: A Study in the Heredity of Feeble-Mindedness*. New York: Macmillan, 1912.

Goddard, Tim, and Randolph Myers. "Against Evidence-Based Oppression: Marginalized Youth and the Politics of Risk-Based Assessment and Intervention." *Theoretical Criminology* 21, no. 2 (2017): 151–67.

Godrej, Farah. *Freedom Inside? Yoga and Meditation in the Carceral State*. New York: Oxford University Press, 2022.

———. "Yoga, Meditation, and Neoliberal Penality: Compliance or Resistance?" *Political Research Quarterly* 75, no. 1 (2020): 47–60.

Goldstein, Robert Justin. *Political Repression in Modern America from 1870 to 1976*. Urbana: University of Illinois Press, 2001.

Gonce, Richard A. "John R. Commons: Five Big Years, 1899–1904." *American Journal of Economics and Sociology* 61, no. 4 (October 2002): 755–77.

Goodman, Philip, Joshua Page, and Michelle Phelps. *Breaking the Pendulum: The Long Struggle over Criminal Justice*. New York: Oxford University Press, 2017.

Gordon, Colin. *New Deals: Business, Labor, and Politics in America, 1920–1935*. New York: Cambridge University Press, 1994.

Gottschalk, Marie. *Caught: The Prison State and the Lockdown of American Politics*. Princeton, NJ: Princeton University Press, 2015.

———. "Kamala Harris' Disturbing Brand of Criminal Justice Reform." *In These Times*, January 25, 2019. https://inthesetimes.com/article/kamala-harris-criminal-justice-reform-mass-incarceration-progress.

———. *The Prison and the Gallows: The Politics of Mass Incarceration in America*. New York: Cambridge University Press, 2006.

Gould, Lewis. *The Presidency of Theodore Roosevelt*. 1991. 2nd ed. Lawrence: University of Kansas, 2011.

Gould, Stephen Jay. *The Mismeasure of Man*. New York: Norton, 1980.

"Gov. Wilson Signs the Sterilization Bill." *New York Tribune*, May 4, 1911.

Gowan, Peter. "Permanently Nationalize the Banks during the Next Crisis." People's Policy Project, July 3, 2018. https://www.peoplespolicyproject.org/2018/07/03/permanently-nationalize-the-banks-during-the-next-financial-crisis.

Graber, Jennifer. *The Furnace of Affliction: Prisons and Religion in Antebellum America*. Chapel Hill: University of North Carolina Press, 2011.

Gramlich, John. "America's Incarceration Rate Falls to Lowest Level since 1995." Pew Research Center, August 16, 2021. https://www.pewresearch.org/fact-tank/2021/08/16/americas-incarceration-rate-lowest-since-1995.

Grant, Madison. *The Passing of the Great Race; or, The Racial Basis of European History*. New York: Charles Scribner's Sons, 1916.

Grant, Roger. Review of *The First Tycoon: The Epic Life of Cornelius Vanderbilt*. *Journal of American History* 98, no. 2 (2011): 544.

Grant, Wyn, and Graham K. Wilson. "Preface to the Paperback Edition." In *The Consequences of the Global Financial Crisis: The Rhetoric of Reform and Regulation*, ed. Wyn Grant and Graham K. Wilson, v–xii. New York: Oxford University Press, 2012.

Grasso, Anthony. "Broken beyond Repair: Rehabilitative Penology and American Political Development." *Political Research Quarterly* 70, no. 2 (2017): 394–407.

———. "'No Bodies to Kick or Souls to Damn': The Political Origins of Corporate Criminal Liability." *Studies in American Political Development* 35, no. 1 (2021): 57–75.

Grawert, Ames. "Brennan Center's Public Comment on the First Step Act's Risk and Needs Assessment Tool." Brennan Center for Justice, September 4, 2019. https://www.brennancenter.org/our-work/research-reports/brennan-centers-public-comment-first-step-acts-risk-and-needs-assessment.

———. "What Is the First Step Act—and What's Happening with It?" Brennan Center for Justice, June 23, 2020. https://www.brennancenter.org/our-work/research-reports/what-first-step-act-and-whats-happening-it.

Green, Bruce. "After the Fall: The Criminal Law Enforcement Response to the S&L Crisis." *Fordham Law Review* 59, no. 6 (1991): S155–S192.

Greenberg, Douglas. *Crime and Law Enforcement in the Colony of New York, 1691–1776.* Ithaca, NY: Cornell University Press, 1976.

Gyauch-Lewis, Dylan. "An Overview of the History of American Financial Regulation." *Revolving Door Project* (blog), February 21, 2023. https://therevolvingdoorproject.org/an-over view-of-the-history-of-american-financial-regulation.

Hacker, Jacob S., and Paul Pierson. *Winner-Take-All Politics: How Washington Made the Rich Richer—and Turned Its Back on the Middle Class.* New York: Simon & Schuster, 2010.

Hagan, John. *Who Are the Criminals? The Politics of Crime Policy from the Age of Roosevelt to the Age of Reagan.* Princeton, NJ: Princeton University Press, 2010.

Hamilton, Jesse. "Banks Get Easier Volcker Rule and $40 Billion Break on Swaps." Bloomberg Law, June 25, 2020. https://news.bloomberglaw.com/banking-law/banks-get-easier-volcker -rule-and-40-billion-reprieve-on-swaps.

Hanna, Thomas. "The Crisis Next Time: Planning for Public Ownership as an Alternative to Corporate Bank Bailouts." Democracy Collaborative, July 2, 2018. https://drive.google.com /file/d/1vjOfQx54Fgq5Sp7sf1RqLvTrOq_QApKk/view.

Hannah-Moffat, Kelly. "Criminogenic Needs and the Transformative Risk Subject." *Punishment and Society* 7, no. 1 (2005): 29–51.

Hansen, Randall, and Desmond King. *Sterilized by the State: Eugenics, Race, and the Population Scare in Twentieth-Century America.* New York: Cambridge University Press, 2013.

Harbinson, Erin, Michael L. Benson, and Edward J. Latessa. "Assessing Risk among White-Collar Offenders under Federal Supervision in the Community." *Criminal Justice and Behavior* 46, no. 2 (2019): 261–79.

Harcourt, Bernard. *The Illusion of Free Markets.* Cambridge, MA: Harvard University Press, 2011.

———. "Risk as a Proxy for Race: The Dangers of Risk Assessment." *Federal Sentencing Reporter* 27, no. 4 (2015): 237–43.

Harpending, Henry, and Patricia Draper. "Antisocial Behavior and the Other Side of Cultural Evolution." In *Biological Contributions to Crime Causation,* ed. Terrie Moffitt and Sarnoff Mednick, 294–307. Dordrecht: Martinus Nijhoff, 1988.

Harpine, William. *From the Front Porch to the Front Page: McKinley and Bryan in the 1896 Presidential Campaign.* College Station: Texas A&M University Press, 2005.

Harring, Sidney. *Policing a Class Society: The Experience of American Cities, 1865–1915.* New Brunswick, NJ: Rutgers University Press, 1983.

Harris, Lee O. *The Man Who Tramps: A Story of To-Day.* Indianapolis: Douglass & Carlon, 1878.

Harris, Richard, and Sidney Milkis. *The Politics of Regulatory Change: A Tale of Two Agencies.* 1989. 2nd ed. New York: Oxford University Press, 1996.

Harvey, David. *A Brief History of Neoliberalism.* New York: Oxford University Press, 2005.

Haskell, Thomas. *The Emergence of Professional Social Science: The American Social Science Association and the Nineteenth-Century Crisis of Authority.* Urbana: University of Illinois Press, 1977.

Hattam, Victoria. *Labor Visions and State Power: The Origins of Business Unionism in the United States.* Princeton, NJ: Princeton University Press, 1993.

Haugh, Todd. "Exactly Wrong: Why the Trump Administration's Stated Policies Will Increase Corporate Crime." *Federal Sentencing Reporter* 29, nos. 2–3 (2017): 91–92.

Hawkins, Keith. "Compliance Strategy, Prosecution Policy and Aunt Sally." *British Journal of Criminology* 30, no. 4 (1990): 444–66.

Hazlett, Thomas W. "The Legislative History of the Sherman Act Re-Examined." *Economic Inquiry* 30, no. 2 (April 1, 1992): 263–76.

Henderson, Charles R. "Business Men and Social Theorists." *American Journal of Sociology* 1, no. 4 (1896): 385–97.

———. *An Introduction to the Study of the Dependent, Defective, and Delinquent Classes.* 1893. 2nd ed. Boston: Heath, 1901.

Henderson, David. "Are We Ailing from Too Much Deregulation." *Cato Institute Policy Report*, December 2008. https://www.cato.org/policy-report/november/december-2008/are-we-ailing-too-much-deregulation.

Hennelly, Robert. "Dodd-Frank at 5: Landmark Law, or Unfinished Business?" July 20, 2015. CBS News. https://www.cbsnews.com/news/dodd-frank-at-5-landmark-law-or-unfinished-business.

Henning, Peter J. "Is Deterrence Relevant in Sentencing White-Collar Criminals?" *Wayne Law Review* 61, no. 1 (2015): 27–59.

Henry, Leslie. "The Jurisprudence of Dignity." *University of Pennsylvania Law Review* 160, no. 1 (2011): 169–234.

Herndon, Thomas, and Mark Paul. "A Public Banking Option as a Mode of Regulation for Household Financial Services in the US." *Journal of Post Keynesian Economics* 43, no. 4 (2020): 576–607.

Herrnstein, Richard J., and Charles Murray. *The Bell Curve: Intelligence and Class Structure in American Life.* New York: Free Press, 1994.

"The Hidden Discrimination in Criminal Risk-Assessment Scores." NPR.org, May 24, 2016. https://www.npr.org/2016/05/24/479349654/the-hidden-discrimination-in-criminal-risk-assessment-scores.

Hinton, Elizabeth. *From the War on Poverty to the War on Crime: The Making of Mass Incarceration in America.* Cambridge, MA: Harvard University Press, 2017.

Hoffman, Frederick L. *Race Traits and Tendencies of the American Negro.* New York: Macmillan, 1896.

Hofstadter, Richard. *The Age of Reform.* New York: Vintage, 1955.

———. *Social Darwinism in American Thought.* 1944. Rev. ed. Boston: Beacon, 1955.

Holland, Joshua. "Hundreds of Wall Street Execs Went to Prison during the Last Fraud-Fueled Bank Crisis." BillMoyers.com, September 17, 2013. https://billmoyers.com/2013/09/17/hundreds-of-wall-street-execs-went-to-prison-during-the-last-fraud-fueled-bank-crisis.

Holmes, Oliver Wendell. "The Path of the Law." *Harvard Law Review* 10, no. 8 (1897): 457–78.

Hoofnagle, Christopher Jay. *The Federal Trade Commission: Privacy Law and Policy.* New York: Cambridge University Press, 2016.

Hubbard, R. Glenn, Hal Scott, and Luigi Zingales. "Banks Need Fewer Carrots and More Sticks." *Wall Street Journal*, May 6, 2009.

Hudson, James F. *The Railways and the Republic.* New York: Harper & Bros., 1886.

Hunter, Joel. "Sterilization of Criminals: Report of Committee 'F' of the Institute." *Journal of the American Institute of Criminal Law and Criminology* 7, no. 3 (1916): 373–78.

Hyatt, John. "Sam Bankman-Fried's Donations to Effective Altruism Nonprofits Tied to an Oxford Professor Are at Risk of Being Clawed Back." *Forbes*, November 17, 2022. https://www.forbes.com/sites/johnhyatt/2022/11/17/disgraced-crypto-trader-sam-bankman-fried-was-a-big-backer-of-effective-altruism-now-that-movement-has-a-big-black-eye/?sh=32f6d1b04ce7.

Illinois Association for Criminal Justice and Chicago Crime Commission. *The Illinois Crime Survey.* Chicago: Illinois Association for Criminal Justice, 1929.

Illinois Board of Charities. *Biennial Report of the Board of State Commissioners of Public Charities*. Springfield: Illinois State Journal Co., 1909.

———. *Seventeenth Biennial Report of the Board of State Commissioners of Public Charities*. Springfield, IL: Phillips Bros., 1902.

Illinois Board of Commissioners of Public Charities. *Eighth Biennial Report of the Board of State Commissioners of Public Charities*. Springfield, IL: H. W. Rokker, 1885.

———. *Tenth Biennial Report of the Board of State Commissioners of Public Charities*. Springfield, IL: Springfield Printing, 1888.

———. *Sixteenth Biennial Report of the Board of State Commissioners of Public Charities*. Springfield, IL: Phillips Bros., 1900.

Indiana State Board of Charities. *Second Annual Report of the Board of State Charities*. Indianapolis: Wm. B. Burford, 1891.

———. *Third Report of the Board of State Charities*. Indianapolis: Wm. B. Burford, 1893.

———. *Fourth Annual Report of the Board of State Charities*. Indianapolis: Wm. B. Burford, 1894.

———. *Fourteenth Annual Report of the Board of State Charities*. Indianapolis: Wm. B. Burford, 1904.

"Inside the Criminal Mind: Understanding How Bad People Think." *Time Life*, January 1, 2018.

Jackson, Amanda. "Tennessee County Inmates Get Reduced Jail Time for Getting a Vasectomy." CNN.com, July 20, 2017. http://www.cnn.com/2017/07/20/us/white-county-inmate-vasec tomy-trnd/index.html.

James, Scott C. *Presidents, Parties, and the State: A Party System Perspective on Democratic Regulatory Choice, 1884–1936*. New York: Cambridge University Press, 2006.

Johnson, Ryan S., Shawn Kantor, and Price V. Fishback. "Striking at the Roots of Crime: The Impact of Social Welfare Spending on Crime during the Great Depression." Working Paper no. 12825. National Bureau of Economic Research, 2007. https://www.nber.org/system/files /working_papers/w12825/w12825.pdf.

Jordan, David Starr. "The Training of the Physician: Commencement Address at Cooper Medical College, 1892." In *The Care and Culture of Men: A Series of Addresses on the Higher Education*, 133–49. San Francisco: Whitaker & Ray, 1896.

Kamin, Sam. "Marijuana Regulation in the United States." In *Dual Markets: Comparative Approaches to Regulation*, ed. Ernesto U. Savona, Mark A. R. Kleiman, and Francesco Calderoni, 105–19. Cham: Springer International, 2017.

Karmen, Andrew. *Crime Victims: An Introduction to Victimology*. 1984. 5th ed. Belmont, CA: Thomson Wadsworth, 2004.

Katz, Rebecca. "United States." In *Encyclopedia of White-Collar and Corporate Crime* (2 vols.), ed. Lawrence Salinger, 2:838–41. Thousand Oaks, CA: Sage Reference, 2005.

Katznelson, Ira. *Fear Itself: The New Deal and the Origins of Our Time*. New York: Norton, 2013.

———. "Was the Great Society a Lost Opportunity?" In *The Rise and Fall of the New Deal Order, 1930–1980*, ed. Steve Fraser and Gary Gerstle, 185–211. Princeton, NJ: Princeton University Press, 1989.

Kauper, Thomas. "The History, Effect, and Scope of Clayton Act Orders of the Federal Trade Commission." *Michigan Law Review* 66, no. 6 (1968): 1095–1210.

Kazin, Michael, Rebecca Edwards, and Adam Rothman. *The Concise Princeton Encyclopedia of American Political History*. Princeton, NJ: Princeton University Press, 2011.

Kennedy, Joseph P. *Address of Hon. Joseph P. Kennedy Chairman of Securities Exchange Commission at the National Press Club*. Washington, DC: US Government Printing Office, July 25, 1934. https://www.sec.gov/news/speech/1934/072534kennedy.pdf.

Keyssar, Alexander. *Out of Work: The First Century of Unemployment in Massachusetts*. New York: Cambridge University Press, 1986.

Khanna, Vikramaditya S. "Corporate Crime Legislation: A Political Economy Analysis." *Washington University Law Review* 82, no. 1 (2004): 95–141.

———. "Corporate Criminal Liability: What Purpose Does It Serve?" *Harvard Law Review* 109, no. 7 (1996): 1477–1534.

Kim, Sung Hui. "The Failure of Federal Incorporation Law: A Public Choice Perspective." Law-Econ Research Paper no. 17-08. Los Angeles: UCLA School of Law, 2017.

King, Gilbert. "The Man Who Busted the 'Banksters.'" *Smithsonian Magazine*, November 29, 2011. https://www.smithsonianmag.com/history/the-man-who-busted-the-banksters-932416.

Kirkland, Edward C. *Industry Comes of Age: Business, Labor, and Public Policy, 1860–1897*. New York: Holt, Rinehart & Winston, 1961.

Klarman, Michael J. "Is the Supreme Court Sometimes Irrelevant? Race and the Southern Criminal Justice System in the 1940s." *Journal of American History* 89, no. 1 (2002): 119–53.

Knight, Kathleen. "Transformations of the Concept of Ideology in the Twentieth Century." *American Political Science Review* 100, no. 4 (2006): 619–26.

Kohler-Hausmann, Issa. *Misdemeanorland: Criminal Courts and Social Control in an Age of Broken Windows Policing*. Princeton, NJ: Princeton University Press, 2018.

Kolasky, William. "The Election of 1912: A Pivotal Moment in Antitrust History." *Antitrust* 25, no. 3 (2011): 82–88.

Kolko, Gabriel. *Railroads and Regulation, 1877–1916*. Princeton, NJ: Princeton University Press, 1965.

———. *The Triumph of Conservatism: A Reinterpretation of American History, 1900–1916*. New York: Free Press, 1963.

Kopan, Tal. "Report: Think Tanks Tied to Kochs." *Politico*, November 13, 2013. https://www.politico.com/story/2013/11/koch-brothers-think-tank-report-099791.

Krawiec, Kimberly. "Don't 'Screw Joe the Plummer': The Sausage-Making of Financial Reform." *Arizona Law Review* 55 (2013): 53–103.

Kress, Jeremy. "Solving Banking's 'Too Big to Manage' Problem." *Minnesota Law Review* 104, no. 1 (2019): 171–242.

Krippner, Greta. "The Financialization of the American Economy." *Socio-Economic Review* 3, no. 2 (2005): 173–208.

Kupiec, Paul. "Bank Regulators Were Asleep at the Wheel: Their Wake-Up Call Is Overdue." *The Hill*, March 14, 2023. https://thehill.com/opinion/finance/3899477-bank-regulators-were-asleep-at-the-wheel-their-wake-up-call-is-overdue.

Kusmer, Kenneth L. *Down and Out, on the Road: The Homeless in American History*. New York: Oxford University Press, 2001.

Lamoreaux, Naomi R. *The Great Merger Movement in American Business, 1895–1904*. New York: Cambridge University Press, 1988.

Lancaster, Roger. *The Trouble with Nature: Sex in Science and Popular Culture*. Berkeley: University of California Press, 2003.

Landis, James. *The Administrative Process*. New Haven, CT: Yale University Press, 1938.

Lane, Roger. *Policing the City: Boston, 1822–1885*. Cambridge, MA: Harvard University Press, 1967.

———. "Urban Police and Crime in Nineteenth-Century America." *Crime and Justice: A Review of Research* 15 (1992): 1–50.

Larner, Wendy. "Neo-Liberalism: Policy, Ideology, and Governmentality." *Studies in Political Economy* 63, no. 1 (2000): 5–25.

Laufer, William S. *Corporate Bodies and Guilty Minds: The Failure of Corporate Criminal Liability.* Chicago: University of Chicago Press, 2006.

Laufer, William S., and Matthew Caulfield. "Wall Street and Progressivism." *Yale Journal on Regulation Bulletin* 37 (2019): 36–51.

Laughlin, Harry H. *Eugenical Sterilization in the United States.* Chicago: Psychopathic Laboratory of the Municipal Court of Chicago, 1922.

———. *Report of the Committee to Study and to Report on the Best Practical Means of Cutting Off the Defective Germ-Plasm in the American Population: The Legal, Legislative, and Administrative Aspects of Sterilization.* Bulletin no. 10B. New York: Eugenics Record Office, 1914.

Laws of the Various States Relating to Vagrancy. Rev. Lansing, MI: State Printer, 1916.

"Lax Methods in Stock Exchange—Money Trust Probe Shows That Manipulation Is Well Approved." *Milwaukee Journal*, December 14, 1912.

Leadership Conference on Civil and Human Rights. "Vote 'No' on the First Step Act." May 21, 2018. http://civilrightsdocs.info/pdf/policy/letters/2018/Short_Oppose%20FIRST%20STEP%20Act_5.21.18_FINAL.pdf.

Leadership Conference on Civil and Human Rights and American Civil Liberties Union. "The ACLU and the Leadership Conference Urge You to Support S.756, the First Step Act." December 19, 2018. http://civilrightsdocs.info/pdf/policy/letters/2018/Letter-of-Support-on-First-Step-Act-%28ACLU-and-LC%29-12-19-18-HOUSE-Final.pdf.

Lehman, Charles Fain. "Contra 'Root Causes.'" *City Journal*, Summer 2021. https://www.city-journal.org/article/contra-root-causes.

Leland, Eugene R. "What Mr. Leland Got No Chance to Say." In *Herbert Spencer on the Americans and the Americans on Herbert Spencer: Being a Full Report of His Interview, and of the Proceedings of the Farewell Banquet of Nov. 11, 1882*, 80–83. New York: D. Appleton, 1883.

Leonard, Thomas. *Illiberal Reformers: Race, Eugenics, and American Economics in the Progressive Era.* Princeton, NJ: Princeton University Press, 2016.

———. "Origins of the Myth of Social Darwinism: The Ambiguous Legacy of Richard Hofstadter's *Social Darwinism in American Thought*." *Journal of Economic Behavior and Organization* 71, no. 1 (2009): 37–51.

Leuchtenburg, William. *In the Shadow of FDR: From Harry Truman to Barack Obama.* 1983. 4th ed. Ithaca, NY: Cornell University Press, 2009.

Levi, Michael. "Sentencing Respectable Offenders." In *The Oxford Handbook of White-Collar Crime*, ed. Shanna R. Van Slyke, Michael L. Benson, and Francis T. Cullen, 582–602. New York: Oxford University Press, 2016.

Levy, Scott. "Spending Money to Make Money: CBO Scoring of Secondary Effects." *Yale Law Journal* 127, no. 4 (February 2018): 936–1105.

Lichtblau, Eric, David Johnston, and Ron Nixon. "F.B.I. Struggles to Handle Financial Fraud Cases." *New York Times*, October 18, 2018. https://www.nytimes.com/2008/10/19/washington/19fbi.html.

Lichtenstein, Alex. *Twice the Work of Free Labor: The Political Economy of Convict Labor in the New South.* New York: Verso, 1996.

Lichtenstein, Nelson. "From Corporatism to Collective Bargaining: Organized Labor and the Eclipse of Social Democracy in the Postwar Era." In *The Rise and Fall of the New Deal Order,*

1930–1980, ed. Steven Fraser and Gary Gerstle, 122–52. Princeton, NJ: Princeton University Press, 1989.

Lieberman, Robert C. "Ideas, Institutions, and Political Order: Explaining Political Change." *American Political Science Review* 96, no. 4 (2002): 697–712.

———. *Shifting the Color Line: Race and the American Welfare State*. Cambridge, MA: Harvard University Press, 1998.

Lindblom, Charles Edward. *Politics and Markets: The World's Political Economic Systems*. New York: Basic, 1977.

Lindsey, Edward. "The Bill to Establish a Criminological Laboratory at Washington." *Journal of the American Institute of Criminal Law and Criminology* 1, no. 2 (1910): 103–17.

Liptak, Adam. "Supreme Court Skeptical of Argument That Could Hobble Consumer Watchdog." *New York Times*, October 3, 2023. https://www.nytimes.com/2023/10/03/us/supreme-court-cfpb.html.

Lisle, John. "Vagrancy Law: Its Faults and Their Remedy." *Journal of the American Institute of Criminal Law and Criminology* 5, no. 4 (November 1914): 498–513.

Logan, Wayne. *The Ex Post Facto Clause: Its History and Role in a Punitive Society*. New York: Oxford University Press, 2023.

Lombroso, Cesare. *Criminal Man*. 1876. Edited by Mary Gibson and Nicole Hahn Rafter. Durham, NC: Duke University Press, 2006.

———. "Illustrative Studies in Criminal Anthropology: III, The Physiognomy of the Anarchists." *The Monist* 1, no. 3 (1891): 336–43.

———. "Why Homicide Has Increased in the United States." *North American Review* 165, no. 493 (1897): 641–48.

Lombroso-Ferrero, Gina. *Criminal Man according to the Classification of Cesare Lombroso*. New York: G. P. Putnam's Sons, 1911.

Lydston, G. Frank. *The Diseases of Society: The Vice and Crime Problem*. Philadelphia: J. B. Lippincott, 1906.

MacDonald, Arthur. *Criminology*. New York: Funk & Wagnalls, 1893.

MacDougall, Ian. "Bill Barr Promised to Release Prisoners Threatened by Coronavirus—Even as the Feds Secretly Made It Harder for Them to Get Out." *ProPublica*, May 26, 2020. https://www.propublica.org/article/bill-barr-promised-to-release-prisoners-threatened-by-coronavirus-even-as-the-feds-secretly-made-it-harder-for-them-to-get-out.

Maestro, Marcello. *Cesare Beccaria and the Origins of Penal Reform*. Philadelphia: Temple University Press, 1973.

Makuen, G. Hudson. "Some Measures for the Prevention of Crime, Pauperism, and Mental Deficiency." *Bulletin of the American Academy of Medicine* 5, no. 1 (1900): 1–15.

Malcolm, John. "Criminal Justice Reform: Testimony Before the Committee on Oversight and Government Reform, U.S. House of Representatives on July 15, 2015." Testimony: Crime and Justice, Heritage Foundation, July 24, 2015. https://www.heritage.org/testimony/criminal-justice-reform.

Mancini, Matthew. *One Dies, Get Another: Convict Leasing in the American South, 1866–1928*. Columbia: University of South Carolina Press, 1996.

Mangual, Rafael A. "Ideas for the New Administration: Criminal Justice." Manhattan Institute, January 27, 2021. https://media4.manhattan-institute.org/sites/default/files/ideas-new-government-criminal-justice-RM.pdf.

———. "New York: Look to Other States If You Want to Do Bail Reform Right." Commentary, Manhattan Institute, February 19, 2020. https://www.manhattan-institute.org/new-york-other-states-bail-reform-right.

Mann, Kenneth. *Defending White-Collar Crime*. New Haven, CT: Yale University Press, 1985.

Marchand, Roland. *Creating the Corporate Soul: The Rise of Public Relations and Corporate Imagery in American Big Business*. Berkeley: University of California Press, 1998.

Marcus, Alfred. *Promise and Performance: Choosing and Implementing an Environmental Policy*. Westport, CT: Greenwood, 1980.

Markoff, Gabriel. "Arthur Andersen and the Myth of the Corporate Death Penalty: Corporate Criminal Convictions in the Twenty-First Century." *University of Pennsylvania Journal of Business Law* 15, no. 3 (2013): 797–824.

Marshall, Wesley, and Louis-Philippe Rochon. "Public Banking and Post-Keynesian Economic Theory." *International Journal of Political Economy* 48, no. 1 (2019): 60–75.

Martinson, Robert. "New Findings, New Views: A Note of Caution Regarding Sentencing Reform." *Hofstra Law Review* 7, no. 2 (1979): 243–58.

———. "Prison Notes of a Freedom Rider." *The Nation*, January 6, 1962, 4–6.

———. "What Works? Questions and Answers about Prison Reform." *The Public Interest* 35 (1974): 22–54.

McCall, Patricia L., Kenneth C. Land, and Karen F. Parker. "An Empirical Assessment of What We Know about Structural Covariates of Homicide Rates: A Return to a Classic 20 Years Later." *Homicide Studies* 14, no. 3 (August 1, 2010): 219–43.

McCann, Michael. *Taking Reform Seriously: Perspectives on Public Interest Liberalism*. Ithaca, NY: Cornell University Press, 1986.

McCord, Charles. *The American Negro as a Dependent, Defective, and Delinquent*. Nashville: Benson, 1914.

McGerr, Michael. *A Fierce Discontent: The Rise and Fall of the Progressive Movement in America, 1870–1920*. New York: Oxford University Press, 2005.

McKim, William Duncan. *Heredity and Human Progress*. New York: G. P. Putnam's Sons, 1900.

McLennan, Rebecca. *The Crisis of Imprisonment: Protest, Politics, and the Making of the American Penal State, 1776–1941*. New York: Cambridge University Press, 2008.

Mednick, Sarnoff, W. F. Gabrielli, and B. Hutching. "Genetic Influences in Criminal Convictions: Evidence from an Adoption Court." *Science* 224, no. 4651 (1984): 891–94.

Mellow, Nicole. "The Democratic Fit: Party Reform and the Eugenics Tool." In *The Progressives' Century: Political Reform, Constitutional Government, and the Modern American State*, ed. Stephen Skowronek, Stephen M. Engel, and Bruce Ackerman, 197–218. New Haven, CT: Yale University Press, 2016.

Mettler, Suzanne. *Dividing Citizens: Gender and Federalism in New Deal Public Policy*. Ithaca, NY: Cornell University Press, 1998.

Michaels, Samantha. "Trump Keeps Celebrating Prison Reform. His Administration's Latest Move Could Sabotage It." *Mother Jones*, April 11, 2019. https://www.motherjones.com/crime-justice/2019/04/trump-first-step-act-hudson-institute-risk-assessment-committee.

Michaels, Walter Benn. "Race into Culture: A Critical Genealogy of Cultural Identity." *Critical Inquiry* 18, no. 4 (1992): 655–85.

Michel, Norbert J. "The Myth of Financial Market Deregulation." Report, Heritage Foundation, April 28, 2016. https://www.heritage.org/report/the-myth-financial-market-deregulation.

———. "Profit and Deregulation Are Not Four-Letter Words." Commentary: Markets and Finance, Heritage Foundation, February 27, 2019. https://www.heritage.org/markets-and-finance /commentary/profit-and-deregulation-are-not-four-letter-words.

Milkis, Sidney M. *The President and the Parties: The Transformation of the American Party System since the New Deal*. New York: Oxford University Press, 1993.

———. *Theodore Roosevelt, the Progressive Party, and the Transformation of American Democracy*. Lawrence: University Press of Kansas, 2009.

Miller, Jerome. "The Debate on Rehabilitating Criminals: Is It True That Nothing Works?" *Washington Post*, March 1989. https://www.prisonpolicy.org/scans/rehab.html.

Miller, Lisa. *The Myth of Mob Rule: Violent Crime and Democratic Politics*. New York: Oxford University Press, 2016.

Millis, Harry. "The Law Affecting Immigrants and Tramps." *Charities Review* 7 (September 1897): 587–94.

"Minnesota Has Its Baumes Law: 'New Measure Rids Society of Criminals' Menace,' Official Declares." *Christian Science Monitor*, April 22, 1927.

Missouri Association for Criminal Justice and Guy A. Thompson. *The Missouri Crime Survey*. New York: Macmillan, 1926.

Mitchell, Kelly Lyn. "State Sentencing Guidelines: A Garden Full of Variety." *Federal Probation* 81 (2017): 28–36.

Mitchell, Lawrence. *The Speculation Economy: How Finance Triumphed over Industry*. San Francisco: Berrett-Kohler, 2007.

Mitrani, Sam. *The Rise of the Chicago Police Department: Class and Conflict, 1850–1894*. Urbana: University of Illinois Press, 2013.

"MIT's Johnson Says Too-Big-to-Fail Banks Will Spark New Crisis." *Bloomberg*, March 21, 2010. https://www.bloomberg.com/news/articles/2010-03-21/mit-s-johnson-says-too-big-to-fail -banks-will-spark-new-crisis.

Moger, Allen. *Virginia: Bourbonism to Byrd, 1870–1925*. Charlottesville: University of Virginia Press, 1968.

Monahan, John, and Jennifer Skeem. "Risk Assessment in Criminal Sentencing." *Annual Review of Clinical Psychology* 12, no. 1 (2016): 489–513.

Monkonnen, Eric H. "Cop History to Social History: The Significance of the Police in American History." *Journal of Social History* 15, no. 4 (1982): 575–91.

———. "History of Urban Police." *Crime and Justice* 15 (1992): 547–80.

———. *Police in Urban America, 1860–1920*. Cambridge, MA: Cambridge University Press, 1981.

Montgomery, David. *Citizen Worker: The Experience of Workers in the United States with Democracy and the Free Market during the Nineteenth Century*. New York: Cambridge University Press, 1993.

Moran, Michael. "The Rise of the Regulatory State." In *The Oxford Handbook of Business and Government*, ed. David Coen, Wyn Grant, and Graham Wilson, 383–403. Oxford: Oxford University Press, 2010.

Morgenson, Gretchen. *Reckless Endangerment: How Outsized Ambition, Greed, and Corruption Led to Economic Armageddon*. New York: Times Books, 2011.

Morone, James. *Hellfire Nation: The Politics of Sin in American History*. New Haven, CT: Yale University Press, 2004.

Morris, Norval. *The Future of Imprisonment*. Chicago: University of Chicago Press, 1974.

Muhammad, Khalil Gibran. *The Condemnation of Blackness: Race, Crime, and the Making of Modern Urban America*. Cambridge, MA: Harvard University Press, 2010.

——. "Where Did All the White Criminals Go? Reconfiguring Race and Crime on the Road to Mass Incarceration." *Souls* 13, no. 1 (2011): 72–90.

Mulligan, Casey. "Trump's Vast Deregulatory Landscape Goes Unnoticed by the Experts." Commentary, Manhattan Institute, January 13, 2020. https://economics21.org/trump-deregulation-unnoticed-experts.

Murakawa, Naomi. *The First Civil Right: How Liberals Built Prison America*. New York: Oxford University Press, 2014.

Murphy, Heather. "How White Nationalists See What They Want to See in DNA Tests." *New York Times*, July 12, 2019. https://www.nytimes.com/2019/07/12/us/white-nationalists-dna-tests.html.

Murphy, James B. *L. Q. C. Lamar: Pragmatic Patriot*. Baton Rouge: Louisiana State University Press, 1973.

Murray, Charles. "'The Bell Curve', Explained: Introduction." American Enterprise Institute, May 11, 2017. https://www.aei.org/society-and-culture/the-bell-curve-explained-introduction.

——. "'The Bell Curve', Explained: Part 1, The Emergence of a Cognitive Elite." American Enterprise Institute, May 12, 2017. https://www.aei.org/society-and-culture/the-bell-curve-explained-part-1-the-emergence-of-a-cognitive-elite.

——. "'The Bell Curve', Explained: Part 2, Cognitive Classes and Social Behavior." American Enterprise Institute, May 15, 2017. https://www.aei.org/society-and-culture/the-bell-curve-explained-part-ii-cognitive-classes-and-social-behavior.

National Commission on Financial Institution Reform, Recovery, and Enforcement. *Origins and Causes of the S&L Debacle: A Blueprint for Reform: A Report to the President and Congress of the United States*. Washington, DC: US Government Printing Office, 1993.

National Law Center on Homelessness and Poverty. "No Safe Place: The Criminalization of Homelessness in U.S. Cities." 2014. https://homelesslaw.org/wp-content/uploads/2019/02/No_Safe_Place.pdf.

New York State Board of Public Charities. *Annual Report of the State Board of Charities for the Year 1905*. Albany, NY: Brandow Printing, 1906.

——. *Annual Report of the State Board of Charities for the Year 1907*. Albany, NY: J. B. Lyon, 1908.

New York State Crime Commission. *New York State Crime Commission Report*. Albany, NY: J. B. Lyon, 1927.

Nielson, James. *Shelby M. Cullom: Prairie State Republican*. Urbana: University of Illinois Press, 1962.

Norquist, Grover. "Conservative Principles and Prison." *National Review*, February 10, 2011. https://www.nationalreview.com/2011/02/conservative-principles-and-prison-grover-norquist.

Norris, Floyd. "Oversight for Auditor of Madoff." *New York Times*, January 8, 2009. https://www.nytimes.com/2009/01/09/business/09audit.html.

——. "She's a Candidate for a Job She Devised." *New York Times*, July 22, 2010. https://www.nytimes.com/2010/07/23/business/economy/23norris.html?searchResultPosition=3.

"Notes: Industrial Armies." *American Law Review* 28, no. 3 (1894): 420–28.

Novak, William. "Law and the Social Control of American Capitalism." *Emory Law Journal* 60, no. 2 (2010): 377–406.

——. *The People's Welfare: Law and Regulation in Nineteenth-Century America*. Chapel Hill: University of North Carolina Press, 1996.

Odell, Joseph, ed. *Henry Martyn Boies: Appreciations of His Life and Character*. New York: Knickerbocker, 1904.

Ohio State Board of Charities. *Fifteenth Annual Report of the Board of State Charities*. Columbus, OH: Westbote, 1891.

———. *Sixteenth Annual Report of the Board of State Charities*. Columbus, OH: Westbote, 1892.

———. *Twenty-Fourth Annual Report of the Board of State Charities*. Columbus, OH: Westbote, 1900.

O'Malley, Pat. "Volatile and Contradictory Punishment." *Theoretical Criminology* 3, no. 2 (1999): 175–96.

"Once More the Tramp." *Scribner's Monthly* 15 (April 1878): 882–83.

O'Reilly, Kenneth. "A New Deal for the FBI: The Roosevelt Administration, Crime Control, and National Security." *Journal of American History* 69, no. 3 (1982): 638–58.

Orren, Karen. *Belated Feudalism: Labor, the Law, and Liberal Development in the United States*. New York: Cambridge University Press, 1991.

Orren, Karen, and Stephen Skowronek. *The Search for American Political Development*. New York: Cambridge University Press, 2004.

Oschner, A. J. "Surgical Treatment of Habitual Criminals." *Journal of the American Medical Association* 32, no. 16 (1899): 867–68.

Oshinsky, David. *"Worse Than Slavery": Parchman Farm and the Ordeal of Jim Crow Justice*. New York: Free Press, 1996.

Pandiani, John A. "The Crime Control Corps: An Invisible New Deal Program." *British Journal of Sociology* 33, no. 3 (1982): 348–58.

Park, Madison. "Using Chemical Castration to Punish Child Sex Crimes." CNN.com, September 5, 2012. http://www.cnn.com/2012/09/05/health/chemical-castration-science/index.html.

Parrish, Michael. *Securities Regulation and the New Deal*. New Haven, CT: Yale University Press, 1970.

Parsons, Philip A. *Responsibility for Crime: An Investigation of the Nature and Causes of Crime and a Means of Its Prevention*. New York: Columbia University Press, 1909.

Paternoster, Ray. "Deterring Corporate Crime: Evidence and Outlook." *Criminology and Public Policy* 15, no. 2 (2016): 383–86.

Paul, Arnold. *Conservative Crisis and the Rule of Law: Attitudes of Bar and Bench, 1877–1900*. Ithaca, NY: Cornell University Press, 1960.

Pecora, Ferdinand. *Wall Street under Oath: The Story of Our Modern Money Changers*. New York: A. M. Kelly, 1939. Reprint, New York: A. M. Kelly, 1968.

Pennsylvania Board of Commissioners of Public Charities. *Twentieth Annual Report of the Board of Commissioners of Public Charities*. Harrisburg, PA: Edwin K. Meyers, 1890.

———. *Twenty-Third Annual Report of the Board of Commissioners of Public Charities*. Harrisburg, PA: Edwin K. Meyers, 1893.

———. *Twenty-Seventh Annual Report of the Board of Commissioners of Public Charities*. Harrisburg, PA: Clarence M. Busch, 1896.

———. *Thirty-First Annual Report of the Board of Commissioners of Public Charities*. Harrisburg, PA: Wm. Stanley Ray, 1901.

Perino, Michael. *The Hellhound of Wall Street: How Ferdinand Pecora's Investigation of the Great Crash Forever Changed American Finance*. New York: Penguin, 2010.

"Perpetual Imprisonment: Suggested at the Prison Congress for Habitual Criminals, Paupers, and Drunkards." *Washington Post*, December 6, 1892.

Petersilia, Joan. "Community Corrections: Probation, Parole, and Prisoner Reentry." In *Crime and Public Policy*, ed. James Wilson and Joan Petersilia, 499–531. New York: Oxford University Press, 2011.

Petroni, Susan. "VIDEO: Sen. Warren Asks How Many Wall Street Banks Have Been Prosecuted." Patch.com, September 11, 2014. https://patch.com/massachusetts/framingham/video -sen-warren-asks-how-many-wall-street-banks-have-been-prosecuted-0.

Petteruti, Amanda, and Jason Fenster. "Finding Direction: Expanding Criminal Justice Options by Considering Policies of Other Nations." Washington, DC: Justice Policy Institute, 2011. https://justicepolicy.org/wp-content/uploads/justicepolicy/documents/finding_direction -full_report.pdf.

Pfaff, John. *Locked In: The True Origins of Mass Incarceration and How to Achieve Real Reform.* New York: Basic, 2017.

Phelan, Daniel. "The Mental and Physical Characteristics of the Criminal and Degenerate." In *Proceedings of the Annual Congress of the American Prison Association*, 222–34. Indianapolis: Wm. B. Burford, 1909.

Phillips-Fein, Kim. *Invisible Hands: The Businessmen's Crusade against the New Deal.* New York: Norton, 2009.

Pierson, Paul. "Increasing Returns, Path Dependence, and the Study of Politics." *American Political Science Review* 94, no. 2 (2000): 251–67.

Pinkerton, Allan. *Strikers, Communists, Tramps, and Detectives.* New York: G. W. Carleton, 1878.

Piper, Kelsey. "Sam Bankman-Fried Tries to Explain Himself." *Vox*, November 16, 2022. https:// www.vox.com/future-perfect/23462333/sam-bankman-fried-ftx-cryptocurrency-effective -altruism-crypto-bahamas-philanthropy.

Pisciotta, Alexander. *Benevolent Repression: Social Control and the American Reformatory-Prison Movement.* New York: New York University Press, 1994.

Pleyte, Maria. "White Collar Crime in the Twenty-First Century: Interview with Professor John Poulos." *UC Davis Business Law Journal*, vol. 4, no. 1 (December 1, 2003). https://blj.ucdavis .edu/archives/vol-4-no-1/white-collar-crime-in-the-twenty-first-century.html.

Pontell, Henry, William Black, and Gilbert Geis. "Too Big to Fail, Too Powerful to Jail? On the Absence of Criminal Prosecutions After the 2008 Financial Meltdown." *Crime, Law and Social Change* 61, no. 1 (2014): 1–13.

"Populist Party Platform." From "People's Party Platform." *Omaha Morning World-Herald*, July 5, 1892. https://wwnorton.com/college/history/archive/reader/trial/directory/1890_1914/12 _ch22_04.htm.

Postel, Charles. "The American Populist and Anti-Populist Legacy." In *Transformations of Populism in Europe and the Americas: History and Recent Tendencies*, ed. John Abromeit, York Norman, Gary Marotta, and Bridget Maria Chesterton, 116–35. London: Bloomsbury Academic, 2016.

———. "TR, Wilson, and the Origins of the Progressive Tradition." In *Progressivism in America: Past, Present, and Future*, ed. David B. Woolner and John M. Thompson, 3–13. New York: Oxford University Press, 2016.

Powell, J. C. *The American Siberia; or, Fourteen Years' Experience in a Southern Convict Camp.* Philadelphia: H. J. Smith, 1891.

Powell, Lewis. "Confidential Memorandum: Attack on American Free Enterprise System." August 23, 1971. https://scholarlycommons.law.wlu.edu/cgi/viewcontent.cgi?article=1000&con text=powellmemo.

"President Bush's Comments." *New York Times*, July 8, 2002. https://www.nytimes.com/2002/07/08/politics/president-bushs-comments.html.

President's Commission on Law Enforcement and Administration of Justice. *The Challenge of Crime in a Free Society*. Washington, DC: US Government Printing Office, 1967.

Pressley, Ayanna, and David Stein. "A Federal Job Guarantee: The Unfinished Business of the Civil Rights Movement." *The Nation*, September 2, 2021. https://www.thenation.com/article/politics/federal-job-guarantee.

Proctor, Ben H. *Not without Honor: The Life of John H. Reagan*. Austin: University of Texas Press, 1962.

"Protection against Tramps." *Chicago Daily Tribune*, July 12, 1877.

"The Question of 'Tramps.'" *New York Times*, February 6, 1875.

Quinney, Richard. *Critique of Legal Order: Crime Control in Capitalist Society*. Boston: Little, Brown, 1973.

Rackhill, Stephen J. "Printzlein's Legacy, the 'Brooklyn Plan,' A.K.A. Deferred Prosecution." *Federal Probation* 60, no. 2 (1996): 8–15.

Rader, Katie, and Carissa Guadron. "What Running on a Jobs Guarantee Could Mean for Democrats." *The Nation*, June 15, 2023. https://www.thenation.com/?post_type=article&p=447711.

Rafter, Nicole Hahn. *Creating Born Criminals*. Urbana: University of Illinois Press, 1997.

Raine, Adrian. *The Anatomy of Violence: The Biological Roots of Crime*. New York: Pantheon, 2013.

Raine, Adrian, William S. Laufer, Yaling Yang, Katherine L. Narr, Paul Thompson, and Arthur W. Toga. "Increased Executive Functioning, Attention, and Cortical Thickness in White-Collar Criminals." *Human Brain Mapping* 33, no. 12 (2012): 2932–40.

Rakoff, Jed S. "The Financial Crisis: Why Have No High-Level Executives Been Prosecuted?" *New York Review of Books*, January 9, 2014. https://www.nybooks.com/articles/2014/01/09/financial-crisis-why-no-executive-prosecutions.

Randolph, A. Philip, and Bayard Rustin. "A 'Freedom Budget' for All Americans: A Summary." New York: A. Philip Randolph Institute, January 1967. https://www.prrac.org/pdf/Freedom Budget.pdf.

Raper, Charles Lee. *Railway Transportation: A History of Its Economics and of Its Relation to the State*. New York: G. P. Putnam's Sons, 1912.

Raphael, Steven, and David F. Weiman. "The Impact of Local Labor-Market Conditions on the Likelihood That Parolees Are Returned to Custody." In *Barriers to Reentry? The Labor Market for Released Prisoners in Post-Industrial America*, ed. Shawn Bushway, Michael A. Stoll, and David F. Weiman, 304–32. New York: Russell Sage, 2007.

Raphael, Steven, and Rudolf Winter-Ebmer. "Identifying the Effect of Unemployment on Crime." *Journal of Law and Economics* 44, no. 1 (2001): 259–83.

"Read the Full Transcript from the First Presidential Debate between Joe Biden and Donald Trump." *USA Today*, October 4, 2020. https://www.usatoday.com/story/news/politics/elections/2020/09/30/presidential-debate-read-full-transcript-first-debate/3587462001.

Reed, Adolph. "Marx, Race, and Neoliberalism." *New Labor Forum* 22, no. 1 (2013): 49–57.

———. "Revolution as 'National Liberation' and the Origins of Neoliberal Antiracism." *Socialist Register* 53 (2017): 299–322.

Reed, Adolph, and Merlin Chowkwanyun. "Race, Class, Crisis: The Discourse of Racial Disparity and Its Analytical Discontents." In "The Crisis and the Left," ed. Leo Panitch, Gregory Albo, and Vivek Chibber, special issue, *Socialist Register* 48 (2012): 149–75.

Reiman, Jeffrey, and Paul Leighton. *The Rich Get Richer and the Poor Get Prison: Ideology, Class, and Criminal Justice.* 1979. 11th ed. New York: Taylor and Francis, 2016.

Reisig, Michael D. "Community and Problem-Oriented Policing." *Crime and Justice* 39, no. 1 (2010): 1–53.

Reitz, Kevin. "Sentencing." In *Crime and Public Policy*, ed. James Q. Wilson and Joan Petersilia, 467–98. New York: Oxford University Press, 2011.

"Remarks of Mr. Henley of Alabama, and P. D. Sims, Chairman of the Board of Prisons, Tennessee." In *Proceedings of the Annual Congress of the National Prison Association of the United States*, 119–22. Pittsburgh: Shaw Bros., 1891.

"Reveal Stock Pool Clears 5 Million in Week: Senators Learn of Radio Bull Coup." *Chicago Tribune*, May 20, 1932.

Richman, Daniel. "Federal White Collar Sentencing in the United States: A Work in Progress." *Law and Contemporary Problems* 76, no. 1 (2013): 53–74.

Ringenbach, Paul. *Tramps and Reformers, 1873–1916: The Discovery of Unemployment in New York.* Westport, CT: Greenwood, 1973.

Ripley, William Z. *The Races of Europe.* New York: D. Appleton, 1899.

"Risk/Needs Assessment 101: Science Reveals New Tools to Manage Offenders." Public Safety Performance Project, Issue Brief, Pew Center on the States, 2011. https://www.pewtrusts.org/~/media/legacy/uploadedfiles/pcs_assets/2011/pewriskassessmentbriefpdf.pdf.

Risley, S. D. "Some of the Ethical and Sociological Relations of the Physicians to the Community." *Bulletin of the American Academy of Medicine* 5, no. 8 (1901): 569–93.

Rodgers, Daniel. *Contested Truths: Keywords in American Politics since Independence.* New York: Basic, 1987.

———. "In Search of Progressivism." *Reviews in American History* 10, no. 4 (December 1982): 113–32.

Roosevelt, Franklin Delano. "Commonwealth Club Address." September 23, 1932. https://www.americanrhetoric.com/speeches/PDFFiles/FDR%20-%20Commonwealth%20Club%20Address.pdf.

Roosevelt, Theodore. "Applied Idealism." *The Outlook* 104 (1913): 461–78.

———. *The Foes of Our Own Household.* New York: George H. Doran, 1917.

———. "Letter to Edward Alsworth Ross." September 19, 1907. Theodore Roosevelt Digital Archive, Dickinson State University. https://www.theodorerooseveltcenter.org/Research/Digital-Library/Record?libID=o200337.

———. "Message Communicated to the Two Houses of Congress at the Beginning of the First Session of the Fifty-Seventh Congress, December 3, 1901." In *Addresses and Presidential Messages of Theodore Roosevelt, 1902–1904.* New York: G. P. Putnam's Sons, 1904.

———. "State of the Union, 1907." Washington, DC, December 3, 1907. http://www.let.rug.nl/usa/presidents/theodore-roosevelt/state-of-the-union-1907.php.

———. *Theodore Roosevelt: An Autobiography.* New York: Charles Scribner's Sons, 1921.

———. "T. Roosevelt Letter to C. Davenport about 'Degenerates Reproducing.'" January 3, 1913. DNA Learning Center, Cold Springs Harbor Laboratory. https://www.dnalc.org/view/11219-T-Roosevelt-letter-to-C-Davenport-about-degenerates-reproducing-.html.

———. "Twisted Eugenics." *The Outlook* 106 (1914): 30–34.

Rose, Amanda M. "Designing an Efficient Securities-Fraud Deterrence Regime." In *Prosperity Unleashed: Smarter Financial Regulation*, ed. Norbert J. Michel, 255–62. Washington, DC: Heritage Foundation, 2017. https://thf-reports.s3.amazonaws.com/2017/Prosperity Unleashed.pdf.

Ross, Edward. "Recent Tendencies in Sociology, III." *Quarterly Journal of Economics* 17, no. 3 (1903): 438–55.

———. *Sin and Society: An Analysis of Latter-Day Iniquity.* Boston: Houghton Mifflin, 1907.

———. "Social Control." *American Journal of Sociology* 1, no. 5 (1896): 513–35.

———. *Social Control: A Survey of the Foundations of Order.* New York: Macmillan, 1901.

Rothman, David J. *The Discovery of the Asylum: Social Order and Disorder in the New Republic.* Boston: Little, Brown, 1971.

———. "The Structure of State Politics." In *Political Parties in American History, 1828–1890* (3 vols.), ed. Felice Bonadio and Morton Borden, 2:815–39. New York: Putnam, 1974.

Rugaber, Christopher. "Federal Reserve Considering Stronger Bank Rules After SVB Failure, Official Says." *PBS Newshour,* PBS.com, March 28, 2023. https://www.pbs.org/newshour /economy/federal-reserve-considering-stronger-bank-rules-after-svb-failure-official-says.

Ruiz, George. "The Ideological Convergence of Theodore Roosevelt and Woodrow Wilson." *Presidential Studies Quarterly* 19, no. 1 (1989): 159–77.

Ruth, Henry, and Kevin Reitz. *The Challenge of Crime: Rethinking Our Response.* Cambridge, MA: Harvard University Press, 2003.

Sampson, Robert J. *Great American City: Chicago and the Enduring Neighborhood Effect.* Chicago: University of Chicago Press, 2012.

Sampson, Robert J., William Julius Wilson, and Hanna Katz. "Reassessing 'Toward a Theory of Race, Crime, and Urban Inequality': Enduring and New Challenges in 21st Century America." *Du Bois Review* 15, no. 1 (2018): 13–34.

Sanders, Elizabeth. *Roots of Reform: Farmers, Workers, and the American State, 1877–1917.* Chicago: University of Chicago Press, 1999.

Savage, Joanne, Richard Bennett, and Mona Danner. "Economic Assistance and Crime: A Cross-National Investigation." *European Journal of Criminology* 5, no. 2 (2008): 217–38.

Savelsberg, Joachim. "Knowledge, Domination and Criminal Punishment." *American Journal of Sociology* 99, no. 4 (January 1994): 911–43.

Schattschneider, E. E. *The Semisovereign People: A Realist's View of Democracy in America.* Hinsdale, IL: Dryden, 1960.

Schell-Busey, Natalie, Sally S. Simpson, Melissa Rorie, and Mariel Alper. "What Works? A Systematic Review of Corporate Crime Deterrence." *Criminology and Public Policy* 15, no. 2 (2016): 387–416.

Schlesinger, Arthur M., Jr. *The Crisis of the Old Order, 1919–1933.* Boston: Houghton Mifflin, 2003.

Schmidt, Vivien. "Reconciling Ideas and Institutions through Discursive Institutionalism." In *Ideas and Politics in Social Science Research,* ed. Daniel Béland and Robert Henry Cox, 47–64. New York: Oxford University Press, 2011.

Schwartz, Hunter. "Following Reports of Forced Sterilization of Female Prison Inmates, California Passes Ban." *Washington Post,* September 26, 2014. https://www.washingtonpost .com/blogs/govbeat/wp/2014/09/26/following-reports-of-forced-sterilization-of-female -prison-inmates-california-passes-ban.

Shaffer, Gregory C. "Law and Business." In *The Oxford Handbook of Business and Government,* ed. David Coen, Wyn Grant, and Graham Wilson, 63–88. Oxford: Oxford University Press, 2010.

Shapiro, James A. "Comity of Errors: When Federal Sentencing Guidelines Ignore State Law Decriminalizing Sentences." *Akron Law Review* 41, no. 1 (2008): 231–47.

Shapiro, Susan P. *Wayward Capitalists: Targets of the Securities and Exchange Commission.* New Haven, CT: Yale University Press, 1985.

Sharp, Harry. *The Sterilization of Degenerates.* Jeffersonville: Indiana Reformatory, 1909.

——. *Vasectomy: A Means of Preventing Defective Procreation.* Jeffersonville: Indiana Reformatory, 1909.

Shefter, Martin. "Trade Unions and Political Machines: The Organization and Disorganization of the American Working Class in the Late Nineteenth Century." In *Working Class Formation: Nineteenth-Century Patterns in Western Europe and the United States,* ed. Ira Katznelson and Aristide R. Zolberg, 197–276. Princeton, NJ: Princeton University Press, 1986.

Shufeldt, R. W. *The Negro: A Menace to American Civilization.* Boston: Gorham, 1907.

Simon, Jonathan. "'The Criminal Is to Go Free': The Legacy of Eugenic Thought in Contemporary Judicial Realism about American Criminal Justice." *Boston University Law Review* 100, no. 3 (2020): 787–815.

——. "Dignity and Its Discontents: Towards an Abolitionist Rethinking of Dignity." *European Journal of Criminology* 18, no. 1 (2021): 33–51.

——. *Governing through Crime: How the War on Crime Transformed American Democracy and Created a Culture of Fear.* New York: Oxford University Press, 2007.

——. *Poor Discipline: Parole and the Social Control of the Underclass, 1890–1990.* Chicago: University of Chicago Press, 1993.

——. "The Second Coming of Dignity." In *The New Criminal Justice Thinking,* ed. Sharon Dolovich and Alexandra Natapoff, 275–307. New York: New York University Press, 2017.

Simpson, Sally S. *Corporate Crime, Law, and Social Control.* New York: Cambridge University Press, 2002.

Skeel, David A., Jr., and William J. Stuntz. "Christianity and the (Modest) Rule of Law." *University of Pennsylvania Journal of Constitutional Law* 8 (2006): 809–40.

Sklar, Martin. *The Corporate Reconstruction of American Capitalism, 1890–1916: The Market, the Law, and Politics.* New York: Cambridge University Press, 1988.

Skowronek, Stephen. *Building a New American State: The Expansion of National and Administrative Capacities, 1877–1920.* New York: Cambridge University Press, 1982.

——. *The Politics Presidents Make: Leadership from John Adams to Bill Clinton.* Cambridge, MA: Harvard University Press, 1993.

——. "The Reassociation of Ideas and Purposes: Racism, Liberalism, and the American Political Tradition." *American Political Science Review* 100, no. 3 (2006): 385–401.

Skowronek, Stephen, and Stephen Engel. "The Progressives' Century." In *The Progressives' Century: Political Reform, Constitutional Government, and the Modern American State,* ed. Stephen Skowronek, Stephen Engel, and Bruce Ackerman, 1–15. New Haven, CT: Yale University Press, 2016.

Smialek, Jeanna. "How a Trump-Era Rollback Mattered for Silicon Valley Bank's Demise." *New York Times,* March 21, 2023. https://www.nytimes.com/2023/03/31/business/economy/silicon-valley-bank-federal-reserve-supervision.html.

Smith, Andrew. "SEC Cease-and-Desist Orders." *Administrative Law Review* 51, no. 4 (1999): 1197–228.

Smith, Rogers M. *Civic Ideals: Conflicting Visions of Citizenship in U.S. History.* New Haven, CT: Yale University, 1997.

——. "Ideas and the Spiral of Politics: The Place of American Political Thought in American Political Development." *American Political Thought* 3, no. 1 (2014): 126–36.

———. "The Progressive Seedbed: Claims of American Political Community in the Twentieth and Twenty-First Centuries." In *The Progressives' Century: Political Reform, Constitutional Government, and the Modern American State*, ed. Stephen Skowronek, Stephen Engel, and Bruce Ackerman, 264–88. New Haven, CT: Yale University Press, 2016.

———. "Which Comes First, the Ideas or the Institutions?" In *Rethinking Political Institutions: The Art of the State*, ed. Ian Shapiro, Stephen Skowronek, and Daniel Galvin, 23–36. New York: New York University Press, 2006.

Smith, Walker C. "The Floater an Iconoclast." *Industrial Worker*, June 4, 1910.

Soss, Joe, Richard C. Fording, and Sanford F. Schram. *Disciplining the Poor: Neoliberal Paternalism and the Persistent Power of Race*. Chicago: University of Chicago Press, 2011.

Spence, Lester. *Knocking the Hustle: Against the Neoliberal Turn in Black Politics*. New York: Punctum, 2015.

Spillane, Joseph F., and David B. Wolcott. *A History of Modern American Criminal Justice*. Thousand Oaks, CA: Sage, 2012.

Spindel, Donna. *Crime and Society in North Carolina, 1663–1776*. Baton Rouge: Louisiana State University Press, 1989.

Starr, Sonja. "Evidence-Based Sentencing and the Scientific Rationalization of Discrimination." *Stanford Law Review* 66, no. 4 (2014): 803–72.

"Statement from the Press Secretary Regarding Executive Grants of Clemency." White House, February 18, 2020. https://trumpwhitehouse.archives.gov/briefings-statements/statement-press-secretary-regarding-executive-grants-clemency-2.

Stern, Alexandra Minna. *Eugenic Nation: Faults and Frontiers of Better Breeding in Modern America*. Oakland: University of California Press, 2015.

Stimson, Charles. "The First Step Act's Risk and Needs Assessment Program: A Work in Progress." Legal Memorandum no. 265, The Heritage Foundation, June 8, 2022. https://www.heritage.org/sites/default/files/2020-06/LM265_0.pdf.

Stocking, George. *Race, Culture, and Evolution: Essays in the History of Anthropology*. New York: Free Press, 1968. Reprint, Chicago: University of Chicago Press, 1982.

"A Stringent Anti-Vagrant Act Passed." *Los Angeles Times*, February 6, 1891.

Stuntz, William J. *The Collapse of American Criminal Justice*. Cambridge, MA: Belknap Press of Harvard University Press, 2011.

"Sturgis Gives Evidence in Money Trust Inquiry." *Evening News* (Providence, RI), December 13, 1912.

Sumner, William Graham. *The Challenge of Facts: And Other Essays*. New Haven, CT: Yale University Press, 1914.

———. *What Social Classes Owe to Each Other*. New York: Harper & Bros., 1883.

Sutherland, Edwin. *White-Collar Crime*. New York: Dryden, 1949.

———. "White-Collar Criminality." *American Sociological Review* 5, no. 1 (1940): 1–12.

Swenson, Peter. "Arranged Alliance: Business Interests in the New Deal." *Politics and Society* 25, no. 1 (1997): 66–116.

Taft, William Howard. "Address at the Lincoln Birthday Banquet of the Republican Club of the City of New York, February 12, 1910." In *Presidential Addresses and State Papers of William Howard Taft from March 4, 1909, to March 4, 1910*, 1:568–86. New York: Doubleday, 1910.

Taibbi, Matt. *The Divide: American Injustice in the Age of the Wealth Gap*. New York: Spiegel & Grau, 2014.

Tanner, Michael. "A Prison-Reform Bill Passed the House 360–59. It'll Probably Die in the Sen-ate." Cato Institute, June 6, 2018. https://www.cato.org/commentary/prison-reform-bill-passed-house-360-59-itll-probably-die-senate.

Tappan, Paul. "Habitual Offender Laws in the United States." *Federal Probation* 13 (1949): 28–31.

Taub, Jennifer. "Bank Bailouts Are Back." *Washington Monthly*, March 16, 2023. https://washingtonmonthly.com/2023/03/16/bank-bailouts-are-back.

———. *Big Dirty Money: The Shocking Injustice and Unseen Cost of White Collar Crime*. New York: Viking, 2020.

Taussig, Frank. *Principles of Economics*. Vol. 2. New York: Macmillan, 1911.

Tcherneva, Pavlina. "The Federal Jobs Guarantee: Prevention, Not Just a Cure." *Challenge* 62, no. 4 (2019): 253–72.

Terman, Lewis M. *The Measurement of Intelligence: An Explanation of and a Complete Guide for the Use of the Stanford Revision and Extension of the Binet-Simon Intelligence Scale*. Boston: Houghton Mifflin, 1916.

Thompson, Alex. "'Why Are You Pissing in Our Face?' Inside Warren's War with the Obama Team." *Politico*, September 12, 2019. https://www.politico.com/magazine/story/2019/09/12/warren-obama-2020-228068.

Thorelli, Hans. *The Federal Antitrust Policy: Origination of an American Tradition*. Baltimore: Johns Hopkins University Press, 1955.

Tillman, Robert, and Henry Pontell. "Organizations and Fraud in the Savings and Loan Indus-try." *Social Forces* 73, no. 4 (1995): 1439–63.

Tillman, Robert, Henry Pontell, and William Black. *Financial Crime and Crises in the Era of False Profits*. New York: Oxford University Press, 2017.

Tonry, Michael. "Equality and Human Dignity: The Missing Ingredients in American Sentenc-ing." *Crime and Justice* 45, no. 1 (2016): 459–96.

———. *Punishing Race: A Continuing American Dilemma*. New York: Oxford University Press, 2011.

———. *Sentencing Fragments*. New York: Oxford University Press, 2016.

———. *Sentencing Matters*. New York: Oxford University Press, 1996.

Trachtenberg, Alan. *The Incorporation of America: Culture and Society in the Gilded Age*. New York: Hill & Wang, 1982.

Tramontozzi, Paul, and Kenneth Chilton. "US Regulatory Agencies under Reagan, 1960–1988." St. Louis: Center for the Study of American Business, Washington University, 1988.

"The Tramp Problem." *Chicago Daily Tribune*, May 11, 1894.

"Tramps Who Are Criminals." *New York Times*, September 29, 1903.

"Transcript of Obama's Press Conference." Economy and Politics, *MarketWatch*, October 6, 2011. https://www.marketwatch.com/story/transcript-of-obamas-press-conference-2011-10-06.

Uhlmann, David. "The Pendulum Swings: Reconsidering Corporate Criminal Prosecution." *UC Davis Law Review* 49, no. 4 (2016): 1235–83.

Urofsky, Melvin. "Proposed Federal Incorporation in the Progressive Era." *American Journal of Legal History* 26, no. 2 (1982): 160–83.

US Bureau of Corporations. Department of Commerce and Labor. *Annual Report of the Commissioner of Corporations*. Washington, DC: US Government Printing Office, 1906.

———. *Report of the Commissioner of Corporations*. Washington, DC: US Government Printing Office, 1908.

US Center for Disease Control and Prevention. "Regulation: Selected Actions of the US Government Regarding the Regulation of Tobacco Sales, Marketing, and Use." CDC.gov, January 11, 2022. https://www.cdc.gov/tobacco/basic_information/policy/regulation/index.htm.

US Congress Committee of Conference. *Securities Exchange Act of 1934: Conference Report.* S. Rep. No. 73-1838. Washington, DC: US Government Printing Office, 1934.

US Department of Justice. "Criminal Resource Manual Archives, Section 958." n.d. https://www.justice.gov/archives/jm/criminal-resource-manual-958-fraud-affecting-financial-institution.

———. "Department of Justice Announces Enhancements to the Risk Assessment System and Updates on First Step Act Implementation." January 15, 2020. https://www.justice.gov/opa/pr/department-justice-announces-enhancements-risk-assessment-system-and-updates-first-step-act.

———. "First Step Act Implementation: Fiscal Year 2020 90-Day Report." June 2, 2020. https://www.ojp.gov/pdffiles1/nij/254799.pdf.

———. "The First Step Act of 2018: Risk and Needs Assessment System." 2019. https://nij.ojp.gov/sites/g/files/xyckuh171/files/media/document/the-first-step-act-of-2018-risk-and-needs-assessment-system_1.pdf.

US Food and Drug Administration. "Family Smoking Prevention and Tobacco Control Act—an Overview." FDA.gov, October 4, 2022. https://www.fda.gov/tobacco-products/rules-regulations-and-guidance/family-smoking-prevention-and-tobacco-control-act-overview.

———. "The Real Cost Campaign." FDA.gov, January 9, 2023. https://www.fda.gov/tobacco-products/public-health-education-campaigns/real-cost-campaign.

US Government Accounting Office. "Bank and Thrift Criminal Fraud: The Federal Commitment Could Be Broadened." Washington, DC: US Government Accounting Office, January 1993. https://www.gao.gov/assets/ggd-93-48.pdf.

US House Commerce Committee. "Views of the Minority." In "A Bureau of Inter-State Commerce." H.R. Rep. No. 47-1399, June 12, 1882.

US House Committee on Banking and Currency. *Federal Supervision of Traffic in Investment Securities in Interstate Commerce.* H.R. Rep. No. 73-85. Washington, DC: US Government Printing Office, 1933.

US House Committee on Banking and Urban Affairs. *The Savings and Loan Crisis: Field Hearings Before the Committee on Banking, Finance, and Urban Affairs.* 101st Cong., 1st Sess. Washington, DC: US Government Printing Office, 1989.

US House Committee on Banking, Finance, and Urban Affairs. *Federal Asset Disposition Association: Hearing Before the Subcommittee on Financial Institutions Supervision, Regulation, and Insurance.* 100th Cong., 1st Sess. Washington, DC: US Government Printing Office, 1987.

———. *Federal Savings and Loan Insurance Corporation Recapitalization Act of 1987 (H.R. 27): Hearings Before the Committee on Banking, Finance, and Urban Affairs.* 100th Cong., 1st Sess. Washington, DC: US Government Printing Office, 1987.

———. *Financial Condition of the Federal Savings and Loan Insurance Corporation and Federal Deposit Insurance Corporation at Year End 1988: Field Hearings Before the Committee on Banking, Finance, and Urban Affairs.* 101st Cong., 1st Sess. Washington, DC: US Government Printing Office, 1989.

———. *Findings of Booz Allen and Hamilton Study of FHLBB: Hearing Before the Subcommittee on General Oversight and Investigations.* 100th Cong., 1st Sess. Washington, DC: US Government Printing Office, 1987.

———. *The Other Side of the Savings and Loan Industry: Hearing Before the Subcommittee on Financial Institutions, Supervision, and Regulation.* 101st Con., 1st Sess. Washington, DC: US Government Printing Office, 1989.

US House Committee on Commerce. *Arguments and Statements in Relation to Certain Bills Proposing Congressional Regulation of Interstate Commerce: Hearings Before the United States House Committee on Commerce.* 47th Cong., 1st Sess. Washington, DC, 1882.

———. *Arguments and Statements in Relation to Certain Bills Proposing Congressional Regulation of Interstate Commerce: Hearings Before the United States House Committee on Commerce.* 48th Cong., 1st Sess. Washington, DC: US Government Printing Office, 1884.

US House Committee on Financial Services. *Assessing the Madoff Ponzi Scheme and Regulatory Failures: Hearing Before the Subcommittee on Capital Markets, Insurance, and Government Sponsored Enterprises.* 111th Cong., 1st Sess. Washington, DC: US Government Printing Office, 2009.

———. *Systemic Risk and Financial Markets: Hearing Before the Committee on Financial Services.* 110th Cong., 2nd Sess. Washington, DC: US Government Printing Office, 2008.

US House Committee on Government Operations. *Fraud and Abuse by Insiders, Borrowers, and Appraisers in the California Thrift Industry: Hearing Before a Subcommittee of the Committee on Government Operations.* 100th Cong., 1st Sess. Washington, DC: US Government Printing Office, 1987.

US House Committee on Interstate and Foreign Commerce. *Federal Securities Act: Hearing Before the Committee on Interstate and Foreign Commerce.* 73rd Cong., 1st Sess. Washington, DC: US Government Printing Office, 1933.

———. "Interstate Trade Commission." H.R. Rep. No. 63-533. Washington, DC: US Government Printing Office, 1914.

———. *Interstate Trade Commission: Hearings Before the Committee on Interstate and Foreign Commerce.* 63rd Cong., 2nd Sess. Washington, DC: US Government Printing Office, 1914.

———. *Securities Exchange Bill of 1934.* H.R. Rep. No. 73-1383. Washington, DC: US Government Printing Office, 1934.

———. *Stock Exchange Regulation: Hearing Before the Committee on Interstate and Foreign Commerce.* 73rd Cong., 2nd Sess. Washington, DC: US Government Printing Office, 1934.

US House Committee on Oversight and Government Reform. *The Financial Crisis and the Role of Federal Regulators: Hearing Before the Committee on Oversight and Government Reform.* 110th Cong., 2nd Sess. Washington, DC: US Government Printing Office, 2008.

US House Committee on the Judiciary. *Federal Sentencing Revision: Hearings Before the Subcommittee on Criminal Justice.* Pt. 1. 98th Cong., 2nd Sess. Washington, DC: US Government Printing Office, 1987.

———. *Federal Sentencing Revision: Hearings Before the Subcommittee on Criminal Justice.* Pt. 2. 98th Cong., 2nd Sess. Washington, DC: US Government Printing Office, 1987.

———. *Formerly Incarcerated Reenter Society Transformed Safely Transitioning Every Person Act.* H.R. Rep. No. 115-699. Washington, DC: US Government Printing Office, 2018.

———. *Prosecuting Fraud in the Thrift Industry: Hearings Before the Subcommittee on Criminal Justice.* 101st Cong., 1st Sess. Washington, DC: US Government Printing Office, 1989.

———. "Report from the Committee on the Judiciary to Accompany H.R. 15657." H.R. Rep. No. 63-627. Washington, DC: US Government Printing Office, 1914.

———. *Sentencing Revision Act of 1984, Report of the Committee on the Judiciary.* H.R. Rep. No. 98-1017. Washington, DC: US Government Printing Office, 1984.

US House Subcommittee of the Committee on Banking and Currency. *Money Trust Investigation: Investigation of Financial and Monetary Conditions in the United States under House Resolutions nos. 429 and 504.* 62nd Cong. Washington, DC: US Government Printing Office, 1913.

US Industrial Commission. *Report of the Industrial Commission on Prison Labor.* Vol. 3. Washington, DC: US Government Printing Office, 1900.

———. *Report of the Industrial Commission on Labor Legislation.* Vol. 5. Washington, DC: US Government Printing Office, 1900.

———. *Report of the Industrial Commission on the Relations and Conditions of Capital and Labor Employed in Manufactures and General Business (Second Volume on This Subject).* Vol. 14. Washington, DC: US Government Printing Office, 1901.

———. *Reports of the Industrial Commission on Immigration, Including Testimony, with Review and Digest, and Special Reports, and on Education, Including Testimony, with Review and Digest.* Vol. 15. Washington, DC: US Government Printing Office, 1901.

US Interstate Commerce Commission. *Interstate Commerce Commission Reports.* Vol. 1, *Reports and Decisions of the Interstate Commerce Commission of the United States: April 5th, 1887 to April 5th, 1888.* New York: L. K. Strouse & Co., 1888.

US Senate Committee on Banking and Currency. *Regulation of Securities: Report.* S. Rep. No. 73-47. Washington, DC: US Government Printing Office, 1933.

———. *Securities Act: Hearings Before the Committee on Banking and Currency.* 73rd Cong., 1st Sess. Washington, DC: US Government Printing Office, 1933.

———. *Stock Exchange Practices: Hearings Before a Subcommittee on Banking and Currency, United States Senate.* Pt. 2. 72nd Cong., 1st Sess. Washington, DC: US Government Printing Office, 1932.

———. *Stock Exchange Practices: Hearings Before a Subcommittee on Banking and Currency, United States Senate.* Pt. 3. 72nd Cong., 1st Sess. Washington, DC: US Government Printing Office, 1932.

———. *Stock Exchange Practices: Hearings Before a Subcommittee on Banking and Currency, United States Senate.* Pt. 4. 72nd Cong., 2nd Sess. Washington, DC: US Government Printing Office, 1933.

———. *Stock Exchange Practices: Hearings Before a Subcommittee on Banking and Currency, United States Senate.* Pt. 5. 72nd Cong., 2nd Sess. Washington, DC: US Government Printing Office, 1933.

———. *Stock Exchange Practices: Hearings Before a Subcommittee on Banking and Currency, United States Senate.* Pt. 6. 72nd Cong., 2nd Sess. Washington, DC: US Government Printing Office, 1933.

———. *Stock Exchange Practices: Hearings Before a Subcommittee on Banking and Currency, United States Senate.* Pt. 8. 73rd Cong., 2nd Sess. Washington, DC: US Government Printing Office, 1934.

———. *Stock Exchange Practices: Hearings Before a Subcommittee on Banking and Currency, United States Senate.* Pt. 15. 73rd Cong., 1st Sess. Washington, DC: US Government Printing Office, 1934.

———. *Stock Exchange Practices: Hearings Before a Subcommittee on Banking and Currency, United States Senate.* Pt. 16. 73rd Cong., 2nd Sess. Washington, DC: US Government Printing Office, 1934.

———. *Stock Exchange Practices: Report of the Committee on Banking and Currency.* S. Rep. No. 73-1455. Washington, DC: US Government Printing Office, 1934.

US Senate Committee on Banking, Housing, and Urban Affairs. *Consumer Protections in Financial Services: Past Problems, Future Solutions: Hearing Before the Committee on Banking, Housing, and Urban Affairs.* 111th Cong., 1st Sess. Washington, DC: US Government Printing Office, 2009.

——. *Creating a Consumer Financial Protection Agency: A Cornerstone of America's New Economic Foundation: Hearing Before the Committee on Banking, Housing, and Urban Affairs.* 111th Cong., 1st Sess. Washington, DC: US Government Printing Office, 2010.

——. *Modernizing the U.S. Financial Regulatory System: Hearing Before the Committee on Banking, Housing, and Urban Affairs.* 111th Cong., 1st Sess. Washington, DC: US Government Printing Office, 2009.

——. *Mortgage Market Turmoil: Causes and Consequences: Hearing Before the Committee on Banking, Housing, and Urban Affairs.* 110th Cong., 1st Sess. Washington, DC: US Government Printing Office, 2007.

——. *Oversight on the Condition of the Financial Services Industry: Hearings Before the Committee on Banking, Housing, and Urban Affairs.* 100th Cong., 2nd Sess. Washington, DC: US Government Printing Office, 1988.

——. *Problems of the Federal Savings and Loan Insurance Corporation (FSLIC): Hearings Before the Committee on Banking, Housing, and Urban Affairs.* Pt. 1. 101st Cong., 1st Sess. Washington, DC: US Government Printing Office, 1989.

——. *Problems of the Federal Savings and Loan Insurance Corporation (FSLIC): Hearings Before the Committee on Banking, Housing, and Urban Affairs.* Pt. 2. 101st Cong., 1st Sess. Washington, DC: US Government Printing Office, 1989.

——. *Problems of the Federal Savings and Loan Insurance Corporation (FSLIC): Hearings Before the Committee on Banking, Housing, and Urban Affairs.* Pt. 3. 101st Cong., 1st Sess. Washington, DC: US Government Printing Office, 1989.

——. *Recent Developments in US Financial Markets and Regulatory Responses to Them: Hearing Before the Committee on Banking, Housing, and Urban Affairs.* 110th Cong., 2nd Sess. Washington, DC: US Government Printing Office, 2008.

——. *The State of the Securities Markets: Hearing Before the Committee on Banking, Housing, and Urban Affairs.* 110th Cong., 1st Sess. Washington, DC: US Government Printing Office, 2007.

——. *Thrift Charter Enhancement Act of 1988: Hearing Before the Committee on Banking, Housing, and Urban Affairs.* 100th Cong., 2nd Sess. Washington, DC: US Government Printing Office, 1988.

US Senate Committee on Commerce. *Federal Trade Commission Oversight: Hearings Before the Committee on Commerce.* 93rd Cong., 2nd Sess. Washington, DC: US Government Printing Office, 1974.

US Senate Committee on Interstate Commerce. "Federal Trade Commission." S. Rep. No. 63-597. Washington, DC: Government Printing Office, 1914.

——. *Interstate Trade: Hearings Before the Committee on Interstate Commerce.* Vol. 2. 63rd Cong., 2nd Sess. Washington, DC, 1914.

US Senate Committee on the Budget. *Current Conditions in the Federal Savings and Loan Insurance Corporation: Hearing Before the Committee on the Budget.* 100th Cong., 2nd Sess. Washington, DC: US Government Printing Office, 1988.

US Senate Committee on the Judiciary. *Charges of Illegal Practices of Department of Justice: Hearings Before a Subcommittee of the Committee on the Judiciary.* 66th Cong., 3rd Sess. Washington, DC: US Government Printing Office, 1921.

———. *Sentencing Reform Act of 1983: Report of the Committee on the Judiciary on S. 688.* S. Rep. No. 98-223. Washington, DC: US Government Printing Office, 1983.

US Senate Select Committee on Interstate Commerce. *Report of the Senate Select Committee on Interstate Commerce: Testimony as to the Regulation of Interstate Commerce by Congress.* 49th Cong., 1st Sess. Washington, DC: US Government Printing Office, 1886.

———. "Report of the Senate Select Committee on Interstate Commerce, to Accompany Bill H.R. 1093." S. Rep. No. 49-46. January 18, 1886.

US Sentencing Commission. *United States Sentencing Commission Guidelines Manual.* 1987. http://www.ussc.gov/sites/default/files/pdf/guidelines-manual/1987/manual-pdf/1987_Guidelines_Manual_Full.pdf.

———. *United States Sentencing Commission Guidelines Manual.* 1991. https://www.ussc.gov/sites/default/files/pdf/guidelines-manual/1991/manual-pdf/1991_Guidelines_Manual_Full.pdf.

US Temporary National Economic Committee. *Investigation of Concentration of Economic Power: Hearings Before the Temporary National Economic Committee.* Pt. 5. 76th Cong., 1st Sess. Washington, DC: US Government Printing Office, 1939.

———. *Investigation of Concentration of Economic Power: Hearings Before the Temporary National Economic Committee.* Pt. 11. 76th Cong., 1st Sess. Washington, DC: US Government Printing Office, 1939.

———. *Investigation of Concentration of Economic Power: Hearings Before the Temporary National Economic Committee.* Pt. 21. 76th Cong., 2nd Sess. Washington, DC: US Government Printing Office, 1939.

———. *Investigation of Concentration of Economic Power: Letter from the Chairman, Transmitting a Preliminary Report Pursuant to Public Resolution No. 113.* S. Doc. 76-95. 76th Cong., 1st Sess. Washington, DC: US Government Printing Office, 1939.

"Vagrancy Laws." *Chicago Daily Tribune*, March 8, 1877.

Van Dijk, Teun. "Ideology and Discourse Analysis." *Journal of Political Ideologies* 11, no. 2 (2006): 115–40.

Van Dusen, Katherine Teilmann, Sarnoff Mednick, W. F. Gabrielli, and B. Hutching. "Social Class and Crime in an Adoption Court." *Journal of Criminal Law and Criminology* 74, no. 1 (1983): 249–69.

Van Zyl Smit, Dirk, and Sonja Snacken. *Principles of European Prison Law and Policy—Penology and Human Rights.* Oxford: Oxford University Press, 2009.

Veblen, Thorstein. *The Theory of the Leisure Class.* New York: Macmillan, 1899.

Vecoli, Rudolph. "Sterilization: A Progressive Measure?" *Wisconsin Magazine of History* 43, no. 3 (1960): 190–202.

Vogel, David. *Fluctuating Fortunes: The Political Power of Business in America.* Washington, DC: Beard, 1989.

———. "The 'New' Social Regulation in Historical and Comparative Perspective." In *Regulation in Perspective: Historical Essays*, ed. Thomas McCraw, 155–85. Cambridge, MA: Harvard University Press, 1981.

———. *Trading Up: Consumer and Environmental Regulation in a Global Economy.* Cambridge, MA: Harvard University Press, 1995.

———. "Why Businessmen Distrust Their State: The Political Consciousness of American Corporate Executives." *British Journal of Political Science* 8, no. 1 (1978): 45–78.

Von Hirsch, Andrew, and Committee for the Study of Incarceration. *Doing Justice: The Choice of Punishments: Report of the Committee for the Study of Incarceration*. New York: Hill & Wang, 1976.

Wacquant, Loïc. "Deadly Symbiosis: When Ghetto and Prison Meet and Mesh." *Punishment and Society* 3, no. 1 (2001): 95–133.

———. *Punishing the Poor: The Neoliberal Government of Social Insecurity*. Durham, NC: Duke University Press, 2009.

Walker, Samuel. *Popular Justice: A History of American Criminal Justice*. New York: Oxford University Press, 1980.

Walters, John P. "The 'Mass Incarceration' Myth Suffers a Heavy Blow." Hudson Institute, June 2, 2015. https://www.hudson.org/research/11342-the-mass-incarceration-myth-suffers-a-heavy-blow.

Walters, John P., and David Tell. "Criminal Justice Reform and the First Step Act's Recidivism Reduction Provisions: Preliminary Issues for Policymakers." Hudson Institute, January 18, 2019. https://www.hudson.org/research/14776-criminal-justice-reform-and-the-first-step-act-s-recidivism-reduction-provisions-preliminary-issues-for-policymakers.

Wayland, Francis. "The Tramp Question." In *Proceedings of the Conference of Charities, 1877*, 111–26. Boston: A. Williams, 1877.

Wayland, Francis, and F. B. Sanborn. "Report on Tramp Laws and Indeterminate Sentence." In *Proceedings of the Seventh Annual Conference of Charities and Corrections*, ed. F. B. Sanborn, 277–81. Boston: A. Williams, 1880.

Weaver, Vesla. "Frontlash: Race and the Development of Punitive Crime Policy." *Studies in American Political Development* 21, no. 2 (Fall 2007): 230–65.

Weaver, Vesla, and Amy Lerman. *Arresting Citizenship: The Democratic Consequences of American Crime Control*. Chicago: University of Chicago Press, 2014.

Weisburd, David, Stanton Wheeler, Elin Waring, and Nancy Bode. *Crimes of the Middle Class: White-Collar Offenders in the Federal Courts*. New Haven, CT: Yale University Press, 1991.

Werner, Timothy, and Graham Wilson. "Business Representation in Washington, DC." In *The Oxford Handbook of Business and Government*, ed. David Coen, Wyn Grant, and Graham Wilson, 261–84. Oxford: Oxford University Press, 2010.

Western, Bruce. "The Penal System and the Labor Market." In *Barriers to Reentry? The Labor Market for Released Prisoners in Post-Industrial America*, ed. Shawn Bushway, Michael A. Stoll, and David F. Weiman, 335–60. New York: Russell Sage, 2007.

———. *Punishment and Inequality in America*. New York: Russell Sage, 2006.

"What Tramps Cost Nation: Seven Hundred Thousand Hoboes Put $100,000,000 Burden on the Workers." *Washington Post*, June 18, 1911.

Wheeler, Stanton, Kenneth Mann, and Austin Sarat. "Sentencing the White-Collar Criminal." *American Criminal Law Review* 17 (1980): 479–500.

———. *Sitting in Judgment: The Sentencing of White Collar Criminals*. New Haven, CT: Yale University Press, 1988.

Whitman, James Q. *Harsh Justice: Criminal Punishment and the Widening Divide between America and Europe*. New York: Oxford University Press, 2003.

Wiebe, Robert. *The Search for Order, 1877–1920*. New York: Hill & Wang, 1967.

Willrich, Michael. "The Two Percent Solution: Eugenic Jurisprudence and the Socialization of American Law, 1900–1930." *Law and History Review* 16, no. 1 (1998): 63–111.

Wilson, Graham K. "The United States: The Strange Survival of (Neo)Liberalism." In *The Consequences of the Global Financial Crisis: The Rhetoric of Reform and Regulation*, ed. Wyn Grant
and Graham K. Wilson, 51–66. Oxford: Oxford University Press, 2012.

Wilson, Graham, and Wyn Grant. "Business and Political Parties." In *The Oxford Handbook of
Business and Government*, ed. David Coen, Wyn Grant, and Graham Wilson, 191–207. Oxford: Oxford University Press, 2010.

Wilson, James Q. *Bureaucracy: What Government Agencies Do and Why They Do It*. New York:
Basic, 1989.

———. *Political Organizations*. New York: Basic, 1973.

———. *Thinking about Crime*. New York: Basic, 1975.

———. *Thinking about Crime*. 2nd ed. New York: Basic, 1983.

———. "What to Do about Crime." *Commentary*, September 1994. https://www.commentary
.org/articles/james-wilson/what-to-do-about-crime.

Wilson, James Q., and Richard J. Herrnstein. *Crime and Human Nature: The Definitive Study of
the Causes of Crime*. New York: Simon & Schuster, 1985.

Wines, E. C., ed. "Declaration of Principles Adopted and Promulgated by the Congress." In
Transactions of the National Congress on Penitentiary and Reformatory Discipline, 541–47.
Albany, NY: Argus, 1871.

Wyatt, Edward. "Promises Made, and Remade, in S.E.C. Fraud Cases." *New York Times*, November 7, 2011.

Yaffe-Bellany, David. "A Crypto Emperor's Vision: No Pants, His Rules." *New York Times*, May 14,
2022. https://www.nytimes.com/2022/05/14/business/sam-bankman-fried-ftx-crypto.html.

———. "How Sam Bankman-Fried's Crypto Empire Collapsed." *New York Times*, November 14,
2022. https://www.nytimes.com/2022/11/14/technology/ftx-sam-bankman-fried-crypto-bank
ruptcy.html.

Yaffe-Bellany, David, Matthew Goldstein, and Edward J. Moreno. "Sam Bankman-Fried Is Found
Guilty of 7 Counts of Fraud and Conspiracy." *New York Times*, November 2, 2023. https://
www.nytimes.com/2023/11/02/technology/sam-bankman-fried-fraud-trial-ftx.html.

Ydstie, John. "5 Years Later, Legacy of Financial Overhaul Still Being Weighed." NPR.org, July 21,
2015. https://www.npr.org/2015/07/21/425053756/five-years-later-legacy-of-financial-overhaul
-still-being-weighed.

Yeager, Peter. "The Elusive Deterrence of Corporate Crime." *Criminology and Public Policy* 15,
no. 2 (2016): 439–51.

Yglesias, Matthew. "Elizabeth Warren Has a Plan to Save Capitalism." *Vox*, August 15, 2018. https://
www.vox.com/2018/8/15/17683022/elizabeth-warren-accountable-capitalism-corporations.

Zimring, Franklin E., Gordon Hawkins, and Sam Kamin. *Punishment and Democracy: Three
Strikes and You're Out in California*. New York: Oxford University Press, 2001.

Index

The Chicago Series in Law and Society

Edited by John M. Conley, Charles Epp, and Lynn Mather

Series titles, continued from front matter

Working Law: Courts, Corporations, and Symbolic Civil Rights
by Lauren B. Edelman

The Myth of the Litigious Society: Why We Don't Sue
by David M. Engel

Policing Immigrants: Local Law Enforcement on the Front Lines
by Doris Marie Provine, Monica W. Varsanyi, Paul G. Lewis,
and Scott H. Decker

*The Seductions of Quantification: Measuring Human Rights,
Gender Violence, and Sex Trafficking*
by Sally Engle Merry

*Invitation to Law and Society: An Introduction to the Study
of Real Law*, Second Edition
by Kitty Calavita

Pulled Over: How Police Stops Define Race and Citizenship
by Charles R. Epp, Steven Maynard-Moody, and Donald P. Haider-Markel

*The Three and a Half Minute Transaction: Boilerplate and the Limits
of Contract Design*
by Mitu Gulati and Robert E. Scott

This Is Not Civil Rights: Discovering Rights Talk in 1939 America
by George I. Lovell

Failing Law Schools
by Brian Z. Tamanaha

Everyday Law on the Street: City Governance in an Age of Diversity
by Mariana Valverde

Lawyers in Practice: Ethical Decision Making in Context
edited by Leslie C. Levin and Lynn Mather

Collateral Knowledge: Legal Reasoning in the Global Financial Markets
by Annelise Riles

Specializing the Courts
by Lawrence Baum

Asian Legal Revivals: Lawyers in the Shadow of Empire
by Yves Dezalay and Bryant G. Garth

The Language of Statutes: Laws and Their Interpretation
by Lawrence M. Solan